Business
Plans
Handbook

Business Plans

A COMPILATION OF BUSINESS PLANS DEVELOPED BY INDIVIDUALS THROUGHOUT NORTH AMERICA

Handbook

VOLUME

40

GALE
A Cengage Company

Farmington Hills, Mich • San Francisco • New York • Waterville, Maine
Meriden, Conn • Mason, Ohio • Chicago

Business Plans Handbook, Volume 40

Project Editor: Donna Craft

Composition and Electronic Prepress: Evi Seoud

Manufacturing: Rita Wimberley

For product information and technology assistance, contact us at
Gale Customer Support, 1-800-877-4253.
For permission to use material from this text or product,
submit all requests online at **www.cengage.com/permissions**.
Further permissions questions can be emailed to
permissionrequest@cengage.com

Gale, A Cengage Company
27500 Drake Rd.
Farmington Hills, MI 48331-3535

ISBN-13: 978-1-4103-2823-6
1084-4473

Printed in Mexico
1 2 3 4 5 6 7 20 19 18 17

Contents

CONTENTS

Highlights

Business Plans Handbook, Volume 40 (BPH-40) is a collection of business plans compiled by entrepreneurs seeking funding for small businesses throughout North America. For those looking for examples of how to approach, structure, and compose their own business plans, *BPH-40* presents 20 sample plans, including plans for the following businesses:

- Axe Throwing Club
- DJ Service
- Escape Room Franchise
- Fumigation & Pest Control Business
- Investment Advisory Firm
- Medical Waste Disposal Services
- Piano Tuning, Repair & Restoration Service
- Wedding Planner
- Whitewater Rafting Excursion Business
- Whiskey Distillery

FEATURES AND BENEFITS

BPH-40 offers many features not provided by other business planning references including:

- Twenty business plans, each of which represent an attempt at clarifying (for themselves and others) the reasons that the business should exist or expand and why a lender should fund the enterprise.
- Two fictional plans that are used by business counselors at a prominent small business development organization as examples for their clients. (You will find these in the Business Plan Template Appendix.)
- A directory section that includes listings for venture capital and finance companies, which specialize in funding start-up and second-stage small business ventures, and a comprehensive listing of Service Corps of Retired Executives (SCORE) offices. In addition, the Appendix also contains updated listings of all Small Business Development Centers (SBDCs); associations of interest to entrepreneurs; Small Business Administration (SBA) Regional Offices; and consultants specializing in small business planning and advice. It is strongly advised that you consult supporting organizations while planning your business, as they can provide a wealth of useful information.
- A Small Business Term Glossary to help you decipher the sometimes confusing terminology used by lenders and others in the financial and small business communities.
- A cumulative index, outlining each plan profiled in the complete *Business Plans Handbook* series.
- A Business Plan Template which serves as a model to help you construct your own business plan. This generic outline lists all the essential elements of a complete business plan and their components, including the Summary, Business History and Industry Outlook, Market Examination,

Competition, Marketing, Administration and Management, Financial Information, and other key sections. Use this guide as a starting point for compiling your plan.

- Extensive financial documentation required to solicit funding from small business lenders. You will find examples of Cash Flows, Balance Sheets, Income Projections, and other financial information included with the textual portions of the plan.

Introduction

Perhaps the most important aspect of business planning is simply doing it. More and more business owners are beginning to compile business plans even if they don't need a bank loan. Others discover the value of planning when they must provide a business plan for the bank. The sheer act of putting thoughts on paper seems to clarify priorities and provide focus. Sometimes business owners completely change strategies when compiling their plan, deciding on a different product mix or advertising scheme after finding that their assumptions were incorrect. This kind of healthy thinking and re-thinking via business planning is becoming the norm. The Editor of *Business Plans Handbook, Volume 40 (BPH-40)* sincerely hopes that this latest addition to the series is a helpful tool in the successful completion of your business plan, no matter what the reason for creating it.

This volume, like each volume in the series, offers business plans created by real people. *BPH-40* provides 20 business plans. The business and personal names and addresses and general locations have been changed to protect the privacy of the plan authors.

NEW BUSINESS OPPORTUNITIES

As in other volumes in the series, *BPH-40* finds entrepreneurs engaged in a wide variety of creative endeavors. Examples include an Axe Throwing Club, Golf Instructor, Radio Station, and Wedding Planer, among others.

Comprehensive financial documentation has become increasingly important as today's entrepreneurs compete for the finite resources of business lenders. Our plans illustrate the financial data generally required of loan applicants, including Income Statements, Financial Projections, Cash Flows, and Balance Sheets.

ENHANCED APPENDIXES

In an effort to provide the most relevant and valuable information for our readers, we have updated the coverage of small business resources. For instance, you will find a directory section, which includes listings of all of the Service Corps of Retired Executives (SCORE) offices; an informative glossary, which includes small business terms; and a cumulative index, outlining each plan profiled in the complete *Business Plans Handbook* series. In addition we have updated the list of Small Business Development Centers (SBDCs); Small Business Administration Regional Offices; venture capital and finance companies, which specialize in funding start-up and second-stage small business enterprises; associations of interest to entrepreneurs; and consultants, specializing in small business advice and planning. For your reference, we have also reprinted the business plan template, which provides a comprehensive overview of the essential components of a business plan and two fictional plans used by small business counselors.

SERIES INFORMATION

If you already have the first thirty-nine volumes of *BPH*, with this fortieth volume, you will now have a collection of over 700 business plans (not including the updated plans); contact information for hundreds of organizations and agencies offering business expertise; a helpful business plan template; more than 1,500 citations to valuable small business development material; and a comprehensive glossary of terms to help the business planner navigate the sometimes confusing language of entrepreneurship.

ACKNOWLEDGEMENTS

The Editor wishes to sincerely thank the contributors to *BPH-40*, including:

- BizPlanDB.com
- Fran Fletcher
- Paul Greenland
- Claire Moore
- Zuzu Enterprises

COMMENTS WELCOME

Your comments on *Business Plans Handbook* are appreciated. Please direct all correspondence, suggestions for future volumes of *BPH*, and other recommendations to the following:

Project Editor
Business Plans Handbook
Gale, A Cengage Company
27500 Drake Rd.
Farmington Hills, MI 48331-3535
Phone: (248)699-4253
Toll-Free: 800-877-GALE
URL: www.gale.com

Axe Throwing Club

Bad Axe Throwing Sacramento, Inc.

2001 Gateway Oaks Dr.
Sacramento, CA 95833

Claire Moore

Bad Axe Throwing, Inc. is currently the largest urban axe throwing club in the world with 12 locations in Canada and the United States. Bad Axe Throwing Sacramento (BAT Sac) is the newest franchise to open in the United States. Under the umbrella of Zelaya's Bad Axe Throwing, we aim to become among the most popular event locations in the Sacramento area.

EXECUTIVE SUMMARY

From a backyard hobby to a lucrative company with 12 locations in less than two years, Mario Zelaya, founder and owner of Bad Axe Throwing, Inc. transformed a niche activity into one with mass appeal.

"People are looking for new forms of entertainment that are interactive and completely different," said Zelaya in a March 2016 interview for MarketWired.com. "Axe throwing is really a traditional hobby that we've turned into a unique experience. It's perfect to celebrate any occasion or simply get a group of friends together because anyone of any skill can participate and have a lot of fun."

From its origins in Canada, urban axe throwing is a trend that is moving across the United States. In a structured game, teams compete to throw 1.5 pound, 14-inch long axes at a wooden target. Teams of eight or more often compete in leagues on a regular basis.

The World Axe Throwing League (WATL) is the global governing body and league for the sport of urban axe throwing. It is the world's largest axe throwing organization with 23 members in four countries. WATL offers standardized rules and regulations for competition. It also hosts regional leagues twice a year, defines safety protocols and procedures, sets standard training techniques and scoring.

The National Axe Throwing Federation (NATF) maintains rigorous and evolving standards to ensure the safety of both throwers and spectators. The NATF's mandate is to promote universal safety, sportsmanship, and competitive protocol with a vision of creating a standardized rule system to enable broad and accessible competition among players.

Bad Axe Throwing, Inc. is currently the largest urban axe throwing club in the world with 12 locations in Canada and the United States. Bad Axe Throwing Sacramento (BAT Sac) is the newest franchise to open in the United States. Under the umbrella of Zelaya's Bad Axe Throwing, we aim to become among the most popular event locations in the Sacramento area.

Objectives

At BAT Sac we have identified the following objectives for our first three years of operations:

- Launch the venue with a highly publicized grand opening event in the summer of Year 1.

- Exceed $1 million in annual sales by the third year of plan implementation.

- Recruit, train and maintain staff that is committed to our values of safety, fun, and customer satisfaction.

Mission

The mission of Bad Axe Throwing is to bring the thrill of a traditional Canadian backyard pastime to urban communities. Our mission at BAT Sac is to become the premier location for group events and team building in the Sacramento region. We will provide our customers with a safe and friendly environment where they can have fun while they compete.

Keys to Success

Our keys to success are:

- Proven principles and standards of operation time-tested by our parent organization.

- The business expertise of our owner.

- A dedicated and trained staff committed to continuous improvement.

- Excellent customer service.

COMPANY OWNERSHIP AND FINANCING

BAT Sac is a franchise of Bad Axe Throwing. It is structured as a California corporation and is wholly owned by Jackson Trowbridge. The business does not require any outside financing at this time.

Trowbridge holds an MBA in Business from California State University, Sacramento and has held executive positions at Oracle and Blue Cross Blue Shield of California. He is part owner in the Blue Fin Sports Bar in Rocklin, California since 2003.

COMPANY LOCATION AND FACILITY

BAT Sac will house it offices and operations in a 9,000-square foot warehouse located in the Natomas area of Sacramento which is conveniently located near downtown Sacramento.

Our facility is just off of highway 80 which extends west into San Francisco and east all the way to Reno. It is easily accessible from surrounding communities such as Carmichael, Roseville, and Elk Grove.

COMPANY SUMMARY

After 25 years in business, Jackson Trowbridge wanted to explore something new. After a trip to Toronto, Canada, he knew that the next step would include axe throwing. Trowbridge decided to sell 40 percent ownership in his sports bar and invest in a Bad Axe Throwing franchise.

The franchise fee was a modest $25,000 for a 20-year franchise in a protected area that includes a large section of Sacramento, California.

The franchise system included:

- Specifications for fixtures and leasehold improvements

- Assistance in site selection and lease negotiation

- Corporate training for Owner/Operator and Director of Operations/General Managers

- Marketing & press outreach

- Ongoing support from members of the Operations team

- Ongoing updates for increasing profitability

- Scheduling systems

- Operating manuals, policies, and procedures

- Business management systems

- Website development, customer service access & booking systems

According to the franchise agreement, on-going payments include a monthly royalty fee of 9% of gross sales for the term of the license.

BAT Sac will be the first Bad Axe Throwing location in California.

STARTUP SUMMARY

Anticipated and incurred startup costs include legal costs for incorporation, legal consultations and liability management, insurance, marketing, rent, and facility remodeling.

All funding has been contributed by the owner and we do not anticipate the need for outside funding at this time. While we wish to remain debt-free we recognize that as expansion of the business becomes a reality, debt or outside investment could be an option.

Startup Expenses

Franchise fee	$ 25,000
Rent	$ 6,000
Furniture/equipment	$ 5,500
Office/stationery	$ 500
Licenses and taxes	$ 550
Web design	$ 1,250
Advertising/promotion	$ 2,000
Legal fees	$ 4,500
Accounting	$ 1,200
Insurance	$ 3,000
Utilities deposits	$ 800
Miscellaneous	$ 1,500
Total	**$51,800**

SERVICES

BAT Sac will provide a safe venue for games and tournaments. Each session will begin with instruction from our axe throwing coach on how to throw an axe. All materials and equipment are provided. Customers must sign an electronic waiver and must be at least 18 years old in order to participate. We only accept payment by credit card and carry no cash on hand. We will be open six days a week.

Hours of operation include:

Monday: 8:00am - 11:00pm

Tuesday: 8:00am - 11:00pm

Wednesday: 8:00am - 11:00pm

Thursday: 8:00am - 11:00pm

Friday: 8:00am - 11:00pm

Saturday: 8:00am - 11:00pm

Sunday: 8:00am - 11:00pm

There are 40 throwing alleys available for booking. Each booking includes at least two alleys depending on the number in the party.

Prices

Axe throwing costs vary depending on three primary uses: 1) Private and Corporate Events 2) Axe Throwing Leagues 3) Public Walk-in Sessions.

For private and corporate events, you will have a dedicated axe throwing coach that will start off by teaching you how to throw an axe in your reserved axe throwing lane (or lanes depending on your group size). They will conduct fun games, then start a group tournament. If you have a corporate event, team building and team-based tournaments will be conducted.

Prices vary from $35.00 to $44.00 (plus tax) per person. The minimum group size will be four persons with the exception of Friday and Saturday nights when the minimum group size will be eight.

We encourage bookings at least three weeks in advance. As we grow in popularity, we will require a longer lead time when booking. Each session will last from 2.5 hours for a group of four to 11 to 3 hours for groups of eight or more. There are no refunds if customers leave before their session time expires.

Event Pricing

BAT Sac will specialize in hosting special events such as:

- Birthday parties

- Corporate/team building

- Bachelor/Bachelorette parties

All of our events are managed by our professional axe throwing coaches who will teach you how to throw an axe and manage fun games, including a tournament for your group.

Our private events last, on average, from 2.5-3 hours by a dedicated Bad Axe Throwing coach. To book an event with a dedicated axe throwing coach, a minimum group size of eight people is required. Private events and bookings cost anywhere from $35 - 44.25 + tax per person.

Walk-In Pricing

Guests that walk-in without a reservation will use a common area for axe throwing where they will be grouped with other walk-in participants. The cost for a public walk-in session is $20 for a minimum session length of one hour. The session includes setup and instruction from one our coaches.

The walk-in schedule is updated every Monday and is posted only one week in advance. It is subject to change so we suggest that the public check our web site prior to coming in.

League Pricing

Leagues run for a total of eight weeks and include a League Appreciation Night where league members may bring family and friends. Each league is comprised of 30 competitors who register online. Total cost is $120 plus tax per person. In eight-week league play, competitors play round robin, with a computer program assigning the pairings.

Limitations

In order to maintain a safe and fun environment we have instituted the following rules:

- We reserve the right to refuse service to any customer who, in our opinion, is not able to participate safely.
- Per the terms of our insurance coverage, customers may only use equipment provided by BAT Sac.
- BAT Sac does not provide food service but customers may bring their own food, beverages, and utensils. A mini refrigerator is provided.
- Alcohol is prohibited on the property, including the parking lot. Anyone assumed to have consumed alcohol will not be allowed to participate.
- Participants must sign a waiver of liability prior to play.
- We ask that participants wear loose, comfortable clothing and flat, close-toed shoes.

Safety Measures

Each event is assigned one of our fully-trained axe throwing coaches who will provide step-by-step instruction and direction throughout the entire session. The coaches inspect and monitor equipment as well as the throwing area.

Axes must be kept at sufficient sharpness to embed into the target yet remain safe to the touch. Each throwing area is designated as a throwing lane. Fences block this area from the rest of the facility to keep throwers and axes contained. Only the two competing throwers and the axe throwing coach are allowed in inside the lane at one time. This includes ensuring the area behind the throwers is clear. For safety reasons, participants are instructed to throw and retrieve their axes in sync with one another.

Onlookers must stand behind the designated lines during axe throwing, keeping a clearance of six feet around the axe thrower.

After initial orientation, coaches oversee players as they prepare to throw, counting down from three, and signaling the throwers when to throw.

Equipment and Games

Only BAT Sac equipment may be used. Two sizes of axes are available in order to accommodate various axe throwing techniques.

The standard throwing axe (hatchet) has the following requirements:

- The axe head must weigh between 1.25 and 1.75 pounds
- The handle must be wood, length must be at least 13 inches long for competition including the handle in the eye of the blade
- The face (blade) of the axe must be no longer than 4"

The big axe (felling axe) has the following requirements:

- The axe head must weigh between 2.25 and 2.75 pounds
- The handle must be wood, length must be at least 25" for competition including the handle in the eye of the blade
- The face (blade) of the axe must be no longer than 4 1/2"

The axe throwing targets are made of axe throwing-grade wood and are mounted on the wall. The rings found on the target each represent points and are designed to resemble the rings found inside a tree once it's been cut down. The target is 60 inches in diameter and contains five scoring areas located in concentric rings around the bull's eye. The center of the bull's eye must be located exactly 60 inches from the ground.

The scoring system works as follows:

- There are 5 rings inside each other, each worth different points.

- The largest ring on the outside is worth 1 point and the smallest is worth 6 points.

- Each successively smaller ring is worth one more point.

- The bullseye is worth 6 points.

- An axe that sticks inside only one ring awards that ring's value.

- An axe that sticks over the line of two rings awards the value of the smallest ring.

- There are two blue balls on the top corners worth 10 points.

Typical axe throwing games include:

Countdown: Two teams start with a score of 100 points each. Points earned in each throw are subtracted with the ultimate goal being to reach zero points exactly. First team to reach zero points wins.

Rings: Teams compete to hit each target ring in the correct order. Having reached the bull's eye, the next goal is to hit the blue balls in the top corners of the target. The first team to successfully hit all targets in the correct order wins.

Tic-Tac-Toe: A tic-tac-toe grid is drawn over the target and each team or player gets to throw. The first to get all X's in a successful tic-tac-toe configuration wins.

Round robins: There are various forms of match-ups where players' scores determine who they compete against in successive rounds.

MARKET ANALYSIS

According to *Entrepreneur* magazine, the current top franchise growth areas include: fitness, children's services, and special events.

Examples of indoor sports/fitness venues include:

- **Sky Zone:** trampoline park

- **iFly World:** indoor sky diving

- **Laser Force Tag:** laser tag

Other indoor sports are also gaining in popularity. However, there are no national companies as yet for these sports:

- Kart racing

- Archery tag

- Paintball

Active.com said that companies are finding ways to create programs that promote health and well-being of their employees. They especially seek activities where employees can interact with one another while exercising.

Proper axe throwing technique works muscle groups in your legs, arms, and core. Moreover, it's a great stress reducer. In an article for *The Star Phoenix*, Matt Wilson, commissioner of the National Axe Throwing Federation said, "The social element is also a big part of the appeal, as society becomes increasingly digital and people crave human interaction."

When Bad Axe Throwing opened its Chicago franchise in 2016, Matt Lindner of the *Chicago Tribune* called the sport, "modern day bowling."

In his article, Lindner cited founder Marion Zelaya, "Zelaya says it doesn't take long for patrons to figure out how to throw an ax and get into a routine. In his experience, women tend to pick up the hang of ax throwing faster than men do, he says."

Bad Axe Throwing was founded by CEO Mario Zelaya in the fall of 2014. In just a few years, it has expanded across Canada and the United States with 12 locations including Toronto, Ottawa, Kitchener, Edmonton, Surrey, Winnipeg and Chicago. Based on our research into axe throwing facilities, we are confident that we can build a loyal following of men and women of all ages and backgrounds.

Sacramento Demographics

The population of Sacramento, California is currently 476,075 with a density of 4,862 persons per square mile. The median age is 33.8 and the ratio of male/female is 1:1. Sixty four percent of households have an income above $40K. Estimated median household income in 2015 was $52,151.

For the population 25 years and older, 30.3 percent have earned a bachelor's degree or higher. Thirty nine percent have never married while 42 percent are currently married. Fifty six percent of Sacramento workers also live in the city.

COMPETITION

We had difficulty locating axe throwing facilities in California but we did note that the trend is moving from the east coast toward the west coast. BAT Sac is well-positioned to establish itself as the premiere axe throwing venue in Sacramento with virtually no competition as yet.

Other fun venues in Sacramento include:

- **Zion Virtual Reality:** arcades and kids' activities
- **Paint Nite:** sip and paint parties
- **Lazer X:** laser tag, arcades, bowling
- **The Rink:** skating

We believe that Sacramentans will be intrigued by the unique experience that BAT Sac offers. At first people may just come to satisfy their curiosity but we feel that many of them will get hooked on the rush of the play.

MARKETING PLAN

Our target market is adults age 18 and over who seek an invigorating social experience. We will encourage new customers with the use of coupons, gift certificates, Groupon discounts and local advertising.

For the most part, our marketing strategy is conducted by our franchisor and will include the following channels:

- **Social media:** Facebook page with regular postings; Bad Axe Throwing has a Facebook rating of 4.9 out of 5 stars

- **Trip Advisor:** Bad Axe Throwing has a rating of 4.9 out of 5 stars

- **Google:** Bad Axe Throwing has a rating of 4.9 out of 5 stars

- **Yelp rankings:** Bad Axe Throwing locations have consistently high ranks on Yelp

- **Web site & blog:** includes video of axe throwing at our facility, reviews from TripAdvisor, League sign-up page, instruction on axe throwing, booking calendar, walk-in schedule, pricing, FAQ, hours of operation, and list of all BAT locations

In addition to the national advertising efforts of our franchisor, we will conduct the following strategies:

- **Local advertising:** newspapers, fliers, mailers to customers

- **Promotional items:** hats, tees, and shot glasses bearing our logo and address will take our brand into far flung regions along with our satisfied customers

- **Networking:** forming and maintaining connections with other business owners for purposes of cross-promotion

Bad Axe Throwing is proud to be a part of the communities where it is located. Our franchises have participated in numerous fundraising events, getting involved in local charities and providing donations to worldwide leadership and support organizations such as United Way. We believe in giving back to the community and helping out where we can. Our campaigns are aimed at supporting families, children and teens in need. Axe throwing events in the community are great opportunities for people to have fun while supporting great causes.

MILESTONES

Milestone	Delivery Date
Business plan	October 2016
Purchase franchise	November 2016
Brochures & cards	January 2017
Facility lease	January 2017
Leasehold improvements	April 2017
Hire/train coaches	May 2017
Grand opening	June 2017

FINANCIAL PROJECTIONS

Our plans call for beginning operations by the summer of 2017. During the first full year of operation, we plan to serve about 2,500 customers per month at an average of $38 per person.

Pro Forma Profit and Loss

	Year 1	Year 2	Year 3
Sales	$1,140,000	$1,425,000	$1,781,250
Direct costs:			
Labor: coaches	$ 530,400	$ 663,000	$ 795,600
Royalty 9%	$ 102,600	$ 128,250	$ 160,313
Total direct costs	**$ 633,000**	**$ 791,250**	**$ 955,913**
Gross profit	**$ 507,000**	**$ 633,750**	**$ 825,338**
Gross profit margin	**44%**	**44%**	**46%**
Expenses			
Admin. payroll	$ 90,000	$ 90,000	$ 90,000
Employee taxes & benefits	$ 93,060	$ 112,950	$ 132,840
Depreciation	$ 5,000	$ 5,020	$ 5,050
Sales & marketing	$ 2,700	$ 2,700	$ 2,800
Phone/Internet	$ 3,600	$ 3,600	$ 3,600
Insurance	$ 10,000	$ 10,000	$ 10,000
Office & postage	$ 750	$ 900	$ 1,100
Auto: gas & maintenance	$ 5,200	$ 6,500	$ 8,000
Utilities	$ 15,000	$ 15,000	$ 15,000
Software app: CRM, scheduling	$ 600	$ 600	$ 600
Software: quickbooks online plus	$ 480	$ 480	$ 480
Repairs & maintenance	$ 1,500	$ 1,500	$ 1,800
Accounting & legal	$ 1,800	$ 1,800	$ 2,000
Professional licenses	$ 1,100	$ 1,100	$ 1,100
Warehouse lease	$ 45,000	$ 45,000	$ 45,000
Other expenses	$ 1,200	$ 1,200	$ 1,499
Total operating expenses	**$ 276,990**	**$ 298,350**	**$ 320,869**
Profit before interest and taxes	**$ 230,010**	**$ 335,400**	**$ 504,469**
Taxes incurred	**$ 72,954**	**$ 114,036**	**$ 171,519**
Net profit	**$ 157,056**	**$ 221,364**	**$ 332,950**
Net profit/sales	**14%**	**16%**	**19%**

Projected Balance Sheet

Assets	Year 1	Year 2	Year 3
Cash in bank	$194,256	$421,040	$759,040
Other current assets			
Total current assets	**$194,256**	**$421,040**	**$759,040**
Fixed assets			
Office furniture & equipment	$ 3,500	$ 3,500	$ 3,500
Equipment	$ 1,500	$ 1,700	$ 2,000
Leasehold improvements	$ 45,000	$ 45,000	$ 45,000
Less: depreciation	(5,000)	$ (10,020)	$ (15,070)
Total assets	**$239,256**	**$461,220**	**$794,470**
Liabilities			
Current liabilities			
Accounts payable	$ 7,200	$ 7,800	$ 8,100
Current maturities loan			
Total current liabilities	**$ 7,200**	**$ 7,800**	**$ 8,100**
Long term liabilities loan	0	0	$ —
Total liabilities	**$ 7,200**	**$ 7,800**	**$ 8,100**
Paid-in capital	$ 75,000	$ 75,000	$ 75,000
Retained earnings	$ —	$157,056	$378,420
Earnings	$157,056	$221,364	$332,950
Total capital	**$232,056**	**$453,420**	**$786,370**
Total liabilities & capital	**$239,256**	**$461,220**	**$794,470**

DJ Service

Party Pro Entertainment, Inc.

PO Box 12234
New York, NY 10107

BizPlanDB.com

The purpose of this business plan is to raise $50,000 for the development of a disc jockey service for events while showcasing the expected financials and operations over the next three years. Party Pro Entertainment, Inc. ("the Company") is a New York-based corporation that will provide disc jockeying and event hosting services to customers in its targeted market. The Company was founded by John Mullins.

1.0 EXECUTIVE SUMMARY

The purpose of this business plan is to raise $50,000 for the development of a disc jockey service for events while showcasing the expected financials and operations over the next three years. Party Pro Entertainment, Inc. ("the Company") is a New York-based corporation that will provide disc jockeying and event hosting services to customers in its targeted market. The Company was founded by John Mullins.

1.1 The Services

As stated above, the Company's revenue will come from DJ services rendered to people that are hosting events such as weddings, sweet sixteen parties, Bar/Bat Mitzvahs, corporate events, and block parties. The Company will charge its services on a per-hour basis with additional ancillary revenues coming from transportation and set up fees.

Mr. Mullins has developed an extensive marketing campaign that the business will use from the onset of operations in order to promote the services offered by Party Pro Entertainment, Inc.

The third section of the business plan will further describe the services offered by Party Pro Entertainment.

1.2 Financing

Mr. Mullins is seeking to raise $50,000 as a bank loan. The interest rate and loan agreement are to be further discussed during negotiation. This business plan assumes that the business will receive a 10-year loan with a 9% fixed interest rate. The financing will be used for the following:

- Development of the Company's office location.

- Financing for the first six months of operation.

- Capital to purchase a company vehicle and mobile DJ equipment.

Mr. Mullins will contribute $10,000 to the venture.

1.3 Mission Statement

Party Pro Entertainment, Inc.'s mission is to provide customers with outstanding event entertainment management services that will make the events memorable and enjoyable.

1.4 Management Team

The Company was founded by John Mullins. Mr. Mullins has more than 10 years of experience in the event entertainment industry. Through his expertise, he will be able to bring the operations of the business to profitability within its first year of operations.

1.5 Sales Forecasts

Mr. Mullins expects a strong rate of growth at the start of operations. Below are the expected financials over the next three years.

Proforma Profit and Loss (Yearly)

Year	1	2	3
Sales	$248,178	$272,996	$300,295
Operating costs	$172,679	$179,117	$185,859
EBITDA	$ 47,695	$ 63,295	$ 80,794
Taxes, interest, and depreciation	$ 25,529	$ 29,609	$ 36,052
Net profit	$ 22,166	$ 33,686	$ 44,741

Sales, Operating Costs, and Profit Forecast

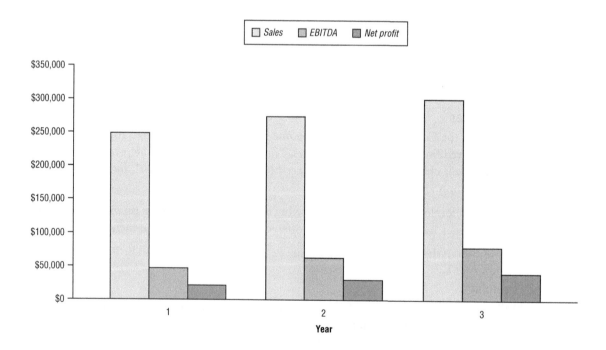

1.6 Expansion Plan

The Founder expects that the business will aggressively expand during the first three years of operation. Mr. Mullins intends to implement marketing campaigns that will effectively target individuals, corporations with event hosting needs, and event planners within the target market.

2.0 COMPANY AND FINANCING SUMMARY

2.1 Registered Name and Corporate Structure
The Company is registered as a corporation in the State of New York.

2.2 Required Funds
At this time, Party Pro Entertainment, Inc. requires $50,000 of debt funds. Below is a breakdown of how these funds will be used:

Projected Startup Costs

Initial lease payments and deposits	$ 5,000
Working capital	$12,500
DJ equipment	$ 7,500
Leasehold improvements	$ 2,000
Security deposits	$ 3,000
Insurance	$ 2,500
Company vehicle	$20,000
Marketing budget	$ 5,000
Miscellaneous and unforeseen costs	$ 2,500
Total startup costs	**$60,000**

Use of Funds

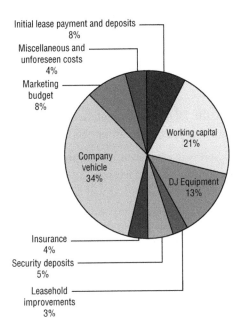

2.3 Investor Equity
Mr. Mullins is not seeking an investment from a third party at this time.

2.4 Management Equity
John Mullins owns 100% of Party Pro Entertainment, Inc.

2.5 Exit Strategy

If the business is very successful, Mr. Mullins may seek to sell the business to a third party for a significant earnings multiple. Most likely, the Company will hire a qualified business broker to sell the business on behalf of Party Pro Entertainment, Inc. Based on historical numbers, the business could fetch a sales premium of up to 3 times earnings.

3.0 SERVICES

Party Pro Entertainment, Inc. through its employed emcees will provide entertainment management for any type of event. As stated in the executive summary, the Company will have the ability to provide services for weddings, corporate events, Bar/Bat Mitzvahs, Sweet Sixteen parties, anniversaries, and other events that often require the services of a DJ or an emcee. Specific benefits of using the Company's service include, but are not limited to:

- Extensive experience in the entertainment management industry.

- Professional grade equipment with backup components.

- Access to thousands of musical titles.

- Wireless microphone systems for blessings and toasts.

- Optional remote DJ set-up for ceremonies and/or cocktail periods.

- Emcee and coordination your event's activities.

- In-person consultations.

- Customized play lists and do not play lists.

4.0 STRATEGIC AND MARKET ANALYSIS

4.1 Economic Outlook

This section of the analysis will detail the economic climate, the DJ and event entertainment industry, the customer profile, and the competition that the business will face as it progresses through its business operations.

Currently, the economic market condition in the United States is moderate. Unemployment rates have declined while asset prices have risen substantially. However, DJ and emcee service companies tend to operate with a strong amount of economic stability as people (and businesses) will continue to host and hold events that require these services. Additionally, DJ service businesses are often a much more economical alternative to having a full band, and as such, these businesses often see that many customers come to them (rather than full band companies) for event entertainment services.

4.2 Industry Analysis

Within the United States, there are 16,500 businesses (and sole proprietors) that provide event entertainment services (which includes DJ and emcee services) to the general public. The aggregate revenue generated by these people and businesses is in excess of $3 billion dollars each year. The industry employs approximately 60,000 people, and disburses $1 billion dollars in payrolls.

During the last economic census, it was found that the number of businesses operated within this industry has increased at a rate of 28% every five years. However, gross receipts have increased 65% over the same period. This is primarily attributed to the fact that the demand among the general public for more lavish and expansive events (especially weddings) has increased substantially. However, with the current economic climate, Management anticipates that this rate will slow to a more moderate level during the next five years.

4.3 Customer Profile

Party Pro Entertainment, Inc. anticipates that its average client will be a couple seeking to get married, a family planning a large gathering, or a corporation planning a large-scale event for clients/employees. Management has outlined several demographics among its target client market, including:

- Has an annual household income of $50,000 or more

- Is seeking to spend approximately $20,000 on their event

- Between the ages of 21 and 60

- Among businesses, has revenues aggregately exceeding $250,000+ per year

4.4 Competition

Competition within the New York metropolitan area market is substantial as it relates to event entertainment businesses. The Company will be able to effectively enter this market given Mr. Mullins's experience within this industry coupled with the moderate pricing point for the business' services. Additionally, Mr. Mullins and the Company's employees will operate within a 100-mile radius of the business' central location.

5.0 MARKETING PLAN

Party Pro Entertainment, Inc. intends to maintain an extensive marketing campaign that will ensure maximum visibility for the business in its targeted market. Below is an overview of the marketing strategies and objectives of the Company.

5.1 Marketing Objectives

- Develop an online presence by developing a website and placing the Company's name and contact information with online directories.

- Implement a local campaign with the Company's targeted market via the use of flyers, local newspaper advertisements, and word-of-mouth.

- Establish relationships with event planners within the targeted market.

5.2 Marketing Strategies

Mr. Mullins intends on using a number of marketing strategies that will allow Party Pro Entertainment, Inc. to easily target people who are hosting events within the target market. These strategies include traditional print advertisements and ads placed on search engines on the Internet. A majority of the Company's marketing operations will be conducted online.

Party Pro Entertainment, Inc.'s primary marketing focus will be online marketing and sales channels. This is very important as many people seeking local services, such as DJs and emcees, use the Internet to conduct their preliminary searches. Mr. Mullins will have this website search engine optimized so that it can be found quickly among major search engines. Additionally, the Company will maintain an expansive presence among major social media platforms including FaceBook, Twitter, and Instagram (showcasing events hosted by the Company's employed DJ's).

The Company will maintain a sizable amount of print and traditional advertising methods within local markets to promote the DJ and emcee services that the Company is selling.

The business will also partner with event planners that will send referrals to the business. Over time, this will become one of the most important aspects to the Company's marketing operations as, once these operations are established, there is minimal ongoing expense related to maintaining these relationships.

5.3 Pricing

Management anticipates that each event will generate $500 to $1,000 for the Company depending on the size of the event and how far an employed DJ needs to travel to the event.

6.0 ORGANIZATIONAL PLAN AND PERSONNEL SUMMARY

6.1 Corporate Organization

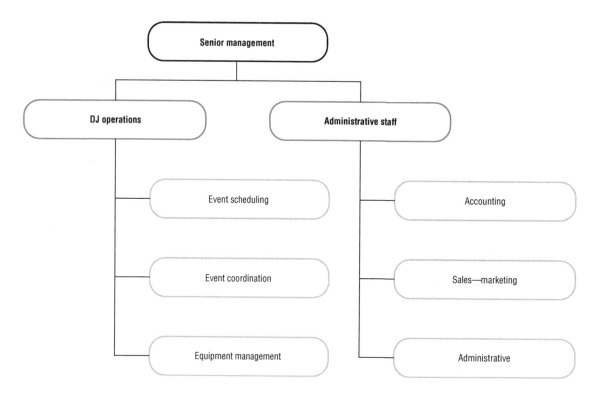

6.2 Organizational Budget

Personnel Plan—Yearly

Year	1	2	3
Owner	$ 30,000	$ 30,900	$ 31,827
Owner's assistant	$ 25,000	$ 25,750	$ 26,523
Emcees (P/T)	$ 40,000	$ 41,200	$ 42,436
Bookkeeper (P/T)	$ 7,500	$ 7,725	$ 7,957
Administrative	$ 17,000	$ 17,510	$ 18,035
Total	**$119,500**	**$123,085**	**$126,778**

Numbers of Personnel

Year	1	2	3
Owner	1	1	1
Owner's assistant	1	1	1
Emcees (P/T)	2	2	2
Bookkeeper (P/T)	1	1	1
Administrative	1	1	1
Totals	**6**	**6**	**6**

Personnel Expense Breakdown

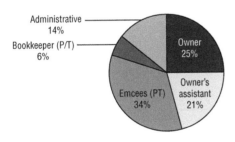

Administrative 14%
Bookkeeper (P/T) 6%
Emcees (PT) 34%
Owner 25%
Owner's assistant 21%

7.0 FINANCIAL PLAN

7.1 Underlying Assumptions

The Company has based its proforma financial statements on the following:

- Party Pro Entertainment, Inc. will have an annual revenue growth rate of 10% per year.

- The Owner will acquire $50,000 of debt funds to develop the business.

- The loan will have a 10-year term with a 9% interest rate.

7.2 Sensitivity Analysis

In the event of an economic downturn, the business may have a decline in its revenues. Event hosting and event entertainment services are luxuries, and during deleterious economic conditions, Mr. Mullins anticipates a slight decline in revenues. However, Party Pro Entertainment, Inc. generates high margin income from its services, and the business will be able to satisfy all financial obligations despite moderate declines in top line income.

7.3 Source of Funds

Financing

Equity contributions

Management investment	$ 10,000.00
Total equity financing	**$10,000.00**
Banks and lenders	
Banks and lenders	$ 50,000.00
Total debt financing	**$50,000.00**
Total financing	**$60,000.00**

7.4 General Assumptions

General Assumptions

Year	1	2	3
Short term interest rate	9.5%	9.5%	9.5%
Long term interest rate	10.0%	10.0%	10.0%
Federal tax rate	33.0%	33.0%	33.0%
State tax rate	5.0%	5.0%	5.0%
Personnel taxes	15.0%	15.0%	15.0%

7.5 Profit and Loss Statements

Proforma Profit and Loss (Yearly)

Year	1	2	3
Sales	**$248,178**	**$272,996**	**$300,295**
Cost of goods sold	$ 27,803	$ 30,584	$ 33,642
Gross margin	88.80%	88.80%	88.80%
Operating income	**$220,375**	**$242,412**	**$266,653**
Expenses			
Payroll	$119,500	$123,085	$126,778
General and administrative	$ 10,800	$ 11,232	$ 11,681
Marketing expenses	$ 4,964	$ 5,460	$ 6,006
Professional fees and licensure	$ 2,500	$ 2,575	$ 2,652
Insurance costs	$ 3,500	$ 3,675	$ 3,859
Travel and vehicle costs	$ 8,000	$ 8,800	$ 9,680
Rent and utilities	$ 4,250	$ 4,463	$ 4,686
Miscellaneous costs	$ 1,241	$ 1,365	$ 1,501
Payroll taxes	$ 17,925	$ 18,463	$ 19,017
Total operating costs	**$172,679**	**$179,117**	**$185,859**
EBITDA	**$ 47,695**	**$ 63,295**	**$ 80,794**
Federal income tax	$ 15,739	$ 19,546	$ 25,430
State income tax	$ 2,385	$ 2,961	$ 3,853
Interest expense	$ 4,369	$ 4,066	$ 3,734
Depreciation expenses	$ 3,036	$ 3,036	$ 3,036
Net profit	**$ 22,166**	**$ 33,686**	**$ 44,741**
Profit margin	**8.93%**	**12.34%**	**14.90%**

Sales, Operating Costs, and Profit Forecast

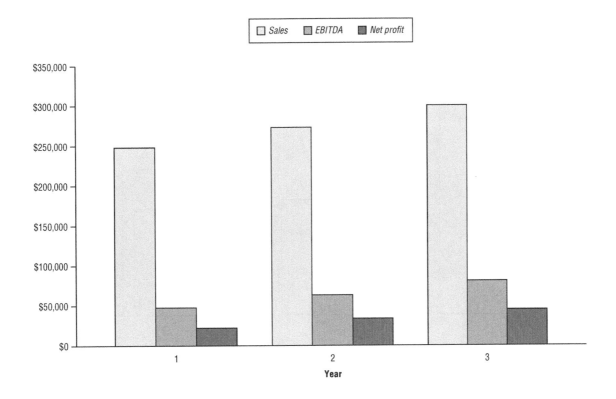

7.6 Cash Flow Analysis

Proforma Cash Flow Analysis—Yearly

Year	1	2	3
Cash from operations	$25,202	$36,722	$47,777
Cash from receivables	$ 0	$ 0	$ 0
Operating cash inflow	**$25,202**	**$36,722**	**$47,777**
Other cash inflows			
Equity investment	$10,000	$ 0	$ 0
Increased borrowings	$50,000	$ 0	$ 0
Sales of business assets	$ 0	$ 0	$ 0
A/P increases	$ 3,790	$ 4,359	$ 5,012
Total other cash inflows	**$63,790**	**$ 4,359**	**$ 5,012**
Total cash inflow	**$88,992**	**$41,081**	**$52,789**
Cash outflows			
Repayment of principal	$ 3,232	$ 3,535	$ 3,866
A/P decreases	$ 2,489	$ 2,987	$ 3,584
A/R increases	$ 0	$ 0	$ 0
Asset purchases	$42,500	$ 9,181	$11,944
Dividends	$16,381	$23,869	$31,055
Total cash outflows	**$64,602**	**$39,572**	**$50,450**
Net cash flow	**$24,390**	**$ 1,509**	**$ 2,339**
Cash balance	**$24,390**	**$25,899**	**$28,238**

Proforma Cash Flow (Yearly)

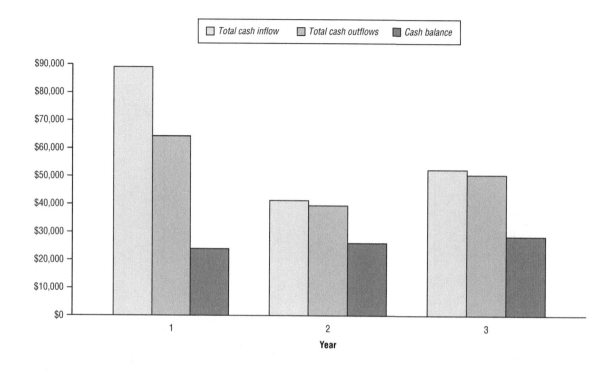

7.7 Balance Sheet

Proforma Balance Sheet—Yearly

Year	1	2	3
Assets			
Cash	$24,390	$25,899	$28,238
Amortized development/expansion costs	$15,000	$15,918	$17,112
Company vehicle	$20,000	$24,590	$30,562
DJ equipment	$ 7,500	$11,172	$15,950
Accumulated depreciation	($ 3,036)	($ 6,071)	($ 9,107)
Total assets	**$63,854**	**$71,508**	**$82,756**
Liabilities and equity			
Accounts payable	$ 1,301	$ 2,673	$ 4,101
Long term liabilities	$46,768	$43,233	$39,699
Other liabilities	$ 0	$ 0	$ 0
Total liabilities	**$48,069**	**$45,906**	**$43,799**
Net worth	**$15,785**	**$25,602**	**$38,957**
Total liabilities and equity	**$63,854**	**$71,508**	**$82,756**

Proforma Balance Sheet

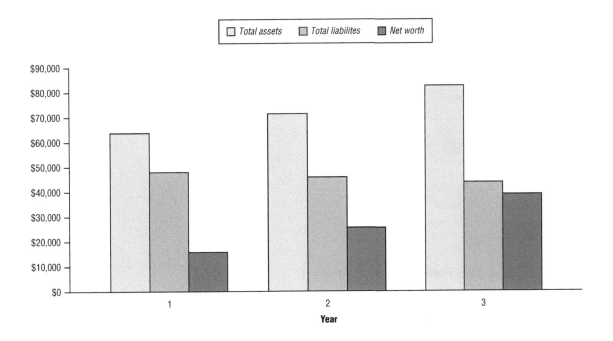

7.8 Breakeven Analysis

Monthly Break Even Analysis

Year	1	2	3
Monthly revenue	$ 16,205	$ 16,810	$ 17,442
Yearly revenue	$194,465	$201,715	$209,308

Break Even Analysis

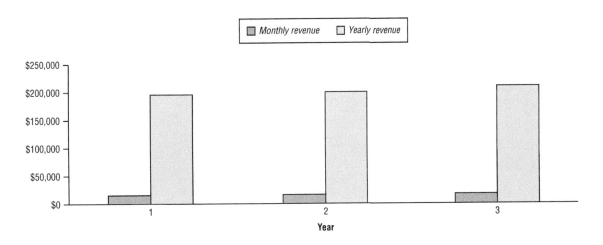

7.9 Business Ratios

Business Ratios—Yearly

Year	1	2	3
Sales			
Sales growth	0.0%	10.0%	10.0%
Gross margin	88.8%	88.8%	88.8%
Financials			
Profit margin	8.93%	12.34%	14.90%
Assets to liabilities	1.33	1.56	1.89
Equity to liabilities	0.33	0.56	0.89
Assets to equity	4.05	2.79	2.12
Liquidity			
Acid test	0.51	0.56	0.64
Cash to assets	0.38	0.36	0.34

7.10 Three Year Profit and Loss Statement

Profit and Loss Statement (First Year)

Months	1	2	3	4	5	6	7
Sales	$19,950	$20,083	$20,216	$20,349	$20,482	$20,615	$20,748
Cost of goods sold	$ 2,235	$ 2,250	$ 2,265	$ 2,280	$ 2,295	$ 2,310	$ 2,324
Gross margin	88.8%	88.8%	88.8%	88.8%	88.8%	88.8%	88.8%
Operating income	$17,715	$17,833	$17,951	$18,069	$18,187	$18,306	$18,424
Expenses							
Payroll	$ 9,958	$ 9,958	$ 9,958	$ 9,958	$ 9,958	$ 9,958	$ 9,958
General and administrative	$ 900	$ 900	$ 900	$ 900	$ 900	$ 900	$ 900
Marketing expenses	$ 414	$ 414	$ 414	$ 414	$ 414	$ 414	$ 414
Professional fees and licensure	$ 208	$ 208	$ 208	$ 208	$ 208	$ 208	$ 208
Insurance costs	$ 292	$ 292	$ 292	$ 292	$ 292	$ 292	$ 292
Travel and vehicle costs	$ 667	$ 667	$ 667	$ 667	$ 667	$ 667	$ 667
Rent and utilities	$ 354	$ 354	$ 354	$ 354	$ 354	$ 354	$ 354
Miscellaneous costs	$ 103	$ 103	$ 103	$ 103	$ 103	$ 103	$ 103
Payroll taxes	$ 1,494	$ 1,494	$ 1,494	$ 1,494	$ 1,494	$ 1,494	$ 1,494
Total operating costs	$14,390	$14,390	$14,390	$14,390	$14,390	$14,390	$14,390
EBITDA	$ 3,325	$ 3,443	$ 3,561	$ 3,679	$ 3,797	$ 3,916	$ 4,034
Federal income tax	$ 1,265	$ 1,274	$ 1,282	$ 1,291	$ 1,299	$ 1,307	$ 1,316
State income tax	$ 192	$ 193	$ 194	$ 196	$ 197	$ 198	$ 199
Interest expense	$ 375	$ 373	$ 371	$ 369	$ 367	$ 365	$ 363
Depreciation expense	$ 253	$ 253	$ 253	$ 253	$ 253	$ 253	$ 253
Net profit	$ 1,240	$ 1,350	$ 1,461	$ 1,571	$ 1,682	$ 1,792	$ 1,902

Profit and Loss Statement (First Year cont.)

Months	8	9	10	11	12	1
Sales	$20,881	$21,014	$21,147	$21,280	$21,413	$248,178
Cost of goods sold	$ 2,339	$ 2,354	$ 2,369	$ 2,384	$ 2,399	$ 27,803
Gross margin	88.8%	88.8%	88.8%	88.8%	88.8%	88.8%
Operating income	$18,542	$18,660	$18,778	$18,896	$19,014	$220,375
Expenses						
Payroll	$ 9,958	$ 9,958	$ 9,958	$ 9,958	$ 9,958	$119,500
General and administrative	$ 900	$ 900	$ 900	$ 900	$ 900	$ 10,800
Marketing expenses	$ 414	$ 414	$ 414	$ 414	$ 414	$ 4,964
Professional fees and licensure	$ 208	$ 208	$ 208	$ 208	$ 208	$ 2,500
Insurance costs	$ 292	$ 292	$ 292	$ 292	$ 292	$ 3,500
Travel and vehicle costs	$ 667	$ 667	$ 667	$ 667	$ 667	$ 8,000
Rent and utilities	$ 354	$ 354	$ 354	$ 354	$ 354	$ 4,250
Miscellaneous costs	$ 103	$ 103	$ 103	$ 103	$ 103	$ 1,241
Payroll taxes	$ 1,494	$ 1,494	$ 1,494	$ 1,494	$ 1,494	$ 17,925
Total operating costs	$14,390	$14,390	$14,390	$14,390	$14,390	$172,679
EBITDA	$ 4,152	$ 4,270	$ 4,388	$ 4,506	$ 4,624	$ 47,695
Federal income tax	$ 1,324	$ 1,333	$ 1,341	$ 1,350	$ 1,358	$ 15,739
State income tax	$ 201	$ 202	$ 203	$ 204	$ 206	$ 2,385
Interest expense	$ 361	$ 359	$ 357	$ 355	$ 353	$ 4,369
Depreciation expense	$ 253	$ 253	$ 253	$ 253	$ 253	$ 3,036
Net profit	$ 2,013	$ 2,123	$ 2,234	$ 2,344	$ 2,455	$ 22,166

Profit and Loss Statement (Second Year)

Quarter	2					
	Q1	Q2	Q3	Q4	2	
Sales	$54,599	$68,249	$73,709	$76,439	$272,996	
Cost of goods sold	$ 6,117	$ 7,646	$ 8,258	$ 8,563	$ 30,584	
Gross margin	88.8%	88.8%	88.8%	88.8%	88.8%	
Operating income	$48,482	$60,603	$65,451	$67,875	$242,412	
Expenses						
Payroll	$24,617	$30,771	$33,233	$34,464	$123,085	
General and administrative	$ 2,246	$ 2,808	$ 3,033	$ 3,145	$ 11,232	
Marketing expenses	$ 1,092	$ 1,365	$ 1,474	$ 1,529	$ 5,460	
Professional fees and licensure	$ 515	$ 644	$ 695	$ 721	$ 2,575	
Insurance costs	$ 735	$ 919	$ 992	$ 1,029	$ 3,675	
Travel and vehicle costs	$ 1,760	$ 2,200	$ 2,376	$ 2,464	$ 8,800	
Rent and utilities	$ 893	$ 1,116	$ 1,205	$ 1,250	$ 4,463	
Miscellaneous costs	$ 273	$ 341	$ 369	$ 382	$ 1,365	
Payroll taxes	$ 3,693	$ 4,616	$ 4,985	$ 5,170	$ 18,463	
Total operating costs	$35,823	$44,779	$48,362	$50,153	$179,117	
EBITDA	$12,659	$15,824	$17,090	$17,723	$ 63,295	
Federal income tax	$ 3,909	$ 4,886	$ 5,277	$ 5,473	$ 19,546	
State income tax	$ 592	$ 740	$ 800	$ 829	$ 2,961	
Interest expense	$ 1,046	$ 1,027	$ 1,007	$ 986	$ 4,066	
Depreciation expense	$ 759	$ 759	$ 759	$ 759	$ 3,036	
Net profit	$ 6,353	$ 8,411	$ 9,247	$ 9,675	$ 33,686	

Profit and Loss Statement (Third Year)

			3		
Quarter	Q1	Q2	Q3	Q4	3
Sales	$60,059	$75,074	$81,080	$84,083	$300,295
Cost of goods sold	$ 6,728	$ 8,411	$ 9,083	$ 9,420	$ 33,642
Gross margin	88.8%	88.8%	88.8%	88.8%	88.8%
Operating income	$53,331	$66,663	$71,996	$74,663	$266,653
Expenses					
Payroll	$25,356	$31,694	$34,230	$35,498	$126,778
General and administrative	$ 2,336	$ 2,920	$ 3,154	$ 3,271	$ 11,681
Marketing expenses	$ 1,201	$ 1,501	$ 1,622	$ 1,682	$ 6,006
Professional fees and licensure	$ 530	$ 663	$ 716	$ 743	$ 2,652
Insurance costs	$ 772	$ 965	$ 1,042	$ 1,080	$ 3,859
Travel and vehicle costs	$ 1,936	$ 2,420	$ 2,614	$ 2,710	$ 9,680
Rent and utilities	$ 937	$ 1,171	$ 1,265	$ 1,312	$ 4,686
Miscellaneous costs	$ 300	$ 375	$ 405	$ 420	$ 1,501
Payroll taxes	$ 3,803	$ 4,754	$ 5,134	$ 5,325	$ 19,017
Total operating costs	$37,172	$46,465	$50,182	$52,041	$185,859
EBITDA	$16,159	$20,198	$21,814	$22,622	$ 80,794
Federal income tax	$ 5,086	$ 6,357	$ 6,866	$ 7,120	$ 25,430
State income tax	$ 771	$ 963	$ 1,040	$ 1,079	$ 3,853
Interest expense	$ 966	$ 945	$ 923	$ 901	$ 3,734
Depreciation expense	$ 759	$ 759	$ 759	$ 759	$ 3,036
Net profit	$ 8,578	$11,174	$12,226	$12,763	$ 44,741

7.11 Three Year Cash Flow Analysis

Cash Flow Analysis (First Year)

Month	1	2	3	4	5	6	7	8
Cash from operations	$ 1,493	$ 1,603	$ 1,714	$ 1,824	$ 1,935	$ 2,045	$ 2,155	$ 2,266
Cash from receivables	$ 0	$ 0	$ 0	$ 0	$ 0	$ 0	$ 0	$ 0
Operating cash inflow	$ 1,493	$ 1,603	$ 1,714	$ 1,824	$ 1,935	$ 2,045	$ 2,155	$ 2,266
Other cash inflows								
Equity investment	$10,000	$ 0	$ 0	$ 0	$ 0	$ 0	$ 0	$ 0
Increased borrowings	$50,000	$ 0	$ 0	$ 0	$ 0	$ 0	$ 0	$ 0
Sales of business assets	$ 0	$ 0	$ 0	$ 0	$ 0	$ 0	$ 0	$ 0
A/P increases	$ 316	$ 316	$ 316	$ 316	$ 316	$ 316	$ 316	$ 316
Total other cash inflows	$60,316	$ 316	$ 316	$ 316	$ 316	$ 316	$ 316	$ 316
Total cash inflow	$61,809	$ 1,919	$ 2,030	$ 2,140	$ 2,250	$ 2,361	$ 2,471	$ 2,582
Cash outflows								
Repayment of principal	$ 258	$ 260	$ 262	$ 264	$ 266	$ 268	$ 270	$ 272
A/P decreases	$ 207	$ 207	$ 207	$ 207	$ 207	$ 207	$ 207	$ 207
A/R increases	$ 0	$ 0	$ 0	$ 0	$ 0	$ 0	$ 0	$ 0
Asset purchases	$42,500	$ 0	$ 0	$ 0	$ 0	$ 0	$ 0	$ 0
Dividends	$ 0	$ 0	$ 0	$ 0	$ 0	$ 0	$ 0	$ 0
Total cash outflows	$42,966	$ 468	$ 470	$ 472	$ 474	$ 476	$ 478	$ 480
Net cash flow	$18,843	$ 1,452	$ 1,560	$ 1,668	$ 1,777	$ 1,885	$ 1,993	$ 2,102
Cash balance	$18,843	$20,295	$21,855	$23,523	$25,300	$27,185	$29,178	$31,280

Cash Flow Analysis (First Year Cont.)

Month	9	10	11	12	1
Cash from operations	$ 2,376	$ 2,487	$ 2,597	$ 2,708	$25,202
Cash from receivables	$ 0	$ 0	$ 0	$ 0	$ 0
Operating cash inflow	**$ 2,376**	**$ 2,487**	**$ 2,597**	**$ 2,708**	**$25,202**
Other cash inflows					
Equity investment	$ 0	$ 0	$ 0	$ 0	$10,000
Increased borrowings	$ 0	$ 0	$ 0	$ 0	$50,000
Sales of business assets	$ 0	$ 0	$ 0	$ 0	$ 0
A/P increases	$ 316	$ 316	$ 316	$ 316	$ 3,790
Total other cash inflows	**$ 316**	**$ 316**	**$ 316**	**$ 316**	**$63,790**
Total cash inflow	**$2 ,692**	**$ 2,802**	**$ 2,913**	**$ 3,023**	**$88,992**
Cash outflows					
Repayment of principal	$ 274	$ 276	$ 278	$ 281	$ 3,232
A/P decreases	$ 207	$ 207	$ 207	$ 207	$ 2,489
A/R increases	$ 0	$ 0	$ 0	$ 0	$ 0
Asset purchases	$ 0	$ 0	$ 0	$ 0	$42,500
Dividends	$ 0	$ 0	$ 0	$16,381	$16,381
Total cash outflows	**$ 482**	**$ 484**	**$ 486**	**$16,869**	**$64,602**
Net cash flow	**$ 2,210**	**$ 2,319**	**$ 2,427**	**−$13,846**	**$24,390**
Cash balance	**$33,490**	**$35,809**	**$38,236**	**$24,390**	**$24,390**

Cash Flow Analysis (Second Year)

Quarter	2				2
	Q1	Q2	Q3	Q4	
Cash from operations	$ 7,344	$ 9,181	$ 9,915	$10,282	$36,722
Cash from receivables	$ 0	$ 0	$ 0	$ 0	$ 0
Operating cash inflow	**$ 7,344**	**$ 9,181**	**$ 9,915**	**$10,282**	**$36,722**
Other cash inflows					
Equity investment	$ 0	$ 0	$ 0	$ 0	$ 0
Increased borrowings	$ 0	$ 0	$ 0	$ 0	$ 0
Sales of business assets	$ 0	$ 0	$ 0	$ 0	$ 0
A/P increases	$ 872	$ 1,090	$ 1,177	$ 1,220	$ 4,359
Total other cash inflows	**$ 872**	**$ 1,090**	**$ 1,177**	**$ 1,220**	**$ 4,359**
Total cash inflow	**$ 8,216**	**$10,270**	**$11,092**	**$11,503**	**$41,081**
Cash outflows					
Repayment of principal	$ 854	$ 874	$ 893	$ 914	$ 3,535
A/P decreases	$ 597	$ 747	$ 806	$ 836	$ 2,987
A/R increases	$ 0	$ 0	$ 0	$ 0	$ 0
Asset purchases	$ 1,836	$ 2,295	$ 2,479	$ 2,571	$ 9,181
Dividends	$ 4,774	$ 5,967	$ 6,445	$ 6,683	$23,869
Total cash outflows	**$ 8,062**	**$ 9,883**	**$10,623**	**$11,004**	**$39,572**
Net cash flow	**$ 155**	**$ 387**	**$ 468**	**$ 499**	**$ 1,509**
Cash balance	**$24,545**	**$24,932**	**$25,400**	**$25,899**	**$25,899**

Cash Flow Analysis (Third Year)

		3			
Quarter	Q1	Q2	Q3	Q4	3
Cash from operations	$ 9,555	$11,944	$12,900	$13,378	$47,777
Cash from receivables	$ 0	$ 0	$ 0	$ 0	$ 0
Operating cash inflow	**$ 9,555**	**$11,944**	**$12,900**	**$13,378**	**$47,777**
Other cash inflows					
Equity investment	$ 0	$ 0	$ 0	$ 0	$ 0
Increased borrowings	$ 0	$ 0	$ 0	$ 0	$ 0
Sales of business assets	$ 0	$ 0	$ 0	$ 0	$ 0
A/P increases	$ 1,002	$ 1,253	$ 1,353	$ 1,403	$ 5,012
Total other cash inflows	**$ 1,002**	**$ 1,253**	**$ 1,353**	**$ 1,403**	**$ 5,012**
Total cash inflow	**$10,558**	**$13,197**	**$14,253**	**$14,781**	**$52,789**
Cash outflows					
Repayment of principal	$ 934	$ 956	$ 977	$ 999	$ 3,866
A/P decreases	$ 717	$ 896	$ 968	$ 1,004	$ 3,584
A/R increases	$ 0	$ 0	$ 0	$ 0	$ 0
Asset purchases	$ 2,389	$ 2,986	$ 3,225	$ 3,344	$11,944
Dividends	$ 6,211	$ 7,764	$ 8,385	$ 8,695	$31,055
Total cash outflows	**$10,251**	**$12,601**	**$13,555**	**$14,043**	**$50,450**
Net cash flow	**$ 307**	**$ 596**	**$ 698**	**$ 738**	**$ 2,339**
Cash balance	**$26,206**	**$26,802**	**$27,500**	**$28,238**	**$28,238**

Electrical Contractor

Henderson Electric LLC

220 5th Street
Roseville, CA 95746

Claire Moore

Henderson Electric LLC is owned and operated by George Henderson whose experience includes 20 years in the industry. Henderson has built his skills and experience from an apprenticeship to certified electrician.

EXECUTIVE SUMMARY

As the construction industry continues its recovery from the 2008 financial crisis, opportunities for expansion in electrical contracting services are showing expansion too. Construction industry trends include owner interest in the use of Building Information Modeling (BIM) even on small projects, Green building practices, growth in single-family construction and in-home remodeling. However, a lack of available construction labor remains a major challenge across all U.S. markets, with labor costs expected to continue to rise over the next year.

Electrical contractors often work as subcontractors on large projects. Services provided typically include the installation and maintenance of electrical power systems, generators, video/data systems, and low-voltage systems (fire alarms). Categories of electrical contracting work include: new construction (50 percent), electrical systems replacement (30 percent), and maintenance/repair/replacement (MRR) (20 percent).

Henderson Electric LLC is owned and operated by George Henderson whose experience includes 20 years in the industry. Henderson has built his skills and experience from an apprenticeship to certified electrician.

Mission

Henderson Electric's mission is to provide expert electrical services in repairing, updating, and servicing home electrical wiring and lighting for indoor and outdoor residential and commercial buildings. We promise our customers the following:

- We will start and finish on time

- We will maintain a neat and clean project

- We ensure high quality

- We handle all the details

- We stand behind our work

Objectives

As we pass the mantle of management to the next generation, Henderson Electric has identified several objectives:

- To expand our customer footprint into nearby counties including El Dorado and Nevada County

- To grow a staff of certified electricians

- To increase brand awareness

- To expand our services to include more green technologies

COMPANY SUMMARY

Henderson Electric has been serving the electrical needs of Placer County for the past 25 years under the direction of company founder, Steve Henderson. The company is now poised to transition control to the next generation with the transfer of management to Steve's son, George Henderson.

Company Ownership

Henderson Electric is structured as a Limited Liability Company in the State of California. The company is owned by Steve and George Henderson.

Company Location and Facilities

The offices and storage facility for Henderson Electric is located on the property of George Henderson in Roseville, California. George's home is on a ten-acre parcel in an agricultural area of the city where there is ample space in a converted barn for the storage of the company truck and van, tools, and supplies as well as office space for administrative activities. The company pays George $1,000 per month to cover rent and utilities for the space used.

STARTUP SUMMARY

Henderson Electric has been in operation for the past 25 years' under the direction of Steve Henderson. If the company were being opened today, the following startup costs are estimated to be incurred:

List of Equipment Needed for Startup

Item	Estimated cost
Computer/printer/copier/scanner/fax	$ 1,500
Office furniture	$ 850
Storage/filing/shelving	$ 300
Adding machine	$ 50
Paper shredder	$ 50
Ladders	$ 1,250
Measuring devices	$ 3,225
Misc tools & safety equipment	$ 650
Uniforms, shoes, work gear	$ 1,750
Power saws, drills, drivers	$ 840
Misc. hand tools	$ 675
Labeling machines	$ 475
Tool bags, belts, pouches	$ 650
Misc. supplies	$ 350
	$12,615
Start-up expenses	
Licenses	$ 550
Van rent deposit	$ 3,000
Advertising	$ 250
Web site development	$ 850
Legal fees incorporation	$ 1,500
Magnetic truck signs	$ 100
Insurance	$ 700
Van customization	$ 2,000
Total start-up expenses	**$ 8,950**
Startup funding	
Cash required	$ 5,000
Startup assets to fund	$12,615
Startup expenses to fund	$ 8,950
Total funding required	**$21,565**

INDUSTRY TRENDS

The "2016 Profile of the Electrical Contractor" report produced by *Electrical Contractor Magazine* found that the industry continues its financial recovery from the 2008 financial crisis and its aftermath. The survey, conducted every two years, garnered more than 2,400 responses.

Survey findings for those in the electrical contractor (EC) profession included:

- Broadening in the kinds of work being performed by ECs

- A larger percentage work in heating, ventilation, and air conditioning (HVAC) both in controls and in mechanical

- 72 percent of respondent firms had 1-9 employees and reported stable employee numbers

- Sustainability-related work types posted significant increases including: electrical vehicle (EV) charging stations, smart or net metering, co-generation, energy storage, smart grid technology, and microgrids

- A significant increase in low-voltage projects especially low-voltage systems integration with almost 60 percent of ECs reporting that they both specify and install lighting

- Billings for smaller companies consist primarily of maintenance, service and repair

- Single-family housing remains the single largest revenue source for ECs, at 36.7 percent of the total, across the entire sample

CALIFORNIA LICENSING REQUIREMENTS

Existing law requires that persons performing work as an electrician under a C-10 licensed contractor be certified pursuant to certification standards established by the Division of Labor Standards Enforcement. "Electricians" is defined as all persons who engage in the connection of electrical devices for electrical contractors licensed pursuant to Section 7058 of the Business and Profession Code, specifically, contractors classified as electrical contractors in the Contractors State License Board Rules and Regulations [Labor Code 108 (c)].

Part of the licensing requirement is that the company must maintain a minimum adequate general liability insurance policy. This is a measure taken to protect the customer/homeowner in the event of a problem. The State also requires that each electrical contractor company be supervised by a licensed Master Electrician. This is a measure that could prevent problems from occurring.

Henderson Electric, LLC has a current and active license with the Contractors State License Board. We encourage all potential customers to check all contractors' licenses before they are hired. Our Insurance is maintained by insurance agencies that provide General Liability, Auto, and Workers Compensation Insurance Policies.

In addition to the required Certification from the State of California, each of our electricians is thoroughly trained with our own Henderson Electric Expert Electrician training. They are also trained to educate the homeowner and inform them of all available options for repairs or additions to their home or business. Henderson Electric also requires that all Certified Electricians maintain their certification with offsite training.

Energy Codes

Title 24 is the specific building energy code standard in California. Like all building codes it is meant to ensure that building construction and installations achieve a minimum level of energy efficiency for both residential and nonresidential buildings. These standards are updated periodically by the California Energy Commission (CEC) to include new energy-efficiency methods. The next set of updates is schedules to be released in 2017. It is projected that new changes will affect projects such as: lighting, HVAC controls, sensors and economizers, computer rooms and data centers, and boiler and water heating systems.

COMPETITIVE ANALYSIS

A review of web sites and Yellow Pages advertisements indicates that there are about seven electrical contracting companies serving the cities in Placer County that we serve. Only two of them appear to be more than one or two-man operations. None have indicated in their materials that they do electrical design nor do they offer Title 24 inspections.

Competitive Advantage

Trends in electrical contracting indicate an increase in the use of Building Information Modeling (BIM) even on small projects, Green building practices, growth in single-family construction, and in-home remodeling. George Henderson's training and experience includes studies in business and electrical engineering and a degree in architecture, which has given him a solid advantage in solving the myriad of residential electrical problems.

Henderson Electric is proud to have been awarded one of the *Sacramento Business Journal's* "Top 25 Sacramento Electrical Contractors" in 2008-2016.

Henderson Electric is a CALCTP-certified installed contractor. We staff CALCTP certified acceptance testing technicians to perform Title 24 acceptance testing at the completion of all of our projects. Our technicians have also completed the CALCTP installation program and are trained on advanced lighting control systems.

MARKET ANALYSIS

Of all the counties in California, Placer County has experienced some of the highest rates in growth of jobs, income, and population in the past 10 years. Over the past 5 to 10 years, the significant expansion in Placer County's housing supply prompted the development of many major retail centers in the area, mostly within the Valley Region and particularly along the Highway 65 Corridor in Roseville and Rocklin.

Many Californians migrate to Placer County for its quality of life, and in some cases, relatively less-expensive housing. Placer County's 10-year growth rate was about 26 percent, almost twice the Sacramento Region's growth rate of around 15 percent, nearly 4 times the Bay Area (7 percent), and close to 3 times California's rate of around 9 percent for total housing unit growth.

Lincoln had the highest housing unit growth of all incorporated cities in Placer County in the 10-year historical period with an increase of 120 percent from 2003 to 2013.

During the next two years of operation we will focus primarily on customers within Placer County. Cities in the county include: Roseville, Lincoln and Rocklin. The Placer County Economic and Demographic Profile for 2014 listed these cities as having the top growth rates in the county.

Overall, the County is projected to see growth of about 18 percent between 2013 and 2023, which is a higher rate than the Sacramento Region's, Bay Area's, and California's respective projected growth of 11 percent, 7 percent, and 10 percent.

The highest population growth from 2012 to 2022 in Placer County, the Sacramento Region, the Bay Area, and California is projected to be in the 60 to 69 and 70 to 79 age groups. Placer County's per capita personal income is projected to increase about 22 percent from 2012 to 2022 to just over $64,000.

SERVICES

The Henderson team is available throughout the greater Lincoln and Roseville areas of Placer County, California six days a week from 7:30 AM to 6:00 PM. Additional hours are available by appointment. We provide free, no obligation estimates.

We will always provide the client with a written contract to secure the arrangement. Each and every electrician at our company is always professional, neat, and courteous, and we make sure we leave the work site as clean and tidy as it was when our representatives started the project. Our team will take care of the debris, left over materials, as well as throw out the trash!

Our staff has extensive knowledge of local and national codes as well as California Title 24 regulation. George Henderson's background in drafting, engineering, and architecture means that we can provide everything needed for a plan submittal.

We serve a number of markets including:

- *Commercial:* office buildings, retail, restaurants, medical

- *Industrial:* manufacturing

- *Construction:* tenant improvements, generators, lighting, design build, value engineering
- *Maintenance:* switchgear, lighting

Services provided include:

- Main Electrical Panels & Sub Panels
- Electrical Upgrades
- Weatherheads and Meter Sockets
- Circuit Breakers, Fuses, Knob & Tube
- Outlets, Switches, Plugs & GFCI
- Ceiling Fan Installation
- Lighting - Indoor, Outdoor & Security
- Rewiring
- Aluminum Wiring
- Exhaust & Attic Fans
- Renovations
- Smoke & CO2 Detectors
- Surge Protection
- Whole House Generators
- 220v Wiring
- Pools & Hot Tubs
- Inspections

Henderson Electric has extensive knowledge of local and national codes as well as California Title 24 regulations. Our in-house design and drafting department can provide everything needed for plan submittal. The design and drafting department can provide everything needed for plan submittal. Henderson Electric also has experience preparing Title 24 and LEED certification documents.

MARKETING PLAN

Henderson Electric will expand its marketing efforts into the digital age with more attention on using the Internet and social media to reach potential customers.

Listings on the Internet will include:

- B2B Yellowpages
- Manta
- Yelp
- The BlueBook
- Facebook
- National Electrical Contractors Assn. NECA Connection
- HomeAdvisor.com
- Angie's List

The company web site, which up to now has consisted of a "brochure" page format, will be expanded to include a blog where we will regularly post articles on topics such as: energy savings, new electrical technologies, green practices, home safety, and more. The site will also house pages that highlight photos of our completed projects. Examples include: Habit Burger in Roseville and the new renovation of K Street on the K Street Mall in downtown Sacramento.

The site will also include a contact feature where visitors can send in questions and requests for services. Our administrative staff will monitor and respond to inquiries each business day.

Our Facebook page will tie in with the web site and blog with an added element of a more personal tone. Visitors can "Like" us and get notifications of our postings, which will be about our company but also about happenings of interest to Placer County home owners.

Another feature of our marketing outreach will be attendance at home/garden shows and home improvement expos. There are about five such events each year in Placer County and we will staff a booth where we can meet the public and inform them about our services, expertise and new technologies in home and commercial electrics.

Other marketing strategies that we will use include:

- Custom magnets on our company van and truck that list our name, phone number, and web site address.

- Yard signs posted at our work locations containing contact information.

- Direct mail of postcards to neighbors in the area of our job locations during our contract.

- Periodic emails to past customers with a useful article about home maintenance and improvement.

- Company uniforms of tees and hats that contain company logo and contact info.

In order to develop our network for referrals, we will develop alliance partners. These are professionals in complementary industries who would benefit from a mutual relationship of referrals. This network includes professionals in the following areas:

- Landscape contractors

- Insurance agents

- Interior designers

- HVAC contractors

- Real estate agents and brokers

- Home stagers

- Architects

- General contractors

We have worked on developing a mailing list for professionals in these categories who serve our area and we have begun an email and LinkedIn campaign to contact them. So far, we have sent our newsletter to them as well as Connect requests at LinkedIn. Our emails include a link to Unsubscribe so that we avoid alienating anyone.

Marketing and the building of our brand will also be a key topic in our continuing education of all staff. We will focus not only on how Henderson Electric can gain a reputation for quality and service, but we will also teach staff how to educate the public about the kinds of products and services that they aren't aware of and that could improve their lives and save them money.

MANAGEMENT SUMMARY

Steve Henderson worked his way up from apprentice to licensed electrical contractor during his 35-year career eventually starting Henderson Electric 25 years ago. Steve's wife, Janis, is the office manager/bookkeeper. Janis runs the office and fields all calls and customer inquiries.

Beginning at the age of 13, George worked with his father, Steve, every weekend and summer vacation in homes throughout Placer County repairing and rewiring all levels of residential electrical systems.

In college, George studied business and electrical engineering, earning a degree in architecture which has given him a solid advantage in solving the myriad of residential electrical problems.

PERSONNEL PLAN

We have developed the following plan for staffing Henderson Electric.

Personnel	Year 1	Year 2	Year 3
Electrician Steve	$ 50,000	$ 55,000	$ 60,000
Electrician George	$ 40,000	$ 45,000	$ 50,000
Electricians (2)	$ 64,000	$ 68,000	$ 72,000
Helpers (apprentices) (4)	$ 72,000	$ 72,000	$ 72,000
Office mgr/bookkeeper	$ 24,000	$ 24,000	$ 24,000
Office assistant	$ 18,000	$ 18,000	$ 18,000
Totals	**$268,000**	**$282,000**	**$296,000**
Total people	**8**	**8**	**8**

FINANCIAL PLAN

As Henderson Electric moves into the future under new management, we project the following financial statistics.

Pro Forma Profit and Loss

	Year 1	Year 2	Year 3
Sales	$635,000	$650,000	$720,000
Direct costs:			
Labor	$226,000	$240,000	$299,000
Material, supplies	$222,250	$227,500	$252,000
Total direct costs	**$448,250**	**$467,500**	**$551,000**
Gross profit	$186,750	$182,500	$169,000
Gross profit margin	29%	28%	23%
Expenses			
Admin. payroll	$ 42,000	$ 42,000	$ 42,000
Employee taxes & benefits	$ 40,200	$ 42,300	$ 51,150
Depreciation	$ 6,820	$ 6,820	$ 6,820
Continuing education	$ 1,250	$ 1,300	$ 1,400
Bid documents, bonds	$ 2,700	$ 2,700	$ 2,800
Phone/Internet	$ 3,600	$ 3,600	$ 3,600
Insurance	$ 7,500	$ 8,000	$ 8,500
Professional dues/memberships	$ 1,000	$ 1,000	$ 1,000
Advertising: print	$ 3,200	$ 3,200	$ 3,200
Advertising: Web site and Internet marketing	$ 3,000	$ 3,000	$ 3,000
Office & postage	$ 750	$ 900	$ 1,100
Auto: gas & maintenance	$ 5,200	$ 6,500	$ 8,000
Software: estimating	$ 1,800	$ 1,800	$ 1,800
Software app: CRM, scheduling	$ 600	$ 600	$ 600
Software: quickbooks online plus	$ 480	$ 480	$ 480
Van rental	$ 9,600	$ 9,600	$ 9,600
Repairs & maintenance	$ 1,500	$ 1,500	$ 1,800
Accounting & legal	$ 1,800	$ 1,800	$ 2,000
Professional licenses	$ 1,100	$ 1,100	$ 1,100
Rent/utilities	$ 12,000	$ 12,000	$ 12,000
Other expenses	$ 1,200	$ 1,200	$ 1,500
Total operating expenses	**$147,300**	**$151,400**	**$163,450**
Profit before interest and taxes	$ 39,450	$ 31,100	$ 5,550
Taxes incurred	$ 5,918	$ 4,665	$ 835
Net profit	**$ 33,532**	**$ 26,435**	**$ 4,715**
Net profit/sales	**5%**	**4%**	**1%**

Projected Balance Sheet

Assets	Year 1	Year 2	Year 3
Cash in bank	$ 3,100	$ 15,030	$ 5,970
Accounts receivable	$ 1,500	$ 12,700	$ 13,200
Inventory	$ 1,000	$ 1,600	$ 1,800
Other current assets	$ 9,000	$ 20,000	$ 40,000
Total current assets	**$14,600**	**$49,330**	**$60,970**
Fixed assets			
Office furniture & equipment	$ 3,200	$ 3,200	$ 3,200
Truck	$47,000	$ 47,000	$ 47,000
Equipment	$18,000	$ 18,000	$ 18,000
Less: depreciation	(18,200)	$(25,020)	$(31,840)
Total assets	**$64,600**	**$92,510**	**$97,330**
Liabilities			
Current liabilities			
Accounts payable	$ 2,100	$ 3,575	$ 3,680
Current maturities loan			
Total current liabilities	**$ 2,100**	**$ 3,575**	**$ 3,680**
Long term liabilities loan	0	0	0
Total liabilities	**$ 2,100**	**$ 3,575**	**$ 3,680**
Paid-in capital	$25,000	$ 25,000	$ 25,000
Retained earnings	$37,500	$ 63,935	$ 68,650
Total capital	**$37,500**	**$63,935**	**$68,650**
Total liabilities & capital	**$64,600**	**$92,510**	**$97,330**

Escape Room Franchise

The Great Escape Plan, Inc.

2755 Maple Avenue, Suite D
Santa Rosa, CA 95404

Claire Moore

The Great Escape Plan (GEP) is a franchise company that offers a variety of escape room designs available for franchise. Upon purchase, the escape plan can be modified to suit the space of the franchisee. We will customize the plan based on the floor plan. We also offer mobile room designs that can fit into a large travel trailer. Because we serve only the Western United States, our staff is also available to make a site visit and help with the initial setup of the room. The owners currently have $450,000 invested and are not seeking additional funding at this time.

EXECUTIVE SUMMARY

An escape room is a live game environment where players are placed in a room and have to use elements of that room to solve a series of puzzles to escape or solve the mystery within a set time limit. Games are set in a variety of fictional locations and scenarios. It is an experience that encourages teamwork and stimulates the creative brain in a fun and exciting environment.

The Great Escape Plan (GEP) is a franchise company that offers a variety of escape room designs available for franchise. Upon purchase, the escape plan can be modified to suit the space of the franchisee. We will customize the plan based on the floor plan. We also offer mobile room designs that can fit into a large travel trailer. Because we serve only the Western United States, our staff is also available to make a site visit and help with the initial setup of the room.

Our designs, practices, and procedures have been fully implemented, tested, and refined over the past five years. Our rooms are designed for two-to-ten people to experience an immersion into their selected room's theme. Participants will be challenged to solve puzzles and think strategically.

The owners currently have $450,000 invested and are not seeking additional funding at this time.

Objectives
Our objectives for the first three years of operations include:

- Finalize business plan and legal documents

- Sell franchises licenses to three to five locations a year

- Establish our brand as a high-quality game experience

- Establish GEP as the premier provider of escape room equipment and props

Mission

Our mission is to become a key player in the escape room industry serving escape room operators and our franchisees in the United States.

Keys to Success

We are confident in our ability to grow our franchise business based on our success in growing our escape room business. Franchisees will choose to purchase a GEP license because of our ability to provide:

- *Escape room design*: a number of customer-tested designs customized to fit the space of the franchisee.

- *Set up assistance*: training programs to help ensure that our franchisees achieve ROI and profits the first year.

- *Continued support*: in addition to annual updates of game designs, our staff is available to answer questions and provide assistance to our franchisees.

- *Time tested*: our operational procedures have been developed over the five years that we ran the Great Escape Experience, thus saving new operators years of trial-and-error.

- *Unique props and designs*: franchisees may take advantage of our ability to negotiate lower prices on furniture, props, equipment, supplies and other inventory.

COMPANY OWNERSHIP AND FINANCING

Great Escape Plans, Inc. is structured as a California corporation. Kurt Wood and Peter Tinker have invested $450,000 of their own capital into the business and own 52 percent of the stock in the company. Thirty percent of shares are owned by members of the GEP management team. Remaining shares are available to interested investors.

Management Team

GEP has assembled a team of experts in business, game design, system engineering, and marketing. Together, we are poised to grow GEP across the United States by assisting budding entrepreneurs in achieving their dream of business ownership.

Kurt Wood, President, Sales and Marketing: Owner Kurt Woods earned his bachelor's degree in Business Management from University of California Berkeley and joined Cisco full-time after graduation. During his 20 years with Cisco, Kurt developed marketing campaigns for new product roll-outs.

Kurt became a fan of escape games in 2011 when he was an account manager for Cisco in Hong Kong. He participated in several games and became hooked on the concept. When he returned to the United States in 2013 and found that there were few escape rooms, he decided to start his own with his friend Peter Tinker.

Peter Tinker, Vice President, Chief Design Engineer: Peter Tinker is retired from his career as a senior system engineer at Disney Parks & Resorts. His talents contributed to the design of such experiences as "Guardians of the Galaxy—Mission Breakout" and "Sorcerer's Workshop." Peter is now Chief Design Engineer for GEP where he will be developing rooms designs and props for escape rooms.

Peter Jerich, Game Developer: Peter began his career as a video game creator in the 1980s with Karateka and Prince of Persia, two of the first Apple II games to combine arcade action with realistic animation and cinematic storytelling. Both title became #1 bestsellers and all-time classics. Peter later became the first game creator to successfully adapt his own work as a film screenwriter with Disney/Bruckheimer's Prince of Persia.

Teri Milton, Game Developer: Teri is that rare creature, an award-winning female game developer. Teri was a key talent in the development of Riot Games' League of Legends, a game that is played by over 27 million players every day.

Sylvia Garner, Finance Manager: After earning her MBA in Accounting from California State University, Sacramento, Sylvia rose through the financial ranks at Intel and Gilbert Associate, CPAs.

Arnold Pointer, Sales Manager: Arnold had focused his business career in the entertainment industry by working for such companies as LucasArts Games and The Walt Disney Company.

COMPANY SUMMARY

GEP is an escape room franchisor owned and managed by its primary stockholders, Kurt Wood and Peter Tinker. These owners represent sales/marketing and management operations, respectively. Funding has been provided by majority stockholders from their own savings, which will cover startup expenses and provide a financial cushion for the first months of operation.

GEP plans to establish a strong marketing position in the escape room industry in the United States due to the owners' industry experience and access to superior talent and resources.

Company History

GEP began five years ago as a small escape room facility in Santa Rosa, California. With an investment of $8,000, Kurt Woods opened the facility. By the end of year two, The Great Escape Experience had annual gross revenue of $1,000,000.

Marketing efforts consisted mainly of social media and reaching out to lifestyle bloggers. Once word began to spread, business gained by leaps and bounds. Over the next four years, with Tinker now aboard, the team expanded the business to four locations in Northern California, Oregon, and Nevada. Franchising the operation was the next logical step in the process of growing the enterprise. It was seen as the best way to take advantage of the growing trend in escape rooms.

The benefits of franchising the Great Escape Experience include:

- *Better market penetration*: franchisees generally live within their territory, know the area and its population, and have a commitment to its growth.

- *Faster expansion*: a franchised network can be expanded more quickly than a company-run network.

- *Scalability*: franchisees are motivated to be successful and do not require the same detailed level of management as employees; they are also responsible for hiring and managing their own employees.

Opportunities and Threats

GEP has seen the escape room market grow from a handful of rooms in Asia to thousands of rooms worldwide with more being added daily. We believe that there is still plenty of room for growth, especially for those operators who know how to craft compelling storylines and utilize the latest in entertainment technologies.

Opportunities: In a June, 26, 2016 article for RoomEscapeArtist.com, Lisa Spira outlined the growth of escape rooms in the United States. According to Spira, in 2009 there were 22 rooms in the United States, and by mid-2016 there were over 900 rooms. EscapeRoomDirectory.com tracks the number of escape rooms worldwide and at this writing there are 2,919 sites and 7,030 rooms worldwide in 101 countries.

Based on our research, we believe that the escape room boom has yet to reach its peak, especially in the Western U.S. And we believe that like other businesses involving a physical experience (paintball or trampoline) there will be plenty of business to be had even after the peak growth has been reached.

Using paintball as an example, we believe that survival will depend on location, keeping costs in check, and outstanding customer service. We learned this early in developing GEP and created methods and procedures that will ensure that each of our franchisees will achieve record profits in their first year, thus giving them a distinct advantage over the competition.

Threats: Where a game developer might have been able to start on a shoestring, as popularity has grown, the public expect a more refined game experience. Increased competition has led to more investment in high tech elements such as keypads, remote control devices, revolving trap doors, and laser mazes. This trend presents a challenge to room operators as they desire to constantly upgrade their technology. However, we feel that in the end, it is really the quality of the game design that drives the user experience and not the technology. Unless you have a compelling story that draws you in, all the tech effects in the world won't help.

Not only does GEP have immersive story lines, our team has developed automated systems and impressive technologies that increase the impact of the user experience beyond the typical escape room.

Perhaps the most significant challenge to the escape room operator is the fact that once a room has been experienced, there is little reason to return to it. If an operator is to build repeat business, then change and innovation will be required to make the game experience fresh.

Thanks to Peter Tinker's years of experience at Disney and our talented management team, we believe that GEP is well-placed to continuously improve its escape experiences.

FRANCHISE PLAN

We sell single-unit franchises, which allow the franchisee to operate their own Great Escape Room in a protected territory. We require that each franchisee be prepared to operate a location that houses at least four escape rooms on site in order to reach optimal revenues.

Franchisees will receive the following services from GEP:

- Project management of launch through onsite and remote project meetings, sharing schedules, work milestones, and daily status

- A detailed launch schedule that includes roles and responsibilities and a check list for critical processes such as control room review and facility review

- Creation of an ongoing marketing schedule with itemized daily and weekly tasks to streamline the marketing process while reducing expenses

- Consultation on setting targets for revenues and costs such as labor, rent, utilities, insurance, etc.

- Review of key metrics for standards and benchmarks related to sales, corporate sales, per room revenue, customer experience rating, etc.

- Training in operations review processes such as hiring and training of staff, game operations, employee scheduling, customer communications, and more

- 24/7 assistance from a member of our support team

- Monthly training webinars

- A step-by-step guide on room setup and a detailed puzzle description for how the room is played

- A detailed list of all props needed for the chosen game room and the control room with a list of vendors (franchisees receive preferential service and pricing for props sold by GEP)

- A personalized blueprint that includes: templates for daily operations and reporting metrics for each area to maximize revenue

- A Great Escape micro web site and booking system and print assets for localization of the franchise facility

GEP will market and sell it licenses, trademarks, and methods to franchisees for an initial investment of $75,000. The length of the franchise agreement is for five years during which the franchisee will pay a monthly royalty fee of five percent of gross revenues. The agreement may be extended for another five years if both parties agree. The franchisee who wishes to sell his business must submit a written request to transfer ownership.

Terms of the franchise agreement dictate that franchisees may only use games developed by GEP, yet they may customize them for their location with GEP approval. GEP will provide guidance on securing the proper location and negotiating a lease but does not intend to hold the lease on any premises operated by franchisees.

Upon final site approval, GEP will begin the architectural design of the facility and assist franchisees in competing the permitting and construction process.

Franchisees will travel to the GEP headquarters in Santa Rosa, California, for our five-day management training program. Our trainers will also advise franchisees on the use of the GEP social media channels, their own GEP micro website and print assets for localization to their own GEP facility. One of our Game Masters will arrive on-site to support the franchisee and their staff during the first week of operations.

GEP will provide franchisees the opportunity to purchase specialized equipment for their rooms. We offer a complete control room setup that includes cameras, sensors, lighting, screens, computers, leader board, microphones, cables and splitters, audio control panel, and a waiver management system.

GEP also offers new and upgraded themes every year so that our franchisees can develop a loyal following of customers.

GEP may terminate a franchise agreement without notice in the following circumstances:

- The franchisee becomes bankrupt

- The franchisee abandons the franchise

- The franchisee is convicted of a serious offense

- The franchisee has committed fraud against the franchisor

- The franchisee has done serious damage to the brand name

- The franchisee has failed to follow GEP's requirements for conducting its games and has failed to remedy its conduct after receiving notice of breach

If the franchisee wishes to end the agreement prior to the termination of the contract, a buyout fee equal to the previous year's total royalty payments will be due.

Upon termination of the franchise agreement, the franchisee must stop using franchisor's trade name and trademarks. All equipment, props and intellectual property including games, themes, narratives, characters, and operations and training materials must be returned to GEP. Further, the franchisee is barred from competing with the franchisor in the franchise area for the next five years. All customer lists are to be returned to the franchisor.

Future Plans

Thanks to Peter Tinker's years of experience in creating animatronics and other devices and props for Disney theme park attractions, GEP has access to a network of talented designers and developers of props that can be used in escape rooms. In the near term, we plan to contract props and devices for our franchisees and charge cost plus a ten percent markup. By year five, we plan to start our own on-site shop where we will create and sell props and mechanical devices to all escape room operators.

GEP is also working on the creation of mobile escape rooms that can be transported to any location, thus increasing the earnings potential of our franchisees.

MARKET ANALYSIS

The first escape room opened in 2007. By mid-2016 there were about 900 escape rooms within North America. The cities with the highest number of escape rooms are New York and Los Angeles with more than 40 rooms each. Cities with at least 20 escape rooms include: Chicago, Denver, Philadelphia, Phoenix, and Boston.

The escape game experience appeals to all ages and genders but is especially popular with young professionals between 24 and 35 years of age. For this demographic, a night out might begin at a bar or karaoke and progress to other activities. The escape experience is yet another way for millennials to have a social experience with friends that is interactive and can encompass other media.

Based on our research, 37 percent of groups who book escape rooms have players over 21 years of age. Fourteen percent of bookings are from families and include parents and children. Players under age 21 comprise 19 percent of groups.

What escape games offer is a way to bring the video game experience into real life allowing the player to be the protagonist in their own adventure.

Escape room bookings are popular for the following groups and venues:

- Birthday parties

- Holiday parties

- Groups

- Team building

- Cruise ships

- Family/friends

Based on our experience and those of other escape room operators who we interviewed, the average costs and time lines associated with escape room startup include the following.

Design and build	$35k to $90k	30 to 60 days
Site assembly		2 to 4 days
Franchise costs	$25k to $80k	
Franchise royalty fee	10% to 20%	
Time to build revenue		30 to 45 days
ROI to profit/recap investment		60 to 70 days from plan start

COMPETITION

The escape room industry is a competitive market very likely due to the fact that intellectual property laws do not cover game design. Therefore, as in the computer game industry, it is easy for another company to come out with a knock-off version of your game within days of its release. However, this environment also makes it possible for game ideas to grow and evolve rapidly.

There are several escape room franchise companies in operation. These companies are located throughout the world, specifically:

- Russia

- Hungary

- United Kingdom

- Canada

- United States

The escape room franchise companies that we found include:

- *PaniqeEscapeRoom (World of Escapes)* : Designed game room assembled and shipped; suggests that franchisees have over $100,000 to invest in room.

- *Escape Room Franchise*: builds game to suit; no monthly fees.

- *Escape Hunt*: Up-front fee plus 10 percent of net revenues, a monthly support fee and a monthly game design fee to cover updates and support.

- *TRAP*: provides layout of purchased games in AutoCAD complete with circuit plans and a tutorial on operating the game.

- *Escapology*: requests that franchisees have at least $100,000 to invest.

- *Boyd Escapes*: located in Arizona, Franchisors and Consultants; operates 10 escape rooms.

While there are over two thousand escapes rooms in the United States, there are none that appear to have a solid brand identity in the minds of the general public. All of the escape room franchisors that we found in the United Staters have been operating as a franchisor for less than five years. We believe that there is still plenty of room for an escape room franchise to thrive, especially if the company is dedicated to quality, originality, and customer service.

MARKETING PLAN

The ideal candidate for the GEP franchise displays the following characteristics:

- Has experience in business ownership

- Is an avid escape room player

- Has at least $200,000 of available financing to get started

- Can secure approximately 2,000 to 3,000 square feet of space to house 4 to 6 rooms or 3,000 to 5,000 square feet to house 7 to 10 rooms

In order to attract potential franchisees, GEP will employ the following marketing methods.

- *Social media*: Facebook, Twitter, and InstaGram feeds will highlight our success story and those of our franchise locations.

- **Blog**: Our GEP blog will house articles on the escape industry as well as article of general interest on ways to plan a corporate event or family vacation.

- **Sales force**: Kurt Woods' experience in corporate marketing will be invaluable in leading our sales force. We especially want to market our rooms to businesses for the purposes of team building and for incentive rewards. We see this as a revenue streams with repeat business potential.

- **Web site**: Our web site will be the hub for all of our other marketing efforts as it will house links to our blog and social media feeds.

- **Articles**: Our sales force will reach out to magazines and newspapers both print and online. In addition, we have hired a social media consultant who will monitor our feeds and will post regularly in forums frequented by game enthusiasts and new entrepreneurs.

- **Listings**: We will ensure that the GEP brand figures prominently in online directories of escape rooms and franchise opportunity sites.

- **Trade shows/conferences**: Our sales team will attend events aimed at escape room aficionados, those interested in franchises, business, and entertainment.

FINANCIAL PROJECTION

GEP has estimated annual revenues based on a conservative projection of an average $425,000 in gross revenues per franchise sold and a 15 percent growth rate per year. Net profit is calculated after payroll for all principals and employees.

GEP Projected Revenues	Year 1	Year 2	Year 3
Franchise fee	$150,000	$ 300,000	$ 375,000
Royalties	$127,500	$ 439,875	$ 927,403
Control room rents	$ 12,000	$ 36,000	$ 66,000
Prop sales	$150,000	$ 275,000	$ 400,000
Mobile escape rooms		$ 50,000	$ 90,000
Total revenues	**$439,500**	**$1,100,875**	**$1,858,403**
Franchise units sold	2	4	5
Total franchise units	2	6	11
Profit			
Gross profit	$439,500	$ 1,100,875	$ 1,858,403
Net profit	$ 35,160	$ 121,096	$ 278,760
Assumptions			
Average annual revenue per franchise	$425,000	$ 488,750	$ 562,063

MILESTONES

GEP has plotted the following milestones for startup.

Milestones	Date	Cost
Name selection	2016	
Incorporation	2016	$ 2,000
Obtain federal id number	2016	$ —
Open bank account	2016	$ —
Trademark	2016	$ 2,500
State registration	2016	$ 675
Federal registration	2016	$ —
Franchise disclosure document	2017	$25,000
Operations manual & training materials	2017	$ 7,500
Sale of first franchise	2017	$ —

Florist

The Perfect Bloom, Inc.

88991 E 23 rd St.
New York, NY 10002

BizPlanDB.com

1.0 EXECUTIVE SUMMARY

The purpose of this business plan is to raise $125,000 for the development of a franchised flower shop while showcasing the expected financials and operations over the next three years. The Perfect Bloom, Inc. ("the Company") is a New York-based corporation that will provide arrangements of flowers and delivery services to customers in its targeted market. The Company was founded by Chad Murphy.

1.1 The Services

The Perfect Bloom will operate a moderately sized retail location that will provide an extensive variety of flowers and floral arrangements. The business will also generate substantial income from providing large-scale floral arrangements for weddings, funerals, and other major events.

The business' secondary revenue center will come from delivery services provided to customers.

The third section of the business plan will further describe the services offered by The Perfect Bloom.

1.2 Financing

Mr. Murphy is seeking to raise $125,000 from a bank loan. The interest rate and loan agreement are to be further discussed during negotiation. This business plan assumes that the business will receive a 10-year loan with a 9% fixed interest rate. The financing will be used for the following:

- Development of the Company's location.

- Initial franchise fee.

- Financing for the first six months of operation.

- Capital to purchase a company vehicle.

Mr. Murphy will contribute $25,000 to the venture.

1.3 Mission Statement

The Perfect Bloom's mission is to become the recognized local leader in its targeted market for flower arrangement and delivery services.

1.4 Management Team

The Company was founded by Chad Murphy. Mr. Murphy has more than 10 years of experience as a florist. Through his expertise, he will be able to bring the operations of the business to profitability within its first year of operations.

1.5 Sales Forecasts

Mr. Murphy expects a strong rate of growth at the start of operations. Below are the expected financials over the next three years.

Proforma Profit and Loss (Yearly)

Year	1	2	3
Sales	$567,378	$680,854	$796,599
Operating costs	$301,220	$317,216	$333,639
EBITDA	$ 39,633	$ 91,808	$144,919
Taxes, interest, and depreciation	$ 30,090	$ 45,296	$ 64,964
Net profit	$ 9,543	$ 46,512	$ 79,955

Sales, Operating Costs, and Profit Forecast

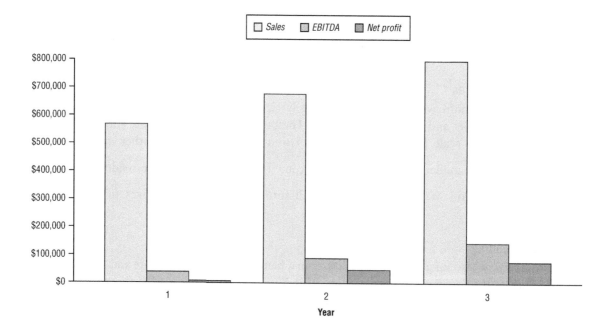

1.6 Expansion Plan

The Founder expects that the business will aggressively expand during the first three years of operation. Mr. Murphy intends to implement marketing campaigns that will effectively target individuals, wedding planners, event planners, and funeral homes within the target market.

2.0 COMPANY AND FINANCING SUMMARY

2.1 Registered Name and Corporate Structure

The Company is registered as a corporation in the State of New York.

2.2 Required Funds

At this time, The Perfect Bloom requires $125,000 of debt funds. Below is a breakdown of how these funds will be used:

Projected Startup Costs

Franchise fee	$ 25,000
Working capital	$ 57,500
FF&E	$ 20,000
Leasehold improvements	$ 5,000
Initial flower inventory	$ 7,500
Insurance	$ 2,500
Company vehicle	$ 10,000
Marketing budget	$ 17,500
Miscellaneous and unforeseen costs	$ 5,000
Total startup costs	**$150,000**

Use of Funds

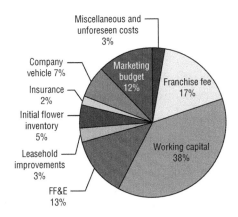

2.3 Investor Equity

Mr. Murphy is not seeking an investment from a third party at this time.

2.4 Management Equity

Chad Murphy owns 100% of The Perfect Bloom, Inc.

2.5 Exit Strategy

If the business is very successful, Mr. Murphy may seek to sell the business to a third party for a significant earnings multiple. Most likely, the Company will hire a qualified business broker to sell the business on behalf of The Perfect Bloom. Based on historical numbers, the business could fetch a sales premium of up to 3 to 5 times earnings.

3.0 PRODUCTS AND SERVICES

Below is a description of the floral arrangement and delivery services offered by The Perfect Bloom.

3.1 Sales of Flowers and Floral Arrangements

The primary source of revenue for the business will be the direct sale of flowers and floral arrangements for both walk in customers and customers that are planning large-scale events. At the onset of operations, Management will source several vendors that can provide The Perfect Bloom with a variety of flowers for the Company's floral arrangements. As stated in the executive summary, the business will generate substantial revenue from the sale of flowers for major events such as weddings, anniversaries, corporate events, and funerals.

The business will have substantial spikes in revenue during holiday months and in the month of May, when many proms are held. Mother's Day is also in May, and will provide the business with significant sales during that time.

3.2 Delivery Services

The Company will also generate secondary revenue from delivery services provided in conjunction with the floral arrangements. Mr. Murphy expects that this aspect of the business will generate 20% of the Company's aggregate income. Delivery services are expected to generate contribution margins of 30%.

4.0 STRATEGIC AND MARKET ANALYSIS

4.1 Economic Outlook

This section of the analysis will detail the economic climate, the florist industry, the customer profile, and the competition that the business will face as it progresses through its business operations.

Currently, the economic market condition in the United States is moderate. Unemployment rates have declined while asset prices have risen substantially. As such, now is a strong economic climate for starting a florist shop. In most economic climates, floral businesses are generally able to remain profitable given that people will continue to host events that require flowers. The gross margins generated from floral products are extremely high. Additionally, The Perfect Bloom will receive substantial marketing support from the Company's franchisor in order to ensure continued visibility for the business.

4.2 Industry Analysis

Within the United States, there are approximately 24,000 companies that provide floral arrangements and sales of flowers on a retail level. In each of the last five years, aggregate revenues have exceeded $7 billion dollars. The industry employs 125,000 people and provides annual payrolls in excess of $1.9 billion dollars.

This is a mature industry, and the future growth rate is expected to equal that of the general economy. However, recent advances in Internet technology have allowed florists to operate with greater economic efficiency as orders can now be placed over the internet through major flower brokers (such as Teleflora and 1800flowers.com) and routed to local florists to fulfill the order. As such, the industry as a whole may see an increase in its baseline profitability due to these technological advances.

4.3 Customer Profile

The Perfect Bloom's average client will be a middle- to upper-middle-class man or woman living in the Company's target market. Common traits among clients will include:

- Annual household income exceeding $50,000.

- Lives or works no more than 15 miles from the Company's location.

- Will spend $25 to $100 per visit to The Perfect Bloom.

- For events, will spend $1,000 to $3,000 for floral arrangements with the Company.

Within the Company's target market of the greater New York metropolitan area, there are more than 4 million potential customers for the business.

4.4 Competition

Within the greater New York metropolitan area, there are approximately 400 flower shops in operation. As such, it is difficult to gauge the exact competition that the business will face as it launches operations. One of the foremost ways that the business will maintain a competitive advantage is via the Company's relationship with the franchisor. The franchisor maintains an expansive national level marketing campaign, which creates substantial brand name visibility. The Perfect Bloom will benefit tremendously from this relationship. The business will also be able to source any type of flower for an arrangement via a customer's request.

5.0 MARKETING PLAN

The Perfect Bloom intends to maintain an extensive marketing campaign that will ensure maximum visibility for the business in its targeted market. Below is an overview of the marketing strategies and objectives of The Perfect Bloom.

5.1 Marketing Objectives

- Establish relationships with event and wedding planners within the target market.

- Maintain a very strong marketing relationship with the Company's franchisor.

- Establish relationships with funeral homes within the target market.

5.2 Marketing Strategies

Foremost, the business will benefit tremendously from its relationship with the Franchisor. The business will pay the franchisor 5% of aggregate sales. In exchange for ongoing royalties, the business will receive ongoing marketing support from this nationally recognized franchisor. The brand name associated with the franchisor will ensure immediate visibility for the Company's location.

The Perfect Bloom will also partner with major online portals such as 1800flowers.com, FTD, and TeleFlora.com (all of which have expansive online ordering websites and operate in conjunction with the franchisor). The business will also develop strategic partnerships with other smaller online flower brokerages so that the Company can receive orders from anywhere in the country that need to be delivered within the Company's local market. In conjunction with the franchisor, the Company will maintain its own website. The Franchisor's website will provide the location and contact information for the Company's location.

Mr. Murphy intends to develop ongoing relationships with event/wedding planners as well as funeral directors that will outsource their client's flower needs to the Company. Over time, this will become an invaluable method of generating revenue for The Perfect Bloom. Once these relationships are developed, there is very little need for ongoing marketing in order to maintain ongoing orders from these businesses.

5.3 Pricing

Management anticipates that each individual order will generate $50 of revenue for the business. Revenues from large flower sales for events/funerals will generate $750 to $3,000.

6.0 ORGANIZATIONAL PLAN AND PERSONNEL SUMMARY

6.1 Corporate Organization

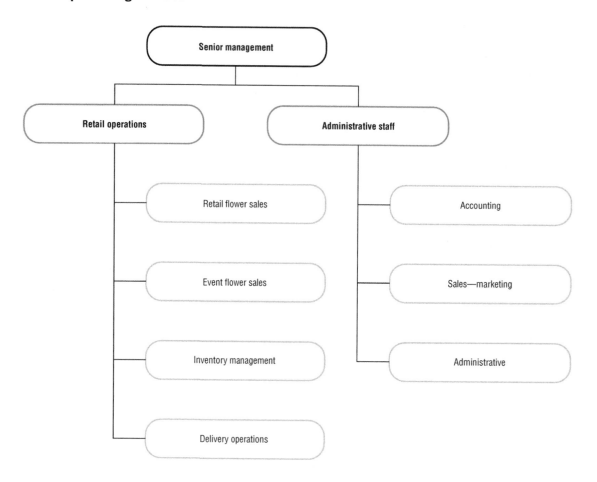

6.2 Organizational Budget

Personnel Plan—Yearly

Year	1	2	3
Owner	$ 40,000	$ 41,200	$ 42,436
Store manager	$ 35,000	$ 36,050	$ 37,132
Store florists	$ 66,000	$ 67,980	$ 70,019
Delivery driver	$ 34,000	$ 35,020	$ 36,071
Administrative and bookkeeper	$ 22,000	$ 22,660	$ 23,340
Total	**$197,000**	**$202,910**	**$208,997**

Numbers of Personnel

Year	1	2	3
Owner	1	1	1
Store manager	1	1	1
Store florists	3	3	3
Delivery driver	2	2	2
Administrative and bookkeeper	1	1	1
Totals	**8**	**8**	**8**

Personnel Expense Breakdown

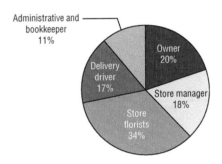

7.0 FINANCIAL PLAN

7.1 Underlying Assumptions

The Company has based its proforma financial statements on the following:

- The Perfect Bloom will have an annual revenue growth rate of 14% per year.

- The Owner will acquire $125,000 of debt funds to develop the business.

- The loan will have a 10-year term with a 9% interest rate.

7.2 Sensitivity Analysis

In the event of an economic downturn, the business may have a decline in its revenues. However, The Perfect Bloom will earn substantial margins on the sales of flowers from walk in customers and from customers holding large-scale events. As such, the business will be able to remain cash flow positive and profitable despite moderate declines in revenues.

7.3 Source of Funds

Financing

Equity contributions

Management investment	$ 25,000.00
Total equity financing	**$ 25,000.00**
Banks and lenders	
Banks and lenders	$ 125,000.00
Total debt financing	**$125,000.00**
Total financing	**$150,000.00**

7.4 General Assumptions

General Assumptions

Year	1	2	3
Short term interest rate	9.5%	9.5%	9.5%
Long term interest rate	10.0%	10.0%	10.0%
Federal tax rate	33.0%	33.0%	33.0%
State tax rate	5.0%	5.0%	5.0%
Personnel taxes	15.0%	15.0%	15.0%

7.5 Profit and Loss Statements

Proforma Profit and Loss (Yearly)

Year	1	2	3
Sales	**$567,378**	**$680,854**	**$796,599**
Cost of goods sold	$226,525	$271,830	$ 318,041
Gross margin	60.08%	60.08%	60.08%
Operating income	**$340,853**	**$409,024**	**$478,558**
Expenses			
Payroll	$197,000	$202,910	$ 208,997
General and administrative	$ 13,200	$ 13,728	$ 14,277
Marketing expenses	$ 2,837	$ 3,404	$ 3,983
Professional fees and licensure	$ 5,219	$ 5,376	$ 5,537
Insurance costs	$ 3,987	$ 4,186	$ 4,396
Franchise fees	$ 28,369	$ 34,043	$ 39,830
Rent and utilities	$ 14,250	$ 14,963	$ 15,711
Miscellaneous costs	$ 6,809	$ 8,170	$ 9,559
Payroll taxes	$ 29,550	$ 30,437	$ 31,350
Total operating costs	**$301,220**	**$317,216**	**$333,639**
EBITDA	**$ 39,633**	**$ 91,808**	**$144,919**
Federal income tax	$ 13,079	$ 26,942	$ 44,743
State income tax	$ 1,982	$ 4,082	$ 6,779
Interest expense	$ 10,922	$ 10,164	$ 9,335
Depreciation expenses	$ 4,107	$ 4,107	$ 4,107
Net profit	**$ 9,543**	**$ 46,512**	**$ 79,955**
Profit margin	**1.68%**	**6.83%**	**10.04%**

Sales, Operating Costs, and Profit Forecast

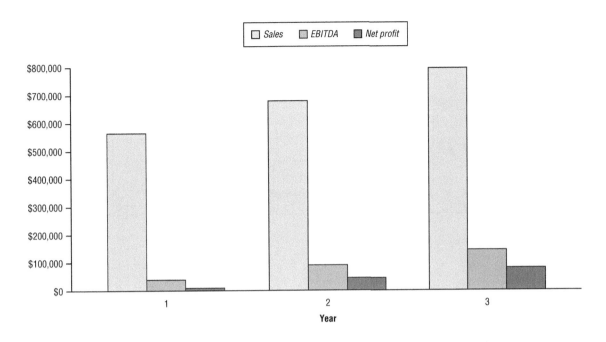

7.6 Cash Flow Analysis

Proforma Cash Flow Analysis—Yearly

Year	1	2	3
Cash from operations	$ 13,650	$50,619	$ 84,062
Cash from receivables	$ 0	$ 0	$ 0
Operating cash inflow	**$ 13,650**	**$50,619**	**$ 84,062**
Other cash inflows			
Equity investment	$ 25,000	$ 0	$ 0
Increased borrowings	$125,000	$ 0	$ 0
Sales of business assets	$ 0	$ 0	$ 0
A/P increases	$ 37,902	$43,587	$ 50,125
Total other cash inflows	**$187,902**	**$43,587**	**$ 50,125**
Total cash inflow	**$201,552**	**$94,206**	**$134,187**
Cash outflows			
Repayment of principal	$ 8,079	$ 8,837	$ 9,666
A/P decreases	$ 24,897	$29,876	$ 35,852
A/R increases	$ 0	$ 0	$ 0
Asset purchases	$ 72,500	$12,655	$ 21,015
Dividends	$ 9,555	$35,433	$ 58,843
Total cash outflows	**$115,032**	**$86,802**	**$125,377**
Net cash flow	**$ 86,521**	**$ 7,405**	**$ 8,811**
Cash balance	**$ 86,521**	**$93,926**	**$102,736**

Proforma Cash Flow (Yearly)

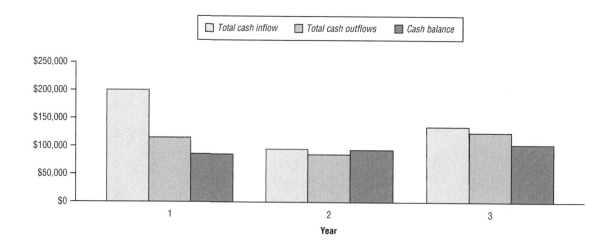

7.7 Balance Sheet

Proforma Balance Sheet—Yearly

Year	1	2	3
Assets			
Cash	$ 86,521	$ 93,926	$102,736
Amortized development/expansion costs	$ 35,000	$ 36,265	$ 38,367
Company vehicle and lease deposits	$ 10,000	$ 11,265	$ 13,367
FF&E	$ 20,000	$ 25,062	$ 33,468
Inventory	$ 7,500	$ 12,562	$ 20,968
Accumulated depreciation	($ 5,179)	($ 10,357)	($ 15,536)
Total assets	**$153,842**	$168,723	$193,371
Liabilities and equity			
Accounts payable	$ 13,005	$ 26,716	$ 40,990
Long term liabilities	$116,921	$108,084	$ 99,247
Other liabilities	$ 0	$ 0	$ 0
Total liabilities	**$129,926**	**$134,800**	**$140,236**
Net worth	**$ 23,917**	**$ 33,924**	**$ 53,135**
Total liabilities and equity	**$153,842**	**$168,723**	**$193,371**

Proforma Balance Sheet

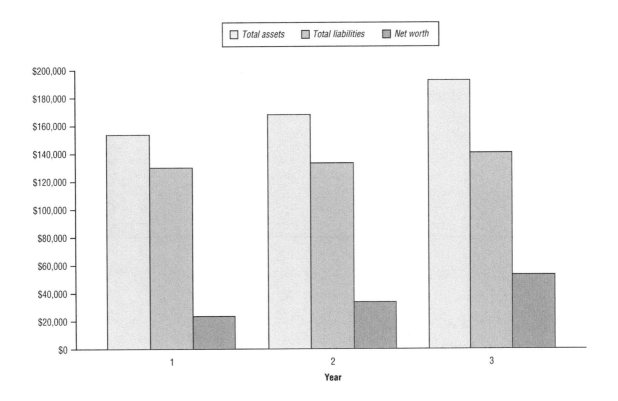

7.8 Breakeven Analysis

Monthly Break Even Analysis

Year	1	2	3
Monthly revenue	$ 41,784	$ 44,003	$ 46,281
Yearly revenue	$501,406	$528,032	$555,369

Break Even Analysis

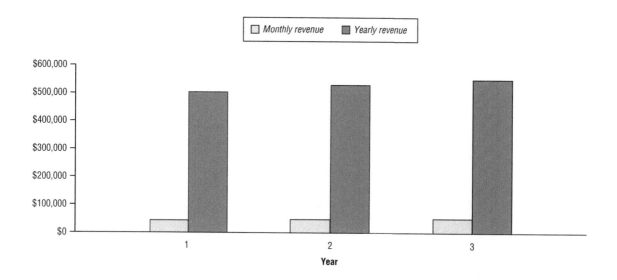

7.9 Business Ratios

Business Ratios—Yearly

Year	1	2	3
Sales			
Sales growth	0.0%	20.0%	17.0%
Gross margin	60.1%	60.1%	60.1%
Financials			
Profit margin	1.49%	6.67%	9.90%
Assets to liabilities	1.18	1.25	1.38
Equity to liabilities	0.18	0.25	0.38
Assets to equity	6.43	4.97	3.64
Liquidity			
Acid test	0.67	0.70	0.73
Cash to assets	0.56	0.56	0.53

7.10 THREE YEAR PROFIT AND LOSS STATEMENT

Profit and Loss Statement (First Year)

Months	1	2	3	4	5	6	7
Sales	**$46,550**	**$46,683**	**$46,816**	**$46,949**	**$47,082**	**$47,215**	**$47,348**
Cost of goods sold	$18,585	$18,638	$18,691	$18,744	$18,797	$18,851	$18,904
Gross margin	60.1%	60.1%	60.1%	60.1%	60.1%	60.1%	60.1%
Operating income	**$27,965**	**$28,045**	**$28,125**	**$28,205**	**$28,285**	**$28,365**	**$28,444**
Expenses							
Payroll	$16,417	$16,417	$16,417	$16,417	$16,417	$16,417	$16,417
General and administrative	$ 1,100	$ 1,100	$ 1,100	$ 1,100	$ 1,100	$ 1,100	$ 1,100
Marketing expenses	$ 236	$ 236	$ 236	$ 236	$ 236	$ 236	$ 236
Professional fees and licensure	$ 435	$ 435	$ 435	$ 435	$ 435	$ 435	$ 435
Insurance costs	$ 332	$ 332	$ 332	$ 332	$ 332	$ 332	$ 332
Franchise fees	$ 2,364	$ 2,364	$ 2,364	$ 2,364	$ 2,364	$ 2,364	$ 2,364
Rent and utilities	$ 1,188	$ 1,188	$ 1,188	$ 1,188	$ 1,188	$ 1,188	$ 1,188
Miscellaneous costs	$ 567	$ 567	$ 567	$ 567	$ 567	$ 567	$ 567
Payroll taxes	$ 2,463	$ 2,463	$ 2,463	$ 2,463	$ 2,463	$ 2,463	$ 2,463
Total operating costs	**$25,102**	**$25,102**	**$25,102**	**$25,102**	**$25,102**	**$25,102**	**$25,102**
EBITDA	**$ 2,863**	**$ 2,943**	**$ 3,023**	**$ 3,103**	**$ 3,183**	**$ 3,263**	**$ 3,343**
Federal income tax	$ 1,073	$ 1,076	$ 1,079	$ 1,082	$ 1,085	$ 1,088	$ 1,091
State income tax	$ 163	$ 163	$ 164	$ 164	$ 164	$ 165	$ 165
Interest expense	$ 938	$ 933	$ 928	$ 923	$ 918	$ 913	$ 908
Depreciation expense	$ 342	$ 342	$ 342	$ 342	$ 342	$ 342	$ 342
Net profit	**$ 348**	**$ 429**	**$ 510**	**$ 592**	**$ 673**	**$ 754**	**$ 836**

Profit and Loss Statement (First Year Cont.)

Months	8	9	10	11	12	1
Sales	**$47,481**	**$47,614**	**$47,747**	**$47,880**	**$48,013**	**$567,378**
Cost of goods sold	$18,957	$19,010	$19,063	$19,116	$19,169	$226,525
Gross margin	60.1%	60.1%	60.1%	60.1%	60.1%	60.1%
Operating income	**$28,524**	**$28,604**	**$28,684**	**$28,764**	**$28,844**	**$340,853**
Expenses						
Payroll	$16,417	$16,417	$16,417	$16,417	$16,417	$197,000
General and administrative	$ 1,100	$ 1,100	$ 1,100	$ 1,100	$ 1,100	$ 13,200
Marketing expenses	$ 236	$ 236	$ 236	$ 236	$ 236	$ 2,837
Professional fees and licensure	$ 435	$ 435	$ 435	$ 435	$ 435	$ 5,219
Insurance costs	$ 332	$ 332	$ 332	$ 332	$ 332	$ 3,987
Franchise fees	$ 2,364	$ 2,364	$ 2,364	$ 2,364	$ 2,364	$ 28,369
Rent and utilities	$ 1,188	$ 1,188	$ 1,188	$ 1,188	$ 1,188	$ 14,250
Miscellaneous costs	$ 567	$ 567	$ 567	$ 567	$ 567	$ 6,809
Payroll taxes	$ 2,463	$ 2,463	$ 2,463	$ 2,463	$ 2,463	$ 29,550
Total operating costs	**$25,102**	**$25,102**	**$25,102**	**$25,102**	**$25,102**	**$301,220**
EBITDA	**$ 3,423**	**$ 3,503**	**$ 3,582**	**$ 3,662**	**$ 3,742**	**$ 39,633**
Federal income tax	$ 1,095	$ 1,098	$ 1,101	$ 1,104	$ 1,107	$ 13,079
State income tax	$ 166	$ 166	$ 167	$ 167	$ 168	$ 1,982
Interest expense	$ 903	$ 898	$ 893	$ 887	$ 882	$ 10,922
Depreciation expense	$ 342	$ 342	$ 342	$ 342	$ 342	$ 4,107
Net profit	**$ 917**	**$ 999**	**$ 1,080**	**$ 1,162**	**$ 1,243**	**$ 9,543**

Profit and Loss Statement (Second Year)

Quarter	Q1	Q2	Q3	Q4	2
Sales	**$136,171**	**$170,213**	**$183,830**	**$190,639**	**$680,854**
Cost of goods sold	$ 54,366	$ 67,957	$ 73,394	$ 76,112	$271,830
Gross margin	60.1%	60.1%	60.1%	60.1%	60.1%
Operating income	**$ 81,805**	**$102,256**	**$110,437**	**$114,527**	**$409,024**
Expenses					
Payroll	$ 40,582	$ 50,728	$ 54,786	$ 56,815	$202,910
General and administrative	$ 2,746	$ 3,432	$ 3,707	$ 3,844	$ 13,728
Marketing expenses	$ 681	$ 851	$ 919	$ 953	$ 3,404
Professional fees and licensure	$ 1,075	$ 1,344	$ 1,451	$ 1,505	$ 5,376
Insurance costs	$ 837	$ 1,047	$ 1,130	$ 1,172	$ 4,186
Franchise fees	$ 6,809	$ 8,511	$ 9,192	$ 9,532	$ 34,043
Rent and utilities	$ 2,993	$ 3,741	$ 4,040	$ 4,190	$ 14,963
Miscellaneous costs	$ 1,634	$ 2,043	$ 2,206	$ 2,288	$ 8,170
Payroll taxes	$ 6,087	$ 7,609	$ 8,218	$ 8,522	$ 30,437
Total operating costs	**$ 63,443**	**$ 79,304**	**$ 85,648**	**$ 88,821**	**$317,216**
EBITDA	**$ 18,362**	**$ 22,952**	**$ 24,788**	**$ 25,706**	**$ 91,808**
Federal income tax	$ 5,388	$ 6,736	$ 7,274	$ 7,544	$ 26,942
State income tax	$ 816	$ 1,021	$ 1,102	$ 1,143	$ 4,082
Interest expense	$ 2,615	$ 2,566	$ 2,517	$ 2,466	$ 10,164
Depreciation expense	$ 1,027	$ 1,027	$ 1,027	$ 1,027	$ 4,107
Net profit	**$ 8,515**	**$ 11,603**	**$ 12,868**	**$ 13,526**	**$ 46,512**

Profit and Loss Statement (Third Year)

Quarter	Q1	Q2	Q3	Q4	3
Sales	**$159,320**	**$199,150**	**$215,082**	**$223,048**	**$796,599**
Cost of goods sold	$ 63,608	$ 79,510	$ 85,871	$ 89,051	$318,041
Gross margin	60.1%	60.1%	60.1%	60.1%	60.1%
Operating income	**$ 95,712**	**$119,640**	**$129,211**	**$133,996**	**$478,558**
Expenses					
Payroll	$ 41,799	$ 52,249	$ 56,429	$ 58,519	$208,997
General and administrative	$ 2,855	$ 3,569	$ 3,855	$ 3,998	$ 14,277
Marketing expenses	$ 797	$ 996	$ 1,075	$ 1,115	$ 3,983
Professional fees and licensure	$ 1,107	$ 1,384	$ 1,495	$ 1,550	$ 5,537
Insurance costs	$ 879	$ 1,099	$ 1,187	$ 1,231	$ 4,396
Franchise fees	$ 7,966	$ 9,957	$ 10,754	$ 11,152	$ 39,830
Rent and utilities	$ 3,142	$ 3,928	$ 4,242	$ 4,399	$ 15,711
Miscellaneous costs	$ 1,912	$ 2,390	$ 2,581	$ 2,677	$ 9,559
Payroll taxes	$ 6,270	$ 7,837	$ 8,464	$ 8,778	$ 31,350
Total operating costs	**$ 66,728**	**$ 83,410**	**$ 90,083**	**$ 93,419**	**$333,639**
EBITDA	**$ 28,984**	**$ 36,230**	**$ 39,128**	**$ 40,577**	**$144,919**
Federal income tax	$ 8,949	$ 11,186	$ 12,081	$ 12,528	$ 44,743
State income tax	$ 1,356	$ 1,695	$ 1,830	$ 1,898	$ 6,779
Interest expense	$ 2,414	$ 2,361	$ 2,307	$ 2,252	$ 9,335
Depreciation expense	$ 1,027	$ 1,027	$ 1,027	$ 1,027	$ 4,107
Net profit	**$ 15,238**	**$ 19,961**	**$ 21,883**	**$ 22,872**	**$ 79,955**

7.11 THREE YEAR CASH FLOW ANALYSIS

Cash Flow Analysis (First Year)

Month	1	2	3	4	5	6	7	8
Cash from operations	$ 690	$ 771	$ 853	$ 934	$ 1,015	$ 1,097	$ 1,178	$ 1,259
Cash from receivables	$ 0	$ 0	$ 0	$ 0	$ 0	$ 0	$ 0	$ 0
Operating cash inflow	**$ 690**	**$ 771**	**$ 853**	**$ 934**	**$ 1,015**	**$ 1,097**	**$ 1,178**	**$ 1,259**
Other cash inflows								
Equity investment	$ 25,000	$ 0	$ 0	$ 0	$ 0	$ 0	$ 0	$ 0
Increased borrowings	$125,000	$ 0	$ 0	$ 0	$ 0	$ 0	$ 0	$ 0
Sales of business assets	$ 0	$ 0	$ 0	$ 0	$ 0	$ 0	$ 0	$ 0
A/P increases	$ 3,159	$ 3,159	$ 3,159	$ 3,159	$ 3,159	$ 3,159	$ 3,159	$ 3,159
Total other cash inflows	**$153,159**	**$ 3,159**	**$ 3,159**	**$ 3,159**	**$ 3,159**	**$ 3,159**	**$ 3,159**	**$ 3,159**
Total cash inflow	**$153,849**	**$ 3,930**	**$ 4,011**	**$ 4,092**	**$ 4,174**	**$ 4,255**	**$ 4,337**	**$ 4,418**
Cash outflows								
Repayment of principal	$ 646	$ 651	$ 656	$ 661	$ 666	$ 671	$ 676	$ 681
A/P decreases	$ 2,075	$ 2,075	$ 2,075	$ 2,075	$ 2,075	$ 2,075	$ 2,075	$ 2,075
A/R increases	$ 0	$ 0	$ 0	$ 0	$ 0	$ 0	$ 0	$ 0
Asset purchases	$ 72,500	$ 0	$ 0	$ 0	$ 0	$ 0	$ 0	$ 0
Dividends	$ 0	$ 0	$ 0	$ 0	$ 0	$ 0	$ 0	$ 0
Total cash outflows	**$ 75,221**	**$ 2,726**	**$ 2,730**	**$ 2,735**	**$ 2,740**	**$ 2,745**	**$ 2,750**	**$ 2,755**
Net cash flow	**$ 78,628**	**$ 1,204**	**$ 1,281**	**$ 1,357**	**$ 1,433**	**$ 1,510**	**$ 1,586**	**$ 1,663**
Cash balance	**$ 78,628**	**$79,832**	**$81,113**	**$82,470**	**$83,904**	**$85,413**	**$87,000**	**$88,662**

Cash Flow Analysis (First Year Cont.)

Month	9	10	11	12	1
Cash from operations	$ 1,341	$ 1,422	$ 1,504	$ 1,586	$ 13,650
Cash from receivables	$ 0	$ 0	$ 0	$ 0	$ 0
Operating cash inflow	**$ 1,341**	**$ 1,422**	**$ 1,504**	**$ 1,586**	**$ 13,650**
Other cash inflows					
Equity investment	$ 0	$ 0	$ 0	$ 0	$ 25,000
Increased borrowings	$ 0	$ 0	$ 0	$ 0	$125,000
Sales of business assets	$ 0	$ 0	$ 0	$ 0	$ 0
A/P increases	$ 3,159	$ 3,159	$ 3,159	$ 3,159	$ 37,902
Total other cash inflows	**$ 3,159**	**$ 3,159**	**$ 3,159**	**$ 3,159**	**$187,902**
Total cash inflow	**$ 4,499**	**$ 4,581**	**$ 4,662**	**$ 4,744**	**$201,552**
Cash outflows					
Repayment of principal	$ 686	$ 691	$ 696	$ 701	$ 8,079
A/P decreases	$ 2,075	$ 2,075	$ 2,075	$ 2,075	$ 24,897
A/R increases	$ 0	$ 0	$ 0	$ 0	$ 0
Asset purchases	$ 0	$ 0	$ 0	$ 0	$ 72,500
Dividends	$ 0	$ 0	$ 0	$ 9,555	$ 9,555
Total cash outflows	**$ 2,760**	**$ 2,766**	**$ 2,771**	**$12,331**	**$115,032**
Net cash flow	**$ 1,739**	**$ 1,815**	**$ 1,892**	**−$ 7,587**	**$ 86,521**
Cash balance	**$90,401**	**$92,216**	**$94,108**	**$86,521**	**$ 86,521**

Cash Flow Analysis (Second Year)

Quarter	Q1	Q2	Q3	Q4	2
Cash from operations	$10,124	$12,655	$13,667	$14,173	$50,619
Cash from receivables	$ 0	$ 0	$ 0	$ 0	$ 0
Operating cash inflow	**$10,124**	**$12,655**	**$13,667**	**$14,173**	**$50,619**
Other cash inflows					
Equity investment	$ 0	$ 0	$ 0	$ 0	$ 0
Increased borrowings	$ 0	$ 0	$ 0	$ 0	$ 0
Sales of business assets	$ 0	$ 0	$ 0	$ 0	$ 0
A/P increases	$ 8,717	$10,897	$11,769	$12,204	$43,587
Total other cash inflows	**$ 8,717**	**$10,897**	**$11,769**	**$12,204**	**$43,587**
Total cash inflow	**$18,841**	**$23,552**	**$25,436**	**$26,378**	**$94,206**
Cash outflows					
Repayment of principal	$ 2,136	$ 2,184	$ 2,233	$ 2,284	$ 8,837
A/P decreases	$ 5,975	$ 7,469	$ 8,067	$ 8,365	$29,876
A/R increases	$ 0	$ 0	$ 0	$ 0	$ 0
Asset purchases	$ 2,531	$ 3,164	$ 3,417	$ 3,543	$12,655
Dividends	$ 7,087	$ 8,858	$ 9,567	$ 9,921	$35,433
Total cash outflows	**$17,728**	**$21,675**	**$23,284**	**$24,114**	**$86,802**
Net cash flow	**$ 1,113**	**$ 1,876**	**$ 2,152**	**$ 2,264**	**$ 7,405**
Cash balance	**$87,634**	**$89,510**	**$91,662**	**$93,926**	**$93,926**

Cash Flow Analysis (Third Year)

Quarter	Q1	Q2	Q3	Q4	3
Cash from operations	$16,812	$21,015	$ 22,697	$ 23,537	$ 84,062
Cash from receivables	$ 0	$ 0	$ 0	$ 0	$ 0
Operating cash inflow	**$16,812**	**$21,015**	**$ 22,697**	**$ 23,537**	**$ 84,062**
Other cash inflows					
Equity investment	$ 0	$ 0	$ 0	$ 0	$ 0
Increased borrowings	$ 0	$ 0	$ 0	$ 0	$ 0
Sales of business assets	$ 0	$ 0	$ 0	$ 0	$ 0
A/P increases	$10,025	$12,531	$ 13,534	$ 14,035	$ 50,125
Total other cash inflows	**$10,025**	**$12,531**	**$ 13,534**	**$ 14,035**	**$ 50,125**
Total cash inflow	**$26,837**	**$33,547**	**$ 36,231**	**$ 37,572**	**$134,187**
Cash outflows					
Repayment of principal	$ 2,336	$ 2,389	$ 2,443	$ 2,498	$ 9,666
A/P decreases	$ 7,170	$ 8,963	$ 9,680	$ 10,038	$ 35,852
A/R increases	$ 0	$ 0	$ 0	$ 0	$ 0
Asset purchases	$ 4,203	$ 5,254	$ 5,674	$ 5,884	$ 21,015
Dividends	$11,769	$14,711	$ 15,888	$ 16,476	$ 58,843
Total cash outflows	**$25,478**	**$31,316**	**$ 33,685**	**$ 34,897**	**$125,377**
Net cash flow	**$ 1,359**	**$ 2,230**	**$ 2,546**	**$ 2,675**	**$ 8,811**
Cash balance	**$95,285**	**$97,515**	**$100,061**	**$102,736**	**$102,736**

Freelance Indexer

Donahue Indexing Services, Inc.

PO Box 91123
New York, NY 10018

BizPlanDB.com

The purpose of this business plan is to raise $30,000 for the development of a freelance indexer business while showcasing the expected financials and operations over the next three years. Donahue Indexing Services, Inc. ("the Company") is a New York-based corporation that will provide indexing and limited copyright editing to authors. The Company was founded by Jack Donahue.

1.0 EXECUTIVE SUMMARY

The purpose of this business plan is to raise $30,000 for the development of a freelance indexer business while showcasing the expected financials and operations over the next three years. Donahue Indexing Services, Inc. ("the Company") is a New York-based corporation that will provide indexing and limited copyright editing to authors. The Company was founded by Jack Donahue.

1.1 The Services

The primary service offered by the business to its customers will consist of indexing books, manuscripts, and documentation on behalf of authors and book publishing businesses. Indexing is a complicated process, and it requires someone with a great deal of knowledge of writing to complete this task. The Company will charge $1,000 to $3,000 per indexed book.

The business will also develop an online ordering platform so that the business can generate sales on a worldwide basis. Manuscripts and documentation can be sent directly to Mr. Donahue and his assistant to be indexed.

The third section of the business plan will further describe the services offered by Donahue Indexing Services.

1.2 Financing

Mr. Donahue is seeking to raise $30,000 from a bank loan. The interest rate and loan agreement are to be further discussed during negotiation. This business plan assumes that the business will receive a 10-year loan with a 6.25% fixed interest rate. The financing will be used for the following:

- Development of the Company's office location.
- Financing for the first six months of operation.
- Financing for computer acquisitions.

Mr. Donahue will contribute $5,000 to the venture.

1.3 Mission Statement

To provide outstanding indexing and limited editing services to a broad spectrum of non-fiction authors and book publishers on a worldwide basis.

1.4 Management Team

The Company was founded by Jack Donahue. Mr. Donahue has more than 10 years of experience as a writer. Through his expertise, he will be able to bring the operations of the business to profitability within its first year of operations.

1.5 Sales Forecasts

Mr. Donahue expects a strong rate of growth at the start of operations. Below are the expected financials over the next three years.

Proforma Profit and Loss (Yearly)

Year	1	2	3
Sales	$156,600	$172,260	$189,486
Operating costs	$113,001	$117,435	$122,085
EBITDA	$ 35,769	$ 46,212	$ 57,927
Taxes, interest, and depreciation	$ 16,975	$ 20,166	$ 24,523
Net profit	$ 18,794	$ 26,046	$ 33,403

Sales, Operating Costs, and Profit Forecast

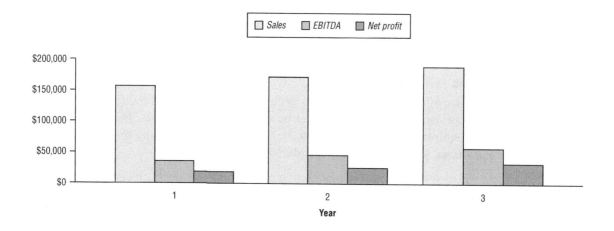

1.6 Expansion Plan

Mr. Donahue intends to implement marketing campaigns that will effectively target individual authors as well as small independent book publishing businesses within the target market. Once these relationships are established, the business will require minimal ongoing marketing.

2.0 COMPANY AND FINANCING SUMMARY

2.1 Registered Name and Corporate Structure

The Company is registered as a corporation in the State of New York.

2.2 Required Funds

At this time, Donahue Indexing Services requires $30,000 of debt funds. Below is a breakdown of how these funds will be used:

Projected Startup Costs

Professional fees and licensure	$ 2,000
Working capital	$13,000
FF&E	$15,000
Initial marketing budget	$ 3,500
Misc. development costs	$ 1,500
Total startup costs	**$35,000**

Use of Funds

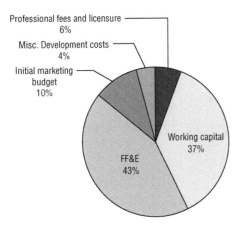

2.3 Investor Equity

Mr. Donahue is not seeking an investment from a third party at this time.

2.4 Management Equity

Jack Donahue owns 100% of Donahue Indexing Services, Inc.

3.0 FREELANCE INDEXER OPERATIONS

Donahue Indexing Services will be actively engaged in the process of indexing the content of non-fiction books for authors and smaller book publishing businesses. Mr. Donahue will do a vast majority of the work himself, but he will have an assistant present to manage his schedule and to work with clients on an ongoing basis.

On an infrequent basis, Mr. Donahue will assist with the editing of a non-fiction text. These services will generally accompany the indexing services offered by Mr. Donahue and the business.

4.0 STRATEGIC AND MARKET ANALYSIS

4.1 Economic Outlook

This section of the analysis will detail the economic climate, the professional writing industry, the customer profile, and the competition that the business will face as it progresses through its business operations.

Currently, the economic market condition in the United States is moderate. Interest rates have remained stable while asset values have increased significantly. Unemployment figures are at historical lows.

4.2 Industry Analysis

The specialized writing and word processing industry is a highly fragmented group of individual practitioners, small firms, and large publishing institutions. There are over 20,000 professional writing firms in the United States. The industry generates over $3 billion dollars a year, and employs over 39,000 Americans.

The demand for outsourced indexing, editing, and related writing services is expected to increase as publishing companies want to reduce their personnel overhead costs.

4.3 Customer Profile

By acting in a multifaceted freelance indexing and editing capacity, the Company will be able to provide its services to a broad spectrum of independent publishers and self-publishing authors. Below is a demographic profile of the businesses that Management will continue to target as potential clientele:

Independent Publishers
- Is a privately-owned business

- Has less than $1,000,000 per year of revenue

- Has EBITDA of $50,000 to $250,000 per year

Authors
- Specializes in non-fiction writing

- Has an indexing budget of $1,500

- Lives within the United States

- Is a full-time professional writer

4.4 Competition

There are many writers and indexers that operate on a freelance basis within the United States that can render similar services to that of the business. As such, competition is difficult to determine as there are thousands of professional writers that market their services online. The business will differentiate itself from other indexing companies by offering its services at extremely competitive rates while concurrently focusing on Mr. Donahue's extensive experience as an index writer.

5.0 MARKETING PLAN

Donahue Indexing Services intends to maintain an extensive marketing campaign that will ensure maximum visibility for the business in its targeted market. Below is an overview of the marketing strategies and objectives of Donahue Indexing Services.

5.1 Marketing Objectives
- Maintain profiles on popular freelancing websites such as Freelancer.com, Elance.com, and Odesk.com.

- Develop an online presence by creating a website and placing the Company's name and contact information with online directories.

5.2 Marketing Strategies

Foremost, the Company intends to use third party freelancing websites including Freelancer.com, Elance.com, and Odesk.com to promote the services offered. These companies allow individuals (and small businesses) to bid on projects that are currently advertised among authors seeking editing and indexing work. There are no upfront fees for using these services. For each successful project completed, these companies take a fee equal to 10% of the value of the job. This will be one of the early and primary methods that the business uses in order to generate sales.

Donahue Indexing Services, for its own website, will use several methods of online advertising including search engine optimization techniques and pay-per-click advertising. The SEO technique will be completed by a third-party web development firm that will enter Donahue Indexing Services's website into a number of online directories that will increase the website's visibility throughout the Internet. The secondary method for creating traffic to the Company's website will be through pay-per-click advertising which allows Donahue Indexing Services's website to appear on the front page of several websites. This method of adverting works as each time a person clicks on the advertisement a small debit is made to the Company's account. Popular search engines that use this business model include Google, Yahoo, Excite, and many other forms of advertising. The website will feature samples of Mr. Donahue's indexing work, contact information, and preliminary pricing information.

Finally, Mr. Donahue will develop relationships with small New York area independent publishing businesses that will use the business for indexing their non-fiction work.

5.3 Pricing

Mr. Donahue anticipates that the business will generate $1,500 per indexing job completed by the business.

6.0 ORGANIZATIONAL PLAN AND PERSONNEL SUMMARY

6.1 Corporate Organization

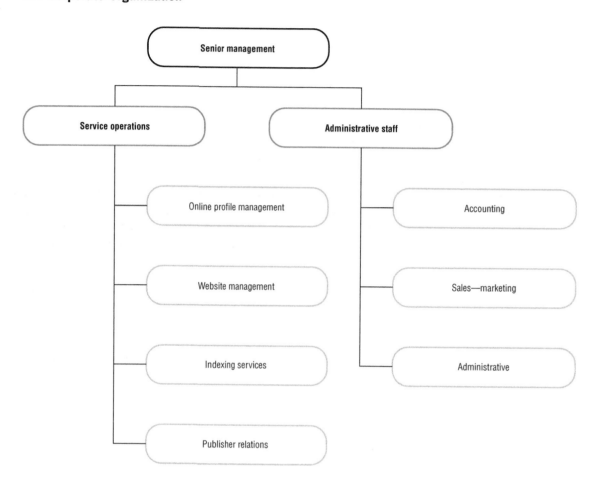

6.2 Organizational Budget

Personnel Plan—Yearly

Year	1	2	3
Mr. Doe	$42,500	$43,775	$45,088
Owner's assistant	$27,500	$28,325	$29,175
Total	**$70,000**	**$72,100**	**$74,263**

Numbers of Personnel

Year	1	2	3
Mr. Doe	1	1	1
Owner's assistant	1	1	1
Totals	**2**	**2**	**2**

Personnel Expense Breakdown

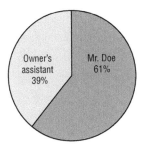

7.0 FINANCIAL PLAN

7.1 Underlying Assumptions

The Company has based its proforma financial statements on the following:

- Donahue Indexing Services will have an annual revenue growth rate of 10% per year.

- The Owner will acquire $30,000 of debt funds to develop the business.

- The loan will have a 10-year term with a 6.25% interest rate.

- The business will settle most short-term payables on a monthly basis.

7.2 Sensitivity Analysis

Donahue Indexing Services's revenues are moderately sensitive to changes in the general economy. During times of economic recession, the Company may have issues relating to generating top line income. However, Donahue Indexing Services's targeted demographics will continue to require indexing services in order to have their works successfully published. As such, the business should be able to remain profitable in any economic climate.

7.3 Source of Funds

Financing

Equity contributions	
Management investment	$ 5,000.00
Total equity financing	**$ 5,000.00**
Banks and lenders	
Banks and lenders	$ 30,000.00
Total debt financing	**$30,000.00**
Total financing	**$35,000.00**

7.4 General Assumptions

General Assumptions

Year	1	2	3
Federal tax rate	33.0%	33.0%	33.0%
State tax rate	5.0%	5.0%	5.0%
Personnel taxes	15.0%	15.0%	15.0%

7.5 Profit and Loss Statements

Proforma Profit and Loss (Yearly)

Year	1	2	3
Sales	**$156,600**	**$172,260**	**$189,486**
Cost of goods sold	$ 7,830	$ 8,613	$ 9,474
Gross margin	95.00%	95.00%	95.00%
Operating income	**$148,770**	**$163,647**	**$180,012**
Expenses			
Payroll	$ 70,000	$ 72,100	$ 74,263
General and administrative	$ 2,520	$ 2,621	$ 2,726
Marketing expenses	$ 4,698	$ 5,168	$ 5,685
Professional fees and licensure	$ 1,500	$ 1,545	$ 1,591
Insurance costs	$ 12,000	$ 12,600	$ 13,230
Travel and vehicle costs	$ 3,500	$ 3,850	$ 4,235
Rent and utilities	$ 7,500	$ 7,875	$ 8,269
Miscellaneous costs	$ 783	$ 861	$ 947
Payroll taxes	$ 10,500	$ 10,815	$ 11,139
Total operating costs	**$113,001**	**$117,435**	**$122,085**
EBITDA	**$ 35,769**	**$ 46,212**	**$ 57,927**
Federal income tax	$ 11,804	$ 14,699	$ 18,616
State income tax	$ 1,788	$ 2,227	$ 2,821
Interest expense	$ 1,812	$ 1,668	$ 1,516
Depreciation expenses	$ 1,571	$ 1,571	$ 1,571
Net profit	**$ 18,794**	**$ 26,046**	**$ 33,403**
Profit margin	**12.00%**	**15.12%**	**17.63%**

Sales, Operating Costs, and Profit Forecast

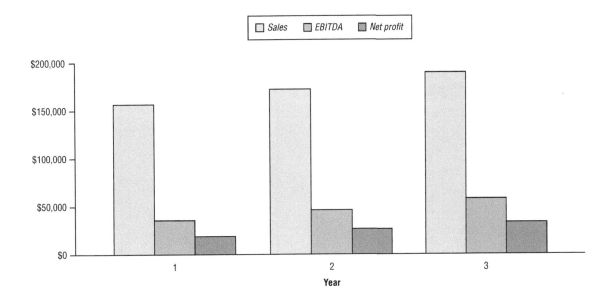

7.6 Cash Flow Analysis

Proforma Cash Flow Analysis—Yearly

Year	1	2	3
Cash from operations	$20,365	$27,617	$34,975
Cash from receivables	$ 0	$ 0	$ 0
Operating cash inflow	**$20,365**	**$27,617**	**$34,975**
Other cash inflows			
Equity investment	$ 5,000	$ 0	$ 0
Increased borrowings	$30,000	$ 0	$ 0
Sales of business assets	$ 0	$ 0	$ 0
A/P increases	$37,902	$43,587	$50,125
Total other cash inflows	**$72,902**	**$43,587**	**$50,125**
Total cash inflow	**$93,267**	**$71,204**	**$85,100**
Cash outflows			
Repayment of principal	$ 2,230	$ 2,374	$ 2,526
A/P decreases	$24,897	$29,876	$35,852
A/R increases	$ 0	$ 0	$ 0
Asset purchases	$22,000	$ 6,904	$ 8,744
Dividends	$14,255	$19,332	$24,482
Total cash outflows	**$63,383**	**$58,486**	**$71,604**
Net cash flow	**$29,884**	**$12,718**	**$13,496**
Cash balance	**$29,884**	**$42,602**	**$56,098**

Proforma Cash Flow (Yearly)

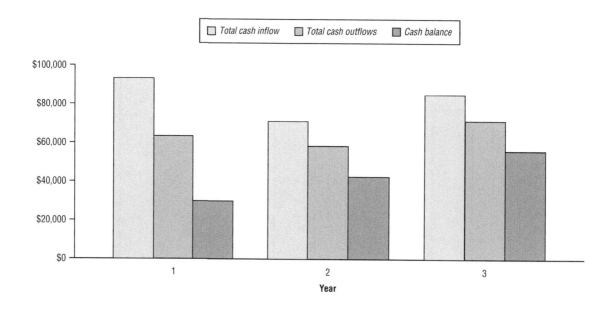

7.7 Balance Sheet

Proforma Balance Sheet—Yearly

Year	1	2	3
Assets			
Cash	$29,884	$42,602	$56,098
Amortized development/expansion costs	$ 7,000	$ 7,690	$ 8,565
FF&E	$15,000	$21,214	$29,083
Accumulated depreciation	($ 1,571)	($ 3,143)	($ 4,714)
Total assets	**$50,313**	**$68,364**	**$95,590**
Liabilities and equity			
Accounts payable	$13,005	$26,716	$40,990
Long term liabilities	$27,770	$25,396	$23,022
Other liabilities	$ 0	$ 0	$ 0
Total liabilities	**$40,775**	**$52,112**	**$64,012**
Net worth	**$ 9,538**	**$16,252**	**$31,578**
Total liabilities and equity	**$50,313**	**$68,364**	**$95,590**

Proforma Balance Sheet

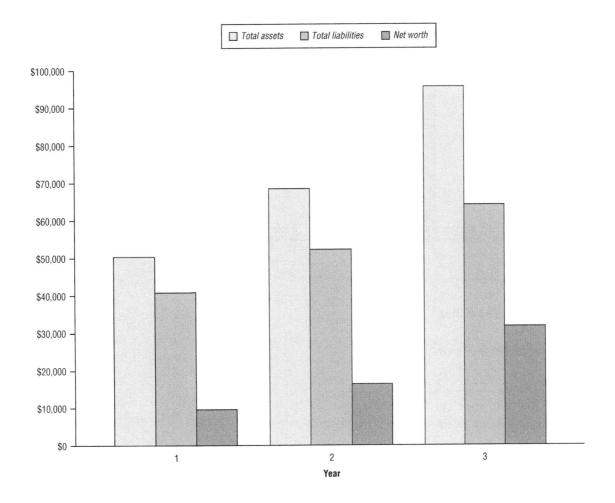

7.8 Breakeven Analysis

Monthly Break Even Analysis

Year	1	2	3
Monthly revenue	$ 9,912	$ 10,301	$ 10,709
Yearly revenue	$118,948	$123,616	$128,511

Break Even Analysis

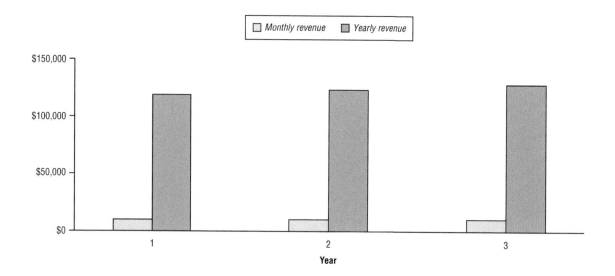

7.9 Business Ratios

Business Ratios—Yearly

Year	1	2	3
Sales			
Sales growth	0.0%	10.0%	10.0%
Gross margin	95.0%	95.0%	95.0%
Financials			
Profit margin	12.00%	15.12%	17.63%
Assets to liabilities	1.23	1.31	1.49
Equity to liabilities	0.23	0.31	0.49
Assets to equity	5.27	4.21	3.03
Liquidity			
Acid test	0.73	0.82	0.88
Cash to assets	0.59	0.62	0.59

7.10 Three Year Profit and Loss Statement

Profit and Loss Statement (First Year)

Months	1	2	3	4	5	6	7
Sales	$12,500	$12,600	$12,700	$12,800	$12,900	$13,000	$13,100
Cost of goods sold	$ 625	$ 630	$ 635	$ 640	$ 645	$ 650	$ 655
Gross margin	95.0%	95.0%	95.0%	95.0%	95.0%	95.0%	95.0%
Operating income	$11,875	$11,970	$12,065	$12,160	$12,255	$12,350	$12,445
Expenses							
Payroll	$ 5,833	$ 5,833	$ 5,833	$ 5,833	$ 5,833	$ 5,833	$ 5,833
General and administrative	$ 210	$ 210	$ 210	$ 210	$ 210	$ 210	$ 210
Marketing expenses	$ 392	$ 392	$ 392	$ 392	$ 392	$ 392	$ 392
Professional fees and licensure	$ 125	$ 125	$ 125	$ 125	$ 125	$ 125	$ 125
Insurance costs	$ 1,000	$ 1,000	$ 1,000	$ 1,000	$ 1,000	$ 1,000	$ 1,000
Travel and vehicle costs	$ 292	$ 292	$ 292	$ 292	$ 292	$ 292	$ 292
Rent and utilities	$ 625	$ 625	$ 625	$ 625	$ 625	$ 625	$ 625
Miscellaneous costs	$ 65	$ 65	$ 65	$ 65	$ 65	$ 65	$ 65
Payroll taxes	$ 875	$ 875	$ 875	$ 875	$ 875	$ 875	$ 875
Total operating costs	$ 9,417	$ 9,417	$ 9,417	$ 9,417	$ 9,417	$ 9,417	$ 9,417
EBITDA	$ 2,458	$ 2,553	$ 2,648	$ 2,743	$ 2,838	$ 2,933	$ 3,028
Federal income tax	$ 942	$ 950	$ 957	$ 965	$ 972	$ 980	$ 987
State income tax	$ 143	$ 144	$ 145	$ 146	$ 147	$ 148	$ 150
Interest expense	$ 156	$ 155	$ 154	$ 153	$ 152	$ 151	$ 151
Depreciation expense	$ 131	$ 131	$ 131	$ 131	$ 131	$ 131	$ 131
Net profit	$ 1,086	$ 1,173	$ 1,261	$ 1,348	$ 1,435	$ 1,522	$ 1,610

Profit and Loss Statement (First Year Cont.)

Months	8	9	10	11	12	1
Sales	$13,200	$13,300	$13,400	$13,500	$13,600	$156,600
Cost of goods sold	$ 660	$ 665	$ 670	$ 675	$ 680	$ 7,830
Gross margin	95.0%	95.0%	95.0%	95.0%	95.0%	95.0%
Operating income	$12,540	$12,635	$12,730	$12,825	$12,920	$148,770
Expenses						
Payroll	$ 5,833	$ 5,833	$ 5,833	$ 5,833	$ 5,833	$ 70,000
General and administrative	$ 210	$ 210	$ 210	$ 210	$ 210	$ 2,520
Marketing expenses	$ 392	$ 392	$ 392	$ 392	$ 392	$ 4,698
Professional fees and licensure	$ 125	$ 125	$ 125	$ 125	$ 125	$ 1,500
Insurance costs	$ 1,000	$ 1,000	$ 1,000	$ 1,000	$ 1,000	$ 12,000
Travel and vehicle costs	$ 292	$ 292	$ 292	$ 292	$ 292	$ 3,500
Rent and utilities	$ 625	$ 625	$ 625	$ 625	$ 625	$ 7,500
Miscellaneous costs	$ 65	$ 65	$ 65	$ 65	$ 65	$ 783
Payroll taxes	$ 875	$ 875	$ 875	$ 875	$ 875	$ 10,500
Total operating costs	$ 9,417	$ 9,417	$ 9,417	$ 9,417	$ 9,417	$113,001
EBITDA	$ 3,123	$ 3,218	$ 3,313	$ 3,408	$ 3,503	$ 35,769
Federal income tax	$ 995	$ 1,002	$ 1,010	$ 1,018	$ 1,025	$ 11,804
State income tax	$ 151	$ 152	$ 153	$ 154	$ 155	$ 1,788
Interest expense	$ 150	$ 149	$ 148	$ 147	$ 146	$ 1,812
Depreciation expense	$ 131	$ 131	$ 131	$ 131	$ 131	$ 1,571
Net profit	$ 1,697	$ 1,784	$ 1,872	$ 1,959	$ 2,046	$ 18,794

Profit and Loss Statement (Second Year)

Quarter	Q1	Q2	Q3	Q4	2
Sales	$34,452	$43,065	$46,510	$48,233	$172,260
Cost of goods sold	$ 1,723	$ 2,153	$ 2,326	$ 2,412	$ 8,613
Gross margin	95.0%	95.0%	95.0%	95.0%	95.0%
Operating income	$32,729	$40,912	$44,185	$45,821	$163,647
Expenses					
Payroll	$14,420	$18,025	$19,467	$20,188	$ 72,100
General and administrative	$ 524	$ 655	$ 708	$ 734	$ 2,621
Marketing expenses	$ 1,034	$ 1,292	$ 1,395	$ 1,447	$ 5,168
Professional fees and licensure	$ 309	$ 386	$ 417	$ 433	$ 1,545
Insurance costs	$ 2,520	$ 3,150	$ 3,402	$ 3,528	$ 12,600
Travel and vehicle costs	$ 770	$ 963	$ 1,040	$ 1,078	$ 3,850
Rent and utilities	$ 1,575	$ 1,969	$ 2,126	$ 2,205	$ 7,875
Miscellaneous costs	$ 172	$ 215	$ 233	$ 241	$ 861
Payroll taxes	$ 2,163	$ 2,704	$ 2,920	$ 3,028	$ 10,815
Total operating costs	$23,487	$29,359	$31,707	$32,882	$117,435
EBITDA	$ 9,242	$11,553	$12,477	$12,939	$ 46,212
Federal income tax	$ 2,940	$ 3,675	$ 3,969	$ 4,116	$ 14,699
State income tax	$ 445	$ 557	$ 601	$ 624	$ 2,227
Interest expense	$ 431	$ 422	$ 413	$ 403	$ 1,668
Depreciation expense	$ 393	$ 393	$ 393	$ 393	$ 1,571
Net profit	$ 5,033	$ 6,507	$ 7,102	$ 7,404	$ 26,046

Profit and Loss Statement (Third Year)

Quarter	Q1	Q2	Q3	Q4	3
Sales	$37,897	$47,372	$51,161	$53,056	$189,486
Cost of goods sold	$ 1,895	$ 2,369	$ 2,558	$ 2,653	$ 9,474
Gross margin	95.0%	95.0%	95.0%	95.0%	95.0%
Operating income	$36,002	$45,003	$48,603	$50,403	$180,012
Expenses					
Payroll	$14,853	$18,566	$20,051	$20,794	$ 74,263
General and administrative	$ 545	$ 681	$ 736	$ 763	$ 2,726
Marketing expenses	$ 1,137	$ 1,421	$ 1,535	$ 1,592	$ 5,685
Professional fees and licensure	$ 318	$ 398	$ 430	$ 446	$ 1,591
Insurance costs	$ 2,646	$ 3,308	$ 3,572	$ 3,704	$ 13,230
Travel and vehicle costs	$ 847	$ 1,059	$ 1,143	$ 1,186	$ 4,235
Rent and utilities	$ 1,654	$ 2,067	$ 2,233	$ 2,315	$ 8,269
Miscellaneous costs	$ 189	$ 237	$ 256	$ 265	$ 947
Payroll taxes	$ 2,228	$ 2,785	$ 3,008	$ 3,119	$ 11,139
Total operating costs	$24,417	$30,521	$32,963	$34,184	$122,085
EBITDA	$11,585	$14,482	$15,640	$16,219	$ 57,927
Federal income tax	$ 3,723	$ 4,654	$ 5,026	$ 5,212	$ 18,616
State income tax	$ 564	$ 705	$ 762	$ 790	$ 2,821
Interest expense	$ 394	$ 384	$ 374	$ 364	$ 1,516
Depreciation expense	$ 393	$ 393	$ 393	$ 393	$ 1,571
Net profit	$ 6,512	$ 8,346	$ 9,085	$ 9,460	$ 33,403

7.11 Three Year Cash Flow Analysis

Cash Flow Analysis (First Year)

Month	1	2	3	4	5	6	7	8
Cash from operations	$ 1,217	$ 1,304	$ 1,392	$ 1,479	$ 1,566	$ 1,653	$ 1,741	$ 1,828
Cash from receivables	$ 0	$ 0	$ 0	$ 0	$ 0	$ 0	$ 0	$ 0
Operating cash inflow	**$ 1,217**	**$ 1,304**	**$ 1,392**	**$ 1,479**	**$ 1,566**	**$ 1,653**	**$ 1,741**	**$ 1,828**
Other cash inflows								
Equity investment	$ 5,000	$ 0	$ 0	$ 0	$ 0	$ 0	$ 0	$ 0
Increased borrowings	$30,000	$ 0	$ 0	$ 0	$ 0	$ 0	$ 0	$ 0
Sales of business assets	$ 0	$ 0	$ 0	$ 0	$ 0	$ 0	$ 0	$ 0
A/P increases	$ 3,159	$ 3,159	$ 3,159	$ 3,159	$ 3,159	$ 3,159	$ 3,159	$ 3,159
Total other cash inflows	**$38,159**	**$ 3,159**	**$ 3,159**	**$ 3,159**	**$ 3,159**	**$ 3,159**	**$ 3,159**	**$ 3,159**
Total cash inflow	**$39,376**	**$ 4,463**	**$ 4,550**	**$ 4,637**	**$ 4,725**	**$ 4,812**	**$ 4,899**	**$ 4,986**
Cash outflows								
Repayment of principal	$ 181	$ 182	$ 182	$ 183	$ 184	$ 185	$ 186	$ 187
A/P decreases	$ 2,075	$ 2,075	$ 2,075	$ 2,075	$ 2,075	$ 2,075	$ 2,075	$ 2,075
A/R increases	$ 0	$ 0	$ 0	$ 0	$ 0	$ 0	$ 0	$ 0
Asset purchases	$22,000	$ 0	$ 0	$ 0	$ 0	$ 0	$ 0	$ 0
Dividends	$ 0	$ 0	$ 0	$ 0	$ 0	$ 0	$ 0	$ 0
Total cash outflows	**$24,255**	**$ 2,256**	**$ 2,257**	**$ 2,258**	**$ 2,259**	**$ 2,260**	**$ 2,261**	**$ 2,262**
Net cash flow	**$15,120**	**$ 2,207**	**$ 2,293**	**$ 2,379**	**$ 2,465**	**$ 2,552**	**$ 2,638**	**$ 2,724**
Cash balance	**$15,120**	**$17,327**	**$19,620**	**$21,999**	**$24,464**	**$27,016**	**$29,654**	**$32,379**

Cash Flow Analysis (First Year Cont.)

Month	9	10	11	12	1
Cash from operations	$ 1,915	$ 2,003	$ 2,090	$ 2,177	$20,365
Cash from receivables	$ 0	$ 0	$ 0	$ 0	$ 0
Operating cash inflow	**$ 1,915**	**$ 2,003**	**$ 2,090**	**$ 2,177**	**$20,365**
Other cash inflows					
Equity investment	$ 0	$ 0	$ 0	$ 0	$ 5,000
Increased borrowings	$ 0	$ 0	$ 0	$ 0	$30,000
Sales of business assets	$ 0	$ 0	$ 0	$ 0	$ 0
A/P increases	$ 3,159	$ 3,159	$ 3,159	$ 3,159	$37,902
Total other cash inflows	**$ 3,159**	**$ 3,159**	**$ 3,159**	**$ 3,159**	**$72,902**
Total cash inflow	**$ 5,074**	**$ 5,161**	**$ 5,248**	**$ 5,336**	**$93,267**
Cash outflows					
Repayment of principal	$ 188	$ 189	$ 190	$ 192	$ 2,230
A/P decreases	$ 2,075	$ 2,075	$ 2,075	$ 2,075	$24,897
A/R increases	$ 0	$ 0	$ 0	$ 0	$ 0
Asset purchases	$ 0	$ 0	$ 0	$ 0	$22,000
Dividends	$ 0	$ 0	$ 0	$14,255	$14,255
Total cash outflows	**$ 2,263**	**$ 2,264**	**$ 2,265**	**$16,522**	**$63,383**
Net cash flow	**$ 2,811**	**$ 2,897**	**$ 2,983**	**−$11,186**	**$29,884**
Cash balance	**$35,189**	**$38,087**	**$41,070**	**$29,884**	**$29,884**

Cash Flow Analysis (Second Year)

Quarter	Q1	Q2	Q3	Q4	2
Cash from operations	$ 5,523	$ 6,904	$ 7,457	$ 7,733	$27,617
Cash from receivables	$ 0	$ 0	$ 0	$ 0	$ 0
Operating cash inflow	**$ 5,523**	**$ 6,904**	**$ 7,457**	**$ 7,733**	**$27,617**
Other cash inflows					
Equity investment	$ 0	$ 0	$ 0	$ 0	$ 0
Increased borrowings	$ 0	$ 0	$ 0	$ 0	$ 0
Sales of business assets	$ 0	$ 0	$ 0	$ 0	$ 0
A/P increases	$ 8,717	$10,897	$11,769	$12,204	$43,587
Total other cash inflows	**$ 8,717**	**$10,897**	**$11,769**	**$12,204**	**$43,587**
Total cash inflow	**$14,241**	**$17,801**	**$19,225**	**$19,937**	**$71,204**
Cash outflows					
Repayment of principal	$ 580	$ 589	$ 598	$ 607	$ 2,374
A/P decreases	$ 5,975	$ 7,469	$ 8,067	$ 8,365	$29,876
A/R increases	$ 0	$ 0	$ 0	$ 0	$ 0
Asset purchases	$ 1,381	$ 1,726	$ 1,864	$ 1,933	$ 6,904
Dividends	$ 3,866	$ 4,833	$ 5,220	$ 5,413	$19,332
Total cash outflows	**$11,802**	**$14,617**	**$15,748**	**$16,319**	**$58,486**
Net cash flow	**$ 2,439**	**$ 3,184**	**$ 3,477**	**$ 3,618**	**$12,718**
Cash balance	**$32,323**	**$35,507**	**$38,984**	**$42,602**	**$42,602**

Cash Flow Analysis (Third Year)

Quarter	Q1	Q2	Q3	Q4	3
Cash from operations	$ 6,995	$ 8,744	$ 9,443	$ 9,793	$34,975
Cash from receivables	$ 0	$ 0	$ 0	$ 0	$ 0
Operating cash inflow	**$ 6,995**	**$ 8,744**	**$ 9,443**	**$ 9,793**	**$34,975**
Other cash inflows					
Equity investment	$ 0	$ 0	$ 0	$ 0	$ 0
Increased borrowings	$ 0	$ 0	$ 0	$ 0	$ 0
Sales of business assets	$ 0	$ 0	$ 0	$ 0	$ 0
A/P increases	$10,025	$12,531	$13,534	$14,035	$50,125
Total other cash inflows	**$10,025**	**$12,531**	**$13,534**	**$14,035**	**$50,125**
Total cash inflow	**$17,020**	**$21,275**	**$22,977**	**$23,828**	**$85,100**
Cash outflows					
Repayment of principal	$ 617	$ 627	$ 636	$ 646	$ 2,526
A/P decreases	$ 7,170	$ 8,963	$ 9,680	$10,038	$35,852
A/R increases	$ 0	$ 0	$ 0	$ 0	$ 0
Asset purchases	$ 1,749	$ 2,186	$ 2,361	$ 2,448	$ 8,744
Dividends	$ 4,896	$ 6,121	$ 6,610	$ 6,855	$24,482
Total cash outflows	**$14,432**	**$17,896**	**$19,287**	**$19,988**	**$71,604**
Net cash flow	**$ 2,588**	**$ 3,379**	**$ 3,690**	**$ 3,840**	**$13,496**
Cash balance	**$45,190**	**$48,569**	**$52,258**	**$56,098**	**$56,098**

Fumigation & Pest Control Business

Walker Pest Management Services Inc.

21 Park St.
Johnson Creek, MS 22119

Paul Greenland

Walker Pest Management Services Inc. is a pest control business that offers fumigation services and other types of applications.

EXECUTIVE SUMMARY

Homeowners often can prevent, control, and eliminate common household pests on their own using common sense and over-the-counter products. However, in some cases professional assistance is needed or desired. Through a combination of on-the-job experience and formal training, professional exterminators can help customers to safely eliminate extensive pest problems. Termites, beetles, and bed bugs, in particular, may require fumigation services, in which a residence is sealed with vinyl tarps and a fumigant (pesticide) is injected into the home to eliminate pests. Walker Pest Management Services is a pest control business that offers fumigation services and other types of applications. The newly-established business is operated by the husband-and-wife team of Trent and Cindy Walker who, after working for a major national pest control company, have decided to establish their own business in the Johnson Creek area.

INDUSTRY ANALYSIS

Pest control is big business. According to *Market Share Reporter*, the pest control industry generated revenues of approximately $12 billion during the mid-2010s. Residential homes accounted for 65.6 percent of the market, while commercial establishments accounted for 31.8 percent and government institutions accounted for 2.6 percent. *Market Share Reporter* indicated that industry revenues were benefiting from an increase in bed bug infestations. By pest category, industry revenues broke down as follows:

- Termites (42%)

- Bed Bugs (15%)

- Cockroaches (15%)

- Rodents (8%)

- Ants (6%)

- Mosquitoes (4%)

- Birds (3%)

- Other (7%)

Some pest control businesses focus on either residential or commercial markets, while others serve both. Seasonal fluctuations can affect sales depending on the region of the United States in which a business operates, and its corresponding climate.

MARKET ANALYSIS

Overview

Walker Pest Management Services specializes in serving residential customers in a 50-mile radius surrounding the community of Johnson Creek, Mississippi, which features a humid, warm climate characterized by mild and brief winters and long, hot summers. Termites, in particular, are ubiquitous in Mississippi, providing ample opportunity for businesses that provide professional treatment services.

Competitive Landscape

In 2016, the publication *Pest Control Technology*, revealed that, as of 2015, several large companies competed in the pest control market. These companies, which generated revenues in the billions of dollars, included:

- Rollins (32.23%)

- Terminix International (17.89%)

- Rentokil North America (6.88%)

- Ecolab (6.3%)

- Massey Services (3.13%)

However, U.S. Census Bureau data released in late 2016 found that, during the middle of the decade, the U.S. pest control market was dominated by small businesses. For example, in 2014 there were approximately 11,437 businesses operating in the exterminating and pest control services industry. Of these, more than 66 percent had fewer than five employees. Nearly 94 percent had fewer than 20 employees.

Johnson Creek, Mississippi, mirrors the national market, with pest control services provided by several national leaders. Additionally, there are several locally-owned pest management companies, including:

- Honest Pest Management Inc.

- Bug Busters LLC

- Ernie's Extermination

Of these three primary competitors, Honest Pest Management has agreed to be acquired by one of the large national service providers in the coming months. Although Bug Busters is an established mid-sized service provider, it recently underwent a change in ownership and has developed a poor reputation for quality and customer service. Finally, Ernie's Extermination does not offer fumigation services. Therefore, Trent and Cindy Walker believe that there is excellent opportunity to establish Walker Pest Management Services in the local market.

Target Market

Citing the results of a Harris Interactive survey, PestWorld.org provided insight into the mindset of consumers in the residential market. According to the survey, women (87%) were slightly more concerned about pests during the summer months than men (82%). In terms of concerns about specific types of summer pests, most respondents were concerned by mosquitoes (62%), followed by ticks (30%), spiders (26%), other pests (14%), and bed bugs (11%). Additionally, 90 percent of respondents with children were concerned about having any type of pests in their home, and some 54 percent of respondents were worried about contracting a disease from household pests.

SERVICES

Walker Pest Management Services will provide prevention and extermination services for a variety of household and lawn pests, including:

- Ants
- Aphids
- Armyworm
- Azalea caterpillar
- Bagworms
- Bed bugs
- Bees
- Beetle
- Boxelder bugs
- Carpenter bees
- Carpet beetles
- Centipedes
- Chiggers
- Chinch bugs
- Cluster flies
- Cockroaches
- Crickets
- Earwigs
- Fleas
- Flies
- Grasshopper
- Grubs
- Japanese beetles
- Leaf-feeding caterpillars
- Millipedes

- Mites
- Mosquitos
- Moths
- Silverfish
- Spiders
- Termites
- Wasps

Process

Although every situation is different, Walker Pest Management will take the following general approach when working with its customers:

1. Perform comprehensive inspection, searching for evidence of past problems/infestations.

2. Identify appropriate treatments/solutions.

3. Perform calculations to determine the physical size of the area requiring pest management.

4. Develop an accurate time and cost estimate and a comprehensive pest management plan based on the scope/magnitude of the problem, intended treatment, and property size.

5. Apply pesticides, bait, and set traps inside/outside the property as appropriate.

6. Perform periodic evaluations and make adjustments as needed.

Application Methods

Pesticide applications often will involve using a tank sprayer to provide the appropriate treatment, usually outside of a customer's home. For lawn treatments, a granular spreader may be used. Typically, it is safe for humans and animals to be in the vicinity following the application of pesticides used by Walker Pest Management once the chemicals have dried. Specialized equipment may be used when targeting a specific type of pest. For example, baiting tools may be used to target underground termites, and light traps may be used during flea infestations.

Walker Pest Management also will provide specialized fumigation services, in which a residence is sealed with vinyl tarps and a fumigant (pesticide) is injected into the home to eliminate pests. This approach typically is used to treat certain types of termites, as well as wood-destroying beetles and bed bugs. A detailed process has been developed to perform fumigation safely, beginning with extensive preparation work that involves the removal of food, food preparation items, and plants from the residence. Additionally, pilot lights on gas appliances are turned off to prevent the possibility of an explosion. Landscaping near the outside of the home also is covered or cut back to prevent damage from pesticide emissions in the area immediately adjacent to the vinyl tarps.

Once a residence has been properly prepared, the Walkers will utilize specialized equipment and chemicals to fumigate the home. The time required for fumigation can vary, ranging from only a few hours to as long as one week. On average, Walker Pest Management is able to cover the average-sized home with tarps in about two hours. Larger residences may take additional time. A variety of factors can impact the amount of time required, including the size of the home, the scope and magnitude of the infestation, and temperature. Typically, termite treatments take three days, while beetle treatments may take four days. Customers must provide ample time before going back into their homes. Once the atmosphere inside the residence is safe, Walker Pest Management recommends that customers contract with a sanitation professional to clean their home prior to re-entry.

Natural Treatments

For customers seeking the most environmentally-friendly treatment methods, or who are concerned about the use of chemicals in their homes, Walker Pest Management will offer a limited number of natural treatments that can be tried initially. For example, some termite infestations can be treated using natural oils, including orange oil or clove bud oil, as well as aloe vera. However, like pesticides, these also can be harmful when not handled appropriately.

PERSONNEL

Walker Pest Management Services is owned and operated by the husband-and-wife team of Trent and Cindy Walker, who met (and eventually got married) while working for the local branch of a major national pest management firm.

Cindy Walker

Cindy began working as an office manager and eventually became a pest management technician as well. In this regard, she gained distinction by becoming the first female exterminator in the Johnson Creek area. The fact that she was a woman was very attractive to female customers (especially stay-at-home moms), who were more comfortable having a woman provide services in their home. Cindy not only is unique in her profession, but also has a specialized blend of business management and technical skills that will be extremely beneficial to Walker Pest Management. Cindy will oversee the administrative aspects of the business, including bookkeeping, recordkeeping, materials management/inventory, payments/collections, and licensure. She also will play a lead role in communicating with customers and managing relationships with them. Cindy will spend about half of her time performing pest management services.

Trent Walker

Trent's career in pest management began shortly after he graduated from high school. While working for a local restaurant, Trent became interested in the field while speaking with an exterminator who provided regular pest management service. Eventually, the exterminator offered Trent an opportunity to begin working as an entry-level pest management technician. After gaining the appropriate training and certification, Trent embarked on a five-year career with a leading national service provider, gaining valuable front-line experience and, importantly, developing relationships with homeowners throughout the Johnson Creek community. Trent will take a lead role in providing pest management services, and will spend the majority of his time in the field.

Staff

The owners will be the business' sole employees during the first year of operations. They plan to hire one pest control technician during each of years two and three, based on customer volume.

Professional & Advisory Support

Walker Pest Management has established a business banking account with Johnson Creek Community Bank, including a merchant account for accepting credit card payments. Tax advisement is provided by Loretta Stevens Price Tax Service.

OPERATIONS

The following items will need to be purchased for the business at startup:

Equipment

- Heavy-Duty Fumigation Tarp (40'x60') (4): $300/each
- Heavy-Duty Fumigation Tarp (50'x50') (2): $500/each
- Heavy-Duty Fumigation Tarp (50'x100') (2): $700/each
- Heavy-Duty Fumigation Tarp (100'x100') (1): $1,300
- Tank Sprayers (3): $50/each
- Granular Spreader (2): $75/each
- Fogging Equipment (2): $360/each
- Bait Guns: $40
- Safety Equipment: $125
- Bee Suits: $150
- Foamer: $65
- UV Flashlights (2): $70
- Respirators (2): $150
- Chemical Gloves: $35
- Work Gloves (2): $20
- Spill Kit: $110
- Bug Vacuum: $220

Supplies

The Walkers also will need supplies on an ongoing basis, the majority of which will be pesticides and other chemicals needed for treatment applications. The owners have determined that they will need the following startup supply inventory:

- Termite Baits (150): $40
- Sprayer Cleaner: $25
- Pesticides: $150
- Fumigants: $350
- Shoe & Boot Covers (50): $40
- Mist Concentrates: $200
- Natural Oils: $100

Location

The owners have identified an affordable facility in an industrial area of Johnson Creek that can be leased for Walker Pest Management. The facility includes a small office area, a kitchenette, bathroom facilities, a storage area for chemicals and equipment, and garage space for up to four commercial vehicles.

Vehicles

The Walkers have purchased a used pickup truck and trailer that they will use to transport chemicals and supplies to their customers' homes. An additional truck/trailer combination will be purchased during each of years two and three based on customer demand.

Hours of Operations

The nature of the pest management business requires service providers to work evenings and weekends in order to meet the needs of their customers. Walker Pest Management will maintain a flexible service call schedule based on customer demand. Generally, the Walkers will be available to answer calls from, and establish appointments with, new customers during regular business hours.

Fees

Walker Pest Management's fees will vary depending on each specific job. However, the owners will use the following average fees for calculation purposes:

- Fumigation: $3,000 ($2/square foot/1,500-square-foot home)

- Exterior pesticide application: $125 (1,500-square-foot home) *$25 per additional 1,000 square feet

- Interior pesticide application: $75 (1,500-square-foot home) *$25 per additional 1,000 square feet

- Carpenter ants: $300

- Bedbugs: $750

- Fleas: $150

- Bees/wasps: $100

Communications

Walker Pest Management has obtained a dedicated phone line with call forwarding capabilities so that the Walkers can accept customer calls when out in the field. Additionally, the business has developed an intake form on its Web site, which is mobile friendly, enabling customers to submit information regarding their particular pest management situation in advance. Customers also can attach up to five photos that can be submitted with the intake form. This will expedite planning/scheduling and allow the Walkers to provide the most effective and responsive customer service. In the future, the Walkers hope to work with an independent developer to create a mobile app for their business, which will provide the same functionality as the online intake form, but also provide current customers with a regular means of interacting with the business when problems arise, and allow them to schedule/reschedule service calls and pay any outstanding balances via credit card or other forms of mobile payment.

LEGAL

Walker Pest Management has obtained all necessary licenses, certifications, and registrations. The business has obtained a five-year license from the Mississippi Department of Agriculture. In addition, an adequate level of liability insurance ($100,000/property damage, $300,000/bodily injury), has been secured.

MARKETING & SALES

Walker Pest Management's owners will use the following tactics to promote the business during its first three years of operations:

1. A unique logo/tagline for the business, developed in partnership with a local advertising agency.

2. A content management strategy involving a bi-weekly blog on pest management topics.

3. A media relations strategy in which the Walkers will make themselves available for interviews with local media (especially affiliates of the major national TV networks), positioning themselves as local experts on trending national topics (e.g., bed bugs, etc.).

4. Printed collateral describing the business.

5. Marketing on social media channels, including Facebook and LinkedIn.

6. Magnetic business cards, which the Walkers will distribute around the community.

7. Membership in the Johnson Creek Chamber of Commerce and the Better Business Bureau.

8. Regular print advertisements in the *Johnson Creek Gazette*, a free weekly newspaper distributed throughout the community.

9. A mobile-friendly Web site with complete details about the business, including a convenient intake form for prospective customers.

10. A seasonal direct-mail campaign targeting area households during late winter/early spring, in preparation for the hot summer months when insects are most active.

11. A customer loyalty program that provides a 15 percent discount to those referring a friend or family member.

12. Mobile marketing (vehicle graphics displaying the business' name, Web site address, phone number, and tagline).

BUSINESS STRATEGY

The Walkers began developing a roadmap for the formation of their business while still working for their previous employer. In addition to taking a small business management course at their local community college, the owners identified a name and identity for their business, calculated startup costs, performed market research, incorporated with the assistance of a local business attorney, performed cash flow projections with an accountant, and opened a business checking account at a local bank.

Following this thoughtful preparation, the owners are well-prepared to begin independent operations. While working for their former employer, customers often told the Walkers, "If you ever go into business for yourself, I want to be your first customer!" With this in mind, the Walkers carefully alerted some of these individuals about their plans to go independent. This has allowed them to begin operations with a handful of customers with whom they already have relationships.

From this nucleus of core customers, the owners plan to grow the business steadily during the first three years of operations, and have identified the following annual volume service targets:

	2017	2018	2019
Fumigations (termites)	22	36	50
Exterior applications	720	900	1,080
Interior applications	540	720	900
Bed bugs	86	108	130
Fleas	58	72	86
Bees/wasps	36	50	65
Carpenter ants	65	79	94

FINANCIAL ANALYSIS

Following is a breakdown of projected revenue, expenses, and net income for Walker Pest Management's first three years of operations. The owners anticipate that chemicals and supplies will account for approximately 15 percent and 5 percent of gross sales, respectively. The owners are anticipating profits of approximately $100,000 per year, which they plan to use as capital for expansion in years four and five, potentially through the acquisition of a pest management business in a surrounding community. The Walkers will cover startup costs for equipment and supplies (approximately $8,000) from their own personal savings, and also will contribute an additional $5,000 in financial capital. They are seeking a $20,000 business loan to cover cash flow and other expenses during the first year of operations. Additional financial projections are available upon request.

	2017	2018	2019
Income			
Total sales	$291,780	$395,100	$498,420
Cost of goods sold	$ 58,356	$ 79,020	$ 99,684
Labor cost	$ 70,000	$135,000	$200,000
Total cost of goods sold	$128,356	$214,020	$299,684
Gross profit	$163,424	$181,080	$198,736
Expenses			
Advertising & marketing	$ 15,000	$ 20,000	$ 25,000
Accounting	$ 1,500	$ 1,600	$ 1,700
Insurance	$ 850	$ 900	$ 950
Vehicles	$ 0	$ 20,000	$ 20,000
Rent	$ 8,500	$ 8,500	$ 8,500
Utilities	$ 2,500	$ 3,000	$ 3,500
Telephone	$ 1,128	$ 1,128	$ 1,128
Office supplies	$ 750	$ 750	$ 750
Equipment	$ 2,500	$ 2,500	$ 2,500
Legal	$ 935	$ 935	$ 935
Postage	$ 1,500	$ 2,000	$ 2,500
Professional development	$ 3,500	$ 4,000	$ 4,500
Fees & regulatory	$ 500	$ 500	$ 500
Health insurance	$ 11,000	$ 14,000	$ 17,000
Total expenses	$ 50,163	$ 79,813	$ 89,463
Net income before taxes	$113,261	$101,267	$109,273

Golf Instructor

Willow Ridge Golf Club

6651 Elm St.
Parker, CO 80134

Zuzu Enterprises

Willow Ridge Gold Club is focused on beginning players and instruction as a relatively inexpensive yet quality place to learn the basics and hone your skills. It is a place to discover and realize your love of the game before investing in costly private membership clubs.

EXECUTIVE SUMMARY

Paker, Colorado is the ideal place for golf. It features a population that has the means to play a somewhat costly sport and the weather and land to provide excellent playing conditions. It is close to major markets as well as ample transportation, and is a destination spot for golfers of all skill levels. While there is significant local competition, Willow Ridge Gold Club is focused on beginning players and instruction as a relatively inexpensive yet quality place to learn the basics and hone your skills. It is a place to discover and realize your love of the game before investing in costly private membership clubs.

INDUSTRY ANALYSIS

The sports coaching industry has an annual revenue of $8 billion dollars, with an annual growth rate of 3%. There are over 138,000 businesses in the industry, employing more than 240,000 people. This industry includes one-on-one sports training at athletic facilities as well as camps and schools that offer instruction in athletic activities to groups or individuals. Overnight and day sports instruction camps are also included in this industry.

Increased participation in sports and rising disposable income will support the industry in the near future. Sports camps have become increasingly popular alternatives to summer camps, and increased promotional and governmental support for sports participation will benefit the industry even more.

In 2017, sports camps are expected to account for 47.0% of the industry's revenue.

MARKET ANALYSIS

Parker, Colorado, was founded in 1864 and was incorporated in 1981. Located 20 miles southeast of Denver, Parker sits at an elevation of 5,900 feet above sea level. The town of Parker is 21.5 square miles with a current population of approximately 50,677 people residing within the incorporated Town boundaries.

Parker features an abundance of local amenities including area parks, restaurants, and other cultural and recreational activities. It features a high income per capita and higher home values than the state and national averages. Unemployment is lower here than either the state or national averages. With a crime rate that is 62% lower than that of the rest of the state and great weather year-round, Parker is a great place to live, work, and play.

Access

The Town of Parker has easy access to downtown Denver, the Denver Technology Center (DTC), Denver International Airport (DIA) and Centennial Airport. The E-470 tollway, Lincoln Avenue, Mainstreet and Hess Road all provide connections to I-25. South Parker Road (Highway 83) is a major north/south roadway that connects Parker to Aurora and Colorado Springs.

Distance from Major Markets
*   Downtown Denver: 25 miles, 34 minutes by car
*   Colorado Springs: 54 miles, 1 hour by car
*   Denver Tech Center: 10 miles, 15 minutes by car

Airports
*   Denver International Airport—40 miles northeast
*   Colorado Springs Municipal Airport—58 miles south
*   Centennial Airport (general aviation)—7 miles west

Regional Transportation District
*   The Regional Transportation District (RTD) serves the community by providing a full menu of rapid transit services, including a call-and-ride system and bus services connecting to surrounding communities and the regional light rail system.

Population

The population density in Parker is 4,526% higher than Colorado while the median age is 6% lower than the state average. The population size has increased 111.6% since 2000 and is expected to grow to nearly 60,000 by the year 2021.

Population (2014): 49,857 (99% urban, 1% rural)

Males: 25,168 (50.5%)

Females: 24,689 (49.5%)

Median resident age: 35.1 years

Colorado median age: 36.4 years

The median age for residents is below the state average, while the percentage of the population with a bachelor's degree or higher is above the state average.

Income

The median household income is above state average and it is rising. The estimated median household income in 2015 was $105,041, up from $74,116 in 2000. This is more than $40,000 higher than the state average on Colorado ($63,909).

2016 Household Income

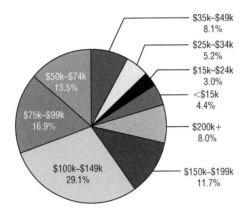

Source of Income

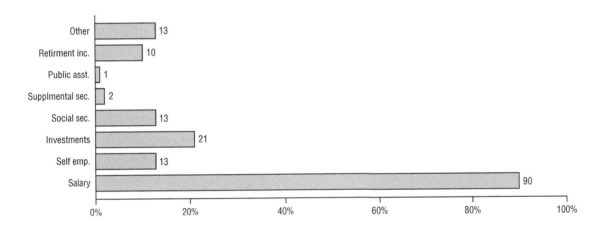

Housing

The estimated median house or condo value in 2015 was $342,583, an significant increase from 2000 when it was $194,000. This is also higher than the state average of $283,800.

In addition to home values increasing, the number of construction projects in the area is up significantly since 2009 as well. The number of single-family new house construction building permits trend is:

2009: 43 buildings, average cost: $357,000

2010: 112 buildings, average cost: $290,300

2011: 185 buildings, average cost: $299,000

2012: 407 buildings, average cost: $284,900

2013: 335 buildings, average cost: $355,700

2014: 348 buildings, average cost: $345,500

Number of permits per 10,000 residents

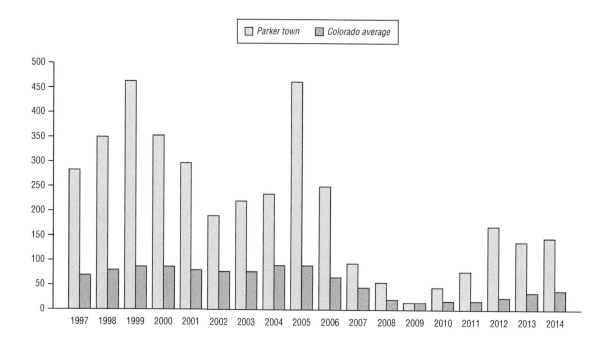

Average cost (in $1,000s)

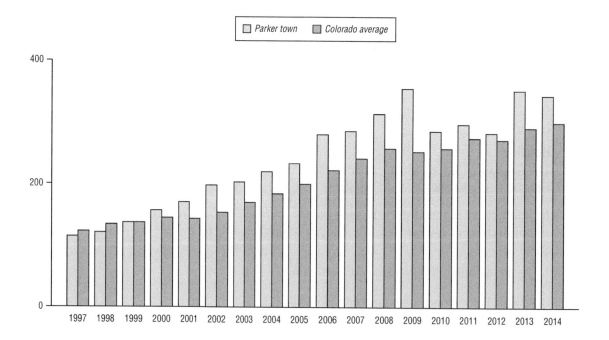

The number of rooms per house is above the state average, while the house age is significantly below the state average.

Unemployment

The percentage of unemployed persons is significantly below state average.

Unemployment in September 2015:

Parker: 3.0%

Colorado: 3.3%

Unemployment in September 2015

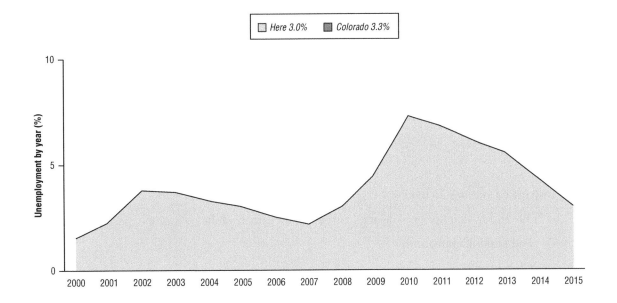

Business

Key industries in Parker include:

- Communications and Broadcasting

- Creative Industries

- Financial Industry

- Health Sciences

- Health and Wellness

- Professional Services including Engineering, Finance, and Business Services

- Retail

- Specialty Manufacturing

- Tourism and Recreation, specifically Golf and Equine

Competition

1. Colorado Golf Club—Features a championship golf course and has hosted the 71st Senior PGA Championship. Also includes a short course and practice facilities.

2. Black Bear Golf Club/Blackstone Country Club—Features a championship golf course and 36 holes of golf over 7,313 yards of play.

3. Pinery Country Club—Features 27 holes and a practice facility. Golf is one of many amenities, including tennis, swimming, and a fitness center.

4. The Club at Pradera—Features a 7,200-yard championship layout and a practice facility.

All of these golf clubs are well known and popular, but can be very costly. There is enough interest in the sport to support all of these clubs as well as Willow Ridge Gold Club. What sets Willow Ridge apart is its short course and practice facilities with a focus on instruction at a reasonable cost. Discovering a love of golf doesn't have to require an immense outlay of cash. With just 3,024 yards, our par 36, 9 hole course is the perfect starting point for beginning golfers.

PERSONNEL

The instruction staff will be comprised of several PGA teaching professionals. Each has at least 2 years of instruction experience as well as customer service training.

SERVICES

Instruction options include:

- 30- and 60-minute one-on-one instruction for either adults or juniors
- Ball striking evaluations
- Club fitting
- Half day workshops
- Ball striking workshops
- Short game workshops
- Putting workshops
- Women's group instruction
- Junior group instruction
- Junior golf camp

Private One-on-One Instruction

One-on-one instruction is provided to either adults or juniors. Instruction is tailored to the unique skills and needs of the individual golfer. Available in either 30- or 60-minute increments. Discounts are available if a series of lessons are purchased at one time.

Ball Striking Evaluation

This 90-minute evaluation will examine participants' ball striking technique. Aspects that will be covered include: what the clubs should do through impact, developing ball flight control and trajectory control, and important differences between iron shots and driving. Video analysis will be done to show participants where to improve.

Club Fitting

A one-hour custom club fitting will match a player's swing to the right equipment. The shaft, length, loft, lie and grip will all be examined. Players will loosen up with their current clubs while being evaluated by staff. The club fitter's job is to observe, analyze and determine what head/shaft/grip combination is best suited for the individual and have their custom golf clubs built accordingly.

Half Day Workshops

We've specifically designed these half day workshops to help intermediate to advanced level golfers develop skills needed to lower scores by improving their ball striking, short games, and putting in small group formats, which allows for substantial instruction time at affordable rates. All areas of ball striking, the short game, and putting will be addressed in half day formats. The Half Day Workshops consists of 3.5 hours of instruction. The minimum class size is two students with a 4:1 student/teacher ratio.

Ball Striking Workshops

This workshop will cover the most important areas involved in developing higher levels of ball striking: what the clubs should do through impact, developing ball flight control and trajectory control, and important differences between iron shots and driving. The ball striking half day workshops will include video analysis for participants. This workshop consists of 3.5 hours of instruction. The minimum class size is two students with a 4:1 student/teacher ratio.

Short Game Workshops

This workshop will cover the most important areas involved in developing higher levels of short game skills. The workshop will focus upon developing important essentials in chipping, pitching, lob shots, and bunker shots. The workshop will also include developing skills for situational assessment and proper shot selection.

Putting Workshops

This workshop will cover the most important areas involved in developing a high level of putting ability. The workshop will focus heavily on developing consistent stroke mechanics, developing strength in the area of distance and speed control, as well as touching upon green reading development. Video analysis may be included for technique.

Women's Group Instruction

Four consecutive weeks of instruction covering putting, chipping and pitching, and the full golf swing. This women's group lesson series is for beginner to intermediate female golfers. However, a custom group lesson program can be put together by our staff for groups of ladies of any ability. The student/teacher ratio is 5 to 1, with a maximum class size of ten students and a minimum class size of three students.

Junior Group Lessons

This is an opportunity for 7-17-year-olds to learn basic golf fundamentals in a group setting, including putting, chipping, pitching, and full swing. These four consecutive group clinics are designed for beginner level junior golfers. Best efforts will be made to group juniors by age and ability level. The student/teacher ratio is 5 to 1, with a maximum class size of 10 students and a minimum class size of three students.

Junior Golf Camp

This camp is designed to help junior golfers improve their golf game, develop good work habits, develop sound values, and most importantly have a good time. The camp provides basic instruction covering every skill area and a general understanding of rules and etiquette. It includes on-course instruction and practice time. Lunch and refreshments will be provided. The student/teacher ratio is 6 to 1, with a maximum class size of 24 students and a minimum class size of four students.

PRICING

Individual lesson rates include:

   60-Minute Lesson—$120

   30-Minute Lesson—$65

   5-Hour Series—$500

   60-Minute Junior Lesson—$90

   30-Minute Junior Lesson—$45

   Ball Striking Evaluation—$99

   Club fitting—$120

Special program rates are:

   Half Day Workshop—$200 per person

   Ball Striking Workshop—$200 per person

   Short Game Workshop—$149 per person

   Putting Workshop—$149 per person

   Women's Group Instruction—$149 per person

   Junior Group Lessons—$129 per person

   Junior Golf Camp—$250 per person

Investment Advisory Firm

Albertson's Investments, Inc.

55449 N. Broad Ave.
New York, NY 10018

BizPlanDB.com

1.0 EXECUTIVE SUMMARY

The purpose of this business plan is to raise $100,000 for the development of an investment advisory firm, while showcasing the expected financials and operations over the next three years. Albertson's Investments, Inc. ("the Company") is a New York-based corporation that will provide financial advice, asset management, and sales of insurance/annuities to customers in its targeted market. The Company was founded by Charles Albertson.

1.1 The Services

The primary revenue stream for the Company will come from the assets that are managed by Mr. Albertson and his staff. Each calendar year, the Company will charge a 1% fee equal to the aggregate assets managed in a client's account. The business will also generate per hour investment advisory fees related to advice provided for clients.

Albertson's Investments will also generate revenues from the sale of insurance products (especially life insurance) as well as annuities.

The third section of the business plan will further describe the services offered by Albertson's Investments.

1.2 Financing

Mr. Albertson is seeking to raise $100,000 from a bank loan. The interest rate and loan agreement are to be further discussed during negotiation. This business plan assumes that the business will receive a 10-year loan with a 9% fixed interest rate. The financing will be used for the following:

- Development of the Company's location.

- Financing for the first six months of operation.

- Capital to purchase a company vehicle.

Mr. Albertson will contribute $10,000 to the venture.

1.3 Mission Statement

Albertson's Investments mission is to become the recognized local leader in its targeted market for financial advisory and asset management services.

1.4 Management Team

The Company was founded by Charles Albertson. Mr. Albertson has more than 10 years of experience in the asset management industry. Through his expertise, he will be able to bring the operations of the business to profitability within its first year of operations.

1.5 Sales Forecasts

Mr. Albertson expects a strong rate of growth at the start of operations. Below are the expected financials over the next three years.

Proforma Profit and Loss (Yearly)

Year	1	2	3
Sales	$327,978	$393,574	$460,481
Operating costs	$262,503	$272,474	$282,815
EBITDA	$ 45,008	$ 96,538	$148,929
Taxes, interest, and depreciation	$ 29,948	$ 45,833	$ 65,331
Net profit	$ 15,060	$ 50,705	$ 83,599

Sales, Operating Costs, and Profit Forecast

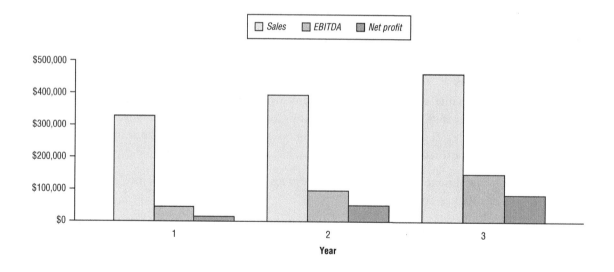

1.6 Expansion Plan

The Founder expects that the business will aggressively expand during the first three years of operation. Mr. Albertson intends to implement marketing campaigns that will effectively target individuals (with a focus on upper-middle-income professionals and small business owners) within the target market. The Company will also continually add new financial products that will assist clients with retirement and college saving needs.

2.0 COMPANY AND FINANCING SUMMARY

2.1 Registered Name and Corporate Structure

The Company is registered as a corporation in the State of New York.

2.2 Required Funds

At this time, Albertson's Investments requires $100,000 of debt funds. Below is a breakdown of how these funds will be used:

Projected Startup Costs

Initial lease payments and deposits	$ 10,000
Working capital	$ 35,000
FF&E	$ 23,000
Leasehold improvements	$ 5,000
Security deposits	$ 5,000
Insurance	$ 2,500
Company vehicle	$ 17,000
Marketing budget	$ 7,500
Miscellaneous and unforeseen costs	$ 5,000
Total startup costs	**$110,000**

Use of Funds

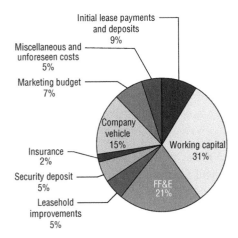

2.3 Investor Equity

Mr. Albertson is not seeking an investment from a third party at this time.

2.4 Management Equity

Charles Albertson owns 100% of Albertson's Investments, Inc.

2.5 Exit Strategy

If the business is very successful, Mr. Albertson may seek to sell the business to a third party for a significant earnings multiple. Most likely, the Company will hire a qualified business broker to sell the business on behalf of Albertson's Investments. Based on historical numbers, the business could fetch a sales premium of up to 4 times earnings.

3.0 PRODUCTS AND SERVICES

Below is a description of the investment advisory services offered by Albertson's Investments.

3.1 Financial Services

The Company will offer a wide variety of financial products that will help clients plan for their future retirement, college savings, and other financial needs. The firm will offer its clients:

- Retirement Plans

- General Investment Advisory Services

- Annuities and Mutual Funds

- Traditional and Roth IRA Accounts

The sale of these products will generate significant streams of commission based on recurring income. Each year, the business would receive fees of approximately 1% of the dollar amount of assets under management. These fees will comprise approximately 70% of the revenue generated by the Company during the next five years of operation.

3.2 Sales of Insurance Products and Annuities

Prior to the onset of operations, the business will develop underwriting relationships with life insurance and annuity companies so that the Company can generate commission revenue from the sale of these financial products to Albertson's Investments clients. Whole life insurance and annuities are a very important part of a client's financial/estate planning, and the Company will generate a significant income stream from the sale of these products.

4.0 STRATEGIC AND MARKET ANALYSIS

4.1 Economic Outlook

This section of the analysis will detail the economic climate, the investment advisory industry, the customer profile, and the competition that the business will face as it progresses through its business operations.

Currently, the economic market condition in the United States is moderate. Unemployment rates have declined while asset prices have risen substantially. As such, now is a strong economic climate to launch an investment advisory firm. It should be noted that the Company will be able to remain profitable and cash flow positive, at all times, given the highly recurring streams of revenue generated from managed account services.

4.2 Industry Analysis

The financial services sector has become one of the fastest growing business segments in the U.S. economy. Computerized technologies allow financial firms to operate advisory and brokerage services anywhere in the country. In previous decades, most financial firms needed to be within a close proximity to Wall Street in order to provide their clients the highest level of service. This is no longer the case as a firm can access almost every facet of the financial markets through Internet connections and specialized trading and investment management software. With these advances, several new firms have been created to address the needs of people in rural and suburban areas. The Bureau of Labor Statistics estimates that there are approximately 94,000 investment advisors currently employed throughout the United States. The average annual income for an investment advisor is $62,700. Salaries are expected to increase at a rate of 2.1% a year as inflation increases.

In the last study conducted by the U.S. Economic Census, it was found that the revenues of the investment advisory industry increased from $14.8 billion dollars in 2012 to over $52.9 billion dollars by 2014. This represents a five-year growth rate of 257%. The number of investment advisory establishments increased 61.5% over the same period. This trend is expected to continue as the 'baby boomer' generation begins to move into retirement age.

4.3 Customer Profile

Albertson's Investments average client will be a middle- to upper-middle-class man or woman living in the Company's target market. Common traits among clients will include:

- Annual household income exceeding $50,000.

- Lives or works no more than 15 miles from the Company's location.

- Has a net worth exceeding $500,000.

- Owns their own home.

- Has investible assets exceeding $250,000.

4.4 Competition

Competition in the investment advisory and brokerage industry is fierce. The highly recurring streams of revenue generated by these businesses has driven many independent and associated registered investment advisors into the industry. This trend is expected to continue in perpetuity. One of the ways that Albertson's Investments will retain a competitive advantage over other companies is that the business will be independent of any major brokerage firm. The business will be able to provide a plethora of financial products that can appropriately assist clients with their financial planning and investment needs.

5.0 MARKETING PLAN

Albertson's Investments intends to maintain an extensive marketing campaign that will ensure maximum visibility for the business in its targeted market. Below is an overview of the marketing strategies and objectives of the business.

5.1 Marketing Objectives

- Establish relationships with accountants and attorneys within the targeted market.

- Maintain an expansive online presence for the Company.

- Develop relationships with referring registered investment advisories that will direct smaller net worth clients to Albertson's Investments, Inc.

5.2 Marketing Strategies

Mr. Albertson intends on using a number of marketing strategies that will allow Albertson's Investments to easily target individuals and families within the target market. These strategies include traditional print advertisements and ads placed on search engines on the Internet. Print advertisements will be distributed in local newspapers and circulars within a 25-mile radius of the Company's location.

A presence on the internet is of extensive importance to the business given that most people now find local and regional businesses via online marketing channels. Prior to the onset of operations, Mr. Albertson will have a web development firm produce a website that clearly showcases the Company's services, backgrounds of staff investment advisors, hours of operation, and location information. This website will be listed among all major search engines. Additionally, the Company will maintain a significant presence among social networking platforms. For social media marketing, the business will frequently post commentary and articles related to the state of the economy and overall stock market performance.

Frequently, Mr. Albertson will host seminars that focus on retirement and college planning. These seminars are expected to generate substantial leads among people that can potentially become clients of the firm. Each year, two of these seminars will be held within the New York metropolitan area. Although these events will be expensive, the anticipated return on investment is significant.

5.3 Pricing

Albertson's Investments, Inc. will charge a fee equal to 1% of a client's assets on a yearly basis. Specialized financial planning services will be billed at a rate of $150 per hour.

6.0 ORGANIZATIONAL PLAN AND PERSONNEL SUMMARY

6.1 Corporate Organization

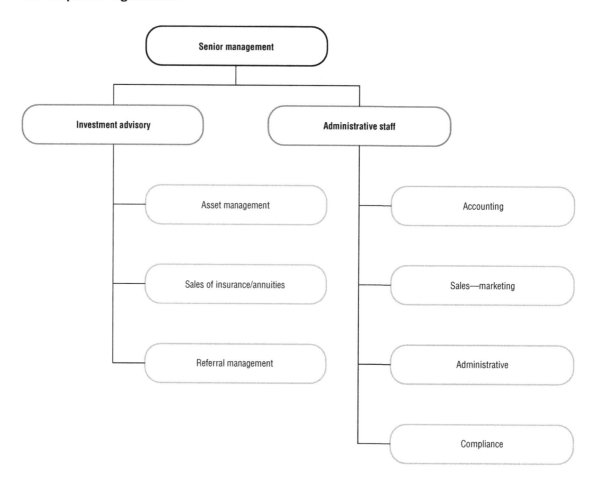

6.2 Organizational Budget

Personnel Plan—Yearly

Year	1	2	3
Owner	$ 40,000	$ 41,200	$ 42,436
Firm manager	$ 35,000	$ 36,050	$ 37,132
On staff investment advisor	$ 65,000	$ 66,950	$ 68,959
Bookkeeper (P/T)	$ 12,500	$ 12,875	$ 13,261
Receptionist	$ 22,000	$ 22,660	$ 23,340
Total	**$174,500**	**$179,735**	**$185,127**

Numbers of Personnel

Year	1	2	3
Owner	1	1	1
Firm manager	1	1	1
On staff investment advisor	2	2	2
Bookkeeper (P/T)	1	1	1
Receptionist	1	1	1
Totals	**6**	**6**	**6**

Personnel Expense Breakdown

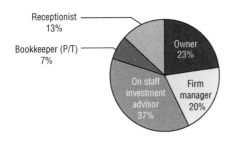

7.0 FINANCIAL PLAN

7.1 Underlying Assumptions

The Company has based its proforma financial statements on the following:

- Albertson's Investments, Inc. will have an annual revenue growth rate of 16% per year.

- The Owner will acquire $100,000 of debt funds to develop the business.

- The loan will have a 10-year term with a 9% interest rate.

7.2 Sensitivity Analysis

In the event of an economic downturn, the business may have a decline in its revenues. The Company's revenues are directly linked to the value of the clients' accounts, and a decline in the publicly traded asset markets may cause a decline in top line income. However, these fees are generated on a recurring basis, and the business will be able to remain profitable even during an economic recession.

7.3 Source of Funds

Financing

Equity contributions

Management investment	$ 10,000.00
Total equity financing	**$ 10,000.00**
Banks and lenders	
Banks and lenders	$100,000.00
Total debt financing	**$100,000.00**
Total financing	**$110,000.00**

7.4 General Assumptions

General Assumptions

Year	1	2	3
Short term interest rate	9.5%	9.5%	9.5%
Long term interest rate	10.0%	10.0%	10.0%
Federal tax rate	33.0%	33.0%	33.0%
State tax rate	5.0%	5.0%	5.0%
Personnel taxes	15.0%	15.0%	15.0%

7.5 Profit and Loss Statements

Proforma Profit and Loss (Yearly)

Year	1	2	3
Sales	**$327,978**	**$393,574**	**$460,481**
Cost of goods sold	$ 20,468	$ 24,561	$ 28,737
Gross margin	93.76%	93.76%	93.76%
Operating income	**$307,510**	**$369,012**	**$431,744**
Expenses			
Payroll	$174,500	$179,735	$185,127
General and administrative	$ 25,200	$ 26,208	$ 27,256
Marketing expenses	$ 1,640	$ 1,968	$ 2,302
Professional fees and licensure	$ 5,219	$ 5,376	$ 5,537
Insurance costs	$ 3,987	$ 4,186	$ 4,396
Travel and vehicle costs	$ 7,596	$ 8,356	$ 9,191
Rent and utilities	$ 14,250	$ 14,963	$ 15,711
Miscellaneous costs	$ 3,936	$ 4,723	$ 5,526
Payroll taxes	$ 26,175	$ 26,960	$ 27,769
Total operating costs	**$262,503**	**$272,474**	**$282,815**
EBITDA	**$ 45,008**	**$ 96,538**	**$148,929**
Federal income tax	$ 14,852	$ 29,174	$ 46,682
State income tax	$ 2,250	$ 4,420	$ 7,073
Interest expense	$ 8,738	$ 8,131	$ 7,468
Depreciation expenses	$ 4,107	$ 4,107	$ 4,107
Net profit	**$ 15,060**	**$ 50,705**	**$ 83,599**
Profit margin	**4.59%**	**12.88%**	**18.15%**

Sales, Operating Costs, and Profit Forecast

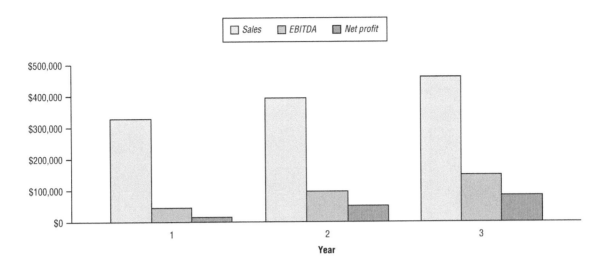

7.6 Cash Flow Analysis

Proforma Cash Flow Analysis—Yearly

Year	1	2	3
Cash from operations	$ 19,167	$54,812	$ 87,706
Cash from receivables	$ 0	$ 0	$ 0
Operating cash inflow	**$ 19,167**	**$54,812**	**$ 87,706**
Other cash inflows			
Equity investment	$ 10,000	$ 0	$ 0
Increased borrowings	$100,000	$ 0	$ 0
Sales of business assets	$ 0	$ 0	$ 0
A/P increases	$ 37,902	$43,587	$ 50,125
Total other cash inflows	**$147,902**	**$43,587**	**$ 50,125**
Total cash inflow	**$167,069**	**$98,400**	**$137,831**
Cash outflows			
Repayment of principal	$ 6,463	$ 7,070	$ 7,733
A/P decreases	$ 24,897	$29,876	$ 35,852
A/R increases	$ 0	$ 0	$ 0
Asset purchases	$ 57,500	$13,703	$ 21,926
Dividends	$ 13,417	$38,369	$ 61,394
Total cash outflows	**$102,277**	**$89,018**	**$126,905**
Net cash flow	**$ 64,792**	**$ 9,382**	**$ 10,926**
Cash balance	**$ 64,792**	**$74,174**	**$ 85,100**

Proforma Cash Flow (Yearly)

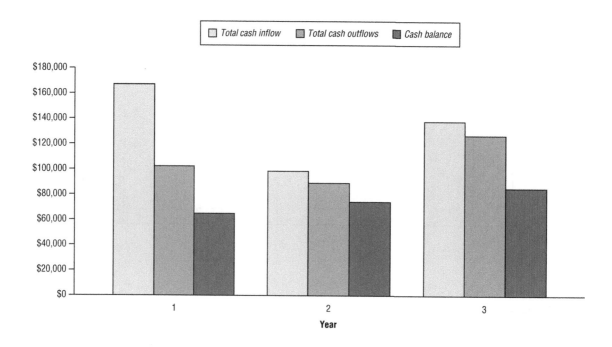

7.7 Balance Sheet

Proforma Balance Sheet—Yearly

Year	1	2	3
Assets			
Cash	$ 64,792	$ 74,174	$ 85,100
Amortized development/expansion costs	$ 17,500	$ 27,777	$ 44,222
Company vehicle	$ 17,000	$ 18,370	$ 20,563
FF&E	$ 23,000	$ 25,055	$ 28,344
Accumulated depreciation	($ 4,107)	($ 8,214)	($ 12,321)
Total assets	**$118,185**	**$137,162**	**$165,908**
Liabilities and equity			
Accounts payable	$ 13,005	$ 26,716	$ 40,990
Long term liabilities	$ 93,537	$ 86,467	$ 79,397
Other liabilities	$ 0	$ 0	$ 0
Total liabilities	**$106,542**	**$113,183**	**$120,387**
Net worth	**$ 11,643**	**$ 23,979**	**$ 45,521**
Total liabilities and equity	**$118,185**	**$137,162**	**$165,908**

Proforma Balance Sheet

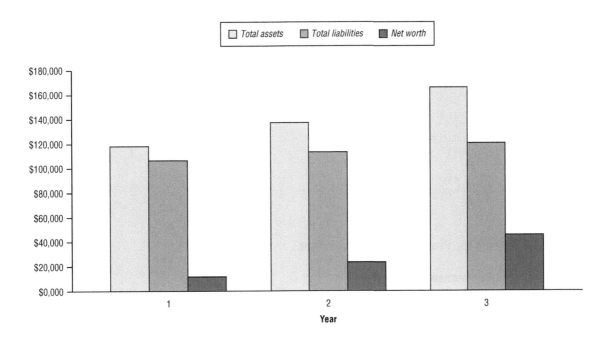

7.8 Breakeven Analysis

Monthly Break Even Analysis

Year	1	2	3
Monthly revenue	$ 23,331	$ 24,217	$ 25,137
Yearly revenue	$279,975	$290,610	$301,639

Break Even Analysis

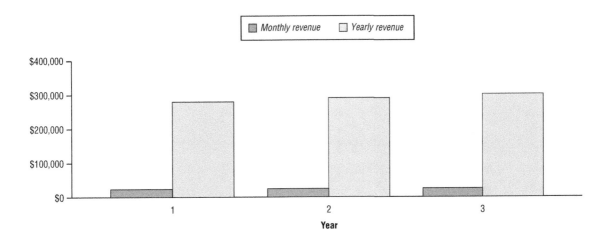

7.9 Business Ratios

Business Ratios—Yearly

Year	1	2	3
Sales			
Sales growth	0.0%	20.0%	17.0%
Gross margin	93.8%	93.8%	93.8%
Financials			
Profit margin	4.59%	12.88%	18.15%
Assets to liabilities	1.11	1.21	1.38
Equity to liabilities	0.11	0.21	0.38
Assets to equity	10.15	5.72	3.64
Liquidity			
Acid test	0.61	0.66	0.71
Cash to assets	0.55	0.54	0.51

7.10 Three Year Profit and Loss Statement

Profit and Loss Statement (First Year)

Months	1	2	3	4	5	6	7
Sales	$26,600	$26,733	$26,866	$26,999	$27,132	$27,265	$27,398
Cost of goods sold	$ 1,660	$ 1,668	$ 1,677	$ 1,685	$ 1,693	$ 1,702	$ 1,710
Gross margin	93.8%	93.8%	93.8%	93.8%	93.8%	93.8%	93.8%
Operating income	$24,940	$25,065	$25,189	$25,314	$25,439	$25,564	$25,688
Expenses							
Payroll	$14,542	$14,542	$14,542	$14,542	$14,542	$14,542	$14,542
General and administrative	$ 2,100	$ 2,100	$ 2,100	$ 2,100	$ 2,100	$ 2,100	$ 2,100
Marketing expenses	$ 137	$ 137	$ 137	$ 137	$ 137	$ 137	$ 137
Professional fees and licensure	$ 435	$ 435	$ 435	$ 435	$ 435	$ 435	$ 435
Insurance costs	$ 332	$ 332	$ 332	$ 332	$ 332	$ 332	$ 332
Travel and vehicle costs	$ 633	$ 633	$ 633	$ 633	$ 633	$ 633	$ 633
Rent and utilities	$ 1,188	$ 1,188	$ 1,188	$ 1,188	$ 1,188	$ 1,188	$ 1,188
Miscellaneous costs	$ 328	$ 328	$ 328	$ 328	$ 328	$ 328	$ 328
Payroll taxes	$ 2,181	$ 2,181	$ 2,181	$ 2,181	$ 2,181	$ 2,181	$ 2,181
Total operating costs	$21,875	$21,875	$21,875	$21,875	$21,875	$21,875	$21,875
EBITDA	$ 3,065	$ 3,189	$ 3,314	$ 3,439	$ 3,564	$ 3,688	$ 3,813
Federal income tax	$ 1,205	$ 1,211	$ 1,217	$ 1,223	$ 1,229	$ 1,235	$ 1,241
State income tax	$ 183	$ 183	$ 184	$ 185	$ 186	$ 187	$ 188
Interest expense	$ 750	$ 746	$ 742	$ 738	$ 734	$ 730	$ 726
Depreciation expense	$ 342	$ 342	$ 342	$ 342	$ 342	$ 342	$ 342
Net profit	$ 585	$ 707	$ 829	$ 950	$ 1,072	$ 1,194	$ 1,316

Profit and Loss Statement (First Year Cont.)

Months	8	9	10	11	12	1
Sales	$27,531	$27,664	$27,797	$27,930	$28,063	$327,978
Cost of goods sold	$ 1,718	$ 1,726	$ 1,735	$ 1,743	$ 1,751	$ 20,468
Gross margin	93.8%	93.8%	93.8%	93.8%	93.8%	93.8%
Operating income	$25,813	$25,938	$26,062	$26,187	$26,312	$307,510
Expenses						
Payroll	$14,542	$14,542	$14,542	$14,542	$14,542	$174,500
General and administrative	$ 2,100	$ 2,100	$ 2,100	$ 2,100	$ 2,100	$ 25,200
Marketing expenses	$ 137	$ 137	$ 137	$ 137	$ 137	$ 1,640
Professional fees and licensure	$ 435	$ 435	$ 435	$ 435	$ 435	$ 5,219
Insurance costs	$ 332	$ 332	$ 332	$ 332	$ 332	$ 3,987
Travel and vehicle costs	$ 633	$ 633	$ 633	$ 633	$ 633	$ 7,596
Rent and utilities	$ 1,188	$ 1,188	$ 1,188	$ 1,188	$ 1,188	$ 14,250
Miscellaneous costs	$ 328	$ 328	$ 328	$ 328	$ 328	$ 3,936
Payroll taxes	$ 2,181	$ 2,181	$ 2,181	$ 2,181	$ 2,181	$ 26,175
Total operating costs	$21,875	$21,875	$21,875	$21,875	$21,875	$262,503
EBITDA	$ 3,938	$ 4,062	$ 4,187	$ 4,312	$ 4,436	$ 45,008
Federal income tax	$ 1,247	$ 1,253	$ 1,259	$ 1,265	$ 1,271	$ 14,852
State income tax	$ 189	$ 190	$ 191	$ 192	$ 193	$ 2,250
Interest expense	$ 722	$ 718	$ 714	$ 710	$ 706	$ 8,738
Depreciation expense	$ 342	$ 342	$ 342	$ 342	$ 342	$ 4,107
Net profit	$ 1,438	$ 1,559	$ 1,681	$ 1,803	$ 1,925	$ 15,060

Profit and Loss Statement (Second Year)

	2				
Quarter	Q1	Q2	Q3	Q4	2
Sales	$78,715	$98,393	$106,265	$110,201	$393,574
Cost of goods sold	$ 4,912	$ 6,140	$ 6,632	$ 6,877	$ 24,561
Gross margin	93.8%	93.8%	93.8%	93.8%	93.8%
Operating income	$73,802	$92,253	$ 99,633	$103,323	$369,012
Expenses					
Payroll	$35,947	$44,934	$ 48,528	$ 50,326	$179,735
General and administrative	$ 5,242	$ 6,552	$ 7,076	$ 7,338	$ 26,208
Marketing expenses	$ 394	$ 492	$ 531	$ 551	$ 1,968
Professional fees and licensure	$ 1,075	$ 1,344	$ 1,451	$ 1,505	$ 5,376
Insurance costs	$ 837	$ 1,047	$ 1,130	$ 1,172	$ 4,186
Travel and vehicle costs	$ 1,671	$ 2,089	$ 2,256	$ 2,340	$ 8,356
Rent and utilities	$ 2,993	$ 3,741	$ 4,040	$ 4,190	$ 14,963
Miscellaneous costs	$ 945	$ 1,181	$ 1,275	$ 1,322	$ 4,723
Payroll taxes	$ 5,392	$ 6,740	$ 7,279	$ 7,549	$ 26,960
Total operating costs	$54,495	$68,119	$ 73,568	$ 76,293	$272,474
EBITDA	$19,308	$24,135	$ 26,065	$ 27,031	$ 96,538
Federal income tax	$ 5,835	$ 7,294	$ 7,877	$ 8,169	$ 29,174
State income tax	$ 884	$ 1,105	$ 1,193	$ 1,238	$ 4,420
Interest expense	$ 2,092	$ 2,053	$ 2,013	$ 1,973	$ 8,131
Depreciation expense	$ 1,027	$ 1,027	$ 1,027	$ 1,027	$ 4,107
Net profit	$ 9,470	$12,656	$ 13,955	$ 14,624	$ 50,705

Profit and Loss Statement (Third Year)

	3				
Quarter	Q1	Q2	Q3	Q4	3
Sales	$92,096	$115,120	$124,330	$128,935	$460,481
Cost of goods sold	$ 5,747	$ 7,184	$ 7,759	$ 8,046	$ 28,737
Gross margin	93.8%	93.8%	93.8%	93.8%	93.8%
Operating income	$86,349	$107,936	$116,571	$120,888	$431,744
Expenses					
Payroll	$37,025	$ 46,282	$ 49,984	$ 51,836	$185,127
General and administrative	$ 5,451	$ 6,814	$ 7,359	$ 7,632	$ 27,256
Marketing expenses	$ 460	$ 576	$ 622	$ 645	$ 2,302
Professional fees and licensure	$ 1,107	$ 1,384	$ 1,495	$ 1,550	$ 5,537
Insurance costs	$ 879	$ 1,099	$ 1,187	$ 1,231	$ 4,396
Travel and vehicle costs	$ 1,838	$ 2,298	$ 2,482	$ 2,574	$ 9,191
Rent and utilities	$ 3,142	$ 3,928	$ 4,242	$ 4,399	$ 15,711
Miscellaneous costs	$ 1,105	$ 1,381	$ 1,492	$ 1,547	$ 5,526
Payroll taxes	$ 5,554	$ 6,942	$ 7,498	$ 7,775	$ 27,769
Total operating costs	$56,563	$ 70,704	$ 76,360	$ 79,188	$282,815
EBITDA	$29,786	$ 37,232	$ 40,211	$ 41,700	$148,929
Federal income tax	$ 9,336	$ 11,671	$ 12,604	$ 13,071	$ 46,682
State income tax	$ 1,415	$ 1,768	$ 1,910	$ 1,980	$ 7,073
Interest expense	$ 1,932	$ 1,889	$ 1,846	$ 1,802	$ 7,468
Depreciation expense	$ 1,027	$ 1,027	$ 1,027	$ 1,027	$ 4,107
Net profit	$16,076	$ 20,878	$ 22,824	$ 23,820	$ 83,599

7.11 Three Year Cash Flow Analysis

Cash Flow Analysis (First Year)

Month	1	2	3	4	5	6	7	8
Cash from operations	$ 928	$ 1,049	$ 1,171	$ 1,293	$ 1,414	$ 1,536	$ 1,658	$ 1,780
Cash from receivables	$ 0	$ 0	$ 0	$ 0	$ 0	$ 0	$ 0	$ 0
Operating cash inflow	$ 928	$ 1,049	$ 1,171	$ 1,293	$ 1,414	$ 1,536	$ 1,658	$ 1,780
Other cash inflows								
Equity investment	$ 10,000	$ 0	$ 0	$ 0	$ 0	$ 0	$ 0	$ 0
Increased borrowings	$100,000	$ 0	$ 0	$ 0	$ 0	$ 0	$ 0	$ 0
Sales of business assets	$ 0	$ 0	$ 0	$ 0	$ 0	$ 0	$ 0	$ 0
A/P increases	$ 3,159	$ 3,159	$ 3,159	$ 3,159	$ 3,159	$ 3,159	$ 3,159	$ 3,159
Total other cash inflows	$113,159	$ 3,159	$ 3,159	$ 3,159	$ 3,159	$ 3,159	$ 3,159	$ 3,159
Total cash inflow	$114,086	$ 4,208	$ 4,329	$ 4,451	$ 4,573	$ 4,695	$ 4,816	$ 4,938
Cash outflows								
Repayment of principal	$ 517	$ 521	$ 525	$ 528	$ 532	$ 536	$ 540	$ 545
A/P decreases	$ 2,075	$ 2,075	$ 2,075	$ 2,075	$ 2,075	$ 2,075	$ 2,075	$ 2,075
A/R increases	$ 0	$ 0	$ 0	$ 0	$ 0	$ 0	$ 0	$ 0
Asset purchases	$ 57,500	$ 0	$ 0	$ 0	$ 0	$ 0	$ 0	$ 0
Dividends	$ 0	$ 0	$ 0	$ 0	$ 0	$ 0	$ 0	$ 0
Total cash outflows	$ 60,092	$ 2,595	$ 2,599	$ 2,603	$ 2,607	$ 2,611	$ 2,615	$ 2,619
Net cash flow	$ 53,995	$ 1,612	$ 1,730	$ 1,848	$ 1,966	$ 2,084	$ 2,201	$ 2,319
Cash balance	$ 53,995	$55,607	$57,337	$59,185	$61,151	$63,235	$65,436	$67,755

Cash Flow Analysis (First Year Cont.)

Month	9	10	11	12	1
Cash from operations	$ 1,902	$ 2,024	$ 2,145	$ 2,267	$ 19,167
Cash from receivables	$ 0	$ 0	$ 0	$ 0	$ 0
Operating cash inflow	**$ 1,902**	**$ 2,024**	**$ 2,145**	**$ 2,267**	**$ 19,167**
Other cash inflows					
Equity investment	$ 0	$ 0	$ 0	$ 0	$ 10,000
Increased borrowings	$ 0	$ 0	$ 0	$ 0	$100,000
Sales of business assets	$ 0	$ 0	$ 0	$ 0	$ 0
A/P increases	$ 3,159	$ 3,159	$ 3,159	$ 3,159	$ 37,902
Total other cash inflows	**$ 3,159**	**$ 3,159**	**$ 3,159**	**$ 3,159**	**$147,902**
Total cash inflow	**$ 5,060**	**$ 5,182**	**$ 5,304**	**$ 5,426**	**$167,069**
Cash outflows					
Repayment of principal	$ 549	$ 553	$ 557	$ 561	$ 6,463
A/P decreases	$ 2,075	$ 2,075	$ 2,075	$ 2,075	$ 24,897
A/R increases	$ 0	$ 0	$ 0	$ 0	$ 0
Asset purchases	$ 0	$ 0	$ 0	$ 0	$ 57,500
Dividends	$ 0	$ 0	$ 0	$13,417	$ 13,417
Total cash outflows	**$ 2,623**	**$ 2,627**	**$ 2,632**	**$16,053**	**$102,277**
Net cash flow	**$ 2,437**	**$ 2,555**	**$ 2,672**	**−$10,627**	**$ 64,792**
Cash balance	**$70,192**	**$72,746**	**$75,419**	**$64,792**	**$ 64,792**

Cash Flow Analysis (Second Year)

Quarter	2				2
	Q1	Q2	Q3	Q4	
Cash from operations	$10,962	$13,703	$14,799	$15,347	$54,812
Cash from receivables	$ 0	$ 0	$ 0	$ 0	$ 0
Operating cash inflow	**$10,962**	**$13,703**	**$14,799**	**$15,347**	**$54,812**
Other cash inflows					
Equity investment	$ 0	$ 0	$ 0	$ 0	$ 0
Increased borrowings	$ 0	$ 0	$ 0	$ 0	$ 0
Sales of business assets	$ 0	$ 0	$ 0	$ 0	$ 0
A/P increases	$ 8,717	$10,897	$11,769	$12,204	$43,587
Total other cash inflows	**$ 8,717**	**$10,897**	**$11,769**	**$12,204**	**$43,587**
Total cash inflow	**$19,680**	**$24,600**	**$26,568**	**$27,552**	**$98,400**
Cash outflows					
Repayment of principal	$ 1,708	$ 1,747	$ 1,787	$ 1,827	$ 7,070
A/P decreases	$ 5,975	$ 7,469	$ 8,067	$ 8,365	$29,876
A/R increases	$ 0	$ 0	$ 0	$ 0	$ 0
Asset purchases	$ 2,741	$ 3,426	$ 3,700	$ 3,837	$13,703
Dividends	$ 7,674	$ 9,592	$10,360	$10,743	$38,369
Total cash outflows	**$18,098**	**$22,234**	**$23,913**	**$24,773**	**$89,018**
Net cash flow	**$ 1,582**	**$ 2,366**	**$ 2,655**	**$ 2,779**	**$ 9,382**
Cash balance	**$66,374**	**$68,739**	**$71,394**	**$74,174**	**$74,174**

Cash Flow Analysis (Third Year)

Quarter	Q1	Q2	Q3	Q4	3
Cash from operations	$17,541	$21,926	$23,681	$24,558	$ 87,706
Cash from receivables	$ 0	$ 0	$ 0	$ 0	$ 0
Operating cash inflow	**$17,541**	**$21,926**	**$23,681**	**$24,558**	**$ 87,706**
Other cash inflows					
Equity investment	$ 0	$ 0	$ 0	$ 0	$ 0
Increased borrowings	$ 0	$ 0	$ 0	$ 0	$ 0
Sales of business assets	$ 0	$ 0	$ 0	$ 0	$ 0
A/P increases	$10,025	$12,531	$13,534	$14,035	$ 50,125
Total other cash inflows	**$10,025**	**$12,531**	**$13,534**	**$14,035**	**$ 50,125**
Total cash inflow	**$27,566**	**$34,458**	**$37,214**	**$38,593**	**$137,831**
Cash outflows					
Repayment of principal	$ 1,869	$ 1,911	$ 1,954	$ 1,999	$ 7,733
A/P decreases	$ 7,170	$ 8,963	$ 9,680	$10,038	$ 35,852
A/R increases	$ 0	$ 0	$ 0	$ 0	$ 0
Asset purchases	$ 4,385	$ 5,482	$ 5,920	$ 6,139	$ 21,926
Dividends	$12,279	$15,349	$16,576	$17,190	$ 61,394
Total cash outflows	**$25,703**	**$31,704**	**$34,131**	**$35,367**	**$126,905**
Net cash flow	**$ 1,863**	**$ 2,754**	**$ 3,084**	**$ 3,226**	**$ 10,926**
Cash balance	**$76,037**	**$78,790**	**$81,874**	**$85,100**	**$ 85,100**

Medical Waste Disposal Services

Medi-Waste

1221 Seminole Street
Tallahassee, FL 32308

Fran Fletcher

Medi-Waste is a state certified medical waste transport and disposal company based in Tallahassee, Florida. The company specializes in medical waste transport and disposal services for facilities seeking pick-up and disposal services for biomedical wastes. Medi-Waste is owned and operated by Joshua Whitaker, Willis Crocket, Asher Woods, and Phillip Jenkins. Each brings a unique skill set to Medi-Waste, including backgrounds in business, sales, and environmental regulations.

EXECUTIVE SUMMARY

Medi-Waste is a state certified medical waste transport and disposal company based in Tallahassee, Florida. The company specializes in medical waste transport and disposal services for facilities seeking pick-up and disposal services for biomedical wastes. Medi-Waste is owned and operated by Joshua Whitaker, Willis Crocket, Asher Woods, and Phillip Jenkins. Each brings a unique skill set to Medi-Waste, including backgrounds in business, sales, and environmental regulations.

Biomedical waste must be handled in accordance with state and federal law. A biomedical waste disposal company is the only entity allowed by law to dispose of this type of waste. Biomedical waste must be treated properly before it can be recycled or thrown away in order to protect people from potential hazards.

There are many businesses in need of biomedical waste disposal services, including:

- Hospitals
- Medical offices
- Nursing homes
- Veterinarian offices
- Animal shelters
- Prisons
- Funeral homes
- Tattoo parlors

All of these businesses are required to be licensed as a biomedical waste generator. They have to ensure that generated waste is being handled and stored properly onsite, and then disposed of by a reputable company.

There are similar businesses that provide waste transporting services in the north Florida area, but according to the Florida Department of Health, there are no other registered biomedical waste transporters or treatment facilities located in Tallahassee/Leon County, Florida.

The overall growth strategy of Medi-Waste is to obtain biomedical waste clients in Tallahassee and the surrounding areas. The owners plan to start by providing services in Tallahassee/Leon County and then expand to other surrounding counties in north Florida.

The VP of Sales and Logistics has identified key tactics to support Medi-Waste's growth strategy including meeting with clients to determine their individual needs, advertising in industry journals, mailing brochures to potential clients, and distributing pens, etc. with the company's logo.

The owners are seeking financing in the form of a business loan. The owners estimate that they will need to borrow $243,750 to cover the start-up costs plus operating expenses for the first quarter. The company estimates that it will have the loan repaid at the end of the fourth year.

COMPANY DESCRIPTION

Location

Medi-Waste is located in Tallahassee, Florida. The owners have secured a 30,000 sq. ft. warehouse for storage and treatment in the Leon County Industrial Park.

Hours of Operation
Office Hours and Pick-up

Monday—Friday 9 a.m. to 6 p.m.

Waste Treatment

Monday—Saturday 7 a.m. to 11 p.m.

Personnel

Joshua Whitaker (Chief Executive Officer)
Mr. Whitaker received a B.S. in Environmental Studies from NC State. He has 3 years of experience working at the Florida Department of Environmental Quality. He brings a wealth of knowledge of state regulations and will ensure that the business has the proper certifications to operate in accordance with state hazardous waste laws.

Willis Crocket (VP Technical Operations)
Mr. Crocket has 5 years of experience as a medical waste transporter. He has worked at Archibald Hospital as a biomedical waste manager for the past 2 years. He currently possesses state certification as a licensed biomedical transporter. He has in-depth knowledge of biomedical waste management and will ensure that the waste is transported and handled in accordance with state law.

Asher Woods (Chief Financial Officer)
Mr. Woods received his B.S. in business from North Florida College and his MBA from Florida State University. He has 2 years of experience as an accountant for Craft Cargo, Inc. He has been employed as the VP of Operations for Archibald Hospital for the last 4 years. His accounting and operational knowledge and experience will be valuable as the business starts up and continues operation.

Phillip Jenkins (VP Sales and Logistics)
Mr. Jenkins has served as a salesman for several different local businesses over the last ten years, including Tallahassee Car Mart and Craft Cargo. Most recently, he was the Regional Sales Manager for Eco Systems where he managed 8 sales representatives throughout the state of Florida. His experience will help him to establish service regions and to manage the logistics required for waste pick-ups.

Office Manager
The office manager will be responsible for Accounts Payable and Receivable.

Compliance Administrator
The compliance administrator will be responsible for filing and renewing the required permits with State Health and DOT.

Waste Treatment Supervisor
The waste treatment supervisor will oversee the treatment of biomedical waste and will ensure proper operation of the treatment facilities.

Waste Treatment Operators
The company will employ 8 operators to handle and treat the waste.

Transporters
The company will employ 4 medical waste transporters to pick up biomedical waste from customers and transport the waste to the treatment facility.

MARKET ANALYSIS

Industry Overview
Biomedical waste must be handled in accordance with state and federal law. A biomedical waste disposal company is the only entity allowed by law to dispose of this type of waste. Biomedical waste must be treated properly before it can be recycled or thrown away in order to protect people from potential hazards.

There are many businesses in need of biomedical waste disposal services, including hospitals, medical offices, nursing homes, veterinarian offices, animal shelters, prisons, funeral homes, and tattoo parlors. All of these businesses are required to be licensed as a biomedical waste generator. They have to ensure that generated waste is being handled and stored properly onsite and then disposed of by a reputable company.

The occupational outlook for handling hazardous waste is favorable over the next decade, and jobs in this industry are expected to increase by 7%.

Tallahassee, Florida is home to 3 hospitals, 1 VA clinic, 2 animal shelters, 1 prison, 10 veterinarian hospitals, 8 funeral homes, 12 nursing homes, 10 tattoo parlors, and over 100 medical offices. The United Nations population projections show Tallahassee's population increasing by 71% over the next fifteen years. As the population increases, the number of facilities is expected to increase to meet demand for services.

Target Market
Hospitals, medical offices, nursing homes, veterinarian offices, animal shelters, prisons, funeral homes, and tattoo parlors in Tallahassee/Leon County in need of biomedical waste disposal services are the target market for Medi-Waste.

Competition

There are similar businesses that provide waste transporting services in the north Florida area, but according to the Florida Department of Health, there are no other registered biomedical waste transporters or treatment facilities located in Leon County. Those providing service to Tallahassee/Leon County are:

BioWaste—Gainesville, FL—providing biomedical waste transport in north and central Florida

Florida Biomedical Transport—Jacksonville, FL—serving north Florida

GROWTH STRATEGY

The overall growth strategy of Medi-Waste is to obtain biomedical waste clients in Tallahassee and the surrounding areas.

The owners plan to start by providing services in Tallahassee/Leon County and then slowly expand to other surrounding counties in north Florida.

Sales and Marketing

Phillip Jenkins, the VP of Sales and Logistics, has identified key tactics to support Medi-Waste's growth strategy.

Advertising/marketing will include:

- Meeting with potential clients to determine their needs.

- Advertising in industry and trade journals.

- Mailing business brochures to applicable industries.

- Distributing pens, notepads, etc. with the company's logo.

FINANCIAL ANALYSIS

Start-up Costs

The majority of start-up related costs will be used for purchasing gently used vans and autoclaves for transporting and sterilizing biomedical waste.

Business license	$ 250
Incorporation fees	$ 5,000
Biomedical waste permits	$ 500
Business cards	$ 100
Brochures	$ 500
Biomedical liners	$ 1,000
Autoclaves	$20,000
Office furniture	$ 6,000
Computers	$ 5,000
Transport vans	$30,000
Initial advertising	$ 500
Employee certification	$12,000
Total	**$80,850**

Estimated Monthly Expenses

Phone/Internet	$ 200
Advertising	$ 100
Payroll	$46,000
Loan repayment	$ 5,000
Fleet insurance	$ 1,000
Landfill fee	$ 2,000
Total	**$54,300**

Estimated Monthly Income

The number of clients will determine income. The owners will set up meetings with potential clients prior to starting the business. The following list exhibits the company's sales goals for the first year of operation.

Month 1—Ten clients requiring daily pick-up of 8 bags each. Five clients requiring weekly pick-up of 8 bags each. Ten clients requiring monthly pick-up of 1 sharps box each.

Month 2—Fifteen clients requiring daily pick-up of 8 bags each. Eight clients requiring weekly pick-up of 8 bags each. Fifteen clients requiring monthly pick-up of 1 sharps box each.

Month 3—Twenty clients requiring daily pick-up of 8 bags each. Twelve clients requiring weekly pick-up of 8 bags each. Twenty clients requiring monthly pick-up of 1 sharps box each.

Month 4 and beyond—Volume expected to stay the same.

Price Schedule

Service	Description	Price
Daily pick-up	Cost per bag	$20
Weekly pick-up	Cost per bag	$35
Monthly pick-up (sharps)	Cost per container	$50

Profit/Loss

Mr. Woods is using the company's sales goals as an estimate to determine monthly profit/loss.

Profit/Loss

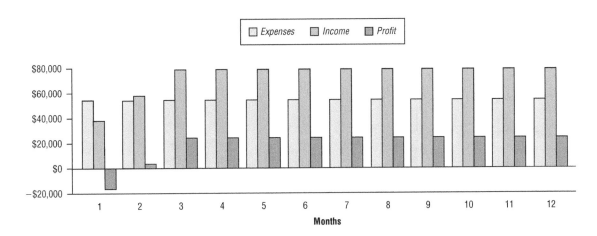

Profit projections show that Medi-Waste will experience a deficit during the first month. A small profit is expected during the second month, then a larger profit during the third month. These profits are expected to continue through the end of the year. Profits will be re-invested to purchase additional equipment. The second year shows a slight increase in income due to an established clientele replacing the small profits of the first month of the first year. The third year is projected to see a 10% increase in both expenses and income.

Year 1–3 Profit Projection

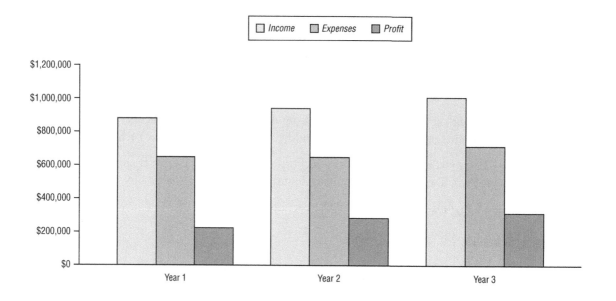

Financing

The owners are seeking financing in the form of a business loan. The owners estimate that they will need to borrow $243,750 to cover the start-up costs plus operating expenses for the first quarter. The company estimates that it will have the loan repaid at the end of the fourth year.

Loan Repayment

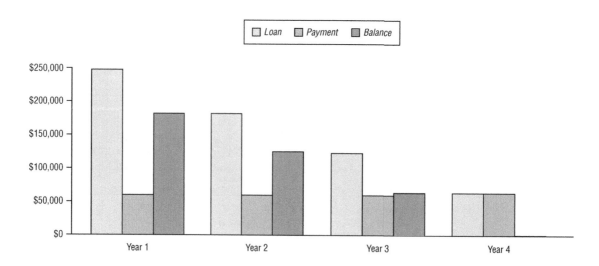

Piano Tuning, Repair & Restoration Service

Jackson Piano Repair, Inc.

21 Montague St., SW
Des Moines, IA 50047

Paul Greenland

Jackson Piano Repair, Inc. provides piano tuning, repair, and restoration services in the Des Moines, Iowa area.

EXECUTIVE SUMMARY

Pianos are complex instruments, involving roughly 9,000-12,000 different parts. Costing anywhere from $3,000 to more than $100,000, pianos are significant investments and require regular care and maintenance for optimal performance. Jackson Piano Repair, Inc. provides piano tuning, repair, and restoration services in the Des Moines, Iowa area. The business is being established by Steven Jackson, a Registered Piano Technician with nearly 20 years of professional experience. In addition to maintaining and repairing pianos, Jackson also is a musician who has played the piano for 35 years.

INDUSTRY ANALYSIS

Professionals in this industry do not necessarily provide both piano tuning and rebuilding/restoration services; some specialize in one or the other. The services of highly-skilled piano technicians are very much in-demand. This especially is the case with professionals providing rebuilding/restoration services, which can be very complex. In the case when such services are not performed correctly, it may be necessary to completely redo the rebuilding/restoration process, which is why consumers and businesses must choose piano technicians carefully.

The Piano Technicians Guild is a leading association for professionals in the piano repair and restoration field. The organization offers a number of resources for teachers, piano owners, pianists, technicians, and tuners, including a journal and educational offerings. The guild provides members with opportunities to become certified in the trade by becoming Registered Piano Technicians (RPT). Members who have not yet passed the required examinations and are still studying piano technology are considered to be associate members. Nationwide, a number of schools provide training programs (both full-time and correspondence-based) to prepare for the exams.

According to the guild, one must pass three different examinations to obtain certification as an RPT: "A written exam tests basic knowledge of piano design, tuning theory, repair techniques, and various other topics relevant to piano technology. Two separate practical, hands-on exams test tuning and technical skills. The practical exams are administered by panels of RPTs under the leadership of examiners trained and certified in standardized exam procedures. Exam procedures are designed to comply with standards of objectivity mandated by US anti-trust legislation, thus assuring that exams are fair and equivalent regardless of where or by whom they are administered."

MARKET ANALYSIS

Jackson Piano Repair will provide piano tuning, repair, and restoration services in Des Moines, Iowa, and nearby communities. Using demographic data available from his local public library, Steven Jackson determined that the Des Moines population included an estimated 215,349 people in 2016. Approximately 72 percent of households were family households, and about 28 percent were non-family households. School-aged children represented an estimated 21 percent of the population.

The average household income in Des Moines, Iowa, was $60,948 in 2016. Jackson Piano Repair will concentrate its marketing efforts on households with income of $60,000 or more. In 2016, approximately 12.2 percent of the Des Moines population had household income between $60,000 and $74,999, and 11.7 percent had household income between $75,000 and $99,999. An estimated 6.5 percent of households had income between $100,000 and $124,999, while 2.8 percent had income between $125,000 and $149,999. Finally, 4.2 percent of households in the Des Moines market had income of more than $150,000.

In addition to individual consumers, Jackson Piano Repair also will provide services to organizations and business establishments with pianos, including schools, daycare centers, nursing homes, churches, nightclubs, and performing arts centers. Specifically, Steven Jackson has identified several key categories of prospects in the local market that are candidates for piano tuning, restoration, and repair, including:

- Churches (163)

- Educational Services (208)

- Hotels, Rooming Houses, Camps, and Other Lodging Places (41)

- Membership Organizations (595)

- Museums, Art Galleries, and Botanical and Zoological Gardens (16)

- Social Services (257)

- Health Services (552)

- Eating and Drinking Places (490)

Although specific data is not available, a market the size of Des Moines will include a sizable number of households, organizations, and business establishments with pianos. Although both new and old pianos require regular tuning, the market for pianos in need of more significant repairs or restoration is considerable. Nationwide, an estimated 8.7 million pianos were sold between 1957 and 2007, according to data from the Bluebook of Pianos. Of these, upright pianos were the most common, accounting for about 85 percent of the total, while grand pianos accounted for 12 percent.

Competition

Piano tuning, repair, and restoration services require specialized knowledge and expertise. For this reason, professionals in this sector of the music industry who provide quality services at competitive rates have excellent opportunities in virtually any market. Steven Jackson will differentiate himself in the local market by offering the capability to provide both piano tuning and rebuilding/restoration services.

Jackson has identified the following primary competitors in the Des Moines market:

1. Daniel M. Peterson, Piano Tuner

2. Dolphin Piano Tuning & Repair

3. Ridgeway Piano Services

4. Foster's Piano Repair Service, Inc.

5. Piano Tuning by Richard Smith

6. Skelly Piano Workshop, LLC

SERVICES

Pianos are complex instruments, involving roughly 9,000-12,000 different parts. Costing anywhere from $3,000 to more than $100,000, pianos are significant investments and require regular care and maintenance for optimal performance. Rebuilding and restoring pianos may involve working on the instrument's action, hammers, strings, frame, pedals, cabinet, and soundboard.

Jackson Piano Repair will offer the following services, with slight rate variations based on customer requirements:

Standard Tuning: ($150)
Because pianos are extremely sensitive to atmospheric changes, including humidity levels, two piano tunings per year are recommended.

Action Regulation:

- Upright ($300)

- Grand ($450)

Key Top Replacement:

- Naturals/White Keys ($500)

- Sharp/Black Keys (in addition to naturals) ($185)

- Individual Keys ($25/each)

Voicing:

- Vertical ($60)

- Grand ($90)

Piano Refinishing:

- Upright: ($2,750 - $3,750)

- Grand ($5,000 - $8,000)

Piano Rebuilding (Refinishing & Restringing):

- Upright ($4,000 - $6,000)

- Grand ($8,000 - $12,500)

OPERATIONS

Business Structure

Steven Jackson has organized his business as an S-corporation, which provides him with certain tax advantages and other benefits. Jackson utilized the services of a local business attorney to file his articles of incorporation and other required paperwork. In addition to drawing a salary, Jackson will take regular profit distributions from the business based on its performance. His accountant will provide assistance with payroll tax payments.

Location

Steven Jackson will provide piano tuning services, and some general repairs, on-location, while complete piano restoration and rebuilding will be performed at his facility. A suitable location has been identified for the business in central Des Moines. Jackson has leased a location that includes a small office, bathroom, kitchenette, as well as a climate-controlled workshop with ample square footage for refinishing/restoring up to four pianos at one time. The workshop includes convenient overhead door access for loading/unloading pianos.

Transportation

Jackson Piano Repair has contracted with a reputable local service to provide piano transportation when required.

Insurance

In partnership with a local insurance agent, Steven Jackson has obtained an appropriate level of liability coverage for his business. Complete documentation is available upon request.

Equipment

Because he has been a registered piano technician for many years, Steven Jackson already has all of the tools needed to operate his business. These include the following essential items, which someone new to the business can purchase for approximately $500:

- Bent Back Check Regulator
- Combination Handle
- Damper Regulator, Offset Angle
- Hammer Head and Butt Borer
- Jaras (4-In-1)
- Offset Key Spacer
- Regulating Screwdriver (7")
- Spoon Bender
- Straight Screwdriver Blade (8")
- Tuning Forks (A and C)

PERSONNEL

Steven Jackson, RPT (Owner)

Steven Jackson is a Registered Piano Technician (RPT) with nearly 20 years of professional experience. In addition to maintaining and repairing pianos, Jackson also is a musician who has played the piano for 35 years. Jackson is a member of the Piano Technicians Guild, and passed all of the necessary examinations needed to become an RPT. Jackson has worked in the Des Moines market for his entire professional career. Until recently, he was employed by Ray's Music Service, a local music store that eventually closed following the owners' retirement. Although the closure of Ray's Music was unfortunate, it has provided an opportunity for Jackson to fulfill his lifelong dream of self-employment.

During its first three years of operations, Jackson will be the business' sole employee, with responsibility for performing piano maintenance and repair, as well as handling all administrative duties. Following three years of successful operations, Steven plans to hire an administrative assistant, which will enable him to increase his capacity. Additionally, he will attempt to recruit another RPT to join him in the business.

Professional & Advisory Support

Jackson Piano Repair has established a business banking account with the Bank of Des Moines, including a merchant account for accepting credit card payments. Tax advisement is provided by Iowa Accounting & Tax Advisory Services, LLC.

GROWTH STRATEGY

Steven Jackson has developed the following growth targets for his business' first three years of operations:

Year One: Perform 500 piano tunings, 96 general repairs, 12 refinishing jobs, and 8 rebuilds. Generate gross sales of $215,000 and net income of $40,397. Operate at 70 percent capacity.

Year Two: Perform 750 piano tunings, 120 general repairs, 15 refinishing jobs, and 10 rebuilds. Generate gross sales of $275,000 and net income of $80,465. Operate at 80 percent of capacity.

Year Three: Perform 1,000 piano tunings, 144 general repairs, 18 refinishing jobs, and 12 rebuilds. Generate gross sales of $335,000 and net income of $120,432. Operate at 90 percent of capacity. Recruit an administrative assistant to join the business during year four, as well as an additional registered piano technician, which will significantly increase capacity and profitability during years four and five.

MARKETING & SALES

Jackson Piano Repair has developed a marketing plan that involves the following main tactics:

1. Word-of-mouth marketing, leveraging Steven Jackson's reputation and experience in the local market, with a goal of generating repeat business.

2. A double-sided color flyer, describing Steven Jackson and the services provided by Jackson Piano Repair, which can be distributed/mailed to prospective customers and referral sources (e.g., piano instructors, music stores, etc.).

3. A quarterly direct mail campaign, consisting of a letter of introduction and a color flyer that will be mailed to key prospects in the Des Moines area.

4. Online directory advertising.

5. Periodic "drop-ins" to key referral sources, including music stores and churches.

6. A Web site with complete details about Jackson Piano Repair, including a service page where customers can request a call-back at their convenience. Additionally, the site will include testimonials from satisfied customers and a gallery showing pianos that Steven Jackson has restored.

7. Membership in the Des Moines Chamber of Commerce and Better Business Bureau.

8. A customer referral program that provides 50 percent off one piano tuning for each new client that is referred.

9. A Facebook page.

10. Expert piano care-related articles, distributed free of charge to school music teachers, choir directors, and private piano instructors in the local market, which can be incorporated into their newsletters for their students.

11. "In Tune," a piano care blog with regular postings regarding piano care and maintenance topics.

12. Vehicle signage to provide mobile advertising when Steven Jackson is in the field.

FINANCIAL ANALYSIS

Steven Jackson will provide $35,000 in startup capital from his personal savings and investments, which will be used to secure the facility lease for Jackson Piano Repair, initial marketing activities, and cash flow for operations. Working in partnership with his accountant, Jackson has developed a series of financial projections for the first three years of his business' operations, which are available upon request. Following is an overview of projected revenue and expenses:

	2017	2018	2019
Income			
Total sales	**$215,000**	**$275,000**	**$335,000**
Cost of goods sold	$ 21,000	$ 26,250	$ 31,500
Labor cost	$ 85,000	$ 90,000	$ 95,000
Total cost of goods sold	**$106,000**	**$116,250**	**$126,500**
Gross profit	**$109,000**	**$158,750**	**$208,500**
Expenses			
Advertising & marketing	$ 15,000	$ 20,000	$ 25,000
Accounting & legal	$ 3,000	$ 3,250	$ 3,500
Insurance	$ 1,850	$ 2,000	$ 2,250
Vehicle	$ 5,500	$ 5,500	$ 5,500
Rent	$ 12,500	$ 12,500	$ 12,500
Utilities	$ 3,600	$ 3,700	$ 3,800
Telephone	$ 1,250	$ 1,500	$ 1,750
Payroll taxes	$ 6,503	$ 6,885	$ 7,268
Office supplies	$ 550	$ 600	$ 650
Tools & equipment	$ 3,500	$ 3,500	$ 3,500
Postage	$ 1,500	$ 2,000	$ 2,500
Professional development	$ 1,700	$ 1,700	$ 1,700
Fees & regulatory	$ 150	$ 150	$ 150
Health insurance	$ 12,000	$ 15,000	$ 18,000
Total expenses	**$ 68,603**	**$ 78,285**	**$ 88,068**
Net income	**$ 40,397**	**$ 80,465**	**$120,432**

Pizzeria

PIZZA TO GO, INC.

3215 Sturges St.
Pittsburg, PA 15233

This plan relies on a proven name and business philosophy to propose the creation of a franchise takeout pizza store. The company does an excellent job of establishing the typical area these franchises are started in, then showing the proposed location to be identical. Ideas for capital cost reduction, as well as the proven success of the other franchises, solidifies this proposal's viability.

This business plan appeared in **Business Plans Handbook, Volume 6.** *It has been updated for this volume.*

INTRODUCTION

Pizza to Go, Inc. is a Pennsylvania corporation, having been incorporated in September of 2016, primarily for the purpose of selling pizza, salads, submarine sandwiches, and various other food products, as a licensed franchisee under the franchise name of "Mama's Pizza." The company presently maintains an office in Pittsburgh, Pennsylvania. The president and principal shareholder of the company is William Becker.

STRATEGIC PLAN

Over the course of the next three years, the company intends to open several franchised retail pizza establishments in the greater Pittsburgh, Pennsylvania area, with its first franchised store scheduled to open in January of 2017. The company's primary thrust will be to locate each of its stores in newly developing, high density, residential areas with little pre-existing competition. The company also will maintain high quality control standards, strictly adhering to the Mama's Pizza "formula," which has, to date, proven successful (Mama's Pizza has previously been voted the "Number 1 Best Tasting Pizza" in Pennsylvania). The company also will utilize midlevel pricing.

THE FRANCHISE/FRANCHISOR

The name of the franchisor is Pizza to Go, Inc., a Pennsylvania corporation formed in 2016 for the purpose of offering and selling Mama's Pizza franchises, and servicing, supporting, and administering all functions inherent in operating the franchise system. William A. Becker is the president, treasurer, director, and 50% shareholder of Pizza to Go, Inc.

The names of Pizza to Go, Inc. predecessors are William A. Becker, Inc. and the Becker Group, Inc., both Pennsylvania corporations. Since its inception in 2010, William A. Becker, Inc. has been engaged in the ownership and operation of Mama's Pizza stores that specialize in the sale of pizza and other food products in the metropolitan Pittsburgh area. Over the last three years William A. Becker, Inc. has owned and operated two Mama's Pizza stores, both located in nearby suburbs. Presently, negotiations are underway for eight franchised Mama's Pizza establishments in the metropolitan Pittsburgh area, with the first franchised store expected to open in January of 2017.

THE FRANCHISE AGREEMENT

On November 12, 2016 the company did execute with Pizza to Go, Inc., the Franchisor's standard franchise agreement with numerous amendments, deletions, and additions. Under the agreement, the company has a protected territory defined as a five-mile radius from each of its stores. Under the agreement, no other Mama's Pizza franchise or company store can be opened within this five-mile radius-protected area. Furthermore, the company has negotiated and the agreement provides that the company has a 30-day right of first refusal anywhere within Washington and Westmoreland counties. This right of first refusal will allow the company, if it chooses, to "lock-in" these counties, thereby becoming and remaining the sole Mama's Pizza franchisee in such counties.

Finally, under the agreement, the company is required to pay an ongoing franchise royalty equal to 3% of gross revenues during the first year of operations and 4% thereafter. An industry-wide review of franchise fees and royalties reveals that the Mama's Pizza royalty is substantially less than those found with competing pizza franchises.

PURPOSE OF FINANCING

The company is seeking financing for the express purpose of providing cash funding to allow: (1) the acquisition of various machinery, equipment, and supplies and (2) the construction of its first franchised retail pizza establishment.

(1) **The Equipment:** Schedule A is a pro-forma list of the equipment and supplies anticipated to be required for the operation of the company's first pizza store, together with a projected aggregate cost of such items. It is important to note that the company has decided to acquire, whenever possible, used equipment and supplies, recognizing that quality used equipment is readily available in the marketplace at substantial savings. The purchase of high quality, well maintained used equipment will allow the company to reduce its capital outlays to approximately 30% of what would otherwise be expected as a result of purchasing new equipment. This will obviously preserve working capital, reduce ongoing interest costs, and increase net profitability.

(2) **The Build-Out:** Schedule B is a list of the items associated with the "Build-Out," which is capable of being financed together with their anticipated cost.

The total cash financing sought for both the equipment and the "Build-Out" is $130,000.

THE INITIAL STORE

The company's initial franchised store will consist of 1,600 square feet of retail space. Indeed, the company has executed a five-year lease with a five-year renewal option at an annual rent of $18.00 per square foot. This results in a monthly rent charge of $2,400, plus common area charges which are anticipated to approximate $450 monthly. The initial store will be located in a plaza consisting of seven retail establishments. The plaza includes two other retail food establishments, an Outback Steak House, which can be described as an "anchor," and Bagel Factory. Neither the Outback Steak House nor Bagel Factory are considered to be direct competitors. Each of their product lines are substantially different and their markets are likewise different. The company is a takeout retail pizza franchise, while both Outback Steak House and Bagel Factory are essentially sit-down restaurants with different product lines. The remaining retail outlets in the plaza include Delta Florist, Century Cellunet, Airway Oxygen, and Benjamin Moore.

THE COMPETITION

The company has examined in detail the geographic area consisting of a two-mile radius from the initial store to determine the extent of competition. It is apparent that little competition exists. The nearest retail pizza establishment west of the initial store is located in a town which is approximately five miles further west. In this town one will find a wide array of pizza establishments, including Little Caesars, Dominos, Pizza Hut, and Hungry Howies. The nearest competing business is approximately one quarter mile to the east and is a nonfranchised, independent pizza establishment known as Jack's Pizza. Approximately two miles to the east are Little Caesars and Papa Mario's. Approximately one and one half miles to the south is a Whatta Pizza. There are no competing pizza establishments within three miles to the north of the initial store.

MARKETING PLAN

The company's marketing thrust will be twofold. First, the company will be participating in and benefiting from the franchise-wide marketing fund. Under the "agreement," each franchisee pays to the franchisor a marketing fee equal to $.15 per pizza box purchased. This amount is then forwarded to the franchisor by the box manufacturer and utilized for the benefit of the franchise. The advertising is not store specific and is geared toward promoting the franchise name and the franchise's product line as a whole. Second, under the "agreement," the company is obligated to expend 1% of its gross revenues on local advertising. However, the company fully expects to exceed the 1% requirement. Indeed, the company's marketing thrust will consist of fliers, discount coupons, and inserts, as well as direct mail promotions.

With respect to packaging, it is important to understand that as a franchisee, the company will be licensed to utilize each and every one of the Mama's Pizza trademarks. Indeed, the "agreement" specifically requires that each of the franchisees strictly adheres to trademark packaging. This is common industry practice.

FINANCIAL STATEMENTS

Schedule C is a pro-forma income statement, before depreciation charges, reflecting the company's anticipated cash flow generated by the initial store during the calendar year ending December 31, 2017.

SCHEDULE A

Equipment

Description	Cost
Middly by marshall 350 double ovens	22,500
Acme sheeter	2,400
Vcm mixer	4,500
3 door pizza prep table	2,700
3 door salad prep table	2,250
Three compartment sink	1,010
Two hand sinks (125ea.)	375
Freezer	600
Three 8' SS tables (275ea.)	1,237
One 6' SS table	188
Smallwares	9,000
Exterior signs	6,000
Interior signs	900
Undercounter cooler	1,350
Proofer	1,650
Phone system	3,900
Car top signs	1,275
Fax machine & cash register	900
Pizza bags	400
8' X 12' walk-in cooler (installed)	7,950
Total	**71,085**
Tax	5,290
Delivery and set-up	100
Total	**$76,475**

SCHEDULE B

Build-Out

Description	Cost
Flooring	$ 5,520
Ceiling	1,260
Walls	6,150
Counters & cabinets	3,000
Hvac	1,500
Makeup air	7,500
Hood sor makeup air	3,000
Electrical	3,900
Plumbing	6,600
Misc. labor & related services	10,800
Misc. extras	1,800
Total	**$50,760**

SCHEDULE C

ProForma Income Statement (First Year)

	Jan.	Feb.	Mar.	Apr.	May	June
Income						
Sales-food	54,000	55,620	57,288	59,007	60,777	62,601
Sales-pop & bottles	2,700	2,781	2,865	2,951	3,039	3,131
Sales-deliv.	3,900	4,017	4,137	4,262	4,389	4,521
Total gross income	**60,600**	**62,418**	**64,290**	**66,219**	**68,207**	**70,253**
Cost of goods sold						
Purchases	15,150	15,605	16,073	16,556	17,052	17,564
Delivery expense	2,430	2,504	2,579	2,655	2,735	2,817
Operating supplies	182	186	192	198	204	210
Total C.O.G. sold	**17,762**	**18,294**	**18,843**	**19,409**	**19,991**	**20,591**
Gross profit	**42,839**	**44,124**	**45,447**	**46,811**	**48,216**	**49,662**
Expenses						
Franchise fee	1,818	1,872	1,929	1,986	2,046	2,108
Insurance	525	525	525	525	525	525
Maintenance & repair	600	600	600	600	600	600
Office supplies	60	63	65	66	68	71
Advertising	5,250	3,000	1,500	1,500	1,500	1,500
Bank charges	60	63	65	66	68	71
Laundry	182	188	194	198	204	212
Rent—office	2,850	2,850	2,850	2,850	2,850	2,850
Equipment lease	2,250	2,250	2,250	2,250	2,250	2,250
Rubbish removal	60	60	60	60	60	60
Telephone	450	450	450	450	450	450
Utilities	788	812	836	861	887	914
Sales tax	3,240	3,338	3,438	3,540	3,647	3,756
Wages	14,847	15,293	15,752	16,224	16,710	17,211
Total expenses	**32,981**	**31,361**	**30,510**	**31,178**	**31,866**	**32,576**
Net operating income	**9,858**	**12,764**	**14,939**	**15,633**	**16,350**	**17,087**
Cumulative net operating income		**22,622**	**37,560**	**53,193**	**69,542**	**86,630**

ProForma Income Statement (First Year Cont.)

	Jul.	Aug.	Sep.	Oct.	Nov.	Dec.
Income						
Sales-food	64,479	66,413	68,406	70,458	72,572	74,748
Sales-pop & bottles	3,224	3,321	3,420	3,524	3,629	3,738
Sales-deliv.	4,658	4,797	4,941	5,088	5,241	5,399
Total gross income	**72,360**	**74,531**	**76,767**	**79,070**	**81,441**	**83,885**
Cost of goods sold						
Purchases	18,090	18,633	19,191	19,767	20,361	20,972
Delivery expense	2,901	2,988	3,078	3,171	3,266	3,365
Operating supplies	216	224	230	237	243	251
Total C.O.G. sold	**21,209**	**21,845**	**22,500**	**23,175**	**23,870**	**24,587**
Gross profit	**51,152**	**52,686**	**54,267**	**55,895**	**57,572**	**59,300**
Expenses						
Franchise fee	2,171	2,237	2,303	2,372	2,444	2,517
Insurance	525	525	525	525	525	525
Maintenance & repair	600	600	600	600	600	600
Office supplies	72	75	77	80	81	84
Advertising	1,500	1,500	1,536	1,581	1,629	1,677
Bank charges	72	75	77	80	81	84
Laundry	218	224	231	237	245	252
Rent—office	2,850	2,850	2,850	2,850	2,850	2,850
Equipment lease	2,250	2,250	2,250	2,250	2,250	2,250
Rubbish removal	60	60	60	60	60	60
Telephone	450	450	450	450	450	450
Utilities	941	969	998	1,028	1,059	1,091
Sales tax	3,869	3,986	4,104	4,227	4,355	4,485
Wages	17,729	18,260	18,807	19,373	19,953	20,552
Total expenses	**33,305**	**34,058**	**34,868**	**35,711**	**36,581**	**37,476**
Net operating income	**17,847**	**18,629**	**19,400**	**20,184**	**20,991**	**21,824**
Cumulative net operating income	**104,475**	**123,105**	**142,505**	**162,689**	**183,680**	**205,502**

Cash Flow

	1/31	2/7	2/14	2/21	2/28	3/7
Beginning balance						
Checking	21,231	18,506	21,801	19,824	22,667	18,795
Sales						
Food	—	4,350	5,003	5,753	6,617	7,608
Pop	—	150	165	182	200	219
Deliveries	—	300	330	363	399	440
Total	**—**	**4,800**	**5,498**	**6,297**	**7,215**	**8,267**
Costs						
Drivers	45	153	176	201	231	264
Food	—	897	1,488	1,649	1,889	2,165
Total	**45**	**1,050**	**1,664**	**1,851**	**2,120**	**2,429**
Subtotal	**21,186**	**22,256**	**25,635**	**24,270**	**27,761**	**24,633**
Expense						
Franchise fee	—	—	—	326	—	405
Insurance maintenance & repair	—	—	—	—	—	504
Office supplies	—	—	75	—	—	75
Advertising bank charges	—	—	885	690	—	750
Laundry	—	—	51	51	51	51
Rent—office	—	—	—	—	2,963	—
Equipment lease	—	—	—	—	—	—
Rubbish removal	—	194	—	192	—	192
Telephone	531	—	—	—	531	—
Utilities	119	—	—	—	525	—
Wages—gross	2,031	—	4,500	—	4,500	—
Taxes	—	261	300	345	398	456
Total expenses	**2,681**	**455**	**5,811**	**1,604**	**8,967**	**2,435**
Ending balance	**18,506**	**21,801**	**19,824**	**22,667**	**18,795**	**22,199**
Labor					**38.2%**	

Cash Flow (Cont.)

	3/14	3/21	3/28	4/7	4/14	4/21	4/28
Beginning balance							
Checking	22,199	22,929	29,219	26,013	34,545	37,028	44,855
Sales							
Food	8,750	10,062	11,571	13,307	13,307	13,307	13,307
Pop	242	266	293	321	321	321	321
Deliveries	483	531	585	644	644	644	644
Total	**9,474**	**10,859**	**12,449**	**14,271**	**14,271**	**14,271**	**14,271**
Costs							
Drivers	303	348	399	456	456	456	456
Food	2,480	2,843	3,258	3,735	4,281	4,281	4,281
Total	**2,784**	**3,189**	**3,656**	**4,191**	**4,739**	**4,739**	**4,739**
Subtotal	**28,890**	**30,599**	**38,012**	**36,095**	**44,079**	**46,560**	**54,389**
Expense							
Franchise fee	—	533	—	699	—	857	—
Insurance maintenance & repair	—	—	504	—	—	—	504
Office supplies	—	—	75	—	—	—	75
Advertising bank charges	—	885	—	—	—	—	—
Laundry	51	51	51	51	51	51	51
Rent—office	—	—	2,963	—	—	—	2,963
Equipment lease	—	—	1,724	—	—	—	1,724
Rubbish removal	—	192	—	—	—	—	—
Telephone	—	—	531	—	—	—	531
Utilities	—	—	750	—	—	—	750
Wages—gross	4,500	—	4,706	—	6,203	—	6,618
Taxes	525	603	695	798	798	798	798
Total expenses	**5,961**	**1,379**	**11,997**	**1,548**	**7,052**	**1,706**	**14,015**
Ending balance	**22,929**	**29,219**	**26,013**	**34,545**	**37,028**	**44,855**	**40,374**
Labor	**29.1%**		**23.1%**		**23.2%**		**23.2%**

Radio Station

RadioXM 95.9

PO Box 67433
New York, NY 10009

BizPlanDB.com

The purpose of this business plan is to raise $1,800,000 for the development of a radio station while showcasing the expected financials and operations over the next three years. RadioXM 95.9 ("the Company") is a New York-based corporation that will provide, develop, and distribute radio programming produced by the business to customers in its targeted market. The Company was founded by Joe Keller.

1.0 EXECUTIVE SUMMARY

The purpose of this business plan is to raise $1,800,000 for the development of a radio station while showcasing the expected financials and operations over the next three years. RadioXM 95.9 ("the Company") is a New York-based corporation that will provide, develop, and distribute radio programming produced by the business to customers in its targeted market. The Company was founded by Joe Keller.

1.1 The Services

As stated above, the Company will be actively engaged in the development and distribution of radio broadcasted programs produced by the business. Once the Company "green lights" a new radio show or format, the business will aggressively produce, distribute, and market the show to the general public.

At this time, the business is acquiring its radio licenses so that the business can immediately begin broadcasting once the requisite capital is in place.

The third section of the business plan will further describe the services offered by RadioXM 95.9.

1.2 Financing

Mr. Keller is seeking to raise $1.8 million from an investor or group of investor(s). On a preliminary basis, Mr. Keller intends to sell a 50% interest in the business in exchange for the capital sought in this business plan. The investor will also receive a seat on the board of directors, as well as a regular stream of dividends from the royalties earned on the radio show programs produced and distributed by the Company. The financing will be used for the following:

- Development of the Company's production operations.

- Financing for the first six months of operation.

- Capital to purchase radio broadcasting and production equipment.

1.3 Mission Statement

To produce quality radio entertainment and other media that provide the Company's audience with enjoyable entertainment.

1.4 Management Team

The Company was founded by Joe Keller. Mr. Keller has more than 10 years of experience in the entertainment industry. Through his expertise, he will be able to bring the operations of the business to profitability within its first year of operations.

1.5 Sales Forecasts

Mr. Keller expects a strong rate of growth at the start of operations. Below are the expected financials over the next three years.

Proforma Profit and Loss (Yearly)

Year	1	2	3
Sales	$6,417,738	$7,701,286	$9,010,504
Operating costs	$3,890,019	$4,415,286	$4,909,040
EBITDA	$1,382,593	$1,911,849	$2,493,707
Taxes, interest, and depreciation	$ 621,814	$ 822,931	$1,044,037
Net profit	$ 760,779	$1,088,918	$1,449,670

Sales, Operating Costs, and Profit Forecast

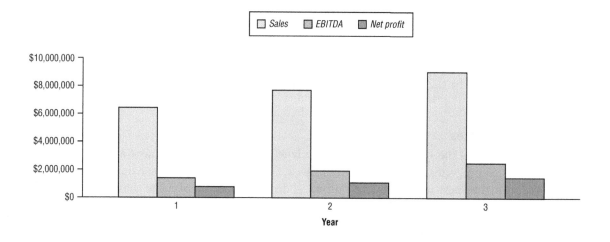

1.6 Expansion Plan

The Founder expects that the business will aggressively expand during the first three years of operation. Mr. Keller intends to implement marketing campaigns that will effectively target quality disc jockeys and on-air personalities that can provide the Company with extensive materials that the Company can produce and distribute via its radio broadcasting operations.

2.0 COMPANY AND FINANCING SUMMARY

2.1 Registered Name and Corporate Structure

The Company is registered as a corporation in the State of New York.

2.2 Required Funds

At this time, RadioXM 95.9 requires $1.8 million of investor funds. Below is a breakdown of how these funds will be used:

Projected Startup Costs

Radio station facility development	$ 750,000
Working capital	$ 200,000
Broadcasting quipment	$ 275,000
Travel expenses	$ 125,000
Security deposits	$ 50,000
Insurance	$ 25,000
FF&E	$ 100,000
Marketing budget	$ 250,000
Miscellaneous and unforeseen costs	$ 25,000
Total startup costs	**$1,800,000**

Use of Funds

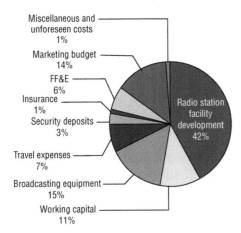

2.3 Investor Equity

At this time, Mr. Keller is seeking to sell a 50% equity interest in the business in exchange for the requisite capital sought in this business plan. The investor will receive a seat on the board of directors and a share of the ongoing royalties generated by the Company's radio broadcasting.

2.4 Management Equity

Once the requisite capital is raised, Mr. Keller will retain a 50% ownership interest in the business.

2.5 Exit Strategy

If the business is very successful, Mr. Keller may seek to sell the business to a third party for a significant earnings multiple. Most likely, the Company will hire a qualified business broker to sell the business on behalf of RadioXM 95.9. Based on historical numbers, the business could fetch a sales premium of up to 10 times earnings if the Company earns substantial royalty income from previous broadcasts.

3.0 PRODUCTS AND SERVICES

Below is a description of RadioXM 95.9's operations.

3.1 Radio Operations

Below is a brief summary of benefits offered to the listener and the advertiser of RadioXM 95.9.

Listeners

- Constant stream of music content that appeals to an independent music audience.

- Regular giveaways of merchandise to listeners that register on the RadioXM 95.9 website.

- Regular updates in the content and music programming offered by the business so the Company may continue to maintain a large, diverse customer base.

Advertisers

- Content that appeals to a wide demographic of world wide listeners.

- Oversight for the listening base of the radio station through third party advertising management.

- The ability to quickly see the results from an advertising campaign.

The business will institute several merchandise giveaways as a promotional campaign for the business' website. This should allow the business to draw more people to the website to register for email updates and notification of new content.

3.2 Advertising Revenues

Among advertising revenue, the primary stream of revenue generated from advertisements will come from the Company's broadcasting station. At the onset of operations, the Company will solicit a third-party advertising agency firm to source all advertisements that will be played on the Company's broadcasting station.

A secondary stream of revenue generated for the business will come from the sale of static and dynamic advertisements throughout the website and during streaming radio content. There are a number of third party advertising providers that will pay the Company directly for hosting their streaming content of advertisements. RadioXM 95.9 will make full use of this content in order to generate predictable streams of revenue on a monthly basis. Management is currently sourcing vendors for this aspect of the Company's revenue generation.

4.0 STRATEGIC AND MARKET ANALYSIS

4.1 Economic Outlook

The business of providing radio broadcasted content with the ability to generate revenue from advertising sales is a complicated business that has many operating facets. Typically, entertainment media content is immune from general changes in the economy, as the content is provided for free, and if people continue to listen to the program, the business will consistently be able to sell advertising space. As such, much of the following market analysis is geared towards the entry plan of the business and the expansion of its customer base.

4.2 Industry Analysis

Within the United States there are more than 7,000 radio program production companies that operate among several thousand markets. Each year these companies aggregately generate $57 billion dollars a year of revenue, while providing jobs for more than 280,000 people. Aggregate payrolls in each of the last five years have reached $9 billion dollars. Radio is a mature industry, and the future expected growth rate will equal that of the general economy.

4.3 Customer Profile

As each radio program and production will target a different demographic, RadioXM 95.9 will conduct an extensive demographic and marketing profile before each new radio program is developed. For the majority of programs developed by the Company, Management has developed the following demographic profile that will be used in conjunction with the business' marketing campaigns:

- Between the ages of 25 to 50

- Enjoys rock, pop, and hip-hop music

- Annual household income of $35,000+

- Lives within 50 miles of a major metropolitan area

Approximately 110 million people fall into the above demographic profile within the United States.

4.4 Competition

As stated above, there are more than 7,000 radio program production companies nationwide. As such, it is difficult to categorize the competition that the business will face as it progresses through its business operations. There are terrestrial, satellite, and online competitors that provide similar content to that of RadioXM 95.9. However, the Company will maintain a strong competitive advantage by playing music for a longer period of time without commercial interruption. Additionally, the business will hire "high-energy" radio personalities to host the Company's programs.

5.0 MARKETING PLAN

RadioXM 95.9 intends to maintain an extensive marketing campaign that will ensure maximum visibility for the business's developed radio programming among its targeted market. Below is an overview of the marketing strategies and objectives.

5.1 Marketing Objectives

- Establish a strong presence in targeted domestic markets.

- Establish connections with entertainment advertising agencies and marketing firms.

- Build a large network of financial backers.

5.2 Marketing Strategies

Management intends on running a number of advertisements within the United States that feature descriptions of the Company's radio programming, its disc jockeys, radio personalities, and descriptions of the format of RadioXM 95.9.

At the onset of operations, the Company will quickly source a number of marketing firms and advertising agencies that place advertisements for businesses on the radio waves. RadioXM 95.9 will develop an extensive information brochure showcasing the listening base and the demographics targeted by the business. As stated earlier, the Company intends to use a third-party advertising firm that will place radio advertisements for the Company's online and traditional broadcasts. This strategy will allow the business to operate profitability from the onset of operations as the advertising revenues will be generated immediately after the business launches. A retained marketing firm is expected to engage in large-scale billboard advertising, as well as guerilla marketing strategies (including flyer distribution within major cities).

RadioXM 95.9 will also maintain an expansive presence via online marketing channels. Beyond the Company's proprietary website, the business will focus on promoting the station, as well as individual programs through social media platforms. For each show and radio personality, the business will maintain a FaceBook and Twitter profile. An in-house marketing manager will be hired in order to manage the Company's social media campaigns.

5.3 Pricing

Management anticipates that it will receive $15 to $20 per thousand listeners for a 30-second radio commercial via traditional broadcasting. For online streaming of the Company's programs, Management anticipates a $7 to $12 CPM.

6.0 ORGANIZATIONAL PLAN AND PERSONNEL SUMMARY

6.1 Corporate Organization

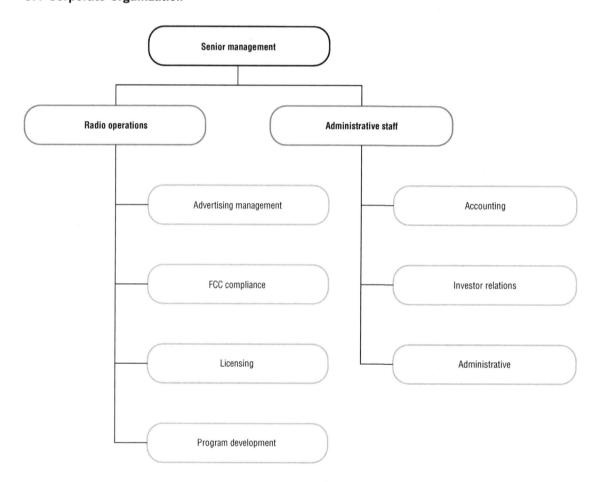

6.2 Organizational Budget

Personnel Plan—Yearly

Year	1	2	3
Senior management	$ 200,000	$ 206,000	$ 212,180
Marketing and distribution staff	$ 390,000	$ 535,600	$ 689,585
Radio production staff	$ 220,000	$ 283,250	$ 291,748
Accounting staff	$ 130,000	$ 133,900	$ 137,917
Administrative staff	$ 225,000	$ 231,750	$ 238,703
Total	**$1,165,000**	**$1,390,500**	**$1,570,132**

Number of Personnel

Year	1	2	3
Senior management	2	2	2
Marketing and distribution staff	6	8	10
Radio production staff	4	5	5
Accounting staff	2	2	2
Administrative staff	6	6	6
Totals	**20**	**23**	**25**

Personnel Expense Breakdown

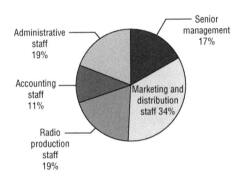

7.0 FINANCIAL PLAN

7.1 Underlying Assumptions

The Company has based its proforma financial statements on the following:

- RadioXM 95.9 will have an annual revenue growth rate of 16% per year.

- The Founder will acquire $1.8 million of equity funds to develop the business.

- The Company shall settle most short-term payables on a monthly basis.

7.2 Sensitivity Analysis

RadioXM 95.9's revenues are moderately sensitive to changes in the general economy. Advertising revenues have a tendency to decline in the event of an economic recession, as content providers compete for smaller amounts of advertising dollars. The high gross margins achieved by the Company will allow the business to remain profitable even in the event of an economic recession.

7.3 Source of Funds

Financing

Equity contributions

Investor(s)	$ 1,800,000.00
Total equity financing	**$1,800,000.00**
Banks and lenders	
Total debt financing	**$0.00**
Total financing	**$1,800,000.00**

7.4 General Assumptions

General Assumptions

Year	1	2	3
Short term interest rate	9.5%	9.5%	9.5%
Long term interest rate	10.0%	10.0%	10.0%
Federal tax rate	33.0%	33.0%	33.0%
State tax rate	5.0%	5.0%	5.0%
Personnel taxes	15.0%	15.0%	15.0%

7.5 Profit and Loss Statements

Proforma Profit and Loss (Yearly)

Year	1	2	3
Sales	**$6,417,738**	**$7,701,286**	**$9,010,504**
Cost of goods sold	$ 1,145,126	$ 1,374,151	$ 1,607,757
Gross margin	82.16%	82.16%	82.16%
Operating income	**$5,272,612**	**$6,327,135**	**$7,402,748**
Expenses			
Payroll	$ 1,165,000	$ 1,390,500	$ 1,570,132
General and administrative	$ 145,200	$ 151,008	$ 157,048
Marketing expenses	$ 256,710	$ 308,051	$ 360,420
Professional fees and licensure	$ 52,190	$ 53,756	$ 55,368
Insurance costs	$ 111,987	$ 117,586	$ 123,466
Production costs	$ 1,175,960	$ 1,293,556	$ 1,422,912
Distribution costs	$ 776,134	$ 853,747	$ 939,122
Miscellaneous costs	$ 32,089	$ 38,506	$ 45,053
Payroll taxes	$ 174,750	$ 208,575	$ 235,520
Total operating costs	**$3,890,019**	**$4,415,286**	**$4,909,040**
EBITDA	**$1,382,593**	**$1,911,849**	**$2,493,707**
Federal income tax	$ 456,256	$ 630,910	$ 822,923
State income tax	$ 69,130	$ 95,592	$ 124,685
Interest expense	$ 0	$ 0	$ 0
Depreciation expenses	$ 96,429	$ 96,429	$ 96,429
Net profit	**$ 760,779**	**$1,088,918**	**$1,449,670**
Profit margin	**11.85%**	**14.14%**	**16.09%**

Sales, Operating Costs, and Profit Forecast

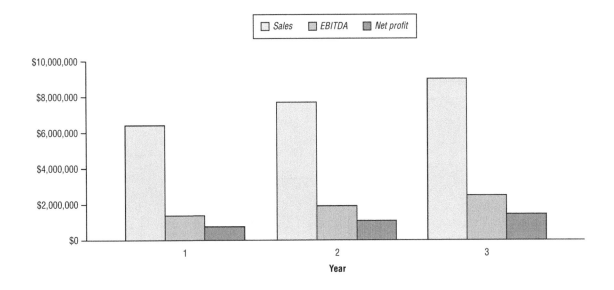

7.6 Cash Flow Analysis

Proforma Cash Flow Analysis—Yearly

Year	1	2	3
Cash from operations	$ 857,208	$ 1,185,346	$ 1,546,099
Cash from receivables	$ 0	$0	$ 0
Operating cash inflow	**$ 857,208**	**$1,185,346**	**$1,546,099**
Other cash inflows			
Equity investment	$ 1,800,000	$ 0	$ 0
Increased borrowings	$ 0	$ 0	$ 0
Sales of business assets	$ 0	$ 0	$ 0
A/P increases	$ 37,902	$ 43,587	$ 50,125
Total other cash inflows	**$1,837,902**	**$ 43,587**	**$ 50,125**
Total cash inflow	**$2,695,110**	**$1,228,934**	**$1,596,224**
Cash outflows			
Repayment of principal	$ 0	$ 0	$ 0
A/P decreases	$ 24,897	$ 29,876	$ 35,852
A/R increases	$ 0	$ 0	$ 0
Asset purchases	$ 1,350,000	$ 296,337	$ 386,525
Dividends	$ 600,046	$ 829,742	$ 1,082,269
Total cash outflows	**$1,974,943**	**$1,155,955**	**$1,504,645**
Net cash flow	**$ 720,167**	**$ 72,978**	**$ 91,579**
Cash balance	**$ 720,167**	**$ 793,146**	**$ 884,724**

Proforma Cash Flow (Yearly)

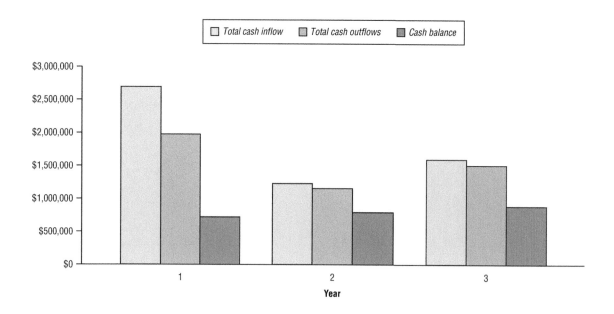

7.7 Balance Sheet

Proforma Balance Sheet—Yearly

Year	1	2	3
Assets			
Cash	$ 720,167	$ 793,146	$ 884,724
Amortized development/expansion costs	$ 225,000	$ 254,634	$ 293,286
General FF&E	$ 100,000	$ 174,084	$ 463,978
Equipment	$ 275,000	$ 319,450	$ 377,429
Intellectual property library	$ 750,000	$ 943,262	$ 943,262
Accumulated depreciation	($ 96,429)	($ 192,857)	($ 289,286)
Total assets	**$1,973,739**	**$2,291,719**	**$2,673,394**
Liabilities and equity			
Accounts payable	$ 13,005	$ 26,716	$ 40,990
Long term liabilities	$ 0	$ 0	$ 0
Other liabilities	$ 0	$ 0	$ 0
Total liabilities	**$ 13,005**	**$ 26,716**	**$ 40,990**
Net worth	**$1,960,734**	**$2,265,003**	**$2,632,404**
Total liabilities and equity	**$1,973,739**	**$2,291,719**	**$2,673,394**

Proforma Balance Sheet

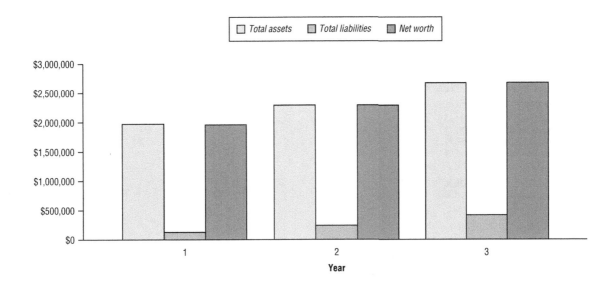

7.8 Breakeven Analysis

Monthly Break Even Analysis

Year	1	2	3
Monthly revenue	$ 394,572	$ 447,851	$ 497,934
Yearly revenue	$4,734,868	$5,374,214	$5,975,204

Break Even Analysis

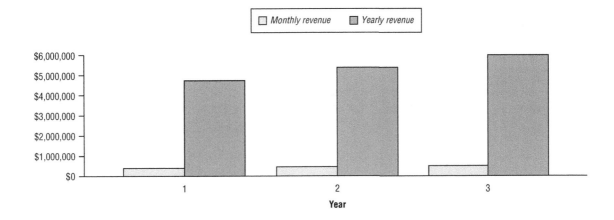

7.9 Business Ratios

Business Ratios—Yearly

Year	1	2	3
Sales			
Sales growth	0.0%	20.0%	17.0%
Gross margin	82.2%	82.2%	82.2%
Financials			
Profit margin	11.85%	14.14%	16.09%
Assets to liabilities	151.77	85.78	65.22
Equity to liabilities	150.77	84.78	64.22
Assets to equity	1.01	1.01	1.02
Liquidity			
Acid test	55.38	29.69	21.58
Cash to assets	0.36	0.35	0.33

7.10 Three Year Profit and Loss Statement

Profit and Loss Statement (First Year)

Months	1	2	3	4	5	6	7
Sales	$ 533,970	$ 534,123	$ 534,276	$ 534,429	$ 534,582	$ 534,735	$ 534,888
Cost of goods sold	$ 95,277	$ 95,304	$ 95,332	$ 95,359	$ 95,386	$ 95,414	$ 95,441
Gross margin	82.2%	82.2%	82.2%	82.2%	82.2%	82.2%	82.2%
Operating income	$ 438,693	$ 438,819	$ 438,944	$ 439,070	$ 439,196	$ 439,322	$ 439,447
Expenses							
Payroll	$ 97,083	$ 97,083	$ 97,083	$ 97,083	$ 97,083	$ 97,083	$ 97,083
General and administrative	$ 12,100	$ 12,100	$ 12,100	$ 12,100	$ 12,100	$ 12,100	$ 12,100
Marketing expenses	$ 21,392	$ 21,392	$ 21,392	$ 21,392	$ 21,392	$ 21,392	$ 21,392
Professional fees and licensure	$ 4,349	$ 4,349	$ 4,349	$ 4,349	$ 4,349	$ 4,349	$ 4,349
Insurance costs	$ 9,332	$ 9,332	$ 9,332	$ 9,332	$ 9,332	$ 9,332	$ 9,332
Production costs	$ 97,997	$ 97,997	$ 97,997	$ 97,997	$ 97,997	$ 97,997	$ 97,997
Distribution costs	$ 64,678	$ 64,678	$ 64,678	$ 64,678	$ 64,678	$ 64,678	$ 64,678
Miscellaneous costs	$ 2,674	$ 2,674	$ 2,674	$ 2,674	$ 2,674	$ 2,674	$ 2,674
Payroll taxes	$ 14,563	$ 14,563	$ 14,563	$ 14,563	$ 14,563	$ 14,563	$ 14,563
Total operating costs	$ 324,168	$ 324,168	$ 324,168	$ 324,168	$ 324,168	$ 324,168	$ 324,168
EBITDA	$ 114,525	$ 114,650	$ 114,776	$ 114,902	$ 115,028	$ 115,153	$ 115,279
Federal income tax	$ 37,961	$ 37,972	$ 37,983	$ 37,994	$ 38,005	$ 38,016	$ 38,027
State income tax	$ 5,752	$ 5,753	$ 5,755	$ 5,757	$ 5,758	$ 5,760	$ 5,762
Interest expense	$ 0	$ 0	$ 0	$ 0	$ 0	$ 0	$ 0
Depreciation expense	$ 8,036	$ 8,036	$ 8,036	$ 8,036	$ 8,036	$ 8,036	$ 8,036
Net profit	$ 62,776	$ 62,889	$ 63,002	$ 63,115	$ 63,229	$ 63,342	$ 63,455

Profit and Loss Statement (First Year Cont.)

Months	8	9	10	11	12	1
Sales	**$ 535,041**	**$ 535,194**	**$ 535,347**	**$ 535,500**	**$ 535,653**	**$ 6,417,738**
Cost of goods sold	$ 95,468	$ 95,495	$ 95,523	$ 95,550	$ 95,577	$ 1,145,126
Gross margin	82.2%	82.2%	82.2%	82.2%	82.2%	82.2%
Operating income	**$ 439,573**	**$ 439,699**	**$ 439,824**	**$ 439,950**	**$ 440,076**	**$ 5,272,612**
Expenses						
Payroll	$ 97,083	$ 97,083	$ 97,083	$ 97,083	$ 97,083	$ 1,165,000
General and administrative	$ 12,100	$ 12,100	$ 12,100	$ 12,100	$ 12,100	$ 145,200
Marketing expenses	$ 21,392	$ 21,392	$ 21,392	$ 21,392	$ 21,392	$ 256,710
Professional fees and licensure	$ 4,349	$ 4,349	$ 4,349	$ 4,349	$ 4,349	$ 52,190
Insurance costs	$ 9,332	$ 9,332	$ 9,332	$ 9,332	$ 9,332	$ 111,987
Production costs	$ 97,997	$ 97,997	$ 97,997	$ 97,997	$ 97,997	$ 1,175,960
Distribution costs	$ 64,678	$ 64,678	$ 64,678	$ 64,678	$ 64,678	$ 776,134
Miscellaneous costs	$ 2,674	$ 2,674	$ 2,674	$ 2,674	$ 2,674	$ 32,089
Payroll taxes	$ 14,563	$ 14,563	$ 14,563	$ 14,563	$ 14,563	$ 174,750
Total operating costs	**$ 324,168**	**$ 324,168**	**$ 324,168**	**$ 324,168**	**$ 324,168**	**$ 3,890,019**
EBITDA	**$ 115,405**	**$ 115,530**	**$ 115,656**	**$ 115,782**	**$ 115,907**	**$ 1,382,593**
Federal income tax	$ 38,038	$ 38,049	$ 38,059	$ 38,070	$ 38,081	$ 456,256
State income tax	$ 5,763	$ 5,765	$ 5,767	$ 5,768	$ 5,770	$ 69,130
Interest expense	$ 0	$ 0	$ 0	$ 0	$ 0	$ 0
Depreciation expense	$ 8,036	$ 8,036	$ 8,036	$ 8,036	$ 8,036	$ 96,429
Net profit	**$ 63,568**	**$ 63,681**	**$ 63,794**	**$ 63,908**	**$ 64,021**	**$ 760,779**

Profit and Loss Statement (Second Year)

			2			
Quarter	Q1	Q2	Q3	Q4	2	
Sales	**$1,540,257**	**$1,925,321**	**$2,079,347**	**$2,156,360**	**$7,701,286**	
Cost of goods sold	$ 274,830	$ 343,538	$ 371,021	$ 384,762	$1,374,151	
Gross margin	82.2%	82.2%	82.2%	82.2%	82.2%	
Operating income	**$1,265,427**	**$1,581,784**	**$1,708,326**	**$1,771,598**	**$6,327,135**	
Expenses						
Payroll	$ 278,100	$ 347,625	$ 375,435	$ 389,340	$1,390,500	
General and administrative	$ 30,202	$ 37,752	$ 40,772	$ 42,282	$ 151,008	
Marketing expenses	$ 61,610	$ 77,013	$ 83,174	$ 86,254	$ 308,051	
Professional fees and licensure	$ 10,751	$ 13,439	$ 14,514	$ 15,052	$ 53,756	
Insurance costs	$ 23,517	$ 29,397	$ 31,748	$ 32,924	$ 117,586	
Production costs	$ 258,711	$ 323,389	$ 349,260	$ 362,196	$1,293,556	
Distribution costs	$ 170,749	$ 213,437	$ 230,512	$ 239,049	$ 853,747	
Miscellaneous costs	$ 7,701	$ 9,627	$ 10,397	$ 10,782	$ 38,506	
Payroll taxes	$ 41,715	$ 52,144	$ 56,315	$ 58,401	$ 208,575	
Total operating costs	**$ 883,057**	**$1,103,821**	**$1,192,127**	**$1,236,280**	**$4,415,286**	
EBITDA	**$ 382,370**	**$ 477,962**	**$ 516,199**	**$ 535,318**	**$1,911,849**	
Federal income tax	$ 126,182	$ 157,728	$ 170,346	$ 176,655	$ 630,910	
State income tax	$ 19,118	$ 23,898	$ 25,810	$ 26,766	$ 95,592	
Interest expense	$ 0	$ 0	$ 0	$ 0	$ 0	
Depreciation expense	$ 24,107	$ 24,107	$ 24,107	$ 24,107	$ 96,429	
Net profit	**$ 212,962**	**$ 272,229**	**$ 295,936**	**$ 307,790**	**$1,088,918**	

Profit and Loss Statement (Third Year)

Quarter	Q1	Q2	Q3	Q4	3
Sales	**$1,802,101**	**$2,252,626**	**$2,432,836**	**$2,522,941**	**$9,010,504**
Cost of goods sold	$ 321,551	$ 401,939	$ 434,094	$ 450,172	$ 1,607,757
Gross margin	82.2%	82.2%	82.2%	82.2%	82.2%
Operating income	**$1,480,550**	**$1,850,687**	**$1,998,742**	**$2,072,769**	**$7,402,748**
Expenses					
Payroll	$ 314,026	$ 392,533	$ 423,936	$ 439,637	$ 1,570,132
General and administrative	$ 31,410	$ 39,262	$ 42,403	$ 43,974	$ 157,048
Marketing expenses	$ 72,084	$ 90,105	$ 97,313	$ 100,918	$ 360,420
Professional fees and licensure	$ 11,074	$ 13,842	$ 14,949	$ 15,503	$ 55,368
Insurance costs	$ 24,693	$ 30,866	$ 33,336	$ 34,570	$ 123,466
Production costs	$ 284,582	$ 355,728	$ 384,186	$ 398,415	$ 1,422,912
Distribution costs	$ 187,824	$ 234,780	$ 253,563	$ 262,954	$ 939,122
Miscellaneous costs	$ 9,011	$ 11,263	$ 12,164	$ 12,615	$ 45,053
Payroll taxes	$ 47,104	$ 58,880	$ 63,590	$ 65,946	$ 235,520
Total operating costs	**$ 981,808**	**$1,227,260**	**$1,325,441**	**$1,374,531**	**$4,909,040**
EBITDA	**$ 498,741**	**$ 623,427**	**$ 673,301**	**$ 698,238**	**$2,493,707**
Federal income tax	$ 164,585	$ 205,731	$ 222,189	$ 230,419	$ 822,923
State income tax	$ 24,937	$ 31,171	$ 33,665	$ 34,912	$ 124,685
Interest expense	$ 0	$ 0	$ 0	$ 0	$ 0
Depreciation expense	$ 24,107	$ 24,107	$ 24,107	$ 24,107	$ 96,429
Net profit	**$ 285,113**	**$ 362,418**	**$ 393,339**	**$ 408,800**	**$1,449,670**

7.11 Three Year Cash Flow Analysis

Cash Flow Analysis (First Year)

Month	1	2	3	4	5	6	7	8
Cash from operations	$ 70,812	$ 70,925	$ 71,038	$ 71,151	$ 71,264	$ 71,377	$ 71,491	$ 71,604
Cash from receivables	$ 0	$ 0	$ 0	$ 0	$ 0	$ 0	$ 0	$ 0
Operating cash inflow	**$ 70,812**	**$ 70,925**	**$ 71,038**	**$ 71,151**	**$ 71,264**	**$ 71,377**	**$ 71,491**	**$ 71,604**
Other cash inflows								
Equity investment	$ 1,800,000	$ 0	$ 0	$ 0	$ 0	$ 0	$ 0	$ 0
Increased borrowings	$ 0	$ 0	$ 0	$ 0	$ 0	$ 0	$ 0	$ 0
Sales of business assets	$ 0	$ 0	$ 0	$ 0	$ 0	$ 0	$ 0	$ 0
A/P increases	$ 3,159	$ 3,159	$ 3,159	$ 3,159	$ 3,159	$ 3,159	$ 3,159	$ 3,159
Total other cash inflows	**$1,803,159**	**$ 3,159**	**$ 3,159**	**$ 3,159**	**$ 3,159**	**$ 3,159**	**$ 3,159**	**$ 3,159**
Total cash inflow	**$1,873,970**	**$ 74,083**	**$ 74,196**	**$ 74,310**	**$ 74,423**	**$ 74,536**	**$ 74,649**	**$ 74,762**
Cash outflows								
Repayment of principal	$ 0	$ 0	$ 0	$ 0	$ 0	$ 0	$ 0	$ 0
A/P decreases	$ 2,075	$ 2,075	$ 2,075	$ 2,075	$ 2,075	$ 2,075	$ 2,075	$ 2,075
A/R increases	$ 0	$ 0	$ 0	$ 0	$ 0	$ 0	$ 0	$ 0
Asset purchases	$ 1,350,000	$ 0	$ 0	$ 0	$ 0	$ 0	$ 0	$ 0
Dividends	$ 0	$ 0	$ 0	$ 0	$ 0	$ 0	$ 0	$ 0
Total cash outflows	**$1,352,075**	**$ 2,075**	**$ 2,075**	**$ 2,075**	**$ 2,075**	**$ 2,075**	**$ 2,075**	**$ 2,075**
Net cash flow	**$ 521,895**	**$ 72,008**	**$ 72,122**	**$ 72,235**	**$ 72,348**	**$ 72,461**	**$ 72,574**	**$ 72,688**
Cash balance	**$ 521,895**	**$593,904**	**$666,025**	**$738,260**	**$810,608**	**$883,069**	**$955,644**	**$1,028,331**

Cash Flow Analysis (First Year Cont.)

Month	9	10	11	12	1
Cash from operations	$ 71,717	$ 71,830	$ 71,943	$ 72,056	$ 857,208
Cash from receivables	$ 0	$ 0	$ 0	$ 0	$ 0
Operating cash inflow	**$ 71,717**	**$ 71,830**	**$ 71,943**	**$ 72,056**	**$ 857,208**
Other cash inflows					
Equity investment	$ 0	$ 0	$ 0	$ 0	$ 1,800,000
Increased borrowings	$ 0	$ 0	$ 0	$ 0	$ 0
Sales of business assets	$ 0	$ 0	$ 0	$ 0	$ 0
A/P increases	$ 3,159	$ 3,159	$ 3,159	$ 3,159	$ 37,902
Total other cash inflows	**$ 3,159**	**$ 3,159**	**$ 3,159**	**$ 3,159**	**$1,837,902**
Total cash inflow	**$ 74,875**	**$ 74,989**	**$ 75,102**	**$ 75,215**	**$2,695,110**
Cash outflows					
Repayment of principal	$ 0	$ 0	$ 0	$ 0	$ 0
A/P decreases	$ 2,075	$ 2,075	$ 2,075	$ 2,075	$ 24,897
A/R increases	$ 0	$ 0	$ 0	$ 0	$ 0
Asset purchases	$ 0	$ 0	$ 0	$ 0	$ 1,350,000
Dividends	$ 0	$ 0	$ 0	$ 600,046	$ 600,046
Total cash outflows	**$ 2,075**	**$ 2,075**	**$ 2,075**	**$602,121**	**$1,974,943**
Net cash flow	**$ 72,801**	**$ 72,914**	**$ 73,027**	**−$526,906**	**$ 720,167**
Cash balance	**$1,101,132**	**$1,174,046**	**$1,247,073**	**$720,167**	**$ 720,167**

Cash Flow Analysis (Second Year)

Quarter	Q1	Q2	Q3	Q4	2
Cash from operations	$237,069	$296,337	$320,043	$331,897	$1,185,346
Cash from receivables	$ 0	$ 0	$ 0	$ 0	$ 0
Operating cash inflow	**$237,069**	**$296,337**	**$320,043**	**$331,897**	**$1,185,346**
Other cash inflows					
Equity investment	$ 0	$ 0	$ 0	$ 0	$ 0
Increased borrowings	$ 0	$ 0	$ 0	$ 0	$ 0
Sales of business assets	$ 0	$ 0	$ 0	$ 0	$ 0
A/P increases	$ 8,717	$ 10,897	$ 11,769	$ 12,204	$ 43,587
Total other cash inflows	**$ 8,717**	**$ 10,897**	**$ 11,769**	**$ 12,204**	**$ 43,587**
Total cash inflow	**$245,787**	**$307,233**	**$331,812**	**$344,101**	**$1,228,934**
Cash outflows					
Repayment of principal	$ 0	$ 0	$ 0	$ 0	$ 0
A/P decreases	$ 5,975	$ 7,469	$ 8,067	$ 8,365	$ 29,876
A/R increases	$ 0	$ 0	$ 0	$ 0	$ 0
Asset purchases	$ 59,267	$ 74,084	$ 80,011	$ 82,974	$ 296,337
Dividends	$165,948	$207,436	$224,030	$232,328	$ 829,742
Total cash outflows	**$231,191**	**$288,989**	**$312,108**	**$323,667**	**$1,155,955**
Net cash flow	**$ 14,596**	**$ 18,245**	**$ 19,704**	**$ 20,434**	**$ 72,978**
Cash balance	**$734,763**	**$753,008**	**$772,712**	**$793,146**	**$ 793,146**

Cash Flow Analysis (Third Year)

	3				
Quarter	Q1	Q2	Q3	Q4	3
Cash from operations	$309,220	$386,525	$417,447	$432,908	$ 1,546,099
Cash from receivables	$ 0	$ 0	$ 0	$ 0	$ 0
Operating cash inflow	**$309,220**	**$386,525**	**$417,447**	**$432,908**	**$1,546,099**
Other cash inflows					
Equity investment	$ 0	$ 0	$ 0	$ 0	$ 0
Increased borrowings	$ 0	$ 0	$ 0	$ 0	$ 0
Sales of business assets	$ 0	$ 0	$ 0	$ 0	$ 0
A/P increases	$ 10,025	$ 12,531	$ 13,534	$ 14,035	$ 50,125
Total other cash inflows	**$ 10,025**	**$ 12,531**	**$ 13,534**	**$ 14,035**	**$ 50,125**
Total cash inflow	**$319,245**	**$399,056**	**$430,980**	**$446,943**	**$1,596,224**
Cash outflows					
Repayment of principal	$ 0	$ 0	0	$ 0	$ 0
A/P decreases	$ 7,170	$ 8,963	$ 9,680	$ 10,038	$ 35,852
A/R increases	$ 0	$ 0	$ 0	$ 0	$ 0
Asset purchases	$ 77,305	$ 96,631	$104,362	$108,227	$ 386,525
Dividends	$216,454	$270,567	$292,213	$303,035	$ 1,082,269
Total cash outflows	**$300,929**	**$376,161**	**$406,254**	**$421,301**	**$1,504,645**
Net cash flow	**$ 18,316**	**$ 22,895**	**$ 24,726**	**$ 25,642**	**$ 91,579**
Cash balance	**$811,461**	**$834,356**	**$859,082**	**$884,724**	**$ 884,724**

Ski Instructor

Tamarack Ski School

PO Box 5543
Tamarack, ID 83615

Zuzu Enterprises

Tamarack Ski School offers a variety of different classes and lessons to suit every age and every schedule. Instructors are experienced in the sport, as well as in teaching, and they take pride in helping others to become successful.

EXECUTIVE SUMMARY

Tamarack Ski School offers a variety of different classes and lessons to suit every age and every schedule. Instructors are experienced in the sport as well as in teaching, and they take pride in helping others to become successful.

INDUSTRY ANALYSIS

The sports coaching industry has an annual revenue of $8 billion dollars, with an annual growth rate of 3%. There are over 138,000 businesses in the industry, employing more than 240,000 people. This industry includes one-on-one sports training at athletic facilities, as well as camps and schools that offer instruction in athletic activities to groups or individuals. Overnight and day sports instruction camps are also included in this industry.

Increased participation in sports and rising disposable income will support the industry in the near future. Sports camps have become increasingly popular alternatives to summer camps, and increased promotional and governmental support for sports participation will benefit the industry even more.

In 2017, sports camps are expected to account for 47.0% of the industry's revenue.

MARKET ANALYSIS

The target market for Tamarack Ski School is Tamarack, Idaho. Tamarack is a very small town, boasting only 760 permanent residents. However, it is located in the shadow of the Bitterroot Mountains north of Boisie, Idaho, and it features a wide variety of terrains perfect for skiing for beginners through advanced skiers. The average annual snowfall is 300 inches, and it features of vertical drop of 2,800 feet. People will gladly travel to Tamarack from the surrounding areas for a chance to ski its slopes.

Demographics

2012 Population growth and population statistics	Tamarack, ID 83615
Total population	**760**
Square miles	115.08
Population density	6.60
1990 population	431
2000 population	642
2010 population	782
5 Year population projection (2017)	775
Population change since 1990	76.48%
Population change since 2000	18.32%
Population change since 2010	−2.84%
Forecasted population change by 2017	1.97%
Population male	52.20%
Population female	47.80%
Median age	47.50

The quality of life in Tamarack is high. It features many recreational, cultural, and dining options, making it the perfect place to relax and have fun for residents and visitors alike.

Quality of Life Indexes

2012 Quality of life indexes	Tamarack, ID 83615	Idaho	United States
Quality of life index	114	96	100
Amusement index	114	104	100
Culture index	106	23	100
Restaurant index	126	42	100

Housing costs in the area are relatively high. Residents of Tamarack and the surrounding areas tend to have more disposable income for recreational activities, and so are likely to spend this income on outdoor activities, including skiing and ski instruction.

Home Values and Rental Rates

2012 Homeowner statistics and home values	Tamarack, ID 83615	Idaho	United States
Owner occupied units	269	407,893	76,294,472
Owner households, with mortgage any	62.30%	70.48%	69.50%
Owner households, with no mortgage	37.70%	29.52%	30.50%
Housing, median value owner households	$268,123	$178,129	$191,717

PERSONNEL

Tamarack Ski School will be staffed by one full-time ski instructor, as well as several part-time instructors on an as-needed basis.

Monica Merkowitz is the owner of Tamarack Ski School, as well as it's one full-time instructor. Monica has been skiing since a very young age and has competed nationally. It is her dream to pass on her love of the sport by teaching others to be successful. She enjoys working with children, teens, and adults, and likes the variety her teaching schedule brings.

Several part-time instructors are also on the schedule, especially during the busy weekend and holiday hours. Most have very flexible availabilities and are happy to pick up as many hours as needed to meet demand.

All instructors are experienced in skiing and snowboarding, as well as teaching. All are certified in First Aid, CPR, and AED, and they are covered under the company's liability insurance.

SERVICES

Tamarack Ski School offers a variety of lessons for skiers and snowboarders of all ability levels and ages. The School is a member of the Professional Ski Instructors of America (PSIA) and uses the American Teaching System. Our instructors are PSIA Certified and offer a simple approach to learning. The techniques have been developed for positive results no matter the ability. Our goal is to emphasize training and safety, but most importantly we want you to have fun skiing and snowboarding.

A variety of different options are available depending on age, length of lesson, and day/time. The current options we have include:

Full Day Children's Lesson (Weekends)

Days Available: Saturdays, Sundays, and Holidays

Ages: Ages 4 to 12 years, ski or snowboard

Start Time: 10:00 am

End Time: 3:00 pm

Duration: 4-hour lesson plus lunch

Note: Lift ticket and equipment rental not included

Half Day Children's Lesson (Weekends)

Days Available: Saturday, Sunday, and Holidays

Ages: Ages 4 to 12 years, ski or snowboard

Start Time: 10:00 am

End Time: 12:00 pm

Duration: 2-hour lesson

Note: Lift ticket and equipment rental not included

Private Full Day Children's Lesson (Weekdays)

Days Available: Monday - Friday, non-holiday

Ages: 4 to 12 years, ski or snowboard

Start Time: 10:00 am

End Time: 3:00 pm

Duration: 4-hour lesson plus lunch

Note: Full day lift ticket and junior equipment included

Private Half Day Children's Lesson (Weekdays)

Days Available: Monday - Friday, non-holiday

Ages: 4 to 12 years, ski or snowboard

Start Time: 10:00am

Duration: 2 hour lesson

Note: Full day lift ticket and junior equipment included

Adult Private Lessons

Ages: 13 and up

Start Times: Every hour starting at 9:00 am

Duration: 2 - 6 hours

Note: Lift ticket and equipment rental not included

Early Bird Private Lesson

Ages: All ages

Start Time: 9:00am ONLY

Duration: 1 hour

Note: Lift ticket and equipment rental not included

Night Owl Private Lesson

Ages: All ages

Start Time: 3:00pm ONLY

Duration: 1 hour

Note: Lift ticket and equipment rental not included

Ski Camp

Days Available: Several week-long camps are held periodically

Ages: Ages 7 to 12 years

Start Time: 10:00 am

End Time: 3:00 pm

Duration: 4-hour lesson plus lunch

Note: Lift ticket and equipment rental not included

Snowboard Camp

Days Available: Several week-long camps are held periodically

Ages: Ages 7 to 12 years

Start Time: 10:00 am

End Time: 3:00 pm

Duration: 4-hour lesson plus lunch

Note: Lift ticket and equipment rental not included

PRICING

Full Day Children's Lesson (Weekends)—$120

Half Day Children's Lesson (Weekends)—$95

Private Full Day Children's Lesson (Weekdays)—$190

Private Half Day Children's Lesson (Weekdays)—$145

Adult Private Lessons 2-hour Weekday—$130

Adult Private Lessons 2-hour Weekend/Holiday—$140

Adult Private Lessons 3-hour Weekday—$180

Adult Private Lessons 3-hour Weekend/Holiday—$190

Adult Private Lessons 6-hour Weekday—$360

Adult Private Lessons 6-hour Weekend/Holiday—$370

Early Bird Private Lesson—$40

Night Owl Private Lesson—$50

Ski Camp—$575

Snowboard Camp—$575

OPERATIONS

Equipment

All instructors are responsible for acquiring and maintaining their own ski and snowboard equipment. Company equipment is limited to:

- Office supplies, including computer, cash register, and printer/copier/fax
- Safety equipment, including first aid kit

Location

While instruction takes place on the slopes, Tamarack Ski School also maintains an office space where clients can meet instructors, schedule lessons, and pay. The office contains a front reception area, restroom, staff area with lockers, and a lounge area.

Hours of Operation

Tamarack Ski School operates daily from 9 am until 4 pm. Private Lessons are available daily, every hour from 9:00 am until 3:00 pm, while Children's Lessons are offered either 10:00 am to 12:00 pm for a half day, or 10:00 am to 3:00 pm for a full day.

Payment

Acceptable forms of payment include cash, check, and major credit cards. Payment is expected at the time of booking, with refunds given only with a minimum 24-hour cancellation notice or in the event of an emergency.

Smoothie and Juice Shop

Suzie's Smoothies

690 LaSalle St.
Ann Arbor, MI 48103

Gerald Rekve

Suzie Cronin has been in the restaurant and food industries for over 20 years, in both ownership and management. This is a key factor why Suzie decided to open a healthy type of restaurant—she sees the need and potential success for serving all healthy food products in a market that has very few restaurants willing or able to do so.

The products will all be produced based on the new health craze, and will include various forms of smoothies and juice drinks. Health drinks like this are made from all natural products like bananas, oranges, pineapples, grapes, mangos, pears, ice, and others. In addition, we will offer meals that are low in fat, high on vitamins, and low on calories.

This business plan appeared in **Business Plans Handbook, Volume 14.** *It has been updated for this volume.*

EXECUTIVE SUMMARY

Suzie Cronin has owned a restaurant for the past four years, and recently sold it after Suzie realized that the long hours and the need for a lot of staff where taking a toll on her. Suzie sold the restaurant with the goal to open another smaller, fast food operation that only served healthy choices for meals and drinks. The smoothie business model matches all of Suzie's requirements. It is a small restaurant, only requires a few staff members to operate, and sells healthy products.

Mission

Suzie's Smoothies will sell healthy food choices for drinks and meals that are high in nutrition and low in fat and calories. Our goal is to gain market share in an even and steady pace, allowing us to enjoy our sales growth.

Our success will be based on our ability to produce products that give our customers healthy food that tastes great. Our mission is to assist our clients in reducing calories and fat intake and to live healthier lives by offering them easy, convenient ways to get healthy, nutritious meals in a hurry.

BUSINESS STRATEGY

After reviewing all of the franchises that are on the market, it was decided that Suzie's Smoothies would be independent. Suzie made this decision based on her needs to operate a small shop—something simple without all the red tape and paperwork that is required of a franchise. By doing this, Suzie understood she would need to develop her own drinks, meals, and so on without the help of a corporate model, but she knew her background in restaurant ownership would give her a solid base from which to operate.

Market Analysis

The target market for Suzie's Smoothies will be the entire city of Ann Arbor, Michigan. Our customers are mainly in the age group of 12 to 35; however, there is a growing trend for the 35 to 46 age group to adopt the healthy life style for food products.

Growth in popularity for smoothie products over the past five years has shown that, once the customer has used this product, they tend to stick with it and tell their friends about it. Healthy food choices are not expensive compared to other food choices. It is just a matter of educating the customer to understand that our food tastes great.

Competition

The current opportunity is greatest right now for our kind of restaurant simply because competing restaurants in the area provide little or no health food choices. Furthermore, even if they were to start offering healthy choices, the branding of their products has been so entrenched in the local market that it will be difficult for restaurants to re-brand themselves as proprietors of healthy options. Our foods, as well as drinks, will be on average lower priced than our competitors.

The future of our business looks bright as long as we open soon enough in order to garner market share. If we have a true competitor open before us, we will lose the ability to get market share. There are no signs of any competitors opening in the near future and we are prepared to open in a very timely fashion.

FINANCIAL ANALYSIS

Here is a breakdown of our financial needs and projected outcomes.

Total amount of funds sought for venture: $48,000

Total amount of estimated startup costs: $24,000

Total amount of projected average monthly expenses: $60,000

Total amount of projected average monthly revenue: $50,400

Start-up Expenses

A chart explaining our needed start-up expenses is included below.

Start-up expenses

Legal	$ 1,800
Stationery etc.	$ 240
Rent	$ 3,120
Expensed equipment	$16,440
Other	$ 2,400
Total start-up expense	**$24,000**
Start-up assets needed	
Cash balance on starting date	$12,000
Start-up inventory	$12,000
Total short-term assets	**$24,000**
Investment	
Owner/founder	$48,000
Total investment	**$48,000**

INDUSTRY ANALYSIS

For a culture that is ever more busy and perpetually on the go, as well as increasingly health conscious, the juice bar is not just a lifestyle stop, but also a gathering place. People are turning away from packaged and canned sugary drinks loaded with high-fructose corn syrup and artificial flavorings. They are reading labels. The vitamin-rich, nutritious alternative is becoming the mainstream choice. Natural sugars and natural ingredients are the calling cards for people who want more green in their diet, but who don't have the time or desire to hit the farmers' market and cook up all those vegetables. While they want these healthy options, they do see barriers that keep them from reaching their healthy eating goals. Among the reasons: availability of products, time constraints, taste concerns, and confusion about what's healthy, including some smoothies. For this reason, cold press juice, which is made by hydraulically chopping and crushing produce such as spinach, kale, and ginger without using heat, thereby yielding highly nutritious juice, has risen to prominence. Suzie's Smoothies makes their juice in this way. Suzie's Smoothies will offer customers the great-tasting, healthy foods they want, quickly and without breaking the bank.

Some relevant statistics include:

- 64% of consumers polled in 2012 agreed that it was important to eat healthy and pay attention to nutrition. That's up from 57% in 2010.

- The Juice and Smoothie Bar Industry is a $5 billion industry with 2.8% growth experienced in the five years from 2011-2016. There are approximately 5,000 businesses employing more than 49,000 people.

- The demographics of the smoothie segment point to demand with a long-term horizon. While just 3.6% of our customers are 55 or older, that number grows to 12.6% for people 45-54, 19.4% for those 35-44, 25.6% for people 25-34, and 26.1% for people 18-24. Smoothies have been mainstream or 20 years—and that is creating more demand as time goes by.

Growth Strategy

The US smoothie market has grown rapidly over the last five years, driven mostly by the consumption habits of Americans who skip meals and often depend on snack foods as a substitute. Since smoothies offer a healthier treat than other snack options, but also taste good and offer convenience and portability, the market is expected to grow at a rate of five to eight percent in the next five years.

The smoothie market has lower barriers of entry because of lower capital investment. But in order to grow, what is required is the quality of the product and brand awareness. Jamba Juice, the leader in the US smoothie market, has clearly taken a lead over its competitors in terms of market share and, most important, brand awareness.

As a result of tremendous growth, many food chains, quick service restaurants, and beverage companies are entering the smoothie segment by opening new stores. The growing interest of large beverage companies in this segment is mostly driven by the declining sales of soft drinks in the United States. There is a possibility of consolidation of the smoothie market, particularly resulting from the inevitable fallout of smoothie brands, which will happen as the market starts to settle.

MARKETING & ADVERTISING

We will utilize various forms of promotion, including:

Word of mouth
- Alliances
- Customer service
- Telemarketing

Advertising
- Billboards
- Direct mail
- Magazines
- Newspapers
- Phone book
- Social media, including Facebook, Instagram, Snapchat, and Twitter

Public Relations
- Demonstrations/booths
- Flyers
- Newsletters
- Press releases
- Promotional products
- Event sponsors

Point of Sale
- Signage
- Web site

OPERATIONS

Suzie's Smoothies will operate our business at 690 LaSalle St. in Ann Arbor, Michigan, as a corporation with one owner.

- We will be open 7 days a week, from 11 am to 7 pm daily.
- We will be closed for major holidays like Thanksgiving and Christmas.
- We will employ 10 full- and part-time staff, including one part-time manager to manage the restaurant when the owner is away. The owner will only work a 40-hour week.

Equipment

In order to operate efficiently, a number of leasehold improvement items and equipment is needed.

These items include:

- Convection ovens
- Electric ovens
- Gas ovens
- Griddle top range

- Microwave ovens
- Walk-In refrigerator
- Walk-In freezer
- Tables
- Booths
- Chairs
- Highchairs and booster seats
- Stools

Other items are needed for food preparation as well, including:

- Aprons
- Blenders
- Can openers
- Chef knives
- Cooking utensils
- Gloves
- Measuring cups
- Storage containers
- Toaster
- Trays
- Work tables
- 20-quart mixers
- Condiment bottles
- Condiment pump

Needed office supplies include:

- Clipboards
- Desks
- Dispenser tape
- Files and filing supplies
- Message pad
- Money bags
- Mounting tape
- Office tape
- Receiving record book
- Safe
- Time clock and time cards

To adequately have dine-in service, we need the following tableware:

- Dishes
- Silverware
- Paper napkins
- Napkin dispensers
- Salt and Pepper shakers

Glassware and beverage essentials include:

- Ice machine—cube
- Ice machine—flaker
- Ice machine—nugget
- Coffee maker
- Coffee filters
- Beverage dispensing systems
- Syrup dispenser
- Tea dispenser
- Plastic cups
- Pitchers
- Straws

Cleaning supplies and equipment we need are:

- Automatic hand dryer
- Compact brooms, mops and wringers
- Under counter cleaning supplies
- Dust mops
- Worktop dusting supplies
- Paper towel dispenser and paper towels
- Soap and soap dispensers
- Sponges
- Trash cans and liners
- Toilet Paper

Other necessary equipment:

- Label dispenser and labels
- Freezer merchandisers
- Signs
- Wet and dry vacuum
- Ice cream case
- First aid supplies

MENU

Smoothies

We have more than 20 delicious, nutritious smoothies all under 500 calories. The smoothie choices include:

- Strawberry kiwi
- Pineapple mango
- Strawberry, pineapple & orange
- Strawberry, pineapple, mango & orange
- Blueberry, strawberry & banana
- Strawberry lime
- Strawberry, pineapple & banana
- Raspberry, strawberry & banana
- Mango, banana, orange & kiwi
- Strawberry banana
- Peach, strawberry & banana
- Carrots, banana & orange
- Spinach, kale, mango, pineapple & banana
- Acai, pomegranate, banana, blueberry & strawberry
- Cucumber, green apple, kale, spinach, celery & kiwi
- Pomegranate, banana & strawberry
- Avocado, pineapple, spinach, coconut & lime
- Peanut butter & banana
- Peanut butter, banana & chocolate
- Blueberry, banana, mango & almonds
- Strawberries, pineapple, white chocolate & coconut

Supplements/Add-ins to the smoothies include:

- Probiotic
- Multivitamins
- Vitamin-C Immune Complex
- Vitamin B-12
- Whey, pea, or soy protein
- Herbal extracts to boost energy or fat burning
- Flax seed
- Almonds
- Spinach
- Kale
- Ginger

- Peanut butter

- Greek yogurt

- Milk

- Almond milk

Food items

Note: All menu options can be made into flatbreads, wraps (tortillas or pita), lettuce wraps, sandwiches, or salads.

- Baja Chicken

- Chicken Caesar

- Chicken Pesto

- Chipotle Turkey

- Cranberry Pecan Chicken Salad

- Hummus Veggie

- Jamaican Jerk Chicken

- King Caesar Chicken

- Southwest Chicken

- Spinach Salad

- Thai Chicken

- Turkey & Swiss

Other food items include:

- Kale & Apple Slaw

- Fruit cup

- Baked chips

- Hummus & pita bread

- Watermelon

Tourist Lodge Business

North Ridge Resort, LLC

2789 Mason Rd.
Twin Bay, WI 54555

Paul Greenland

North Ridge Resort is a tourist business in northern Wisconsin featuring a large main lodge, four cabins, 300 feet of lakefront access, and related amenities.

EXECUTIVE SUMMARY

Northern Wisconsin is a popular tourist destination known for outdoor activities such as fishing, boating, hunting, hiking, and snowmobiling. North Ridge Resort is a tourist business in this region that features a large main lodge, four cabins, 300 feet of lakefront access, and related amenities. The resort is located in the town of Twin Bay, on 4,350-acre Garfield Lake in Lewis County. The lake, which has a maximum depth of 68 feet, contains a variety of fish, including walleye, northern pike, largemouth bass, smallmouth bass, and panfish. Nathan and Deidra Smith have purchased the resort from the family of Leroy Conway, which has owned it since 1953. The lodge's history dates back to 1927, when it was founded by Harley Gunderson, a Norwegian immigrant. The Smiths are committed to providing the same friendly customer service and attention that North Ridge Resort's established customer base has experienced for many years. In addition, they have plans to expand the business by adding capacity to serve additional guests.

INDUSTRY ANALYSIS

Wisconsin is known for its strong tourism industry, especially in the state's northern region. The state attributes 35 percent of all recreational jobs, as well as 23 percent of all food and beverage jobs, to tourist businesses, according to the Wisconsin Department of Tourism. In 2016, Wisconsin's tourism industry had an economic impact of $20 billion. This was a 3.5% increase from the previous year's impact of $19.3 billion, and a 35% increase from 2010. Between 2010 and 2016, the number of visitors to Wisconsin increased by 15.2 million, reaching 107.7 million.

MARKET ANALYSIS

The immediate area that includes Twin Bay and several surrounding communities (primarily most of Lewis County) is home to many popular lodging and accommodation options. From tent and trailer camping to full-service hotels, tourists have a wide range of options when planning their vacations. For those who appreciate the outdoors, the market has something to offer for everyone, from the rustic to the luxurious. The same can be said for available recreational activities, which include, but are not limited to:

- Antiquing
- Fishing
- Boating
- Canoeing
- Kayaking
- Paddle Boarding
- Jet Skiing
- Parasailing
- Hiking
- Biking
- Golf
- Cross-Country Skiing
- Downhill Skiing
- Snowmobiling
- Ice Skating
- Ice Fishing
- Hunting
- Horseback Riding
- Bird/Animal Watching

Visitors are attracted to the Twin Bay area by a number of different annual events, including:

- Twin Bay Arts & Crafts Show
- Cranberry Festival
- Maple Syrup Festival
- Ashton Ridge Snowmobile Derby
- Lewis County Fishing Tournament
- Fourth of July Parade & Festival
- Labor Day Parade & Festival
- Autumn Parade & Festival
- Polar Ice Fishing Tournament
- Lewis County Winter Carnival
- Snow Sculpting Competition
- Pine Mountain Cross Country Ski Tournament

Much of the region's tourist activity takes place in and around its many lakes, including 4,350-acre Garfield Lake, which is stocked with a variety of fish, including:

- Bass
- Perch
- Pike
- Trout
- Musky
- Walleye
- Panfish

SERVICES

Accommodations:

North Ridge Resort offers several different year-round options for tourists seeking accommodations.

Main Lodge: The North Ridge Lodge, which operates as a bed and breakfast, has been the focal point of North Ridge Resort for many years. Since its construction in 1927 by founder Harley Gunderson, a Norwegian immigrant, the lodge has been renovated and expanded several times. It features a rustic knotty pine/stone/log decor throughout. Today, the 6,750-square-foot structure features nine bedrooms, including a private master suite for the owners and eight rooms that are available for guests. Each is equipped with a full bathroom. The structure's mechanicals have been updated and feature in-floor heating. In addition to bedrooms, guests have access to the lodge's great room, which includes a cathedral ceiling, a massive stone fireplace, numerous sitting areas, and a generous supply of books and games. Daily breakfast, prepared from scratch in the lodge's large commercial kitchen, is included for all guests. Delicious dinners, available for an additional fee, are prepared three times per week.

Cabins: In addition to the main lodge, North Ridge Resort also includes four cabins that are available for rent. Two of the cabins include two bedrooms, and two include three bedrooms. Each cabin rental comes with a charcoal grill, a supply of firewood, and a fishing boat. Guests are required to supply their own lifejackets and motor (rental options are available in town). Cabins feature air-conditioning, gas-forced heat, fireplaces, satellite television, full kitchens, coffee makers, and microwaves. Bed linens and towels are provided for guest use. During the peak vacation months of June, July, and August, cabins are available for weekly rentals only. Weekend cabin rentals are available from September through May.

Amenities:

The North Ridge Resort provides the following amenities to all guests at no additional charge:

- Horseshoe Pits (2)
- Fire Pits (6)
- Volleyball Court
- Boat Launch
- Private Piers with Benches for Fishing/Relaxation (2)
- 300 Feet of Lake Frontage
- Private Beach Area
- Private Patios with Grills (3)

- Tennis Court
- Playground Area
- Picnic Tables (8)
- Kayaks (10)
- Canoes (10)
- Paddleboards (5)

In addition to the above, the resort has relationships with local fishing and hunting guides, and provides recommendations regarding/directions to nearby rental services, skiing/snowmobiling/hiking trails, restaurants, supper clubs, and bars.

OPERATIONS

Property Specifications:
- Maintenance Building
- Storage Enclosure
- Outside Storage Area
- Wheelchair Accessibility Features
- 300-Foot Lakefront Access
- 5.4 Acres
- Property Taxes: $13,669
- Recreational Zoning

Pricing & Payments:

Payment is accepted by credit card or check. A 50 percent deposit is required for all reservations. As long as cancellations are made at least 30 days in advance, and assuming that the owners are able to successfully rebook the reservation, deposits will be returned, less a 30 percent processing fee. Pets are allowed in cabins, but not in the main lodge. Pets are required to be with their owners at all times and cannot be left unattended. A refundable $250 damage deposit is required for all guests with pets.

North Ridge Resort's regular-season rates (June-October) are listed below. Rental fees are discounted 35 percent during the off-season months.

Two bedroom/bathroom cabins will accommodate a maximum of five guests.

- *Weekly:* (Deposit: $425/Rental Fee: $850)
- *Weekend:* (Deposit: $215/Rental Fee: $425)

Three bedroom/bathroom cabins will accommodate a maximum of eight guests.

- *Weekly:* (Deposit: $550/Rental Fee: $1,100)
- *Weekend:* (Deposit: $225/Rental Fee: $550)

Main lodge accommodations accommodate a maximum of two guests.

- *Daily:* $60
- *Weekly:* (Deposit: $225/Rental Fee: $550)
- *Weekend:* (Deposit: $90/Rental Fee: $180)

Additional Fees:

- Pets—In addition to the aforementioned deposit, cabin guests with pets must pay an additional $60/week or $30/weekend.

- Extra guests—Rollaway beds are available to accommodate additional cabin guests (above the listed minimum) for $15/night. Additionally, guests must pay $60/week or $30/weekend for the additional guest.

Check-In/Check-Out Times:

During the summer months, weekly cabin rentals are Saturday-Saturday (7 nights). Weekend-only rentals (during the off-season) are Friday-Sunday (2 nights). Guests may check-in after 3 PM on the first day of the reservation. Checkout time is 11 AM on the last day of the guest's reservation.

PERSONNEL

Nathan and Deidra Smith

Nathan and Deidra Smith are both Wisconsin natives with a passion for the outdoors. The couple met on a hunting trip during the late 1990s. Both in their mid-50s, the Smiths are ready to enjoy a "working retirement" by relocating to Northern Wisconsin, where they already spend the majority of their free time hunting, boating, and fishing. Nathan, who has 23 years of experience in residential and commercial construction, and Deidra, who has worked in the hospitality industry as a hotel manager for 17 years, will combine their professional skills and their passions to operate the North Ridge Resort. The couple sold their home in Madison, Wisconsin, and reinvested the equity, along with some of their personal savings, to make the new resort their permanent home. To maximize their prospects for success, the Smiths took advantage of educational opportunities offered by the Small Business Administration, as well as courses offered through a local community college. The Smiths will be joined in the business by their high school-aged children, Tabitha and Jason, who will both work at the resort on a part-time basis, mainly during the busy summer months.

Professional and Advisory Support

North Ridge Resort will utilize a popular software application for bookkeeping, making it easy for the owners to provide regular reports to their accountant, Stanley Anderson. They have established a commercial checking account with Partners Credit Union and will utilize a popular mobile point-of-sale service to accept credit card and debit card payments from customers. Additionally, the owners have purchased a hospitality software package that they can use to manage reservations and guest accounts.

MARKETING & SALES

North Ridge Resort has developed a marketing plan that features the following primary tactics:

1. A color brochure promoting the resort.

2. Regional print advertising in two key Midwestern lifestyle publications.

3. Online directory listings.

4. A Web site with complete details about the resort, along with a scheduling tool that guests can use to check room/cabin availability; a listing of available amenities and nearby attractions; pricing; and terms/conditions.

5. A social media strategy involving Facebook and Instagram, allowing the business to quickly communicate special offers to followers.

6. A semi-annual e-mail/direct mail campaign to former customers, encouraging return visits for summer vacations and fall/winter getaways. The mailers will include an incentive (discount) for booking, and also for referring friends/family.

7. Participation and/or literature distribution at select boating, fishing, and outdoor shows throughout the Midwest.

8. Constant Contact: North Ridge Resort will utilize this e-mail marketing service to stay in touch with prospects and contacts in the company's database, providing the business with another tool for quickly communicating special offers.

GROWTH STRATEGY

Nathan and Deidra Smith estimate that North Ridge Resort will generate profits of approximately $38,000 during the first year of operation. Based on conservative projections prepared in partnership with their accountant, the Smiths estimate that the business will have generated more than $120,000 in profits after its first three years. The owners plan to reinvest most of these profits back into the business, mainly to fund the construction of additional cabins that they will build themselves to save on costs. The Smiths anticipate that the first additional cabin will be available for rental during the fourth year of operations. Long-term, an additional two cabins will be constructed (during years five and six, respectively). The additional three cabins will substantially increase the North Ridge Resort's revenue potential.

FINANCIAL ANALYSIS

The Smiths have sold their home in Madison, Wisconsin, and have relocated to the North Ridge Resort, which is now their permanent year-round home. The owners acquired the lodge and cabins for a total of $1.4 million. After making a 20 percent down payment, the proceeds of which were obtained from equity in their former home and savings, a 30-year mortgage (3.92 percent interest) was obtained for the balance of $1.12 million (payment of $5,296/month or $63,552/year).

The owners have prepared the following projections, showing estimated rental revenues for the business' first year under their ownership:

	Jan.	Feb.	Mar.	Apr.	May	June	July	Aug.	Sept.	Oct.	Nov.	Dec.
2-bedroom cabins(weekly)	$1,658	$1,658	$2,210	$3,315	$4,420	$13,600	$13,600	$13,600	$5,100	$3,400	$1,658	$1,658
3-bedroom cabins (weekly)	$2,145	$2,145	$2,860	$3,575	$5,720	$17,600	$17,600	$17,600	$6,600	$4,400	$2,145	$2,145
2-bedroom cabins (weekend)	$553	$829	$1,105	$1,381	$1,381	$0	$0	$0	$850	$1,700	$1,105	$1,105
3-bedroom cabins (weekend)	$715	$1,073	$1,430	$1,073	$1,073	$0	$0	$0	$1,100	$2,200	$1,430	$1,430
Lodge (daily)	$234	$117	$234	$312	$468	$1,080	$1,080	$1,080	$960	$900	$468	$312
Lodge (weekly)	$715	$715	$1,430	$2,860	$3,575	$13,200	$13,200	$13,200	$8,800	$4,400	$1,430	$715
Lodge (weekend)	$1,170	$936	$1,170	$1,404	$1,638	$1,440	$1,440	$1,440	$2,880	$4,320	$117	$117
	$7,189	**$7,472**	**$10,439**	**$13,920**	**$18,275**	**$46,920**	**$46,920**	**$46,920**	**$26,290**	**$21,320**	**$8,353**	**$7,482**

In addition to $261,500 generated from cabin and room rentals, the owners are anticipating the business will generate an additional $39,225 in fees, resulting in total first-year revenues of $300,725.

The Smiths also have estimated their main fixed and variable costs. The following table provides an overview, showing corresponding percentages of total sales:

Labor	$ 76,000	25%
Utilities	$ 15,690	5%
Equipment	$ 10,460	3%
Marketing	$ 13,075	4%
Insurance	$ 5,230	2%
Mortgage	$ 63,552	21%
Taxes	$ 13,075	4%
Food	$ 39,225	13%
Supplies	$ 7,845	3%
Maintenance	$ 18,305	6%
Total	**$262,457**	

Based on these projections, the Smiths estimate they will generate a profit of $38,268 during the first year of operation. The owners project that they can increase their profits by five percent annually during the second and third years of operation, generating $40,181 and $42,190, respectively. The Smiths plan to reinvest the majority of these profits into the business.

A complete set of financial projections, which the Smiths have prepared in conjunction with their accountant, is available upon request.

Transcription Service

Precision Transcription

873 Woodland Drive
Folkston, GA 31537

Fran Fletcher

Precision Transcription is a medical transcription service owned by Eva Watson. Precision Transcription is located in Folkston, Georgia, a small town between Jacksonville, Florida, and Waycross, Georgia. The Miyo Clinic of Jacksonville attracts many top-level physicians to the area. Many medical clinics in Waycross are members of the Miyo Clinic network and serve as extensions of the Miyo Clinic.

EXECUTIVE SUMMARY

Precision Transcription is a medical transcription service owned by Eva Watson. Precision Transcription is located in Folkston, Georgia, a small town between Jacksonville, Florida, and Waycross, Georgia. The Miyo Clinic of Jacksonville attracts many top-level physicians to the area. Many medical clinics in Waycross are members of the Miyo Clinic network and serve as extensions of the Miyo Clinic.

Ms. Watson earned a medical terminology degree from South Georgia Technical School. She was employed as a medical transcriptionist at Miyo Cardiology Group for five years. She made the tough decision to quit her job when her mother fell ill and needed around-the-clock care in Folkston, Georgia. Her mother has made a partial recovery, so Ms. Watson now has the time to devote to starting her own medical transcription service.

According to the Bureau of Labor Statistics, jobs in the medical transcription industry are expected to stay the same over the next decade. The industry is transitioning to the use of speech recognition technology, and industry professionals will need to be flexible to remain competitive.

Many medical practices are already utilizing speech recognition technology; however, a human must edit these files for errors. Therefore, Ms. Watson will extend her services to include medical file editing.

There are several competitors in the area, but Ms. Watson is confident that Precision Transcription will stand out from its competitors with its 3-day turnaround guarantee. Marketing and advertising will focus on the following customer service features:

- 3-day turnaround time.
- Speech recognition transcription editing.
- Transportation of materials on a set schedule.

Ms. Watson will visit individual medical offices to advertise her services. Referrals and a reputation for quality are essential in the medical transcription field, and Ms. Watson will work hard to gain the respect of clients by providing unparalleled customer service.

Ms. Watson will be not be seeking outside financing at this time. In the beginning, Ms. Watson will work from her home office. Additional medical transcriptionists will be employed as the number of clients and demand for services increase.

COMPANY DESCRIPTION

Location

Precision Transcription is located in Folkston, Georgia. Folkston is conveniently located between Jacksonville, Florida, and Waycross, Georgia. Both cities are home to an abundance of medical practices. Ms. Watson plans to work out of her home office for the first two years.

Hours of Operations

Pick-up/Delivery of Files

Monday and Wednesday 8 AM—11 AM

Office Hours

Monday and Wednesday 1 PM—5 PM

Tuesday, Thursday, and Friday 8 AM—5 PM

Personnel

Eva Watson (Owner/Operator)

Ms. Watson will provide all transcription services until the business becomes established. She has a medical terminology degree from the local technical school. She gained 5 years of experience in medical transcription while working for Miyo Cardiology Group in Jacksonville, Florida.

Medical Transcriptionists

A full-time medical transcriptionist will be hired after 6 months. Additional transcriptionists will be hired as business volume increases.

Services

- Medical Transcription Services
- Speech Recognition Software Editing
- Transportation of materials on a set schedule

MARKET ANALYSIS

Industry Overview

According to the Bureau of Labor Statistics, jobs in the medical transcription industry are expected to stay the same over the next decade. The industry is transitioning to the use of speech recognition technology, and industry professionals will need to be flexible to remain competitive.

Many healthcare providers are opting to use speech recognition technology for medical transcription. However, medical transcriptionists will still be required to edit the files, since the speech recognition transcription will need to be proofed for errors and readability by a human.

The shift to speech recognition software is due to the advancements in technology, the widespread use of computers, and the desire of businesses to decrease operating expenses.

Jacksonville and Waycross are home to hundreds of medical offices that require medical transcription services. Precision Transcription will be available to complete this time-consuming task, which will allow the medical personnel to focus on patient care.

Target Market

Precision Transcription will focus on two target markets.

- Small provider practices—these are often general physicians and other medical professionals who do not wish to employ a large office staff.

- Practices with transcription software—Ms. Watson will offer proofreading and editing services for practices that are utilizing automated software.

Precision Transcription will provide services to medical facilities within a 60-mile radius of the office in Folkston. However, Jacksonville, Florida, and Waycross, Georgia will be the company's primary focus due to the number of potential clients and for the convenience of file pick-up and delivery.

Competition

The following Transcription agencies are located in Jacksonville:

- Jacksonville Transcription Services—8842 Miyo Blvd, Jacksonville, FL—employs approximately 6 medical transcriptionists and provides services to medical facilities in Jacksonville.

- M & M Transcription—2241 W. 6th Street, Jacksonville, FL—employs approximately 3 medical transcriptionists and provides services to medical facilities in Jacksonville.

Precision Transcription will set itself apart from the competition by offering fast turnaround times and friendly service.

GROWTH STRATEGY

The overall strategy of the company is to attract and keep clients who need medical transcription services. Ms. Watson will work alone for the first six months of business operation. After six months, Ms. Watson will take on additional clients and will hire a full-time transcriptionist to assist with the workload. Ms. Watson will then hire additional help as needed to meet customer demand. Precision Transcription wishes to achieve strong financial growth during the first two years of operation, and expand into a larger office space.

Sales and Marketing

Ms. Watson has identified key advertising tactics to obtain customers and build a reputation for quality. Ms. Watson will market that she can provide the services for a fraction of the cost of employing someone solely to provide transcription services in-house.

Precision Transcription will market the following:

- 3-day turnaround time.

- Transcription editing.

- Transportation of files.

Advertising

Advertising will include:

- Visiting potential clients.

- Sending mailers to local medical clinics.

- Utilizing the website transcriptionjobs.com.

In addition to advertising, the company will rely on quality work, great customer service, and fair prices to generate customers through referrals.

FINANCIAL ANALYSIS

Start-up Costs

The start-up costs are minimal since Ms. Watson plans to work from her home office.

Computer	$1,200
Headset system	$ 500
Total	**$1,700**

Prices for Services

The owner will meet with each client and give a free estimate. The type of report preferred or required will dictate which price will be offered to each client.

Service	Price
Transcription	$4 per page
Transcription	$0.14 per gross line
Editing	$4 per page
Editing	$0.14 per gross line

Monthly Expenses

Phone/Internet	$ 100
Gas	$ 120
Wages for Ms. Watson (est.)	$4,000
Total	**$4,220**

Phone/Internet	$ 100
Utilities	$ 120
Wages for All Employees (est.)	$7,000
Total	**$7,220**

Profit/Loss

The statistics used to calculate monthly income is based on clients seeing patients four days per week. Ms. Watson predicts that during the first and second month of operation, she will transcribe for 2 customers that schedule 30 patients per day. No profits are expected during that time. In the third month of operation, she estimates that she will pick up one additional editing client that schedules 30 patients per day.

Ms. Watson estimates $3,840 in income for the first and second months, and $5,760 for the third through sixth months. That will be the maximum amount of files that she can comfortably guarantee a 3-day turnaround time on while working alone. She plans to continue working and building the business unaided for the first six months.

Ms. Watson plans to obtain additional clients during month seven. She estimates that the business will gain two additional medical offices that schedule 30 patients per day. This will increase business expenses to $7,220 per month and increase income to $9,600 per month.

Estimated Profits Months 1–6

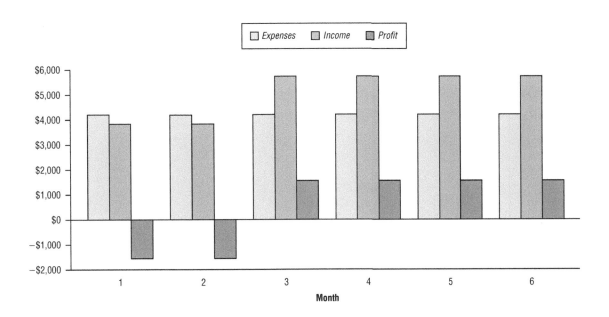

Estimated Profits Months 7–12

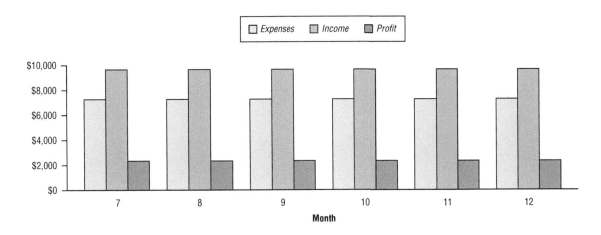

Annual Profit/Loss

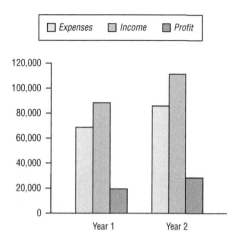

Financing

Ms. Watson is not seeking financing at this time.

Wedding Planner

Perfect Day Wedding Services, Inc.

76654 W 95 th Ave.
New York, NY 10107

BizPlanDB.com

The purpose of this business plan is to raise $60,000 for the development of a wedding planning and consulting firm while showcasing the expected financials and operations over the next three years. Perfect Day Wedding Services, Inc. ("the Company") is a New York-based corporation that will provide wedding planning, design, and management services to customers in its targeted market. The Company was founded by Jeanne Smyth.

1.0 EXECUTIVE SUMMARY

The purpose of this business plan is to raise $60,000 for the development of a wedding planning and consulting firm while showcasing the expected financials and operations over the next three years. Perfect Day Wedding Services, Inc. ("the Company") is a New York-based corporation that will provide wedding planning, design, and management services to customers in its targeted market. The Company was founded by Jeanne Smyth.

1.1 The Services

As state above, Ms. Smyth intends to arrange wedding events that range from $7,500 to over $100,000. Perfect Day Wedding Services will develop and manage each step and aspect of a client's wedding day event. Ms. Smyth will personally manage every event that is hosted by the Company.

For each event, the Company will receive 10 to 25 percent of the aggregate budget for the event. This is a sliding scale, and as the event becomes more costly, the percentage fees received by Perfect Day Wedding Services will decrease. The business will also receive per hour fees for services related to design and wedding day consulting.

The third section of the business plan will further describe the services offered by Perfect Day Wedding Services.

1.2 Financing

Ms. Smyth is seeking to raise $60,000 from a bank loan. The interest rate and loan agreement are to be further discussed during negotiation. This business plan assumes that the business will receive a 10-year loan with a 6.25% fixed interest rate. The financing will be used for the following:

- Development of the Company's office location.

- Financing for the first six months of operation.

- Capital to purchase a company vehicle.

Ms. Smyth will contribute $10,000 to the venture.

1.3 Mission Statement

Ms. Smyth's mission is to develop Perfect Day Wedding Services into a premier wedding planning business within the target market.

1.4 Management Team

The Company was founded by Jeanne Smyth. Ms. Smyth has more than 10 years of experience in the event management industry. Through her expertise, she will be able to bring the operations of the business to profitability within its first year of operations.

1.5 Sales Forecasts

Ms. Smyth expects a strong rate of growth at the start of operations. Below are the expected financials over the next three years.

Proforma Profit and Loss (Yearly)

Year	1	2	3
Sales	$296,058	$355,270	$415,665
Operating costs	$233,735	$242,911	$252,442
EBITDA	$ 32,717	$ 76,832	$121,657
Taxes, interest, and depreciation	$ 19,270	$ 34,479	$ 51,323
Net profit	$ 13,447	$ 42,352	$ 70,334

Sales, Operating Costs, and Profit Forecast

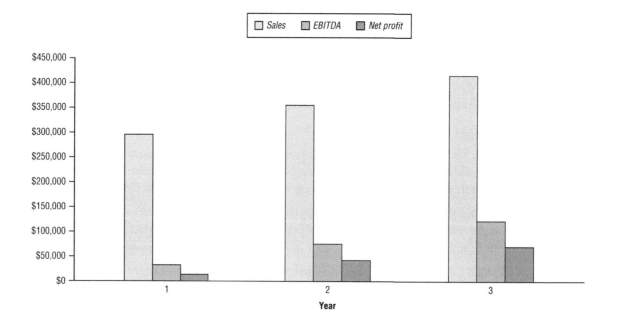

1.6 Expansion Plan

The Founder expects that the business will aggressively expand during the first three years of operation. Ms. Smyth intends to implement marketing campaigns that will effectively target individuals within the target market.

2.0 COMPANY AND FINANCING SUMMARY

2.1 Registered Name and Corporate Structure

The Company is registered as a corporation in the State of New York.

2.2 Required Funds

At this time, Perfect Day Wedding Services requires $60,000 of debt funds. Below is a breakdown of how these funds will be used:

Projected Startup Costs

Professional Fees and Licensure	$ 3,000
Working capital	$13,000
FF&E	$14,000
Leasehold improvements	$ 5,000
Security Deposits	$ 5,000
Insurance	$ 2,500
Company vehicle	$15,000
Marketing budget	$ 7,500
Miscellaneous and unforeseen costs	$ 5,000
Total startup costs	**$70,000**

Use of Funds

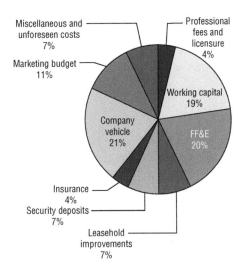

2.3 Investor Equity

Ms. Smyth is not seeking an investment from a third party at this time.

2.4 Management Equity

Jeanne Smyth owns 100% of Perfect Day Wedding Services, Inc.

2.5 Exit Strategy

If the business is very successful, Ms. Smyth may seek to sell the business to a third party for a significant earnings multiple. Most likely, the Company will hire a qualified business broker to sell the business on behalf of Perfect Day Wedding Services. Based on historical numbers, the business could fetch a sales premium of up to 2 times earnings.

3.0 PRODUCTS AND SERVICES

Below is a description of the planning and consulting services offered by Perfect Day Wedding Services.

3.1 Wedding Planning and Management Services

The primary revenue source for the business will come from services related to planning and managing weddings. Ms. Smyth will charge a percentage fee (10% to 25% on a sliding scale) depending on the size and scope of the event. Each aspect of the wedding will be managed by Ms. Smyth and her staff. These services include:

- Catering selection and oversight
- Flower arrangement and oversight
- Cake ordering and delivery management
- Event management
- Music selection and management
- Payment arrangements

3.2 Consulting

The Company will also generate secondary revenues from per hour consulting fees for brides and bridegrooms that are seeking general advice for their wedding event, but do not necessarily want Perfect Day Wedding Services to actively manage each aspect of the wedding. Management expects that 15% of the Company's revenues will come from these services.

4.0 STRATEGIC AND MARKET ANALYSIS

4.1 Economic Outlook

This section of the analysis will detail the economic climate, the event planning industry, the customer profile, and the competition that the business will face as it progresses through its business operations.

Currently, the economic market condition in the United States is moderate. Unemployment rates have declined while asset prices (among all classes) have increased substantially. People are spending more money than ever on weddings. An economic recession may present certain difficulties with revenue generation as people will spend less on their wedding events.

4.2 Industry Analysis

The US Economic Census indicates that there are approximately 5,000 companies that specialize in event management. Each year, these businesses aggregately generate more than $5 billion dollars a year of revenue and provide jobs for more than 40,000 people. The growth of this industry has remained in lockstep with the growth of the economy in general. The number of businesses operating within this industry has increased 15% over last five years while gross receipts have increased almost two-fold.

This industry has exploded as the economic tastes of Americans have changed significantly over the last five years as the overall wealth of the country has grown. As Americans now have more access to capital and an increased borrowing capacity, their ability to spend money on luxury items/services has also increased. With this, the number of people having extravagant and expensive weddings has had a marked increase over the last five years. In 2016, the average wedding exceeded $26,000, excluding transportation costs. In the same year, Americans spend nearly $125 billion dollars on weddings. This trend is expected to continue as the economy remains strong.

4.3 Customer Profile

Perfect Day Wedding Services' anticipates that its average client will be a couple seeking to get married and is concurrently seeking to host a large-scale wedding event. Management has outlined several demographics among its target client market, including:

- Has an annual household income of $50,000 or more

- Is seeking to spend approximately $20,000 on their wedding or event

- Needs an event or wedding planner

- Between the ages of 21 and 35

4.4 Competition

Competition within the wedding planner industry in New York City is substantial. There are many wealthy people within this market, and as such a number of wedding planners operate to cater to the needs of these people. There are also competitive issues regarding venues that maintain their own in-house event and wedding planners. However, the primary differentiating factor that the business will have over other competitors is Ms. Smyth's substantial experience, expertise, and artistry regarding planning and executing wedding events. She is well known within the regional wedding planner industry.

5.0 MARKETING PLAN

Perfect Day Wedding Services intends to maintain an extensive marketing campaign that will ensure maximum visibility for the business in its targeted market. Below is an overview of the marketing strategies and objectives of Perfect Day Wedding Services.

5.1 Marketing Objectives

- Develop an online presence by developing a website and placing the Company's name and contact information with online directories.

- Establish relationships with banquet halls and country clubs within the target market.

- Maintain referral relationships with event planners that do not manage wedding events.

5.2 Marketing Strategies

Ms. Smyth will promote the business through a number of traditional marketing and advertising channels. The foremost marketing strategy that the business will use is to develop connections with local banquet halls and hotels that outsource their event planning to third party wedding planners like Perfect Day Wedding Services. This will greatly decrease the amount of advertising required by the business as, once a rapport is established with these vendors, they will continually refer business to Ms. Smyth.

The business will also maintain an expansive presence on the internet via its own website, as well as social media marketing channels. The Company's website will feature images of previously planned weddings, hours of operation information, preliminary pricing, Ms. Smyth's professional biography, and contact information. The business will maintain profiles on FaceBook, Twitter, and Instagram, which will feature images of recently hosted events (shown with client's permission). The Company will have its web development firm search engine optimize the website so that the business is easily found when a person conducts an online search for wedding planners in New York City.

The business will also take out print advertisements in local and regional magazines and newspapers that deal specifically with wedding planning. Many brides often acquire these periodicals when planning their weddings. As such, Ms. Smyth sees a substantial opportunity to generate additional visibility for the business via these advertising channels.

5.3 Pricing

The Company will receive a fee equal to 10% to 25% of the total cost of the wedding (sliding scale). Perfect Day Wedding Services, Inc. will also charge $50 per hour for consulting services. The average fee charged by the Company will be $3,000.

6.0 ORGANIZATIONAL PLAN AND PERSONNEL SUMMARY

6.1 Corporate Organization

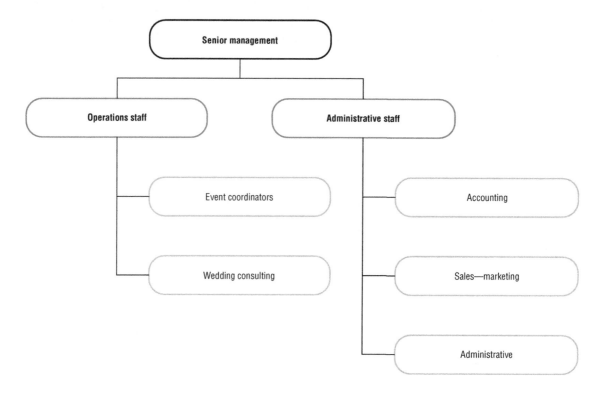

6.2 Organizational Budget

Personnel Plan—Yearly

Year	1	2	3
Owner	$ 40,000	$ 41,200	$ 42,436
Assistant manager	$ 29,000	$ 29,870	$ 30,766
Event coordinators	$ 48,000	$ 49,440	$ 50,923
Bookkeeper (P/T)	$ 9,000	$ 9,270	$ 9,548
Administrative (P/T)	$ 17,000	$ 17,510	$ 18,035
Total	**$143,000**	**$147,290**	**$151,709**

Numbers of Personnel

Year	1	2	3
Owner	1	1	1
Assistant manager	1	1	1
Event coordinators	2	2	2
Bookkeeper (P/T)	1	1	1
Administrative (P/T)	1	1	1
Totals	**6**	**6**	**6**

Personnel Expense Breakdown

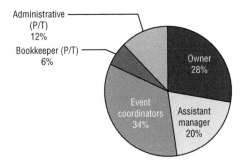

7.0 FINANCIAL PLAN

7.1 Underlying Assumptions

The Company has based its proforma financial statements on the following:

- Perfect Day Wedding Services will have an annual revenue growth rate of 16% per year.

- The Owner will acquire $60,000 of debt funds to develop the business.

- The loan will have a 10-year term with a 6.25% interest rate.

7.2 Sensitivity Analysis

The business' revenues are somewhat sensitive to the overall condition of the economic markets. In the event of a steep economic decline, Management expects that its revenue will decrease as people host weddings at alternative, less expensive venues with less involvement from a wedding planner. In the event of a decline in revenues, the business will be able to maintain profitability because the business generates significantly high gross margins.

7.3 Source of Funds

Financing

Equity contributions

Management investment	$ 10,000.00
Total equity financing	**$10,000.00**

Banks and lenders

Banks and lenders	$ 60,000.00
Total debt financing	**$60,000.00**
Total financing	**$70,000.00**

7.4 General Assumptions

General Assumptions

Year	1	2	3
Short term interest rate	9.5%	9.5%	9.5%
Long term interest rate	10.0%	10.0%	10.0%
Federal tax rate	33.0%	33.0%	33.0%
State tax rate	5.0%	5.0%	5.0%
Personnel taxes	15.0%	15.0%	15.0%

7.5 Profit and Loss Statements

Proforma Profit and Loss (Yearly)

Year	1	2	3
Sales	**$296,058**	**$355,270**	**$415,665**
Cost of goods sold	$ 29,606	$ 35,527	$ 41,567
Gross margin	90.00%	90.00%	90.00%
Operating income	**$266,452**	**$319,743**	**$374,099**
Expenses			
Payroll	$143,000	$147,290	$151,709
General and administrative	$ 25,200	$ 26,208	$ 27,256
Marketing expenses	$ 1,480	$ 1,776	$ 2,078
Professional fees and licensure	$ 5,219	$ 5,376	$ 5,537
Insurance costs	$ 11,987	$ 12,586	$ 13,216
Travel and vehicle costs	$ 7,596	$ 8,356	$ 9,191
Rent and utilities	$ 14,250	$ 14,963	$ 15,711
Miscellaneous costs	$ 3,553	$ 4,263	$ 4,988
Payroll taxes	$ 21,450	$ 22,094	$ 22,756
Total operating costs	**$233,735**	**$242,911**	**$252,442**
EBITDA	**$ 32,717**	**$ 76,832**	**$121,657**
Federal income tax	$ 10,797	$ 24,253	$ 39,146
State income tax	$ 1,636	$ 3,675	$ 5,931
Interest expense	$ 3,624	$ 3,337	$ 3,031
Depreciation expenses	$ 3,214	$ 3,214	$ 3,214
Net profit	**$ 13,447**	**$ 42,352**	**$ 70,334**
Profit margin	**4.54%**	**11.92%**	**16.92%**

Sales, Operating Costs, and Profit Forecast

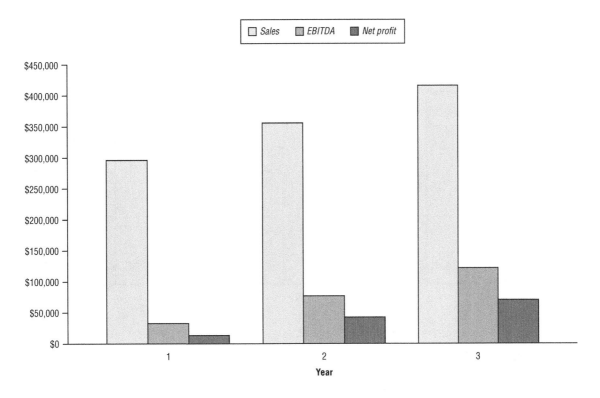

7.6 Cash Flow Analysis

Proforma Cash Flow Analysis—Yearly

Year	1	2	3
Cash from operations	$ 16,661	$45,567	$ 73,548
Cash from receivables	$ 0	$ 0	$ 0
Operating cash inflow	**$ 16,661**	**$45,567**	**$ 73,548**
Other cash inflows			
Equity investment	$ 10,000	$ 0	$ 0
Increased borrowings	$ 60,000	$ 0	$ 0
Sales of business assets	$ 0	$ 0	$ 0
A/P increases	$ 37,902	$43,587	$ 50,125
Total other cash inflows	**$107,902**	**$43,587**	**$ 50,125**
Total cash inflow	**$124,563**	**$89,154**	**$123,673**
Cash outflows			
Repayment of principal	$ 4,461	$ 4,747	$ 5,053
A/P decreases	$ 24,897	$29,876	$ 35,852
A/R increases	$ 0	$ 0	$ 0
Asset purchases	$ 45,000	$ 6,123	$ 10,274
Dividends	$ 9,760	$32,655	$ 54,796
Total cash outflows	**$ 84,118**	**$73,402**	**$105,975**
Net cash flow	**$ 40,445**	**$15,752**	**$ 17,698**
Cash balance	**$ 40,445**	**$56,197**	**$ 73,895**

Proforma Cash Flow (Yearly)

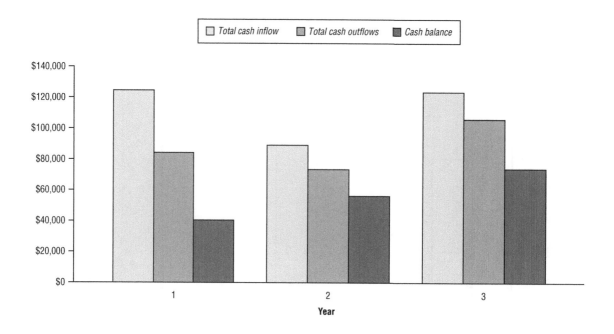

7.7 Balance Sheet

Proforma Balance Sheet—Yearly

Year	1	2	3
Assets			
Cash	$40,445	$ 56,197	$ 73,895
Amortized development/expansion costs	$16,000	$ 19,674	$ 25,838
Company vehicle	$15,000	$ 16,531	$ 19,099
FF&E	$14,000	$ 14,918	$ 16,460
Accumulated depreciation	($ 3,214)	($ 6,429)	($ 9,643)
Total assets	**$82,231**	**$100,891**	**$125,650**
Liabilities and equity			
Accounts payable	$13,005	$ 26,716	$ 40,990
Long term liabilities	$55,539	$ 50,792	$ 46,045
Other liabilities	$ 0	$ 0	$ 0
Total liabilities	**$68,544**	**$ 77,508**	**$ 87,034**
Net worth	**$13,686**	**$ 23,383**	**$ 38,615**
Total liabilities and equity	**$82,231**	**$100,891**	**$125,650**

Proforma Balance Sheet

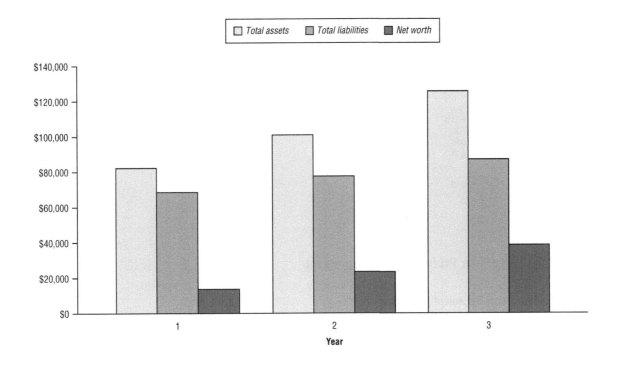

7.8 Breakeven Analysis

Monthly Break Even Analysis

Year	1	2	3
Monthly revenue	$ 21,642	$ 22,492	$ 23,374
Yearly revenue	$259,706	$269,901	$280,491

Break Even Analysis

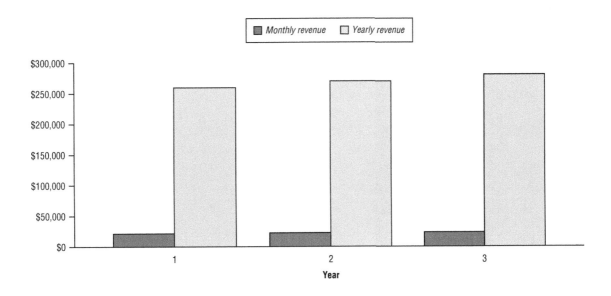

7.9 Business Ratios

Business Ratios—Yearly

Year	1	2	3
Sales			
Sales growth	0.0%	20.0%	17.0%
Gross margin	90.0%	90.0%	90.0%
Financials			
Profit margin	4.54%	11.92%	16.92%
Assets to liabilities	1.20	1.30	1.44
Equity to liabilities	0.20	0.30	0.44
Assets to equity	6.01	4.31	3.25
Liquidity			
Acid test	0.59	0.73	0.85
Cash to assets	0.49	0.56	0.59

7.10 Three Year Profit and Loss Statement

Profit and Loss Statement (First Year)

Months	1	2	3	4	5	6	7
Sales	$23,940	$24,073	$24,206	$24,339	$24,472	$24,605	$24,738
Cost of goods sold	$ 2,394	$ 2,407	$ 2,421	$ 2,434	$ 2,447	$ 2,461	$ 2,474
Gross margin	90.0%	90.0%	90.0%	90.0%	90.0%	90.0%	90.0%
Operating income	$21,546	$21,666	$21,785	$21,905	$22,025	$22,145	$22,264
Expenses							
Payroll	$11,917	$11,917	$11,917	$11,917	$11,917	$11,917	$11,917
General and administrative	$ 2,100	$ 2,100	$ 2,100	$ 2,100	$ 2,100	$ 2,100	$ 2,100
Marketing expenses	$ 123	$ 123	$ 123	$ 123	$ 123	$ 123	$ 123
Professional fees and licensure	$ 435	$ 435	$ 435	$ 435	$ 435	$ 435	$ 435
Insurance costs	$ 999	$ 999	$ 999	$ 999	$ 999	$ 999	$ 999
Travel and vehicle costs	$ 633	$ 633	$ 633	$ 633	$ 633	$ 633	$ 633
Rent and utilities	$ 1,188	$ 1,188	$ 1,188	$ 1,188	$ 1,188	$ 1,188	$ 1,188
Miscellaneous costs	$ 296	$ 296	$ 296	$ 296	$ 296	$ 296	$ 296
Payroll taxes	$ 1,788	$ 1,788	$ 1,788	$ 1,788	$ 1,788	$ 1,788	$ 1,788
Total operating costs	$19,478	$19,478	$19,478	$19,478	$19,478	$19,478	$19,478
EBITDA	$ 2,068	$ 2,188	$ 2,307	$ 2,427	$ 2,547	$ 2,667	$ 2,786
Federal income tax	$ 873	$ 878	$ 883	$ 888	$ 892	$ 897	$ 902
State income tax	$ 132	$ 133	$ 134	$ 134	$ 135	$ 136	$ 137
Interest expense	$ 313	$ 311	$ 309	$ 307	$ 305	$ 303	$ 301
Depreciation expense	$ 268	$ 268	$ 268	$ 268	$ 268	$ 268	$ 268
Net profit	$ 482	$ 598	$ 714	$ 830	$ 946	$ 1,062	$ 1,179

Profit and Loss Statement (First Year Cont.)

Months	8	9	10	11	12	1
Sales	$24,871	$25,004	$25,137	$25,270	$25,403	$296,058
Cost of goods sold	$ 2,487	$ 2,500	$ 2,514	$ 2,527	$ 2,540	$ 29,606
Gross margin	90.0%	90.0%	90.0%	90.0%	90.0%	90.0%
Operating income	$22,384	$22,504	$22,623	$22,743	$22,863	$266,452
Expenses						
Payroll	$11,917	$11,917	$11,917	$11,917	$11,917	$143,000
General and administrative	$ 2,100	$ 2,100	$ 2,100	$ 2,100	$ 2,100	$ 25,200
Marketing expenses	$ 123	$ 123	$ 123	$ 123	$ 123	$ 1,480
Professional fees and licensure	$ 435	$ 435	$ 435	$ 435	$ 435	$ 5,219
Insurance costs	$ 999	$ 999	$ 999	$ 999	$ 999	$ 11,987
Travel and vehicle costs	$ 633	$ 633	$ 633	$ 633	$ 633	$ 7,596
Rent and utilities	$ 1,188	$ 1,188	$ 1,188	$ 1,188	$ 1,188	$ 14,250
Miscellaneous costs	$ 296	$ 296	$ 296	$ 296	$ 296	$ 3,553
Payroll taxes	$ 1,788	$ 1,788	$ 1,788	$ 1,788	$ 1,788	$ 21,450
Total operating costs	$19,478	$19,478	$19,478	$19,478	$19,478	$233,735
EBITDA	$ 2,906	$ 3,026	$ 3,145	$ 3,265	$ 3,385	$ 32,717
Federal income tax	$ 907	$ 912	$ 917	$ 922	$ 926	$ 10,797
State income tax	$ 137	$ 138	$ 139	$ 140	$ 140	$ 1,636
Interest expense	$ 299	$ 297	$ 295	$ 293	$ 291	$ 3,624
Depreciation expense	$ 268	$ 268	$ 268	$ 268	$ 268	$ 3,214
Net profit	$ 1,295	$ 1,411	$ 1,527	$ 1,643	$ 1,759	$ 13,447

Profit and Loss Statement (Second Year)

	2				
Quarter	Q1	Q2	Q3	Q4	2
Sales	$71,054	$88,817	$95,923	$99,475	$355,270
Cost of goods sold	$ 7,105	$ 8,882	$ 9,592	$ 9,948	$ 35,527
Gross margin	90.0%	90.0%	90.0%	90.0%	90.0%
Operating income	$63,949	$79,936	$86,331	$89,528	$319,743
Expenses					
Payroll	$29,458	$36,823	$39,768	$41,241	$147,290
General and administrative	$ 5,242	$ 6,552	$ 7,076	$ 7,338	$ 26,208
Marketing expenses	$ 355	$ 444	$ 480	$ 497	$ 1,776
Professional fees and licensure	$ 1,075	$ 1,344	$ 1,451	$ 1,505	$ 5,376
Insurance costs	$ 2,517	$ 3,147	$ 3,398	$ 3,524	$ 12,586
Travel and vehicle costs	$ 1,671	$ 2,089	$ 2,256	$ 2,340	$ 8,356
Rent and utilities	$ 2,993	$ 3,741	$ 4,040	$ 4,190	$ 14,963
Miscellaneous costs	$ 853	$ 1,066	$ 1,151	$ 1,194	$ 4,263
Payroll taxes	$ 4,419	$ 5,523	$ 5,965	$ 6,186	$ 22,094
Total operating costs	$48,582	$60,728	$65,586	$68,015	$242,911
EBITDA	$15,366	$19,208	$20,745	$21,513	$ 76,832
Federal income tax	$ 4,851	$ 6,063	$ 6,548	$ 6,791	$ 24,253
State income tax	$ 735	$ 919	$ 992	$ 1,029	$ 3,675
Interest expense	$ 862	$ 844	$ 825	$ 806	$ 3,337
Depreciation expense	$ 804	$ 804	$ 804	$ 804	$ 3,214
Net profit	$ 8,115	$10,579	$11,575	$12,083	$ 42,352

Profit and Loss Statement (Third Year)

Quarter	Q1	Q2	Q3	Q4	3
Sales	$83,133	$103,916	$112,230	$116,386	$415,665
Cost of goods sold	$ 8,313	$ 10,392	$ 11,223	$ 11,639	$ 41,567
Gross margin	90.0%	90.0%	90.0%	90.0%	90.0%
Operating income	$74,820	$ 93,525	$101,007	$104,748	$374,099
Expenses					
Payroll	$30,342	$ 37,927	$ 40,961	$ 42,478	$151,709
General and administrative	$ 5,451	$ 6,814	$ 7,359	$ 7,632	$ 27,256
Marketing expenses	$ 416	$ 520	$ 561	$ 582	$ 2,078
Professional fees and licensure	$ 1,107	$ 1,384	$ 1,495	$ 1,550	$ 5,537
Insurance costs	$ 2,643	$ 3,304	$ 3,568	$ 3,700	$ 13,216
Travel and vehicle costs	$ 1,838	$ 2,298	$ 2,482	$ 2,574	$ 9,191
Rent and utilities	$ 3,142	$ 3,928	$ 4,242	$ 4,399	$ 15,711
Miscellaneous costs	$ 998	$ 1,247	$ 1,347	$ 1,397	$ 4,988
Payroll taxes	$ 4,551	$ 5,689	$ 6,144	$ 6,372	$ 22,756
Total operating costs	$50,488	$ 63,110	$ 68,159	$ 70,684	$252,442
EBITDA	$24,331	$ 30,414	$ 32,847	$ 34,064	$121,657
Federal income tax	$ 7,829	$ 9,787	$ 10,570	$ 10,961	$ 39,146
State income tax	$ 1,186	$ 1,483	$ 1,601	$ 1,661	$ 5,931
Interest expense	$ 787	$ 768	$ 748	$ 728	$ 3,031
Depreciation expense	$ 804	$ 804	$ 804	$ 804	$ 3,214
Net profit	$13,725	$ 17,573	$ 19,125	$ 19,910	$ 70,334

7.11 Three Year Cash Flow Analysis

Cash Flow Analysis (First Year)

Month	1	2	3	4	5	6	7	8
Cash from operations	$ 750	$ 866	$ 982	$ 1,098	$ 1,214	$ 1,330	$ 1,446	$ 1,562
Cash from receivables	$ 0	$ 0	$ 0	$ 0	$ 0	$ 0	$ 0	$ 0
Operating cash inflow	$ 750	$ 866	$ 982	$ 1,098	$ 1,214	$ 1,330	$ 1,446	$ 1,562
Other cash inflows								
Equity investment	$ 10,000	$ 0	$ 0	$ 0	$ 0	$ 0	$ 0	$ 0
Increased borrowings	$ 60,000	$ 0	$ 0	$ 0	$ 0	$ 0	$ 0	$ 0
Sales of business assets	$ 0	$ 0	$ 0	$ 0	$ 0	$ 0	$ 0	$ 0
A/P increases	$ 3,159	$ 3,159	$ 3,159	$ 3,159	$ 3,159	$ 3,159	$ 3,159	$ 3,159
Total other cash inflows	$73,159	$ 3,159	$ 3,159	$ 3,159	$ 3,159	$ 3,159	$ 3,159	$ 3,159
Total cash inflow	$73,909	$ 4,025	$ 4,141	$ 4,257	$ 4,373	$ 4,489	$ 4,605	$ 4,721
Cash outflows								
Repayment of principal	$ 361	$ 363	$ 365	$ 367	$ 369	$ 371	$ 373	$ 375
A/P decreases	$ 2,075	$ 2,075	$ 2,075	$ 2,075	$ 2,075	$ 2,075	$ 2,075	$ 2,075
A/R increases	$ 0	$ 0	$ 0	$ 0	$ 0	$ 0	$ 0	$ 0
Asset purchases	$ 45,000	$ 0	$ 0	$ 0	$ 0	$ 0	$ 0	$ 0
Dividends	$ 0	$ 0	$ 0	$ 0	$ 0	$ 0	$ 0	$ 0
Total cash outflows	$ 47,436	$ 2,438	$ 2,440	$ 2,442	$ 2,444	$ 2,445	$ 2,447	$ 2,449
Net cash flow	$ 26,473	$ 1,587	$ 1,701	$ 1,815	$ 1,929	$ 2,043	$ 2,158	$ 2,272
Cash balance	$ 26,473	$ 28,060	$ 29,761	$ 31,576	$ 33,505	$ 35,549	$ 37,706	$ 39,978

Cash Flow Analysis (First Year Cont.)

Month	9	10	11	12	1
Cash from operations	$ 1,679	$ 1,795	$ 1,911	$ 2,027	$ 16,661
Cash from receivables	$ 0	$ 0	$ 0	$ 0	$ 0
Operating cash inflow	**$ 1,679**	**$ 1,795**	**$ 1,911**	**$ 2,027**	**$ 16,661**
Other cash inflows					
Equity investment	$ 0	$ 0	$ 0	$ 0	$ 10,000
Increased borrowings	$ 0	$ 0	$ 0	$ 0	$ 60,000
Sales of business assets	$ 0	$ 0	$ 0	$ 0	$ 0
A/P increases	$ 3,159	$ 3,159	$ 3,159	$ 3,159	$ 37,902
Total other cash inflows	**$ 3,159**	**$ 3,159**	**$ 3,159**	**$ 3,159**	**$ 107,902**
Total cash inflow	**$ 4,837**	**$ 4,953**	**$ 5,069**	**$ 5,185**	**$ 124,563**
Cash outflows					
Repayment of principal	$ 377	$ 378	$ 380	$ 383	$ 4,461
A/P decreases	$ 2,075	$ 2,075	$ 2,075	$ 2,075	$ 24,897
A/R increases	$ 0	$ 0	$ 0	$ 0	$ 0
Asset purchases	$ 0	$ 0	$ 0	$ 0	$ 45,000
Dividends	$ 0	$ 0	$ 0	$ 9,760	$ 9,760
Total cash outflows	**$ 2,451**	**$ 2,453**	**$ 2,455**	**$ 12,218**	**$ 84,118**
Net cash flow	**$ 2,386**	**$ 2,500**	**$ 2,614**	**−$ 7,033**	**$ 40,445**
Cash balance	**$ 42,364**	**$ 44,863**	**$ 47,477**	**$ 40,445**	**$ 40,445**

Cash Flow Analysis (Second Year)

Quarter	2				2
	Q1	Q2	Q3	Q4	
Cash from operations	$ 9,113	$ 11,392	$ 12,303	$ 12,759	$ 45,567
Cash from receivables	$ 0	$ 0	$ 0	$ 0	$ 0
Operating cash inflow	**$ 9,113**	**$ 11,392**	**$ 12,303**	**$ 12,759**	**$ 45,567**
Other cash inflows					
Equity investment	$ 0	$ 0	$ 0	$ 0	$ 0
Increased borrowings	$ 0	$ 0	$ 0	$ 0	$ 0
Sales of business assets	$ 0	$ 0	$ 0	$ 0	$ 0
A/P increases	$ 8,717	$ 10,897	$ 11,769	$ 12,204	$ 43,587
Total other cash inflows	**$ 8,717**	**$ 10,897**	**$ 11,769**	**$ 12,204**	**$ 43,587**
Total cash inflow	**$ 17,831**	**$ 22,289**	**$ 24,072**	**$ 24,963**	**$ 89,154**
Cash outflows					
Repayment of principal	$ 1,159	$ 1,177	$ 1,196	$ 1,215	$ 4,747
A/P decreases	$ 5,975	$ 7,469	$ 8,067	$ 8,365	$ 29,876
A/R increases	$ 0	$ 0	$ 0	$ 0	$ 0
Asset purchases	$ 1,225	$ 1,531	$ 1,653	$ 1,714	$ 6,123
Dividends	$ 6,531	$ 8,164	$ 8,817	$ 9,144	$ 32,655
Total cash outflows	**$ 14,890**	**$ 18,341**	**$ 19,733**	**$ 20,438**	**$ 73,402**
Net cash flow	**$ 2,941**	**$ 3,947**	**$ 4,339**	**$ 4,525**	**$ 15,752**
Cash balance	**$ 43,386**	**$ 47,333**	**$ 51,672**	**$ 56,197**	**$ 56,197**

Cash Flow Analysis (Third Year)

| | 3 | | | | |
Quarter	Q1	Q2	Q3	Q4	3
Cash from operations	$14,710	$18,387	$ 19,858	$ 20,593	$ 73,548
Cash from receivables	$ 0	$ 0	$ 0	$ 0	$ 0
Operating cash inflow	**$14,710**	**$18,387**	**$ 19,858**	**$ 20,593**	**$ 73,548**
Other cash inflows					
Equity investment	$ 0	$ 0	$ 0	$ 0	$ 0
Increased borrowings	$ 0	$ 0	$ 0	$ 0	$ 0
Sales of business assets	$ 0	$ 0	$ 0	$ 0	$ 0
A/P increases	$10,025	$12,531	$ 13,534	$ 14,035	$ 50,125
Total other cash inflows	**$10,025**	**$12,531**	**$ 13,534**	**$ 14,035**	**$ 50,125**
Total cash inflow	**$24,735**	**$30,918**	**$ 33,392**	**$ 34,629**	**$123,673**
Cash outflows					
Repayment of principal	$ 1,234	$ 1,253	$ 1,273	$ 1,293	$ 5,053
A/P decreases	$ 7,170	$ 8,963	$ 9,680	$ 10,038	$ 35,852
A/R increases	$ 0	$ 0	$ 0	$ 0	$ 0
Asset purchases	$ 2,055	$ 2,569	$ 2,774	$ 2,877	$ 10,274
Dividends	$10,959	$13,699	$ 14,795	$ 15,343	$ 54,796
Total cash outflows	**$21,418**	**$26,484**	**$ 28,522**	**$ 29,551**	**$105,975**
Net cash flow	**$ 3,316**	**$ 4,435**	**$ 4,870**	**$ 5,077**	**$ 17,698**
Cash balance	**$59,513**	**$63,948**	**$ 68,818**	**$ 73,895**	**$ 73,895**

Whiskey Distillery

Placer County Distilling Co., Inc.

522 Coloma Rd.
Placerville, CA 95667

Claire Moore

Placer County Distilling Co., Inc. (PCDC) is a craft distillery located in Placerville, California. We will produce about 4,000 cases of distilled spirits in our first year consisting of vodka, gin, aged whiskey, and white whiskey.

EXECUTIVE SUMMARY

Craft distillers produce alcohol beverage spirits by distillation or by infusion through distillation or re-distillation. The maximum production for a craft or artisan distiller in California is limited to 100,000 distillate gallons per year.

While multinational conglomerates dominate the alcohol industry, craft producers set the trends. Their reward for innovation is the ability to command a premium price for their products. Unlike their giant competitors, craft distillers emphasize the eco-values of sustainability and using local ingredients as much as possible.

Placer County Distilling Co., Inc. (PCDC) is a craft distillery located in Placerville, California. We will produce about 4,000 cases of distilled spirits in our first year consisting of vodka, gin, aged whiskey, and white whiskey.

OBJECTIVES

PCDC's objectives for the first five years of operations include the following:

- Establish and maintain the highest quality by utilizing quality ingredients and a motivated staff
- Establish profitability and use the funds for expansion
- Expand our line of spirits with new unique recipes
- Increase direct to consumer sales to 75 percent of sales
- Add a bistro to our facility

COMPANY SUMMARY

In late 2010 Tom White and Jackson Call decided to combine their business experience with their love of crafted spirits to create their own distillery in Placerville, California. Tom White, a medical equipment salesman, had three years of experience distilling products from wheat, rye, and corn produced in the Sacramento Valley. Jackson Call hails from a small village in England where his family has been refining their sloe gin recipe for generations, using sloes hand-picked every autumn along the coastal hills.

After agreeing to form a business together, the two decided to step up their game with training from Chicago's first distillery, Koval. There followed over a year of research and development, which included touring dozens of distilleries on the West Coast, Kentucky, and Tennessee.

Based on their research it was decided that PCDC would use an American still and begin by primarily producing spirits that don't require aging (Vodka, Gin, and White Whiskey).

White attended training at Moonshine University in Kentucky, which lead to the finalization of plans for the equipment and layout of the distillery. Meanwhile, Call developed the logo, labels, and marketing strategy for the products, began work on the company web site and started the search for a distributor.

PCDC is a founding member of the California Artisanal Distiller Guild (CADG), a non-profit that works with peer organizations and the public to spread the word about the California Spirit Industry. The Guild was a key player in furthering Assembly Bill 933 in 2013, which allowed for paid tastings. It was the first time that the state's liquor laws had changed since prohibition in 1934. The CADG then put forth AB 1295, which passed in January 2016 and allows distillers to sell their products directly to consumers.

PCDC is proudly located in the heart of Placerville, California, and the names of our products reflect the town's colorful history.

The history of Placerville represents several important points in California history, from gold mining, to the Pony Express, to railroad history. Today Placerville features many historical buildings and markers, including the Fountain-Tallman Soda Works (now the Fountain & Tallman Museum), the John Pearson Soda Works, the Combellack-Blair House, Confidence Hall, Hangman's Tree, the Church of Our Savior, the Placerville Bell, and the Hangtown Gold Bug Park & Mine.

As of the 2010 Census, Placerville's population was 10,389. Main Street and Downtown are popular tourist destinations, and nearby Apple Hill, known for its wineries and orchards, is east of here. Placerville is located on Highway 50, approximately 44 miles east of Sacramento and 62 miles west of South Lake Tahoe. (SierraNevadaGeotourism.com).

COMPANY OWNERSHIP

PCDC, Inc. is a California corporation owned by Tom White and Jackson Call. Other owner/investors include six investors whose contributions have made our creation possible.

COMPANY LOCATION

The PCDC distillery is located on a ten-acre parcel within minutes of downtown Placerville. This ten-acre parcel was formerly run as a winery and tasting room. It is zoned agricultural and has a special use permit. The existing buildings consisted of a winery, tasting room, equipment barn, greenhouse, and 3-bedroom cottage. The parcel also houses a 3-acre vineyard of Merlot and Sauvignon Blanc varieties. Utilities include electricity, water, and irrigation.

The home has a downstairs suite with separate access. There is also a scenic pond, patio, RV parking space, fireplace, barbecue, and large event area for gatherings and business events. The original buildings had one full and four half-baths.

The purchase price was $620,000. Several modifications were made during the distillery buildout in order to bring the building up to current code for public use, a distillery, and for installation of the equipment.

STARTUP SUMMARY

PCDC has incurred the following costs in its startup phase:

Buildout

Distillery buildout	$300,000
Tasting room	$ 20,000
Parking lot	$ 10,000
Signage	$ 5,000
Landscaping	$ 3,200
Total	**$338,200**

Distilling Equipment—Electric

Stills	$500,000
Chillers 5 HP, 10 HP	$ 15,000
Grain silo	$ 12,000
Receiving tanks	$ 4,500
Floor scale	$ 3,000
Installation costs	$ 3,000
Oak casks	$ 25,000
Cask storage racks	$ 1,500
Measuring equipment	$ 800
Bottling machine—4 spout (2)	$ 5,600
Misc. tools & equipment	$ 5,500
Bottle labeler	$ 1,500
Forklift used	$ 9,000
Total	**$586,400**

Other Startup Costs

Supplies inventory	$ 7,500
TTB application assistance	$ 2,500
Water testing	$ 2,000
Surety bond	$ 2,500
Research & development	$13,000
Legal—incorporation, trademark	$ 5,000
Accounting	$ 2,000
Licenses/permits	$ 1,100
Total	**$35,600**

Other Equipment Purchased

POS system	$ 5,000
Security system	$ 6,000
Furnishings/décor	$12,000
Total other	**$23,000**

INITIAL FINANCING

From the early planning stages of the venture to the first batch from the distillery, took four years and six months. The search for investors began at the end of year one of the startup phase. Thanks to their incomes and that they continue to work at their jobs, White and Call have contributed the bulk of the startup funding.

The financial investments came from the following sources:

- Owners
- Friends/relatives
- Key "Angel" investors
- Kickstarter campaign
- Bank loan guaranteed by White and Call

The Kickstart campaign ran for eight months in late 2015 and garnered nearly $30,000 in funding from 320 backers. Rewards for backers included shot glasses and T-shirts with the PCDC logo and a coupon that can be presented at the tasting room for one free tasting.

In year four of the startup phase PCDC secured a bank loan with a local lender. The loan totaled $425,000 at 4 percent for 10 years.

INDUSTRY REGULATIONS

Distilleries must progress through three levels of registration in order to operate in the United States. These levels include: federal, state, and local (city or county).

Federal Licensing

The federal registration process includes a full background check of owners and inquiries relating to their spouses, investors, and financiers. It also requires that owners provide information concerning facility security and provisions for fire, theft, and internal theft. This means that the applicant must have a facility in place and a plan to protect it.

Every new formulation must be approved. The application must include data sheets on ingredients and on the label design.

A bond is required as part of the federal distillery permit application. It must be issued by a surety, in cash, or through a treasury note/bond. The most common type of bond is obtained as an insurance policy through an insurance company. The purpose of the bond is to provide the government with a guarantee that excise taxes will be paid and provides assurance that the distiller will comply with Federal laws and regulations.

Distillers making Beverage Alcohol only (no industrial or denatured spirits) must file monthly operations reports including a Production Report (F5110.40), Storage Report (F5110.11), and Processing Report (F5110.28) due by the 14th of the next month. In addition, distillers must file and pay a Federal Excise Tax (FET) Return (F5000.24) after every tax period.

Most craft distillers pay $13.50/proof gallon for any cases of beverage alcohol they remove from the bonded distillery space, including cases they move to their gift shop or tasting room areas. Another way to estimate excise tax is $2.14 per 750ml bottle of vodka at 80 proof. For a craft distillery who pays less than $50,000 in excise tax per year (or ~3,700 six pack cases per year), they can pay every quarter

(4 times per year). If a distillery pays more than $50,000/year in one calendar year, they must pay every 15 days and 3 times in September.

When distillers talk about a proof gallon, they traditionally are referring to a volumetric measurement of liquid with regard to proof or percent alcohol. A proof gallon is one liquid gallon of spirits that is 50% alcohol at 60 degrees F. Distilled Spirits bottled at 80 proof (40% alcohol) would be 0.8 proof gallons per gallon of liquid. At 125 proof, a gallon of liquid would be 1.25 proof gallons.

Spirits that are destroyed due to contamination or some other issue must be documented on a Record of Destruction, which should be kept internally in the event of an audit.

A manufacturer and/or processor of alcohol must register with the FDA in accordance with the Bioterrorism Act. Under this Act, any domestic or foreign facilities that manufacture, process, pack, or hold food for human or animal consumption in the United States must register. "Food" includes alcoholic beverages.

State Licensing

Each state has its own set of regulations regarding licensing of a still and how products may be sold and marketed.

Local Licensing

Local authorities will want to authorize operations in regards to zoning, water, draining, and fire regulations.

THE DISTILLERY INDUSTRY IN CALIFORNIA

There has never been a better time to open a craft distillery in California. Thanks to passage of a new law that went into effect on January 1, 2016, distillers may now sell their product on site and at an event. Distilleries may sell up to three 750-ml bottles per customer per day on-site. The law also allows license holders to open an on-site bar or restaurant and have tastings where they can make and sell cocktails and mixed drinks.

On-site sales will increase the profit margins of craft distilleries that, up to now, saw as much as 60 percent of the bottle price go to the wholesalers. However, the federal excise tax on spirits still hovers at about 21 cents per ounce of alcohol.

The new law also defined craft distillers as those that produce up to 100,000 gallons of distilled spirits per fiscal year (July 1—June 30) excluding brandy that it manufactures or is manufactured for the licensee with a brandy manufacturer's license. So far 38 distillers have an active or pending craft distilling license with the California Department of Alcoholic Beverage Control (ABC). There are 133 businesses that have a license to be a distilled spirits manufacturer in the state.

Until January 1, 2016, distilleries in California were required to obtain two California Liquor Licenses: Type 6 (Still License) and Type 4 (Distilled Spirits Manufacturer). Distilleries were not allowed to sell directly to the consumer either on-site. or at off-site events. They could, however, conduct on-site tastings and charge for them. As of June 2015, the state had issued 133 distillery licenses (Type 04).

The industry radically changed with the passage of AB 1295, The Craft Distillers Act of 2015 on January 1, 2016. The State of California defines craft distillers as those distilleries that produce less than 100,000 gallons of distilled spirits per fiscal year, exclusive of brandy.

The Craft Distillers Act of 2015 created a new Type-74 license. Aimed specifically at distilleries that produce less than 100,000 gallons of distillate per year, the law allows distillers to sell three

750-ml bottles to consumers who participate in a tasting. The sales limit is three bottles per customer, per day. The law also allows distilleries to have ownership in up to three restaurants or bars.

Distillers are now required to purchase a new Type-74 craft distiller's license. The application fee is $600 and the annual renewal fee will be $300. Craft distillers must report their production volume to the Alcohol Beverage Control (ABC) when applying for an annual renewal, and if they exceed the production cap their license will be renewed as a Type 4.

Provisions of the Type 74 license require that the licensee must actually manufacture distilled spirits. Second, the Type-74 license authorizes the licensee to package, rectify, mix, flavor, color, label, and export only those distilled spirits manufactured by the licensee. The distillery must still hold a Type 6 (Still) license in order to own and/or operate a still to produce distilled spirits.

For years, the distillery industry in California has lagged behind that of other states. The passage of the Craft Distillers Act of 2015 opens the door to research and experimentation with new recipes because distilleries will be able to market test on site in their tasting rooms.

MANAGEMENT TEAM

While maintaining his day job, Tom distilled on weekends and created his signature first product, Pony Express Vodka, named in an homage to part of Placerville's colorful history. Thanks to his sales contacts, Tom negotiated shelf space at Whole Foods and eventually closed deals with other major chain stores in the state. First year sales totaled $500,000 and by his third-year revenues had reached just over $1 million, earning Tom a profit.

Jackson Call has always loved experimenting with new combinations of ingredients to arrive at new flavors. His designs for products will make PCDC stand out from the competition.

Ever since he immigrated to the United States five years ago, Jackson has run his own consulting service, Distillers Resource Services, which provides general and strategic advisory, business, and financial planning services, as well as assistance with the development and implementation of distillery set-up, product formulation, and marketing.

Tom White will serve as Director of Sales and Marketing for PCDC while Jackson Call will be Director of Operations. For the first three years of operations, White and Call will take limited salaries in order to help lower expenses while the company establishes its cash flow.

PRODUCTS AND SERVICES

PCDC currently sells about 95 percent of its product through distributors. Because of the changing legislative landscape, our goal is to sell 75 percent of our product direct to consumers by year five. Thanks to the years of experience owners, White and Call will be able to sell whiskey products within the first year of PCDC's operations.

Grain to Glass is our focus at PCDC. Every level of the production is handled in-house. Proudly ignoring the industry trends in pursuit of a new legacy—we are steeped in traditional values but fueled by modern taste. We source only the finest non-GMO grains from California and our malted barley is locally smoked with California Cherrywood. Our new, American oak barrels are proudly made in Missouri and Minnesota.

During our first three to five years of operation, PCDC will focus on producing vodka, gin, and whiskey. We will produce both white whiskey and Bourbon whiskey. PCDC will produce two formulations of white whiskey because it does not require aging and can therefore be sold much earlier than Bourbon whiskey, which must be aged.

Another source of revenue will be our client manufacturing service where we offer distilling and bottling to a limited list of clients. We expect to phase out this service as our production increases.

PCDC will also offer a Bourbon whiskey and age it in 5-gallon casks in order to cut the aging time from the typical six-to eight years down to about six months. We expect to increase our offerings of aged whiskey as funds allow. But the initial sales of white spirits will help PCDC establish cash flow and working capital for expansion.

Characteristics of Bourbon whiskey are:

- Must be made in the United States
- Must contain 51 percent corn
- Must be aged in oak barrels
- Must be distilled to no more than 160 proof and entered into barrel at 125 proof
- Must be bottled at no less than 80 proof
- Must not contain any added flavoring, color, or other additives

Our list of current formulas includes:

- **Gold Rush White Whiskey:** This whiskey has a new twist on traditional whiskey with an earthy, grassy unaged single malt base, hints of nectar, honey, and vanilla.
- **Paydirt White Rye Whiskey:** Unaged rye makes for a smooth sipping drink without the aging overtones of oak.
- **Eureka Dry Gin:** Complex combination of juniper, citrus, and coriander exudes a smooth texture uncommon to most gins.
- **Lucky Strike Vodka:** California wine grapes are blended to produce a smooth, light vodka. The taste is clean with a light wine finish. Beautiful in a cocktail or straight up. Wine lovers appreciate the soft taste and smooth feel.
- **Coyote Hole Bourbon Whiskey:** This is a deep, full-flavored Bourbon. Barrel strength filtered once to retain all the color, aroma, and taste of the original cask. Vanilla, caramel, and a smoky oak flavor give a depth and complex aged flavor.

Shop

Our on-site and online shop has a variety of gifts that are emblazoned with the PCDC logo:

- Shot glasses: $7.99
- PCDC T-shirt: $19.33—$25.33
- PCDC sweatshirt: $29.99—$35.99
- PCDC hats in various colors: $24.99

Tours & Tastings

- We are open Wednesday through Sunday for tastings and sales from 11 a.m. to 5 p.m.
- Tastings are $10 per person and include up to six ¼ ounce tastes of our products.

- Distillery tours are on Friday at 2 p.m. and Saturday/Sunday at 11 a.m., 2 p.m., and 4 p.m.

- Tours are $20 per person and include tastings and a commemorative glass.

PRODUCTION

In Year One PCDC will produce Gin, Vodka, and White Whiskey for sale and distribution, as well as Bourbon, which will be aged in 5-gallon barrels. The smaller barrels for aging will allow us to sell this whiskey after six months of aging. Some whiskey was produced and put into storage in late 2015 allowing us to have a full year of Bourbon sales during the first year of operation.

Trends indicate a growing demand for whiskey, especially Irish Whiskey, thanks in part to a broad demographic of consumers, particularly women. This is probably due to the fact that Irish Whiskey is sweeter and smoother than most other whiskeys and is also a natural ingredient in craft cocktails.

PCDC will gradually increase its inventory of aged whiskey in order to take advantage of the continuing trend in whiskey consumption.

By distilling five days a week, we project the following production numbers:

	Year 1	Year 2	Year 3
Cases wholesale	3,200	4,960	7,040
Cases retail	800	1,240	1,760
Total cases	**4,000**	**6,200**	**8,800**
Gallons	9,508	14,737	20,918

Production Year 1	Percentage	Cases	Wholesale	Retail
Gin	30%	1,200	960	240
Vodka	30%	1,200	960	240
Whiskey	40%	1,600	1,280	320
Total cases		**4,000**	**3,200**	**800**

Production Year 2	Percentage	Cases	Wholesale	Retail
Gin	25%	1,550	1,240	310
Vodka	25%	1,550	1,240	310
Whiskey	50%	3,100	2,480	620
Total cases		**6,200**	**4,960**	**1,240**

Production Year 3	Percentage	Cases	Wholesale	Retail
Gin	25%	2,200	1,760	440
Vodka	25%	2,200	1,760	440
Whiskey	50%	4,400	3,520	880
Total cases		**8,800**	**7,040**	**1,760**

Assumptions:

Prices per case	Wholesale	Retail
Gin	$140	$280
Vodka	$140	$280
Whiskey	$195	$390

DISTRIBUTION STRATEGY

Thanks to the Craft Distillers Act of 2015, PCDC can sell product out of our tasting room where we can meet our customers face-to-face. But selling on-site is not enough, so we will work with our distributor, Wine Warehouse, to personally visit sales venues in California. In this way, the sellers will learn about our brand first hand from its creators, an experience that they won't get from the big brands.

Our distributor is a company with a long history of serving the premium beverage industry in California. The company has two offices, one in Southern California and one in Northern California. Its diverse selection of offerings positions the company with a strong and sustainable route to all channels of the California market.

MARKET ANALYSIS SUMMARY

As in many consumer trends, millennials are driving many changes in the alcohol industry. A survey by the industry publication *Beverage Dynamics* revealed the following trends for 2016-2017:

- Millennials are drinking more Bourbon, rye, and Scotch, spurring a whiskey revival

- Thanks to the success of Saerac's Fireball Cinnamon Whiskey, flavored whiskeys are gaining market strength

- Whiskeys from Ireland are also growing in favor, especially among female consumers

- Millennials have embraced tequila as a premium product and appreciate the handmade aura projected by many brands

- Several brands of vodka lost market share in 2015 but overall vodka retains about a one-third share of the market. Brands that promoted its craft and handmade qualities, such as New Amsterdam, increased in sales volume.

- Ciders and hard soda continue to increase in sales and popularity. They appeal equally to males and females and are becoming popular additions to classic cocktail recipes.

- A growing movement of at-home drinking culture is developing partly due to concerns for safety

- Consumers are interested in brand history and craft

- Whiskey is growing in popularity and some industry watchers think that it could surpass vodka in dollar value sales this year

- Bourbon has been trending for more than a decade but Rye and Irish Whiskey are experiencing incredible growth

- According to the Distilled Spirits Council, *Euromonitor International* predicts that Americans will spend about $2.5 billion on Irish whiskey by 2019, a fivefold increase over 2008.

Unlike previous decades, whiskey and other spirits appeal to a wide demographic. There is a large and growing demographic of women who are drinking whiskey, rye, Bourbon, and Irish Whiskey. Consumers are interested in new styles, special releases, and innovation.

As consumers continue to seek out artisan spirit brands, they want to know who made the product and how it was made. It isn't enough to use the word "craft" in marketing. Consumers demand traceability and authenticity in their products and they want to know that people are involved in every step of the process.

COMPETITIVE ADVANTAGE

We are located in Placer County just northeast of the Sacramento Valley, a fertile area that produces such products as wheat, corn, plums, peaches, pears, kiwifruit, and almonds. Placer County is known for its produce, especially its varieties of mandarin oranges.

We use fruit and other locally grown crops in our fermentations. Our plan is to distill traditional products while also exploring the frontiers of the distilling experience. Our acreage is already producing wine grapes, several herbs, and fruits, which will be incorporated into our formulations. The fact that we craft on-site and use local ingredients will be a major feature of our brand.

PCDC will begin by creating gin, vodka, and white whiskey with some production of Bourbon whiskey to be stored and aged. We will use 5-gallon oak barrels instead of the standard 54-gallon barrels, thus cutting the aging time from six to eight years down to three to six months. This shorter aging time will allow PCDC to get its aged whiskey products to the market sooner than other startup distilleries. Because sales of whiskey generate almost twice the revenues of gin and vodka, the additional cost and storage challenges of using the smaller casks is outweighed by the higher revenues during our startup phase. In year two we will begin to incorporate the traditional 54-gallon barrels in our aging process.

In addition to touring our facility and learning about our products first hand, visitors can spend time at our Visitor Center where they can sit by a scenic pond and view the Sierra foothills while eating their picnic lunch. Future plans include the addition of a bistro on our premises where visitors can purchase and enjoy a select menu of tasty fare, coffees, teas, sodas, and distilled beverages.

MARKETING PLAN

Our target market is primarily mid- to upper-class consumers between the ages of 21 and 40. This demographic is interested in transparency of production and true craftsmanship. They also prefer lighter, sweeter products while still appreciating the joy of discovering elegant subtleties and a hint of complexity. Ever mindful of the rising power of the female whiskey consumer, our marketing efforts will address their interest in lighter flavors.

Our marketing efforts will include the following strategies:

- *Print advertising:* Including marketing materials aimed at the tourist visitors to the area and inviting them to visit our tasting room.

- *Web site:* Information on our company, our products, staff, and farm including tours and tastings. The site will include pages about: our history, the historical connections to the names of our products, recipes for using PCDC products, a blog with articles about the distillery, new products, events, new recipe ideas, and a contact page. Google Analytics will provide data about site visits and usage.

- *Social media:* Facebook, Twitter, and Instagram will be used to gain visibility and drive traffic to our web site where they engage more deeply with our brand. Our Sales & Marketing budget includes funds for a social media manager to monitor and maintain our social media accounts.

- *Promotional items:* hats, tees, and shot glasses bearing our logo and address will take our brand into far flung regions along with our satisfied customers.

PERSONNEL PLAN

Salaries

Director of operations	$ 18,000
Director of sales & marketing	$ 18,000
Social media manager	$ 24,000
Office administrator	$ 18,000
Head distiller	$ 45,000
Assistant distiller	$ 35,000
Assistant distiller	$ 35,000
Total	**$193,000**

MILESTONES

Task	Delivery Date
Training at Koval Distillery Chicago	2012
Research & development	2012
Begin business plan	2013
Create product recipes	2013
Begin search for facility location	2013
Begin equipment search	2013
Form corporation, obtain IRS EIN	2013
Finalize logo design and registration of trademark	2013
Begin search for distributor	2013
Begin raising capital investments	2013
Begin market research with bar owners	2013
Training at Moonshine University, KY	2013
Finalize distillery plan and equipment layout	2013
Find location, negotiate lease	2014
Complete label designs	2014
Obtain building permit	2014
Order remaining equipment	2014
Complete buildout and installation	2014
Submit federal permit application with TTB	2014
Submit Certificate of Label Approval (COLA) with TTB	2015
Submit state permit application	2015
Finalize COLA approval and order production labels	2015
Begin work on web site	2015
Complete contracts with local farmers for product purchases	2015
Complete distillery set up	2015
Apply for bank loan	2015
Store first batch of whiskey in casks	2015
Open to the public	2016
Begin distribution	2016

FINANCIAL PLAN

Pro Forma Profit and Loss

	Year 1	Year 2	Year 3
Sales			
Wholesale (after distributor share)	$518,400	$ 830,800	$ 1,179,200
Retail	$259,200	$ 415,400	$ 589,600
Tours	$ 6,500	$ 8,000	$ 10,200
Store sales	$ 3,200	$ 3,700	$ 4,200
Client production runs	$ 38,000	$ 45,000	$ 45,000
Total sales	$825,300	$1,302,900	$ 1,828,200
Cost of goods sold:			
Total direct costs	**$240,000**	**$ 372,000**	**$ 528,000**
Gross profit	$585,300	$ 930,900	$1,300,200
Gross profit %	71%	71%	71%
Expenses			
Excise taxes	$102,720	$ 159,216	$ 225,984
Depreciation	$142,960	$ 142,960	$ 142,960
Labor	$115,000	$ 115,000	$ 115,000
Administrative payroll	$ 78,000	$ 78,000	$ 78,000
Payroll taxes	$ 19,300	$ 19,300	$ 19,300
Employee benefits	$ 9,650	$ 9,650	$ 9,650
Sales & marketing	$ 10,000	$ 10,000	$ 10,000
Utilities/phone	$ 17,000	$ 19,000	$ 21,000
Insurance	$ 3,200	$ 3,200	$ 3,200
Fees/licenses	$ 1,100	$ 1,200	$ 1,200
Office expense	$ 1,400	$ 1,400	$ 1,400
Repairs/maintenance	$ 3,500	$ 7,500	$ 8,000
Legal/accounting	$ 3,600	$ 3,000	$ 3,000
Property tax	$ 7,100	$ 7,100	$ 7,100
Professional dues/subscription	$ 1,285	$ 1,285	$ 1,285
Management tracking software	$ 4,200	$ 4,200	$ 4,200
Research & development	$ 8,000	$ 8,000	$ 5,000
Travel	$ 7,000	$ 6,000	$ 6,000
Other	$ 1,200	$ 2,500	$ 4,500
Total operating expenses	**$536,215**	**$ 598,511**	**$ 666,779**
Earnings before interest and taxes	$ 49,085	$ 332,389	$ 633,421
Interest expense	$ 16,369	$ 14,926	$ 11,200
Net earnings	$ 32,716	$ 317,463	$ 622,221
Income tax	$ 4,907	$ 107,061	$ 211,555
Net profit	**$ 27,809**	**$ 210,402**	**$ 410,666**
Net profit/sales	3%	12%	22%
Average monthly break even revenue	**$ 34,417**		
Assumptions:			
Average percent variable cost	29%		
Estimated monthly fixed costs	**$ 9,925**		
100% of production is sold			

Projected Balance Sheet

Assets	Year 1	Year 2	Year 3
Current assets			
Cash in bank	$ 12,000	$ 107,667	$ 210,993
Account receivable		$ 8,500	$ 9,000
Inventory—raw materials	$ 18,500	$ 15,000	$ 28,000
Inventory—finished goods			
Other current assets			$ 400,000
Total current assets	**$ 30,500**	**$ 131,167**	**$ 647,993**
Fixed assets			
Van	$ 32,000	$ 32,000	$ 32,000
Distillery: buildings	$ 450,000	$ 450,000	$ 450,000
Distillery: improvements	$ 338,200	$ 338,200	$ 338,200
Equipment: distillery	$ 586,400	$ 586,400	$ 586,400
Equipment: other	$ 23,000	$ 23,000	$ 23,000
Less: depreciation	(142,960)	(285,920)	(428,880)
Distillery: land	$ 170,000	$ 170,000	$ 170,000
Total assets	**$1,487,140**	**$1,444,847**	**$1,818,713**
Liabilities			
Current liabilities			
Accounts payable	$ 217,695	$ 2,000	$ 3,200
Current maturities loan	$ 51,636	$ 51,636	$ 51,636
Total current liabilities	**$ 269,331**	**$ 53,636**	**$ 54,836**
Long term liabilities loan	$ 390,000	$ 353,000	$ 315,000
Total liabilities	**$ 659,331**	**$ 406,636**	**$ 369,836**
Paid-in capital	$ 800,000	$ 800,000	$ 800,000
Net profit	**$ 27,809**	**$ 210,402**	**$ 410,666**
Retained earnings		$ 27,809	$ 238,211
Total capital	**$ 827,809**	**$1,038,211**	**$1,448,877**
Total liabilities & capital	**$1,487,140**	**$1,444,847**	**$1,818,713**

Whitewater Rafting Excursion Business

Red Paddle Adventures LLC

14 Golden Gorge Ave., Southwest
Foster Point, CO 33219

Paul Greenland

Red Paddle Adventures LLC offers whitewater rafting excursions for adventurers of all skill levels.

EXECUTIVE SUMMARY

Each year, Colorado's mountain snow melts in the spring, resulting in some of the most exciting opportunities for whitewater rafting in the nation. Red Paddle Adventures is being established by the Jake and Lisa McMurtry, owners of the popular Red Paddle Inn restaurant and hotel, who are seeking additional sources of tourism-related revenue. Already a thriving business, the Red Paddle Inn's guests are always seeking additional entertainment and recreation options, which the business is well-positioned to provide. The owners have converted one of the inn's gift shops into a booking center for the newly-established Red Paddle Adventures, providing prime exposure from a location that gets heavy foot traffic in and out of the establishment.

INDUSTRY ANALYSIS

According to a 2017 report from the Outdoor Industry Association, outdoor recreation is one of the nation's most profitable industry sectors. Personal consumption expenditure data from the Bureau of Economic Analysis reveals that consumer spending on outdoor recreation totaled $887 billion toward the end of the decade. This figure was behind only financial services and insurance ($921 billion), outpatient health care ($931 billion), and hospital care ($964 billion).

Additionally, the outdoor recreation industry supports 7.6 million jobs, ahead of computer technology (6.7 million), construction (6.4 million), finance and insurance (6.0 million), transportation and warehousing (4.8 million), food and beverage service (4.7 million), education (3.5 million), and real estate/rentals and leasing (2.1 million). Specifically, water sports, including whitewater rafting, generate $139.97 billion in retail spending each year, supporting 1.23 million jobs that pay $43.89 billion in annual wages.

Businesses like Red Paddle Adventures benefit from membership in several different trade and professional associations, including the Outdoor Industry Association (www.outdoorindustry.org), American Whitewater (www.americanwhitewater.org) and Colorado Whitewater (www.coloradowhitewater.org).

MARKET ANALYSIS

Located in Garfield County, Colorado, Foster Point is home to approximately 20,000 people. The city is located in close proximity to the Eagle, Colorado, and Roaring Fork Rivers, making it a prime location for outdoor enthusiasts. Tourists visit Foster Point year-round to enjoy activities such as biking, fishing, golf, paragliding, skiing, sightseeing, kayaking, shopping, dining, and more. The region also is home to hot springs, caves, and other natural attractions. Although there is significant competition in the local/regional tourism market, significant opportunities exist for companies that already have an established presence, such as the Red Paddle Inn/Red Paddle Adventures.

SERVICES

From its location near the Eagle, Colorado, and Roaring Fork Rivers, Red Paddle Adventures offers white-water rafting excursions for adventurers of all skill levels. Specifically, the business offers one full-day and two half-day whitewater rafting excursions per day, seven days per week, between April 1 and Labor Day.

Customers book excursions with Red Paddle Adventures at the Red Paddle Inn in Foster Point. After considering the unique needs and makeup (e.g., age, skill level, etc.) of each group, experienced guides accompany participants on a shuttle bus from the Red Paddle Inn to one of several possible "put-ins" on one of the aforementioned rivers. Using a pickup truck and trailer, the business also hauls all of the rafts and equipment to the put-in location. Following the rafting experience, Red Paddle Adventures transports all guests and equipment from the "take-out" location back to the Red Paddle Inn.

Colorado.com, the "Official Site of Colorado Tourism," offers the following brief description of each river on which Red Paddle Adventures operates:

Colorado River: The Colorado River, divided by the upper and lower sections, runs a gauntlet of canyons and ravines that provide exquisite sightseeing intermingled within rapids and calms. Like the Arkansas, it's one of the most diverse, with various stretches that serve up adventures for both the daring and more timid.

Roaring Fork River: The upper section of the Roaring Fork, known as "Slaughterhouse," is packed with challenging rapids and is home to one of Colorado's few commercially rafted waterfalls. The lower section is popular with families and inflatable kayakers for its mellower floats.

Eagle River: One of the few free-flowing (un-dammed) rivers remaining in the West, the Eagle is fed largely from the snowpack on Vail Mountain. Because it relies on that snowpack, it is typically only run in spring and early summer when the snowmelt is at its peak.

Red Paddle Adventures offers two levels of raft options (regular and deluxe). Regular rafts include up to 10 guests and an experienced guide, while deluxe rafts include a maximum of six guests and an experienced guide. Deluxe rafts offer a more individualized experience, and are ideal for groups that wish to have their own private raft.

The following fees have been established for excursions offered by Red Paddle Adventures:

- Full-Day Excursion (Regular) Adult: $129

- Full-Day Excursion (Regular) Youth: $109

- Full-Day Excursion (Deluxe) Adult/Youth: $169

- Half-Day Excursion (Regular) Adult: $79

- Half-Day Excursion (Regular) Youth: $59

- Half-Day Excursion (Deluxe) Adult/Youth: $119

On average, all-day excursions include four hours of time on the water and lunch catered by the Red Paddle Inn. They allow for two hours of total travel time by shuttle. Half-day excursions include about 1.5 hours on the water and an equal amount of travel time. Lunch is not provided, but guests are offered an opportunity to dine at the Red Paddle Inn restaurant at a special discount following their excursion.

Rafts

Red Paddle Adventures will maintain an inventory of two different raft sizes (13-foot and 14-foot). The company has purchased premium, professional-grade rafts that feature welded seams, rubberized handles, stainless steel D-rings, and three-year commercial warranties.

OPERATIONS

Location

Red Paddle Adventures maintains operations at the Red Paddle Inn, a popular hotel and restaurant near the Eagle, Colorado, and Roaring Fork Rivers. The business is seasonal in nature, and maintains operations seven days per week between April 1 and Labor Day. The inn's owners have converted one of its gift shops into a booking center for the newly-established Red Paddle Adventures, providing prime exposure from a location that gets heavy foot traffic in and out of the establishment. Red Paddle Adventures will lease the space from Red Paddle Inn, along with space inside of an existing maintenance building, which will be used for the storage of vehicles, trailers, and equipment.

Communications

All of Red Paddle Adventures' guides will utilize satellite communication equipment, allowing them to maintain constant communications with the main office and notify rescue personnel in the event of an emergency.

Equipment & Vehicles

Red Paddle Adventures will purchase the following equipment during its first three years of operations:

	2017	2018	2019
Aluminum raft trailers	2	1	1
Pickup trucks	2	1	1
Shuttle buses	2	1	1
Whitewater rafts	20	10	10
Paddles	90	50	50
Lifejackets	90	50	50
Water helmets	90	50	50

PERSONNEL

Ownership

Red Paddle Adventures is being established by the Jake and Lisa McMurtry, the owners of the popular Red Paddle Inn, who are seeking additional sources of revenue during Colorado's peak tourism season. Already a thriving business, the Red Paddle Inn's guests are always looking for additional entertainment and recreation options, which the business is well-positioned to provide. The McMurtrys are both natives of Foster Point, and have owned the Red Paddle Inn (which was established in 1958) for five years. Under their ownership, extensive renovations have been made to the restaurant/hotel, which has helped to attract new customers. From this position of strength, the owners are now ready to expand the business.

Management

Although Red Paddle Adventures will be a seasonal business, it will require a full-time manager, who will be responsible for maintaining and managing equipment inventories, coordinating advertising and marketing activities, handling reservations/customer bookings, designing tourism packages, executing contracts with independent contractors (tour guides), communicating with state regulatory agencies and professional advisers (e.g., attorneys and accountants), and maintaining financial records. The owners have developed a detailed job description for this position, which is available upon request, and recently hired Stacy Winters to fill this position. Stacy is a University of Colorado graduate with 15 years of hospitality management experience. Additionally, she is an experienced whitewater rafter who is very familiar with the rivers on which Red Paddle Adventures operates.

Independent Contractors

Experienced rafting guides form the backbone of Red Paddle Adventures. The McMurtrys have identified a core group of experienced independent guides, with whom they will contract on a seasonal basis. The owners have gone to great lengths to select guides whose experience and qualifications significantly exceed the minimum standards set by the state of Colorado. On average, Red Paddle Adventures' guides have more than 1,500 hours of on-river experience. A complete list of the guides, along with details regarding their experience and licensure, is available upon request.

Professional & Advisory Support

Red Paddle Adventures has established a business banking account with Foster Point Community Bank, including a merchant account for accepting credit card payments. Tax advisement is provided by Foster Point Financial Services, Inc. Additionally, the business has obtained an appropriate amount of liability insurance in partnership with the agency Red Rock Partners Inc.

LEGAL

Colorado Parks & Wildlife requires that all river outfitters operating in the state hold a river outfitter license. All of Red Paddle Adventures' guides maintain these licenses and exceed the related requirements outlined in the state's River Outfitter Licensing Program. Complete details regarding application, licensing, inspection, regulation, and statutes in the State of Colorado are available at:

http://cpw.state.co.us/thingstodo/Pages/RiverOutfitterLicensingRegulationsStatutes.aspx

MARKETING & SALES

Red Paddle Adventures has developed a marketing plan that involves the following primary tactics:

1. A logo/brand identity that closely resembles that of the Red Paddle Inn.

2. Color brochures, featuring dramatic outdoor photography, describing the business' rafting excursions. These will be distributed at key tourism information distribution points throughout the region.

3. Regional print advertising in tourism-oriented publications and newspapers.

4. Paid listings in key online directories.

5. A mobile-friendly Web site with complete details about the business; a listing of excursions, pricing, safety requirements/policies, and terms/conditions; and an advance reservation tool.

6. A social media strategy involving Facebook, Twitter, and Instagram.

7. A toll-free number that guests may call to book rafting excursions throughout the continental United States.

8. Co-marketing initiatives with the Foster Point Convention and Visitors Bureau and complementary tourism partners (e.g., Jeep and zip-line tour operators).

9. Participation in regional/state tourism shows.

10. A customer loyalty program that provides a 15 percent discount to customers of the Red Paddle Inn, and to Red Paddle Adventures customers who refer someone to the business.

11. Combination Red Paddle Inn/Red Paddle Adventures travel packages that offer significant savings on lodging, meals, and rafting for one attractive price.

12. Mobile marketing (signage on all company vehicles).

13. Database marketing (e.g., building a customer database and utilizing a popular e-mail marketing service to stay in touch with them/encourage future bookings.

GROWTH STRATEGY

Year One: Begin operations with the capacity to offer one full-day and two half-day whitewater rafting excursions per day (five rafts per excursion). On average, book three rafts with regular customers (10 guests/raft) and two rafts with premium customers (6 guests/raft). Operate at no less than 80 percent of maximum capacity, resulting in gross revenues of about $1.6 million and net income of $184,215.

Year Two: Expand operations by adding the capacity to offer two additional half-day whitewater rafting excursions per day, with the same ratio of regular/premium customers. Introduce an optional half-day zip-lining option in partnership with another local tourism destination, resulting in commissions of $250,000 from the zip-lining tour operator. Operate at no less than 85 percent of maximum capacity, resulting in gross revenues of about $2.8 million and net income of $585,040.

Year Three: Expand operations by adding the capacity to offer two additional half-day whitewater rafting excursions per day, with the same ratio of regular/premium customers. Introduce an optional half-day Jeep tour option in partnership with another local tourism destination, resulting in commissions of $300,000 from the Jeep tour operator. Operate at no less than 90 percent of maximum capacity, resulting in gross revenues of about $4.3 million and net income of $1,018,490.

FINANCIAL ANALYSIS

Following is a breakdown of projected revenue, expenses, and net income for Red Paddle Adventures' first three years of operations. After generating modest profits during the first two years, the business is expected to achieve significant (e.g., more than $1 million) annual profits by year three.

	2017	2018	2019
Income			
Rafting excursions	$ 1,600,000	$ 2,550,000	$ 3,750,000
Tour operator commissions	$ 0	$ 250,000	$ 550,000
Gross income	**$1,600,000**	**$2,800,000**	**$4,300,000**
Expenses			
Advertising & marketing	$ 480,000	$ 840,000	$ 1,290,000
Accounting & legal	$ 10,000	$ 12,000	$ 15,000
Insurance	$ 25,000	$ 27,000	$ 29,000
Independent contractors	$ 640,000	$ 1,120,000	$ 1,720,000
Salaries	$ 60,000	$ 65,000	$ 70,000
Payroll taxes	$ 4,800	$ 5,200	$ 5,600
Vehicles	$ 0	$ 20,000	$ 20,000
Fuel	$ 15,000	$ 20,000	$ 25,000
Rent	$ 12,000	$ 12,000	$ 12,000
Telephone	$ 850	$ 900	$ 950
Office supplies	$ 750	$ 750	$ 750
Equipment	$ 151,750	$ 75,375	$ 75,375
Utilities	$ 935	$ 935	$ 935
Postage	$ 3,500	$ 4,500	$ 5,500
Fees & regulatory	$ 1,200	$ 1,300	$ 1,400
Health insurance	$ 10,000	$10,000	$ 10,000
Total expenses	**$1,415,785**	**$2,214,960**	**$3,281,510**
Net income	**$ 184,215**	**$ 585,040**	**$1,018,490**

Following is a detailed breakdown of projected equipment purchases for Red Paddle Adventures' first three years of operations:

	2017	2018	2019
Aluminum raft trailers	$ 6,000	$ 3,000	$ 3,000
Pickup trucks	$ 30,000	$15,000	$15,000
Shuttle buses	$ 35,000	$17,500	$17,500
Whitewater rafts	$ 48,250	$24,125	$24,125
Paddles	$ 6,300	$ 3,500	$ 3,500
Lifejackets	$ 11,700	$ 6,500	$ 6,500
Water helmets	$ 4,500	$ 2,500	$ 2,500
Communications equipment	$ 2,500	$ 1,250	$ 1,250
Miscellaneous	$ 1,000	$ 1,000	$ 1,000
Computers	$ 1,500	$ 500	$ 500
Office equipment	$ 5,000	$ 500	$ 500
	$151,750	**$75,375**	**$75,375**

The Red Paddle Inn's owners anticipate total start-up cost of $350,000. They will provide half of the funding and are seeking the remainder from the Red Paddle Inn/Red Paddle Adventures' private investors, for whom this business plan has been prepared.

Business Plan Template

USING THIS TEMPLATE

A business plan carefully spells out a company's projected course of action over a period of time, usually the first two to three years after the start-up. In addition, banks, lenders, and other investors examine the information and financial documentation before deciding whether or not to finance a new business venture. Therefore, a business plan is an essential tool in obtaining financing and should describe the business itself in detail as well as all important factors influencing the company, including the market, industry, competition, operations and management policies, problem solving strategies, financial resources and needs, and other vital information. The plan enables the business owner to anticipate costs, plan for difficulties, and take advantage of opportunities, as well as design and implement strategies that keep the company running as smoothly as possible.

This template has been provided as a model to help you construct your own business plan. Please keep in mind that there is no single acceptable format for a business plan, and that this template is in no way comprehensive, but serves as an example.

The business plans provided in this section are fictional and have been used by small business agencies as models for clients to use in compiling their own business plans.

GENERIC BUSINESS PLAN

Main headings included below are topics that should be covered in a comprehensive business plan. They include:

Business Summary

Purpose
Provides a brief overview of your business, succinctly highlighting the main ideas of your plan.

Includes

- Topic Headings and Subheadings
- Page Number References

Table of Contents

Purpose
Organized in an Outline Format, the Table of Contents illustrates the selection and arrangement of information contained in your plan.

Includes

- Name and Type of Business
- Description of Product/Service
- Business History and Development
- Location
- Market

- Competition
- Management
- Financial Information
- Business Strengths and Weaknesses
- Business Growth

Business History and Industry Outlook

Purpose

Examines the conception and subsequent development of your business within an industry specific context.

Includes

- Start-up Information
- Owner/Key Personnel Experience
- Location
- Development Problems and Solutions
- Investment/Funding Information

- Future Plans and Goals
- Market Trends and Statistics
- Major Competitors
- Product/Service Advantages
- National, Regional, and Local Economic Impact

Product/Service

Purpose

Introduces, defines, and details the product and/or service that inspired the information of your business.

Includes

- Unique Features
- Niche Served
- Market Comparison
- Stage of Product/Service Development
- Production

- Facilities, Equipment, and Labor
- Financial Requirements
- Product/Service Life Cycle
- Future Growth

Market Examination

Purpose

Assessment of product/service applications in relation to consumer buying cycles.

Includes

- Target Market
- Consumer Buying Habits
- Product/Service Applications
- Consumer Reactions
- Market Factors and Trends

- Penetration of the Market
- Market Share
- Research and Studies
- Cost
- Sales Volume and Goals

Competition

Purpose

Analysis of Competitors in the Marketplace.

Includes

- Competitor Information
- Product/Service Comparison
- Market Niche

- Product/Service Strengths and Weaknesses
- Future Product/Service Development

Marketing

Purpose

Identifies promotion and sales strategies for your product/service.

Includes

- Product/Service Sales Appeal
- Special and Unique Features
- Identification of Customers
- Sales and Marketing Staff
- Sales Cycles
- Type of Advertising/ Promotion
- Pricing
- Competition
- Customer Services

Operations

Purpose

Traces product/service development from production/inception to the market environment.

Includes

- Cost Effective Production Methods
- Facility
- Location
- Equipment
- Labor
- Future Expansion

Administration and Management

Purpose

Offers a statement of your management philosophy with an in-depth focus on processes and procedures.

Includes

- Management Philosophy
- Structure of Organization
- Reporting System
- Methods of Communication
- Employee Skills and Training
- Employee Needs and Compensation
- Work Environment
- Management Policies and Procedures
- Roles and Responsibilities

Key Personnel

Purpose

Describes the unique backgrounds of principle employees involved in business.

Includes

- Owner(s)/Employee Education and Experience
- Positions and Roles
- Benefits and Salary
- Duties and Responsibilities
- Objectives and Goals

Potential Problems and Solutions

Purpose

Discussion of problem solving strategies that change issues into opportunities.

Includes

- Risks
- Litigation
- Future Competition
- Economic Impact
- Problem Solving Skills

Financial Information

Purpose

Secures needed funding and assistance through worksheets and projections detailing financial plans, methods of repayment, and future growth opportunities.

Includes

- Financial Statements
- Bank Loans
- Methods of Repayment
- Tax Returns

- Start-up Costs
- Projected Income (3 years)
- Projected Cash Flow (3 Years)

Appendices

Purpose

Supporting documents used to enhance your business proposal.

Includes

- Photographs of product, equipment, facilities, etc.
- Copyright/Trademark Documents
- Legal Agreements
- Marketing Materials
- Research and or Studies

- Operation Schedules
- Organizational Charts
- Job Descriptions
- Resumes
- Additional Financial Documentation

Fictional Food Distributor

Commercial Foods, Inc.

3003 Avondale Ave.
Knoxville, TN 37920

This plan demonstrates how a partnership can have a positive impact on a new business. It demonstrates how two individuals can carve a niche in the specialty foods market by offering gourmet foods to upscale restaurants and fine hotels. This plan is fictional and has not been used to gain funding from a bank or other lending institution.

STATEMENT OF PURPOSE

Commercial Foods, Inc. seeks a loan of $75,000 to establish a new business. This sum, together with $5,000 equity investment by the principals, will be used as follows:

- Merchandise inventory $25,000
- Office fixture/equipment $12,000
- Warehouse equipment $14,000
- One delivery truck $10,000
- Working capital $39,000
- Total $100,000

DESCRIPTION OF THE BUSINESS

Commercial Foods, Inc. will be a distributor of specialty food service products to hotels and upscale restaurants in the geographical area of a 50 mile radius of Knoxville. Richard Roberts will direct the sales effort and John Williams will manage the warehouse operation and the office. One delivery truck will be used initially with a second truck added in the third year. We expect to begin operation of the business within 30 days after securing the requested financing.

MANAGEMENT

A. Richard Roberts is a native of Memphis, Tennessee. He is a graduate of Memphis State University with a Bachelor's degree from the School of Business. After graduation, he worked for a major manufacturer of specialty food service products as a detail sales person for five years, and, for the past three years, he has served as a product sales manager for this firm.

B. John Williams is a native of Nashville, Tennessee. He holds a B.S. Degree in Food Technology from the University of Tennessee. His career includes five years as a product development chemist in gourmet food products and five years as operations manager for a food service distributor.

Both men are healthy and energetic. Their backgrounds complement each other, which will ensure the success of Commercial Foods, Inc. They will set policies together and personnel decisions will be made jointly. Initial salaries for the owners will be $1,000 per month for the first few years. The spouses of both principals are successful in the business world and earn enough to support the families.

They have engaged the services of Foster Jones, CPA, and William Hale, Attorney, to assist them in an advisory capacity.

PERSONNEL

The firm will employ one delivery truck driver at a wage of $8.00 per hour. One office worker will be employed at $7.50 per hour. One part-time employee will be used in the office at $5.00 per hour. The driver will load and unload his own trucks. Mr. Williams will assist in the warehouse operation as needed to assist one stock person at $7.00 per hour. An additional delivery truck and driver will be added the third year.

LOCATION

The firm will lease a 20,000 square foot building at 3003 Avondale Ave., in Knoxville, which contains warehouse and office areas equipped with two-door truck docks. The annual rental is $9,000. The building was previously used as a food service warehouse and very little modification to the building will be required.

PRODUCTS AND SERVICES

The firm will offer specialty food service products such as soup bases, dessert mixes, sauce bases, pastry mixes, spices, and flavors, normally used by upscale restaurants and nice hotels. We are going after a niche in the market with high quality gourmet products. There is much less competition in this market than in standard run of the mill food service products. Through their work experiences, the principals have contacts with supply sources and with local chefs.

THE MARKET

We know from our market survey that there are over 200 hotels and upscale restaurants in the area we plan to serve. Customers will be attracted by a direct sales approach. We will offer samples of our products and product application data on use of our products in the finished prepared foods. We will cultivate the chefs in these establishments. The technical background of John Williams will be especially useful here.

COMPETITION

We find that we will be only distributor in the area offering a full line of gourmet food service products. Other foodservice distributors offer only a few such items in conjunction with their standard product line. Our survey shows that many of the chefs are ordering products from Atlanta and Memphis because of a lack of adequate local supply.

SUMMARY

Commercial Foods, Inc. will be established as a foodservice distributor of specialty food in Knoxville. The principals, with excellent experience in the industry, are seeking a $75,000 loan to establish the business. The principals are investing $25,000 as equity capital.

The business will be set up as an S Corporation with each principal owning 50% of the common stock in the corporation.

Fictional Hardware Store

Oshkosh Hardware, Inc.

123 Main St.
Oshkosh, WI 54901

The following plan outlines how a small hardware store can survive competition from large discount chains by offering products and providing expert advice in the use of any product it sells. This plan is fictional and has not been used to gain funding from a bank or other lending institution.

EXECUTIVE SUMMARY

Oshkosh Hardware, Inc. is a new corporation that is going to establish a retail hardware store in a strip mall in Oshkosh, Wisconsin. The store will sell hardware of all kinds, quality tools, paint, and housewares. The business will make revenue and a profit by servicing its customers not only with needed hardware but also with expert advice in the use of any product it sells.

Oshkosh Hardware, Inc. will be operated by its sole shareholder, James Smith. The company will have a total of four employees. It will sell its products in the local market. Customers will buy our products because we will provide free advice on the use of all of our products and will also furnish a full refund warranty.

Oshkosh Hardware, Inc. will sell its products in the Oshkosh store staffed by three sales representatives. No additional employees will be needed to achieve its short and long range goals. The primary short range goal is to open the store by October 1, 1994. In order to achieve this goal a lease must be signed by July 1, 1994 and the complete inventory ordered by August 1, 1994.

Mr. James Smith will invest $30,000 in the business. In addition, the company will have to borrow $150,000 during the first year to cover the investment in inventory, accounts receivable, and furniture and equipment. The company will be profitable after six months of operation and should be able to start repayment of the loan in the second year.

THE BUSINESS

The business will sell hardware of all kinds, quality tools, paint, and housewares. We will purchase our products from three large wholesale buying groups.

In general our customers are homeowners who do their own repair and maintenance, hobbyists, and housewives. Our business is unique in that we will have a complete line of all hardware items and will be able to get special orders by overnight delivery. The business makes revenue and profits by servicing our customers not only with needed hardware but also with expert advice in the use of any product we sell. Our major costs for bringing our products to market are cost of merchandise of 36%, salaries of $45,000, and occupancy costs of $60,000.

219

Oshkosh Hardware, Inc.'s retail outlet will be located at 1524 Frontage Road, which is in a newly developed retail center of Oshkosh. Our location helps facilitate accessibility from all parts of town and reduces our delivery costs. The store will occupy 7500 square feet of space. The major equipment involved in our business is counters and shelving, a computer, a paint mixing machine, and a truck.

THE MARKET

Oshkosh Hardware, Inc. will operate in the local market. There are 15,000 potential customers in this market area. We have three competitors who control approximately 98% of the market at present. We feel we can capture 25% of the market within the next four years. Our major reason for believing this is that our staff is technically competent to advise our customers in the correct use of all products we sell.

After a careful market analysis, we have determined that approximately 60% of our customers are men and 40% are women. The percentage of customers that fall into the following age categories are:

Under 16: 0%
17-21: 5%
22-30: 30%
31-40: 30%
41-50: 20%
51-60: 10%
61-70: 5%
Over 70: 0%

The reasons our customers prefer our products is our complete knowledge of their use and our full refund warranty.

We get our information about what products our customers want by talking to existing customers. There seems to be an increasing demand for our product. The demand for our product is increasing in size based on the change in population characteristics.

SALES

At Oshkosh Hardware, Inc. we will employ three sales people and will not need any additional personnel to achieve our sales goals. These salespeople will need several years experience in home repair and power tool usage. We expect to attract 30% of our customers from newspaper ads, 5% of our customers from local directories, 5% of our customers from the yellow pages, 10% of our customers from family and friends, and 50% of our customers from current customers. The most cost effect source will be current customers. In general our industry is growing.

MANAGEMENT

We would evaluate the quality of our management staff as being excellent. Our manager is experienced and very motivated to achieve the various sales and quality assurance objectives we have set. We will use a management information system that produces key inventory, quality assurance, and sales data on a weekly basis. All data is compared to previously established goals for that week, and deviations are the primary focus of the management staff.

GOALS IMPLEMENTATION

The short term goals of our business are:

1. Open the store by October 1, 1994
2. Reach our breakeven point in two months
3. Have sales of $100,000 in the first six months

In order to achieve our first short term goal we must:

1. Sign the lease by July 1, 1994
2. Order a complete inventory by August 1, 1994

In order to achieve our second short term goal we must:

1. Advertise extensively in Sept. and Oct.
2. Keep expenses to a minimum

In order to achieve our third short term goal we must:

1. Promote power tool sales for the Christmas season
2. Keep good customer traffic in Jan. and Feb.

The long term goals for our business are:

1. Obtain sales volume of $600,000 in three years
2. Become the largest hardware dealer in the city
3. Open a second store in Fond du Lac

The most important thing we must do in order to achieve the long term goals for our business is to develop a highly profitable business with excellent cash flow.

FINANCE

Oshkosh Hardware, Inc. Faces some potential threats or risks to our business. They are discount house competition. We believe we can avoid or compensate for this by providing quality products complimented by quality advice on the use of every product we sell. The financial projections we have prepared are located at the end of this document.

JOB DESCRIPTION-GENERAL MANAGER

The General Manager of the business of the corporation will be the president of the corporation. He will be responsible for the complete operation of the retail hardware store which is owned by the corporation. A detailed description of his duties and responsibilities is as follows.

Sales

Train and supervise the three sales people. Develop programs to motivate and compensate these employees. Coordinate advertising and sales promotion effects to achieve sales totals as outlined in budget. Oversee purchasing function and inventory control procedures to insure adequate merchandise at all times at a reasonable cost.

Finance

Prepare monthly and annual budgets. Secure adequate line of credit from local banks. Supervise office personnel to insure timely preparation of records, statements, all government reports, control of receivables and payables, and monthly financial statements.

Administration

Perform duties as required in the areas of personnel, building leasing and maintenance, licenses and permits, and public relations.

Organizations, Agencies, & Consultants

A listing of Associations and Consultants of interest to entrepreneurs, followed by the Small Business Administration Regional Offices, Small Business Development Centers, Service Corps of Retired Executives offices, and Venture Capital and Finance Companies.

Associations

This section contains a listing of associations and other agencies of interest to the small business owner. Entries are listed alphabetically by organization name.

American Business Women's Association
9820 Metcalf Ave., Ste. 110
Overland Park, MO 66212
(800)228-0007
Fax: (913)660-0101
E-mail: webmail@abwa.org
Website: http://www.abwa.org
Rene Street, Exec. Dir.

American Franchisee Association
53 W Jackson Blvd., Ste. 1256
Chicago, IL 60604
(312)431-0545
Fax: (312)431-1469
E-mail: spkezios@franchisee.org
Website: http://www.franchisee.org
Susan P. Kezios, Pres.

American Independent Business Alliance
222 S Black Ave.
Bozeman, MT 59715
(406)582-1255
Website: http://www.amiba.net
Jennifer Rockne, Co-Dir.
Jeff Milchen, Co-Dir.

American Small Business Coalition
PO Box 2786
Columbia, MD 21045
(410)381-7378
Website: https://www.theasbc.org
Margaret H. Timberlake, Pres.

American Small Business League
3910 Cypress Dr., Ste. B
Petaluma, CA 94954
(707)789-9575

Fax: (707)789-9580
E-mail: jspatola@asbl.com
Website: http://www.asbl.com
Lloyd Chapman, Founder

American Small Business Travelers Alliance
3112 Bent Oak Cir.
Flower Mound, TX 75022
(972)836-8064
E-mail: info@asbta.com
Website: http://www.asbta.com/
Chuck Sharp, Pres./CEO

America's Small Business Development Center
8990 Burke Lake Rd., 2nd Fl.
Burke, VA 22015
(703)764-9850
Fax: (703)764-1234
E-mail: info@americassbdc.org
Website: http://americassbdc.org
Charles Rowe, Pres./CEO

Association for Enterprise Opportunity
1310 L St NW, Ste. 830
Washington, DC 22209
(202)650-5580
E-mail: cevans@aeoworks.org
Website: http://www.aeoworks.org
Connie Evans, Pres./CEO

Association of Printing and Data Solutions Professionals
PO Box 2249
Oak Park, IL 60303
(708)218-7755
E-mail: ed.avis@irga.com
Website: http://www.apdsp.org
Ed Avis, Mng. Dir.

Association of Publishers for Special Sales
PO Box 9725
Colorado Springs, CO 80932-0725

(719)924-5534
Fax: (719)213-2602
E-mail: BrianJud@bookapss.org
Website: http://community.bookapss.org
Brian Jud, Exec. Dir.

BEST Association
17701 Mitchell N
Irvine, CA 92614-6028
866-706-2225
Website: http://www.beassoc.org

Business Planning Institute, LLC
580 Village Blvd., Ste. 150
West Palm Beach, FL 33409
(561)236-5533
Fax: (561)689-5546
E-mail: info@bpiplans.com
Website: http://www.bpiplans.com

Coalition for Government Procurement
1990 M St. NW, Ste. 450
Washington, DC 20036
(202)331-0975
Fax: (202)521-3533
E-mail: rwaldron@thecgp.org
Website: http://thecgp.org
Roger Waldron, Pres.

Ewing Marion Kauffman Foundation
4801 Rockhill Rd.
Kansas City, MO 64110
(816)932-1000
Website: http://www.kauffman.org
Wendy Guillies, Pres./CEO

Family Business Coalition
PO Box 722
Washington, DC 20044
(202)393-8959
E-mail: info@familybusinesscoalition.org
Website: http://familybusinesscoalition.org
Palmer Schoening, Chm.

Family Firm Institute, Inc.
200 Lincoln St., Ste. 201
Boston, MA 02111
(617)482-3045
Fax: (617)482-3049
E-mail: ffi@ffi.org
Website: http://www.ffi.org
Judy Green, Pres.

Film Independent
9911 W Pico Blvd., 11th Fl.
Los Angeles, CA 90035
(310)432-1200
Fax: (310)432-1203
E-mail: jwelsh@filmindependent.org
Website: http://www.filmindependent.org
Josh Welsh, Pres.

HR People and Strategy
1800 Duke St.
Alexandria, VA 223142
(703)535-6056
Fax: (703)535-6490
E-mail: info@hrps.org
Website: http://www.hrps.org
Lisa Connell, Exec. Dir.

Independent Visually Impaired Entrepreneurs
2121 Scott Rd., No. 105
Burbank, CA 91504-1228
(818)238-9321
E-mail: abazyn@bazyncommunications
.com
Website: http://www.ivie-acb.org
Ardis Bazyn, Pres.

International Council for Small Business
Funger Hall, Ste. 315
2201 G St. NW
Washington, DC 20052
(202)994-0704
Fax: (202)994-4930
E-mail: icsb@gwu.edu
Website: http://www.icsb.org
Dr. Ayman El Tarabishy, Exec. Dir.

LearnServe International
PO Box 6203
Washington, DC 20015
(202)370-1865
Fax: (202)355-0993
E-mail: info@learn-serve.org
Website: http://learn-serve.org
Scott Rechler, Dir./CEO

National Association for the Self-Employed
PO Box 241
Annapolis Junction, MD 20701-0241
800-232-6273
800-649-6273 (Alaska and Hawaii only)

E-mail: media@nase.org
Website: http://www.nase.org
Keith R. Hall, CPA, Pres./CEO

National Association of Business Owners
1509 Green Mountain Dr.
Little Rock, AR 72211
(501)227-8423
Website: http://nabo.org

National Association of Small Business Contractors
700 12th St. NW, Ste. 700
Washington, DC 20005
Free: 888-861-9290
Website: http://www.nasbc.org
Cris Young, Pres.

National Business Association
15305 Dallas Pkwy., Ste. 300
Addison, TX 75001
800-456-0440
Fax: (972)960-9149
E-mail: database@nationalbusiness.org
Website: http://www.nationalbusiness.org

National Federation of Independent Business
1201 F St. NW
Washington, DC 20004
(615)872-5800
800-NFIBNOW
Fax: (615)872-5353
Website: http://www.nfib.org
Juanita Duggan, Pres./CEO

National Small Business Association
1156 15th St. NW, Ste. 502
Washington, DC 20005
800-345-6728
E-mail: info@nsba.biz
Website: http://www.nsba.biz
Todd McCracken, Pres.

Professional Association of Small Business Accountants
6405 Metcalf Ave., Ste. 503
Shawnee Mission, KS 66202
866-296-0001
E-mail: director@pasba.org
Website: http://community.pasba.org/
home
Jordan Bennett, Exec. Dir.

Rainbow PUSH Wall Street Project
1441 Broadway, Ste. 5051
New York, NY 10018
(646)569-5889
(212)425-7874
E-mail: info@rainbowpush.org
Website: http://www.rainbowpush.org
Chee Chee Williams, Exec. Dir.

Root Cause
11 Avenue de Lafayette
Boston, MA 02111
(617)492-2300
E-mail: info@rootcause.org
Website: http://www.rootcause.org
Andrew Wolk, Founder/CEO

Sales Professionals USA
1400 W 122nd Ave., No. 101
Westminster, CO 80234
(303)578-2020
E-mail: support@dmdude.com
Website: http://www.salesprofessionals-usa
.com
Peter Brissette, Pres.

Score Association
1175 Herndon Pkwy., Ste. 900
Herndon, VA 20170
(202)205-6762
800-634-0245
E-mail: help@score.org
Website: http://www.score.org
W. Kenneth Yancey, Jr., CEO

Seedco
22 Cortlandt St., 33rd Fl.
New York, NY 10007
(212)473-0255
E-mail: info@seedco.org
Website: http://www.seedco.org
Barbara Dwyer Gunn, Pres./CEO

Small Business and Entrepreneurship Council
301 Maple Ave. W, Ste. 690
Vienna, VA 22180
(703)242-5840
Website: http://www.sbecouncil.org
Karen Kerrigan, Pres./CEO

Small Business Council of America
Brandywine East
1523 Concord Pike, Ste. 300
Wilmington, DE 19803
(302)691-SBCA
E-mail: lredstone@shanlaw.com
Website: http://sbca.net
Leanne Redstone, Exec. Dir.

Small Business Exporters Association of the United States
1156 15th St. NW, Ste. 502
Washington, DC 20005
(202)552-2903
800-345-6728
E-mail: info@sbea.org
Website: http://www.sbea.org
Jody Milanese, VP, Government Affairs

Small Business Investor Alliance
1100 H St. NW, Ste. 1200
Washington, DC 20005
(202)628-5055
E-mail: info@sbia.org
Website: http://www.sbia.org
Brett Palmer, Pres.

Small Business Legislative Council
4800 Hampden Ln., 6th Fl.
Bethesda, MD 20814
(301)652-8302
Website: http://www.sblc.org
Paula Calimafde, Pres.

Small Business Service Bureau, Inc.
554 Main St.
PO Box 15014
Worcester, MA 01615-0014
800-343-0939
E-mail: info@sbsb.com
Website: http://www.sbsb.com
Lisa M. Carroll, MS, MPH, RN, Pres.

Support Services Alliance
165 Main St.
Oneida, NY 13421
(315)363-65842
Website: http://www.oneidachamberny
.org/supportservices.html
Michele Hummel, Contact

United States Association for Small Business and Entrepreneurship
University of Wisconsin
Whitewater College of Business and
Economics
Hyland Hall
809 W Starin Rd.
Whitewater, WI 53190
(262)472-1449
E-mail: psnyder@usasbe.org
Website: http://www.usasbe.org
Patrick Snyder, Exec. Dir.

Consultants

This section contains a listing of consultants specializing in small business development. It is arranged alphabetically by country, then by state or province, then by city, then by firm name.

Canada

Alberta

Dark Horse Strategies
20 Coachway Rd. SW, Ste. 262
Calgary, AB, Canada T3H 1E6

(403)605-3881
E-mail: info@darkhorsestrategies.com
Website: http://www.darkhorsestrategies
.com

Kenway Mack Slusarchuk Stewart L.L.P.
333 11th Ave. SW, Ste. 1500
Calgary, AB, Canada T2R 1L9
(403)233-7750
Fax: (403)266-5267
E-mail: info@kmss.ca
Website: http://www.kmss.ca

Kenway Mack Slusarchuk Stewart L.L.P.
714 10 St., Ste. 3
Canmore, AB, Canada T1W 2A6
(403)675-1010
Fax: (403)675-6789
Website: http://kmss.ca/about-us/
canmore-office/

Tenato Strategy Inc.
1229A 9th Ave. SE
Calgary, AB, Canada T2G 0S9
(403)242-1127
E-mail: info@tenato.com
Website: http://www.tenato.com

Nichols Applied Management Inc.
10104 103rd Ave. NW, Ste. 2401
Edmonton, AB, Canada T5J 0H8
(780)424-0091
Fax: (780)428-7644
E-mail: info@nicholsappliedmanagement
.com
Website: http://nicholsconsulting.com/
WP

Abonar Business Consultants Ltd.
240-222 Baseline Rd., Ste. 212
Sherwood Park, AB, Canada T8H 1S8
(780)862-0282
Fax: (866)405-4510
E-mail: info@abonarconsultants.com
Website: http://www.abonarconsultants
.com/index.html

AJL Consulting
52312 Range Rd. 225, Ste. 145
Sherwood Park, AB, Canada T8C 1E1
(780)467-6040
Fax: (780)449-2993
Website: http://www.ajlconsulting.ca

Taylor Warwick Consulting Ltd.
121 Courtenay Terr.
Sherwood Park, AB, Canada T8A 5S6
(780)669-1605
E-mail: info@taylorwarwick.ca
Website: http://www.taylorwarwick.ca

British Columbia

Stevenson Community Consultants
138 Pritchard Rd.
Comox, BC, Canada V9M 2T2
(250)890-0297
Fax: (250)890-0296
E-mail: dagit@island.net

Andrew R. De Boda Consulting
1523 Milford Ave.
Coquitlam, BC, Canada V3J 2V9
(604)936-4527
Fax: (604)936-4527
E-mail: deboda@intergate.bc.ca

Reality Marketing Associates
3049 Sienna Ct.
Coquitlam, BC, Canada V3E 3N7
(604)944-8603
Fax: (604)944-4708
E-mail: info@realityassociates.com
Website: http://www.realityassociates.com

Landmark Sq. II, 1708 Dolphin Ave., Ste. 806
Kelowna, BC, Canada V1Y 9S4
(250)763-4716
Fax: (877)353-8608
Free: 877-763-4022
E-mail: steve@burnsinnovation.com
Website: http://www.burnsinnovation.com

Kuber Business Consultants Ltd.
3003 Saint John's St., Ste. 202
Port Moody, BC, Canada V3H 2C4
(604)568-3055
Fax: (604)608-2903
E-mail: info@kuberbiz.ca
Website: http://www.kuberbiz.ca

Seajay Consulting Ltd.
800-15355 24th Ave., Ste. 527
Surrey, BC, Canada V4A 2H9
(604)541-0148
E-mail: chris@seajayconsulting.ca
Website: http://www.seajayconsulting.ca

Einblau and Associates Ltd.
999 W Broadway, Ste. 720
Vancouver, BC, Canada V5Z 1K5
(604)684–7164
Fax: (604)873–8256
E-mail: office@einblau.com
Website: http://www.einblau.com

Pinpoint Tactics Business Consulting
5525 West Blvd., Ste. 330
Vancouver, BC, Canada V6M 3W6
(604)263-4698
Fax: (604)909-4916
E-mail: info@pinpointtactics.com
Website: http://www.pinpointtactics.com

Synergy Complete Management Consulting
1489 Marine Dr., Ste. 317
West Vancouver, BC, Canada V7T 1B8
(604)260-5477
Free: 866-866-8755
E-mail: info@synergy-cmc.com
Website: http://www.synergy-cmc.com

Nova Scotia

The Marketing Clinic
1384 Bedford Hwy.
Bedford, NS, Canada B4A 1E2
(902)835-4122
Fax: (902)832-9389
Free: 877-401-9398
E-mail: office@themarketingclinic.ca
Website: http://www.themarketing
clinic.ca

Thyagrissen Consulting Ltd.
35 Talon Ct.
Bible Hill, NS, Canada B2N 7B4
(902)895-1414
Fax: (902)895-5188
E-mail: yvonne@thyagrissenconsulting.ca
Website: http://www.thyagrissen
consulting.ca

Coburg Consultants Ltd.
6100 University Ave.
Halifax, NS, Canada B3H 3J5
E-mail: info@coburgconsultants.ca
Website: http://www.coburgconsultants.ca

MacDonnell Group Consulting Ltd.
1505 Barrington St., Ste. 1100
Halifax, NS, Canada B3J 3K5
(902)425-3980
Fax: (902)423-7593
Website: http://www.macdonnell.com

Ontario

The Cynton Co.
17 Massey St.
Brampton, ON, Canada L6S 2V6
(905)792-7769
Fax: (905)792-8116
E-mail: cynton@cynton.com
Website: http://www.cynton.com

Fresh Insights Consulting
901 Guelph Line
Burlington, ON, Canada L7R 3N8
(905)634-6500
E-mail: info@freshinsightsconsulting.ca
Website: http://freshinsightsconsulting.ca

Globe Consult Corp.
34 Willow Shore Way
Carleton Place, ON, Canada K7C 0B1

(613)257-8265
Fax: (613)253-2436
E-mail: infoid@globeconsult.ca
Website: http://www.globeconsult.ca

KLynn Inc.
4421 Hwy. 45
Cobourg, ON K9A 4J9
(905)373-4909
Free: 888-717-2220
E-mail: info@klynnbusinessconsulting
.com
Website: www.klynnbusinessconsulting
.com

Heaslip Associates
50 West St., Unit 2
Collingwood, ON, Canada L9Y 3T1
(613)537-8900
E-mail: info@heaslipassociates.com
Website: http://www.heaslipassociates
.com

JThomson & Co. CPA
645 Upper James St. S
Hamilton, ON, Canada L9C 2Y9
(905)388-7229
Fax: (905)388-3134
Website: http://www.jthomsonco.com

Queen's Business Consulting
Queen's University
Stephen J.R. Smith School of Business
Goodes Hall, Rm. LL201
Kingston, ON, Canada K7L 3N6
(613)533-2309
Fax: (613)533-2744
E-mail: qbc@business.queensu.ca
Website: http://smith.queensu.ca/
centres/business-consulting/index.php

Fronchak Corporate Development Inc.
23-500 Fairway Rd. S, Ste. 209
Kitchener, ON, Canada N2C 1X3
(519)896-9950
E-mail: mike@fronchak.com
Website: http://www.fronchak.com

Eigenmacht Crackower
345 Renfrew Dr., Ste. 202
Markham, ON, Canada L3R 9S9
(905)305-9722
(905)607-6468
Fax: (905)305-9502
E-mail: jack@eigenmachtcrackower.com
Website: http://www.eigenmachtcrackower
.com

JPL Consulting
236 Millard Ave.
Newmarket, ON, Canada L3Y 1Z2
(416)606-9124

E-mail: jplbiz1984@gmail.com
Website: http://www.jplbiz.ca

Roger Hay & Associates Ltd.
1272 Elgin Cres.
Oakville, ON, Canada L6H 2J7
(416)848-0997
E-mail: info@rogerhay.ca
Website: http://www.rogerhay.ca

Comgate Engineering Ltd.
236 1st Ave.
Ottawa, ON, Canada K1S 2G6
(613)235-4778
Fax: (613)248-4644
E-mail: info_eng@comgate.com
Website: http://www.comgate.com

PMC Training
858 Bank St., Ste. 109
Ottawa, ON, Canada K1S 3W3
(613)234-2020
Fax: (613)569-1333
E-mail: info@pmctraining.com
Website: http://pmctraining.com/

Arbex Forest Resource Consultants Ltd.
1555 Scotch Line Rd. E
Oxford Mills, ON, Canada K0G 1S0
(613)798-3099
Website: http://www.arbex.ca

G.R. Eagleson Consulting Inc.
69436 Mollard Line
RR3
Parkhill, ON, Canada N0M 2K0
(519)238-2676
Fax: (519)238-1224
E-mail: eagleson@hay.net
Website: http://www.eagleson.com/
consulting

Mark H. Goldberg & Associates Inc.
91 Forest Lane Dr.
Thornhill, ON, Canada L4J 3P2
(905)882-0417
Fax: (905)882-2219
E-mail: info@mhgoldberg.com
Website: http://www.mhgoldberg.com

Petersen Consulting
136 Cedar St. S
Timmons, ON, Canada P4N 2G8
(705)264-5323
E-mail: pcmanage@nt.net
Website: http://www.petersenconsulting.ca

Care Concepts & Communications
21 Spruce Hill Rd.
Toronto, ON, Canada M4E 3G2
(416)420-8840
E-mail: info@cccbizconsultants.com
Website: http://www.cccbizconsultants.com

FHG International Inc.
99 Crown's Ln., 1st Fl.
Toronto, ON, Canada M5R 3P4
(416)402-8000
E-mail: info@fhgi.com
Website: http://www.fhgi.com

KLynn Inc.
6 Bartlett Ave., Ste. 8
Toronto, ON M6H 3E6
Free: 888-717-2220
E-mail: info@klynnbusinessconsulting
.com
Website: www.klynnbusinessconsulting
.com

PWR Health Consultants, Inc.
720 Spadina Ave., Ste. 303
Toronto, ON, Canada M5S 2T9
(416)467-1844
Fax: (416)467-5600
Fax: (416)323-3166
E-mail: ldoupe@pwr.ca
Website: http://www.pwr.ca

Ryerson Consulting Group
575 Bay St., Ste. 2-005
Toronto, ON, Canada M5G 2C5
(416)979-5059
E-mail: info@rcginsight.com
Website: http://www.rcginsight.com

David Trahair CPA, CA
15 Coldwater Rd., Ste. 101
Toronto, ON, Canada M3B 1Y8
(416)420-8840
Fax: (416)385-3813
Website: http://www.trahair.com

Quebec

PGP Consulting
17 Linton
Dollard-des-Ormeaux, QC, Canada H9B
1P2
(514)796-7613
(514)862-5837
Fax: (866)750-0947
E-mail: pierre@pgpconsulting.com
Website: http://www.pgpconsulting.com

Conseil Saint-Paul
400 Blvd. Saint-Martin Ouest, Bureau 121
Laval, QC, Canada H7M 3Y8
(450)664-4442
Fax: (450)664-3631
E-mail: info@spaul.ca
Website: http://spaul.ca

KLynn Inc.
2025 Rue de la Visitation
Montreal, QC H2L 3C8

Free: 888-717-2220
E-mail: info@klynnbusinessconsulting.com
Website: www.klynnbusinessconsulting.com

Komand Consulting Inc.
1250 Rene Levesque Blvd. W, Ste. 2200
Montreal, QC, Canada H3B 4W8
(514)934-9281
E-mail: info@komand.ca
Website: http://www.komand.ca

Lemay-Yates Associates Inc.
2015 Peel St., Ste. 425
Montreal, QC, Canada H3A 1T8
(514)288-6555
E-mail: lya@lya.com
Website: http://www.lya.com

Groupe Dancause Inc.
3175 Chemin des Quatre-Bourgeois, Ste.
375
Quebec, QC, Canada G1W 2K7
(418)681-0268
E-mail: groupe@dancause.net
Website: http://www.dancause.net

Saskatchewan

Abonar Business Consultants Ltd.
3110 8th St. E, Ste. 8B-376
Saskatoon, SK, Canada S7H 0W2
Fax: (866)405-4510
Free: 866-405-4510
E-mail: info@abonarconsultants.com
Website: http://www.abonarconsultants
.com/index.html

Banda Marketing Group
3-1124 8th St. E
Saskatoon, SK, Canada S7H 0S4
(306)343-6100
E-mail: brent.banda@bandagroup.com
Website: http://www.bandagroup.com

Hoggard International
435 McKercher Dr.
Saskatoon, SK, Canada S7H 4G3
(306)374-6747
Fax: (306)653-7252
E-mail: bhoggard@shaw.ca
Website: http://hoggardinternational.com

United states

Alabama

Accounting & Business Consultants Inc.
1711 9th Ave. N
Bessemer, AL 35020
E-mail: tclay@abcconsultants.com
Website:http://www.abcconsultants.com

Accounting & Business Consultants Inc.
4120 2nd Ave. S
Birmingham, AL 35222
(205)425-9000
E-mail: tclay@abcconsultants.com
Website: http://www.abcconsultants.com

MILBO, LLC
2214 3rd Ave. N, Ste. 204
Birmingham, AL 35203
(205)543-0645
Website: http://www.milbollc.com

Jackson Thorton Dothan Office
304 Jamestown Blvd.
Dothan, AL 36301
(334)793-7001
Fax: (334)793-7004
Website: http://www.jacksonthornton.com

Mason, Bearden & Diehl, Inc.
4100 Bob Wallace Ave.
Huntsville, AL 35805
(256)533-0806
Fax: (256)533-7742 fax
E-mail: mbd@mbdaccounting.com
Website: http://www.mbdaccounting.com

SEL & Associates
103 Cabot Circ., Ste. 201
Madison, AL 35758
(256)325-9809
Fax: (256)325-9809
E-mail: steven@stevenlevyassociates.com
Website: http://www.stevenlevyassociates
.com

Jackson Thorton Montgomery Office
200 Commerce St.
Montgomery, AL 36104
(334)834-7660
Fax: (334)956-5090
Website: http://www.jacksonthornton.com

Jackson Thorton Auburn/Opelka Office
100 N 9th St.
Opelika, AL 36801
(334)749-8191
Fax: (334)749-9358
Website: http://www.jacksonthornton.com

Jackson Thorton Prattville Office
310 S Washington St.
Prattville, AL 36067
(334)365-1445
Fax: (334)956-5066
Website: http://www.jacksonthornton.com

Jackson Thorton Wetumpka Office
194 Fort Toulouse
Wetumpka, AL 36092
(334)567-3400

Fax: (334)956-5005
Website: http://www.jacksonthornton.com

Alaska

Agnew::Beck Consulting
441 W 5th Ave., Ste. 202
Anchorage, AK 99501
(907)222-5424
Fax: (907)222-5426
E-mail: admin@agnewbeck.com
Website: http://agnewbeck.com

McDowell Group
1400 W Benson Blvd., Ste. 510
Anchorage, AK 99503
(907)274-3200
Fax: (907)274-3201
E-mail: info@mcdowellgroup.net
Website: http://www.mcdowellgroup.net

The Foraker Group
161 Klevin St., Ste. 101
Anchorage AK 99508
(907)743-1200
Fax: (907)276-5014
Free: 877-834-5003
Website: http://www.forakergroup.org

Consulting Professionals of Alaska
17137 Park Place St.
Eagle River, AK, 99577
(907)694-0105
Fax: (907)694-0107
Website: http://www.cpalaska.com

McDowell Group
9360 Glacier Hwy., Ste. 201
Juneau, AK 99801
(907)586-6126
Fax: (907)586-2673
E-mail: info@mcdowellgroup.net
Website: http://www.mcdowellgroup.net

Sheinberg Associates
1107 W 8th St., Ste. 4
Juneau, AK 99801
(907)586-3141
Fax: (907)586-2331
Website: http://www.sheinbergassociates
.com

Arizona

Comgate Telemanagement Ltd.
428 E Thunderbird Rd., Ste. 133
Phoenix, AZ 85022
(602)485-5708
Fax: (602)485-5709
E-mail: info_telemgmt@comgate.com
Website: http://www.comgate.com

Kalil & Associates, LLC
245 S Plumer Ave., Ste. 16
Tucson, AZ 85719
(520)628-4264
Fax: (520)903-0347
E-mail: info@kalilassociates.com
Website: https://www.kalilassociates.com

California

Cayenne Consulting, LLC
155 N Riverview Dr.
Anaheim Hills, CA 92808
Website: https://www.caycon.com

Fessel International, Inc.
20 E Foothill Blvd., Ste. 128
Arcadia, CA 91006
(626)566-3500
Fax: (626)566-3875
Free: 877-432-8380
Website: http://www.fessel.com/
default.asp

Streamline Planning Consultants
1062 G St. Suite I
Arcata, CA 95521
(707)822-5785
Fax: (707)822-5786
Website: http://streamlineplanning.net

The One Page Business Plan Co.
1798 Fifth St.
Berkeley, CA 94710
(510)705-8400
Fax: (510)705-8403
E-mail: info@onepagebusinessplan.com
Website: http://www.onepagebusinessplan
.com

Business Consulting Group
30 Landing Cir. 300
Chico, CA 95973
(530)864-5980
E-mail: info@bcgca.com
Website: http://www.bcgca.com

Go Jade Solutions
9808 Valgrande Way
Elk Grove, CA 95757
(916)538-7561
E-mail: info@gojadesolutions.com
Website: http://gojadesolutions.com

La Piana Consulting
5858 Horton St., Ste. 272
Emeryville, CA 94608-2007
(510)601-9056
Fax: (510)420-0478
E-mail: info@lapiana.org
Website: http://lapiana.org

Norris Bernstein, CMC
9309 Marina Pacifica Dr. N
Long Beach, CA 90803
(562)493-5458
Fax: (562)493-5459
E-mail: norris@norrisbernstein.com
Website: http://www.norrisbernstein.com

Blue Garnet Associates L.L.C.
8055 W Manchester Ave., Ste. 430
Los Angeles, CA 90293
(310)439-1930
E-mail: hello@bluegarnet.net
Website: http://www.bluegarnet.net

Edeska LLC (dba Go Business Plans)
Bldg. D, Fl. 3
12777 W Jefferson Blvd., Ste. 3119
Los Angeles, CA 90066
Free: 855-546-0037
Website: http://edeska.com

Growthink Inc.
12655 W Jefferson Blvd.
Los Angeles, CA 90045
Free: 800-647-6983
E-mail: services@growthink.com
Website: http://www.growthink.com

Paul Yelder Consulting
3964 Hubert Ave.
Los Angeles, CA 90008-2620
(323)295-7652
E-mail: email: consulting@yelder.com
Website: http://www.yelder.com

BizplanSource
1048 Irvine Ave., Ste. 621
Newport Beach, CA 92660
Free: 888-253-0974
Fax: (800)859-8254
E-mail: info@bizplansource.com
Website: http://www.bizplansource.com

MakeGreenGo!
240 3rd St., Ste. 2A
Oakland, CA 94607
(510)250-9890
Website: http://makegreengo.com

Accessible Business, LLC
18325 Keswick St.
Reseda, CA 91335
(818)264-7830
Free: 800-490-8362
Fax: (818)264-7833
E-mail: info@accessiblebusiness.com
Website: https://www.accessiblebusiness
.com

International Business Partners
8045 Darby Pl.

Reseda, CA 91335
(714)875-3604
E-mail: admin@IBPconsultants.com
Website: http://www.ibpconsultants.com/
home.html

Jackson Law Firm, P.C.
979 Golf Course Dr., Ste. 300
Rohnert Park, CA 94928
(707)584-4529
(707)584-9033
E-mail: shawnjackson@business
developmentattorney.com
Website: http://jacksonlawfirm.net/

Business Performance Consultants
9777 Caminito Joven
San Diego, CA 92131
(858)583-4159
E-mail: larrymiller@businessper
formanceconsultants.com
Website: http://businessperformance
consultants.com/

The Startup Garage
San Diego, CA 92109
(858)876-4597
E-mail: info@thestartupgarage.com
Website: https://thestartupgarage.com

Venture Builder, Inc.
1286 University Ave., Ste. 315
San Diego, CA 92103
(619)563-1841
Website: http://www.venturebuilderinc.com

Growthink Inc.
55 2nd St., Ste. 570
San Francisco, CA 94105
Free: 800-647-6983
E-mail: services@growthink.com
Website: http://www.growthink.com

San Francisco Management Group
1048 Union St., Ste. 7
San Francisco, CA 94133
(415)775-3405
E-mail: info@sfmanagementgroup.com
Website: http://www.sfmanagement
group.com/

The Wright Consultants
835 Market St.
San Francisco, CA 94105
(415)928-2071
Website: http://www.thewrightconsultants
.com

Business Group
369-B 3rd St., Ste. 387
San Rafael, CA 94901
(415)491-1896

Fax: (415)459-6472
E-mail: mvh@businessgroup.biz
Website: http://www.businessowners
toolbox.com

Manex Inc.
2010 Crow Canyon Pl., Ste. 320
San Ramon, CA 94583
(925)807-5100
Free: 877-336-2639
Website: http://www.manexconsulting
.com

Bargain Business Plan, Inc.
12400 Ventura Blvd., Ste. 658
Studio City, CA 91604
Free: 800-866-9971
Fax: (800)866-9971
E-mail: info@bargainbusinessplan.com
Website: http://www.bargainbusinessplan
.com

**Out of Your Mind...and Into the
Marketplace**
13381 White Sands Dr.
Tustin, CA 92780-4565
(714)544-0248
Fax: (714)730-1414
Free: 800-419-1513
E-mail: lpinson@aol.com
Website: http://www.business-plan.com

Colorado

Comer & Associates, LLC
5255 Holmes Pl.
Boulder, CO 80303
(303)786-7986
E-mail: info@comerassociates.com
Website: http://www.comerassociates.com

McCord Consulting Group
2525 Arapahoe Ave., Ste. 515
Boulder, CO 80302
(720)443-0894
E-mail: nikki@mcconsultgroup.com
Website: http://mcconsultgroup.com/

The Startup Expert
661 Eldorado Blvd. Ste. 623
Broomfield, CO 80021
(303)534-1019
Website: http://thestartupexpert.com/

Ameriwest Business Consultants, Inc.
PO Box 26266
Colorado Springs, CO 80936
(719)380-7096
Fax: (719)380-7096
E-mail: email@abchelp.com
Website: http://www.abchelp.com

GVNW Consulting Inc.
2270 La Montana Way, Ste. 200
Colorado Springs, CO 80918
(719)594-5800
E-mail: jushio@gvnw.com
Website: http://www.gvnw.com

Wilson Hughes Consulting LLC
2100 Humboldt St., Ste. 302
Denver, CO 80205
(303)680-7889
E-mail: bhughescnm@gmail.com
Website: http://wilsonhughesconsulting
.com/

Extelligent Inc.
8400 E Crescent Pky., Ste. 600
Greenwood Village, CO 80111
(720)201-5672
E-mail: clientrelations@extelligent.com
Website: http://www.extelligent.com

The Schallert Group, Inc.
321 Main St.
Longmont, CO 80501
(303)774-6522
Website: http://jonschallert.com/

Vaughn CPA
210 E 29th St.
Loveland, CO 80538
(970)667-2123
E-mail: vaughn@vaughncpa.com
Website: http://vaughncpa.com/
loveland-cpa-firm

Connecticut

Alltis Corp.
PO Box 1292
Farmington, CT 06034-1292
(860)255-7610
Fax: (860)674-8168
E-mail: info@alltis.com
Website: http://www.alltis.com

Christiansen Consulting
56 Scarborough St.
Hartford, CT 06105
(860)586-8265
Fax: (860)233-3420
E-mail:
Francine@ChristiansenConsulting.
com
Website: http://www.christiansenconsulting
.com/

Musevue360
555 Millbrook Rd.
Middletown, CT 06457
(860)463-7722
Fax: (860)346-3013

E-mail: jennifer.eifrig@musevue360.com
Website: http://www.musevue360.com

Kalba International Inc.
116 McKinley Ave.
New Haven, CT 06515
(203)397-2199
Fax: (781)240-2657
E-mail: kas.kalba@kalbainternational
.com
Website: http://www.kalbainternational
.com

Delaware

Doherty & Associates
Stoney Batter Office Bldg.
5301 Limestone Rd., Ste. 100
Wilmington, DE 19808
(302)239-3500
Fax: (302)239-3600
E-mail: info@dohertyandassociates.com
Website: http://www.dohertyandassociates
.com

Gunnip & Co. LLP
Little Falls Centre 2
2751 Centerville Rd., Ste. 300
Wilmington, DE 19808-1627
(302)225-5000
Fax: (302)225-5100
E-mail: info@gunnip.com
Website: http://www.gunnip.com

Master, Sidlow & Associates, P.A.
2002 W 14th St.
Wilmington, DE 19806
(302)652-3480
Fax: (302)656-8778
E-mail: imail@mastersidlow.com
Website: http://www.mastersidlow.com

Florida

BackBone, Inc.
20404 Hacienda Ct.
Boca Raton, FL 33498
(561)470-0965
Fax: (561)908-4038
E-mail: che@backboneinc.com
Website: http://www.backboneinc.com

Dr. Eric H. Shaw & Associates
500 S Ocean Blvd., Ste. 2105
Boca Raton, FL 33432
(561)338-5151
E-mail: ericshaw@bellsouth.net
Website: http://www.ericshaw.com

Professional Planning Associates, Inc.
1440 NE 35th St.
Oakland Park, FL 33334

(954)829-2523
Fax: (954)537-7945
E-mail: mgoldstein@proplana.com
Website: http://proplana.com

Alfred Endeio LLC
8700 Maitland Summit Blvd., Ste. 214
Orlando, FL 32810
Website: http://www.alfredeconsulting.com

Hughes Consulting Services LLC
522 Alternate 19
Palm Harbor, FL 34683
(727)631-2536
Fax: (727)474-9818
Website: http://consultinghughes.com

Strategic Business Planning Co.
PO Box 821006
South Florida, FL 33082
(954)704-9100
Fax: (888)704-3290
Free: 888-704-9100
E-mail: info@SBPlan.com
Website: http://www.ipplan.com

Cohen & Grieb, P.A.
500 N Westshore Blvd., Ste. 700
Tampa, FL 33609
(813)739-7200
Fax: (813)282-7225
E-mail: info@cohengrieb.com
Website: http://www.cohengrieb.com/
contact

Dufresne Consulting Group, Inc.
13014 N Dale Mabry, Ste. 175
Tampa, FL 33618-2808
(813)264-4775
E-mail: info@dcgconsult.com
Website: http://www.dcgconsult.com

Reliance Consulting, LLC
13940 N Dale Mabry Hwy.
Tampa, FL, 33618
(813)931-7258
Fax: (813)931-5555
Website: http://www.reliancecpa.com

Tunstall Consulting LLC
13153 N Dale Mabry Hwy., Ste. 200
Tampa, FL 33618
(813)968-4461
Fax: (813)961-2315
E-mail: info@tunstallconsulting.com
Website: http://www.tunstallconsulting
.com

The Business Planning Institute, LLC.
580 Village Blvd., Ste. 150
West Palm Beach, FL 33409
(561)236-5533
Fax: (561)689-5546

E-mail: info@bpiplans.com
Website: http://www.bpiplans.com

Georgia

CHScottEnterprises
227 Sandy Springs Pl. NE, Ste. 720702
Atlanta, GA 30358-9032
(770)356-4808
E-mail: info@chscottenterprises.com
Website: http://www.chscottenterprises
.com

Fountainhead Consulting Group, Inc.
3970 Old Milton Pkwy., Ste. 210
Atlanta, GA 30005
(770)642-4220
Website: http://www.fountainhead
consultinggroup.com

PSMJ Resources Inc.
2746 Rangewood Dr.
Atlanta, GA 30345
(770)723-9651
Fax: (815)461-7478
Free: 800-537-7765
Website: http://www.psmj.com

Scullyworks, LLC
PO Box 8641
Atlanta, GA 31106-0641
(404)310-9499
Website: http://www.scullyworks.com

Theisen Consulting LLC
865 Waddington Ct.
Atlanta, GA 30350
(770)396-7344
Fax: (404)393-3527
E-mail: terri@theisenconsulting.com
Website: http://www.theisenconsulting
.com

Sterling Rose Consulting Corp.
722 Collins Hill Rd., Ste. H-307
Lawrenceville, GA 30046
(678)892-8528
E-mail: info@sterlingroseconsulting
corp.com
Website: http://www.sterlingroseconsulting
corp.com

Lemongrass Consulting, Inc.
951 Gettysburg Way
Locust Grove, GA 30248
(678)235-5901
E-mail: chamilton@lemongrassplanning
.com
Website: http://lemongrassplanning.com

Samet Consulting
4672 Oxford Cir.
Macon, GA 31210

(478)757-1070
Fax: (478)757-1984
Website: http://sametconsulting.com/

Hawaii

Maui Venture Consulting LLC
PO Box 81515
Haiku, HI 96708
(808)269-1031
E-mail: df@mauiventure.net
Website: http://www.mauiventure.net

Business Plans Hawaii
3059 Maigret St.
Honolulu, HI 96816
(808)735-5597
E-mail: valerie@
businessplanshawaii.com
Website: http://www.businessplanshawaii
.com

**John V. McCoy Communications
Consultant**
425 Ena Rd., Apt. 1204-B
Honolulu, HI 96815
(510)219-2276
E-mail: mccoy.jv@gmail.com
Website: http://www.busplan.com

Idaho

Agnew::Beck Consulting
802 W Bannock St., Ste. 803
Boise, ID 83702
(208)342-3976
E-mail: admin@agnewbeck.com
Website: http://agnewbeck.com

Kairosys
16645 Plum Rd.
Caldwell, ID 83607
(208)454-0086
E-mail: support@kairosys.net
Website: http://kairosys.net

Illinois

Midwest Business Consulting, LLC
Midway Corporate Ctr.
6640 S Cicero Ave., Ste. 204
Bedford Park, IL 60638
(708)571-3401
Fax: (708)571-3409
E-mail: inquiries@mbconsultingco.com
Website: https://www.mbconsultingco.com

Anchor Advisors, Ltd.
5366 N Elston Ave., Ste. 203
Chicago, IL 60630
(773)282-7677
Website: http://anchoradvisors.com

Brighton Windsor Group, LLC
Chicago, IL 60602
Free: 888-781-1304
E-mail: hello@brightonwindsor.com
Website: http://brightonwindsor.com

Ground Floor Partners, Inc.
150 N Michigan Ave., Ste. 2800
Chicago, IL 60601
(312)726-1981
Website: http://groundfloorpartners.com

Midwest Business Consulting, LLC
Chicago Temple Bldg.
77 W Washington, Ste. 718
Chicago, IL 60602
(312)415-0340
Fax: (312)994-8554
E-mail: inquiries@mbconsultingco.com
Website: https://www.mbconsultingco.com

Gold Consulting, Inc.
18 Exmoor Ct.
Highwood, IL 60040
(847)433-8141
Fax: (847)433-2446
E-mail: ron@goldconsultinginc.com
Website: http://goldconsultinginc.com

Francorp
20200 Governors Dr.
Olympia Fields, IL 60461
(708)481-2900
Free: 800-372-6244
E-mail: francorp@aol.com
Website: http://www.francorp.com

MD Consultants of America, Inc.
6738 N Frostwood Pkwy.
Peoria, IL 61615
Free: 877-272-1631
Fax: (309)414-0298
E-mail: info@mdconsultantus.com
Website: http://www.mdconsultantus.com

Quiet Storm Enterprises Ltd.
3701 Trilling Ave., Ste. 201
Rockford IL 61103-2157
(815)315-0146
Free: 877-958-0160
E-mail: info@qsenterprisesltd.net
Website: http://www.qsenterprisesltd.net

Public Sector Consulting
5718 Barlow Rd.
Sherman, IL 62684
(217)629-9869
Fax: (217)629-9732
E-mail: mail@gotopsc.com
Website: http://www.gotopsc.com

GVNW Illinois
3220 Pleasant Run, Ste. A
Springfield, IL 62711
(217)698-2700
E-mail: jushio@gvnw.com
Website: http://www.gvnw.com

Indiana

Compass CPA Group
435 Ann St.
Fort Wayne, IN 46774
(260)749-2200
Free: 866-788-9789
E-mail: information@compasscpa
group.com
Website: http://www.compasscpagroup
.com

Cox and Co.
3930 Mezzanine Dr. Ste A
Lafayette, IN, 47905
(765)449-4495
Fax: (765)449-1218
E-mail: stan@coxpa.com
Website: http://coxcpa.com

Kimmel Consulting LLC
136 S 9th St Ste 320
Noblesville, IN 46060
(317)773-3810
Fax: (317)770-8787
E-mail: info@kimmelconsultingllc.com
Website: http://www.kimmelconsultingllc
.com

Iowa

**TD&T CPAs and Advisors, P.C.
Burlington Office**
323 Jefferson St.
Burlington, IA 52601
(319)753-9877
Fax: (319)753-1156
E-mail: briani@tdtpc.com
Website: http://www.tdtpc.com/
index.php

**TD&T CPAs and Advisors, P.C. Cedar
Rapids Office**
1700 42nd St. NE
Cedar Rapids, IA 52402
(319)393-2374
Fax: (319)393-2375
E-mail: amandal@tdtpc.com
Website: http://www.tdtpc.com/
index.php

Terry, Lockridge and Dunn
210 2nd St. SE
Cedar Rapids, IA 52407
(319)364-2945

Fax: (319)362-4487
E-mail: info@tld-inc.com
Website: http://www.tld-inc.com

TD&T CPAs and Advisors, P.C. Centerville Office

101 W Van Buren St.
Centerville, IA 52544
(641)437-4296
Fax: (641)437-1574
E-mail: markl@tdtpc.com
Website: http://www.tdtpc.com/index.php

TD&T CPAs and Advisors, P.C. Fairfield Office

2109 W Jefferson Ave.
Fairfield, IA 52556
(641)472-6171
Fax: (641)472-6632
E-mail: jodik@tdtpc.com
Website: http://www.tdtpc.com/index.php

Steve Meyer Consulting LLC

304 E Maple
Garrison, IA 52229
(319)477-5041
E-mail: gfdchief@netins.net
Website: http://www.stevemeyerconsulting.com/

Terry, Lockridge and Dunn

2225 Mormon Trek Blvd.
Iowa City, IA 52246
(319)339-4884
Fax: (319)358-9113
E-mail: info@tld-inc.com
Website: http://www.tld-inc.com

TD&T CPAs and Advisors, P.C. Mount Pleasant Office

204 N Main
Mount Pleasant, IA 52641
(319)385-9718
Fax: (319)385-2612
E-mail: tomh@tdtpc.com
Website: http://www.tdtpc.com/index.php

TD&T CPAs and Advisors, P.C. Muscatine Office

500 Cedar St.
Muscatine, IA 52761
(563)264-2727
Fax: (563)263-7777
E-mail: vickib@tdtpc.com;
dennyt@tdtpc.com
Website: http://www.tdtpc.com/index.php

TD&T CPAs and Advisors, P.C. Oskaloosa Office

317 High Ave. E
Oskaloosa, IA 52577
(641)672-2523
Fax: (641)673-7453
E-mail: joshb@tdtpc.com
Website: http://www.tdtpc.com/index.php

TD&T CPAs and Advisors, P.C. Ottumwa Office

117 S Court
Ottumwa, IA 52501
(641)683-1823
Fax: (641)683-1868
E-mail: dougm@tdtpc.com
Website: http://www.tdtpc.com/index.php

TD&T CPAs and Advisors, P.C. Pella Office

1108 Washington St.
Pella, IA 50219
(641)628-9411
Fax: (641)628-1321
E-mail: justinp@tdtpc.com
Website: http://www.tdtpc.com/index.php

Murk-n-T, Inc.

209 Rose Ave. SW
Swisher, IA 52338
(319)857-4638
Fax: (319)857-4648
E-mail: info@murknt.com
Website: http://www.murknt.com/index.php

TD&T CPAs and Advisors, P.C. West Des Moines Office

1240 Office Plaza Dr.
West Des Moines, IA 50266
(515)657-5800
Fax: (515)657-5801
E-mail: davef@tdtpc.com
Website: http://www.tdtpc.com/index.php

Kansas

Nail CPA Firm, LLC
4901 W 136th St.
Leawood, KS 66224
(913)663-2500
E-mail: info@nailcpafirm.com
Website: http://www.nailcpafirm.com

Shockey Consulting Services, LLC
12351 W 96th Ter., Ste. 107
Lenexa, KS 66215
(913)248-9585

E-mail: solutions@shockeyconsulting.com
Website: http://www.shockeyconsulting.com/

Aspire Business Development
10955 Lowell Ave., Ste. 400
Overland Park, KS 66210
(913)660-9400
Free: 888-548-1504
Website: http://www.aspirekc.com

Wichita Technology Corp.
7829 E Rockhill Rd., Ste. 307
Wichita, KS 67206
(316)651-5900
Free: 866-810-6671
E-mail: wtc@wichitatechnology.com
Website: http://www.wichitatechnology.com

Kentucky

BizFixes
277 E High St.
Lexington, KY 40507
(859)552-5151
Website: http://bizfixes.com

Louisiana

Cathy Denison, PhD & Associates Professional Services, Inc.
9655 Perkins Rd., Ste. C-123
Baton Rouge, LA 70810
(337)502-1911
E-mail: cdenison@denisonassociates.com
Website: http://www.denisonassociates.com

Rabalais Business Consulting
209 Rue Louis XIV, Ste. B
Lafayette, LA 70508
(337)981-2577
Fax: (337)981-2579
Website: http://rabbiz.com

Terk Consulting Business Plans
3819A Magazine St.
New Orleans, LA 70115
(504)237-0480
E-mail: info@terkconsulting.com
Website: https://terkconsulting.com

Maine

PFBF CPAs Bath Office
259 Front St.
Bath, ME 04530
(207)371-8002
Fax: (207)877-7407
E-mail: mail@pfbf.com
Website: http://www.pfbf.com

John Rust Consulting

PO Box 459

Hampden, ME 04444

(207)337-5858

E-mail: john@johnrustconsulting.com

Website: http://www.johnrustconsulting
.com

PFBF CPAs Oakland Office

46 First Park Dr.

Oakland, ME 04963

(207)873-1603

Fax: (207)877-7407

E-mail: mail@pfbf.com

Website: http://www.pfbf.com

Maryland

**Maryland Capital Enterprises, Inc.
Baltimore Area Office**

333 N Charles St.

Baltimore, MD 21201

(410)546-1900

Fax: (410)546-9718

E-mail: info@marylandcapital.org

Website: http://www.marylandcapital.org

Burdeshaw Associates Ltd.

4701 Sangamore Rd.

Bethesda, MD 20816

(301)229-5800

E-mail: jstacy@burdeshaw.com

Website: http://www.burdeshaw.com

Jacoby

2304 Frederick Rd.

Catonsville, MD 21228

(410)744-3900

Fax: (410)747-7850

Free: 877-799-GROW

E-mail: info@artjacoby.com

Black Rock Accounting & Consulting

13424 Burnt Woods Pl.

Germantown, MD 20874

(301)928-7600

Fax: (301)515-1840

E-mail: mike@blackrockaccounting
.com

Website: http://www.blackrockaccounting
.com

L&H Business Consulting

1212 York Rd., Ste. C-300

Lutherville, MD 21093

(410)828-4177

Fax: (410)321-1588

E-mail: info@lhbusinessconsulting.com

Website: http://www.lhbusinessconsulting
.com

**Maryland Capital Enterprises, Inc.
Eastern Shore Office**

144 E Main St.

Salisbury, MD 21801

(410)546-1900

Fax: (410)546-9718

E-mail: info@marylandcapital.org

Website: http://www.marylandcapital.org

Massachusetts

The Carrot Project

89 South St.

Boston, MA 02111

(617)674-2371

E-mail: info@thecarrotproject.org

Website: http://www.thecarrotproject
.org/home

Julia Shanks Food Consulting

37 Tremont St.

Cambridge, MA 02139

(617)945-8718

E-mail: info@juliashanks.com

Website: http://www.juliashanks.com

CYTO Consulting

363 N Emerson Rd.

Lexington, MA 02420

(339)707-0767

E-mail: info@cytoconsulting.com

Website: http://www.cytoconsulting.com

Foxboro Consulting Group Inc.

36 Lancashire Dr.

Mansfield, MA 02048

(774)719-2236

E-mail: moreinfo@foxboro-consulting.com

Website: http://www.foxboro-consulting
.com

Dahn Consulting Group

Newburyport, MA 01950

(978)314-1722

E-mail: info@dahnconsulting.com

Website: http://www.dahnconsulting
.com

PSMJ Resources Inc.

10 Midland Ave.

Newton, MA 02458

(617)965-0055

Fax: (617)965-5152

Free: 800-537-7765

Website: http://www.psmj.com

Spark Business Consulting

167 Washington St.

Norwell, MA 02061

(781)871-1003

Website: http://sparkbusinessconsulting
.com

Bruno P.C.

57 Obery St., Ste. 4

Plymouth, MA 02360

(508)830-0800

Fax: (508)830-0801

E-mail: info@BrunoAccountants.com

Website: https://www.brunoaccountants
.com

Non Profit Capital Management

41 Main St.

Sterling, MA 01564

(781)933-6726

Fax: (978)563-1007

E-mail: info@npcm.com

Website: http://www.npcm.com/

Michigan

Aimattech Consulting LLC

568 Woodway Ct., Ste. 1

Bloomfield Hills, MI 48302-1572

(248)540-3758

Fax: (775)305-4755

E-mail: dweaver@aimattech.com

Website: http://www.aimattech.com

**BBC Entrepreneurial Training &
Consulting LLC**

12671 E Old U.S. 12

Chelsea, MI 48118

(734)930-9741

Fax: (734)930-6629

E-mail: info@bbcetc.com

Website: http://www.bioconsultants.com

LifeLine Business Consulting

1400 Woodbridge St., 4th Fl.

Detroit, MI 48207

(313)965-3155

E-mail: hello@thelifelinenetwork.com

Website: https://thelifelinenetwork.com

TL Cramer Associates LLC

1788 Broadstone Rd.

Grosse Pointe Woods, MI 48236

(313)332-0182

E-mail: info@tlcramerassociates.com

Website: http://www.tlcramerassociates
.com

Jackson Small Business Support Center

950 W Monroe St., Ste. G-100

Jackson, MI 49202

(517)796-8151

Website: http://www.smallbusiness
supportcenter.com

Tedder Whitlock Consulting

17199 N Laurel Park Dr.

Livonia, MI 48152

(734)542-4200

Fax: (734)542-4201
E-mail: info@tedderwhitlock.com
Website: http://www.tedderwhitlock.com

MarketingHelp Inc.
6647 Riverwoods Ct. NE
Rockford, MI 49341
(616)856-0148
Website: http://www.mktghelp.com

Lucid Business Strategies
8187 Rhode Dr., Ste. D
Shelby Township, MI 48317
(586)254-0095
E-mail: results@lucidbusiness.com
Website: http://www.lucidbusiness.com

QT Business Solution
24901 Northwestern Hwy., Ste. 305
Southfield, MI 48075
(248)416-1755
Free: 877-859-6768
E-mail: info@qtbizsolutions.com
Website: http://qtbizsolutions.com

Cool & Associates Inc.
921 Village Green Ln., Ste. 1068
Waterford, MI 48328
(248)683-1130
E-mail: info@cool-associates.com
Website: http://www.cool-associates.com

Griffioen Consulting Group, Inc.
6689 Orchard Lake Rd., Ste. 295
West Bloomfield, MI 48322
Free: 888-262-5850
Fax: (248)855-4084
Website: http://www.griffioenconsulting
.com

NooJoom Immigration Services & Business Plan
35253 Warren Rd.
Westland, MI 48185
(734)728-5755
E-mail: wadak@noojoom.org
Website: http://www.noojoomimmigration
services.com

Minnesota

Devoted Business Development
2434 E 117th St., Ste. 100
Burnsville, Minnesota
(952) 582-4669
E-mail: info@devoted-business.com
Website: http://devoted-business.com

Community & Economic Development Associates (CEDA)
1500 S Hwy. 52
Chatfield, MN 55923
(507)867-3164

E-mail: ron.zeigler@cedausa.com
Website: https://www.cedausa.com

Metropolitan Consortium of Community Developers (MCCD)
Open to Business Program
3137 Chicago Ave.
Minneapolis, MN 55407
(612)789-7337
Fax: (612)822-1489
E-mail: info@opentobusinessmn.org
Website: http://www.opentobusinessmn
.org

Metropolitan Economic Development Association (MEDA)
250 2nd Ave. S, Ste. 106
Minneapolis, MN 55401
(612)332-6332
E-mail: info@meda.net
Website: http://meda.net

WomenVenture
2021 E Hennepin Ave., Ste. 200
Minneapolis, MN 55413
(612)224-9540
Fax: (612)200-8369
E-mail: info@womenventure.org
Website: https://www.womenventure.org/
index.html

Mississippi

The IRON Network, LLC
1636 Popps Ferry Rd., Ste. 201
Biloxi, MS 39532
(412)336-8807
E-mail: sales@theironcom.com
Website: http://theironcom.com/
services/business-consulting

Richardson's Writing Service
3285 Squirrel Lake Rd.
Sledge, MS 38670
(662)326-3996
Website: http://www.richws.com

Missouri

Taylor Management Group, LLC (TMG)
PO Box 50155
Clayton, MO 63015
(314)488-1566
Website: http://taymg.com

Stuff
316 W 63rd St.
Kansas City, MO 64113
(816)361-8222
E-mail: sloaneandcasey@pursue
goodstuff.com

Website: http://www.pursuegoodstuff.com

Westphal-Kelpe Consulting Inc.
4050 Broadway, Ste. 201
Kansas City, MO 64111
(816)931-7141
Fax: (816)931-7180
E-mail: info@wkcrestaurants.com
Website: http://www.westphal-kelpe.com

Shockey Consulting Services, LLC
441 Alice Ave.
Kirkwood, MO 66122
(314)497-3126
E-mail: solutions@shockeyconsulting.com
Website: http://www.shockeyconsulting
.com/

Sanford, Lea & Associates
1655 S Enterprise Ave., Ste. B-4
Springfield, MO 65804
(417)886-2220
Fax: (417)886-3979
E-mail: david@adifferentcpa.com
Website: https://www.adifferentcpa.com

EMD Consulting
11111 Conway Rd.
Saint Louis, MO 63131
(314)692-7551
E-mail: info@emdconsulting.com
Website: http://www.emdconsulting.com

M.A. Birsinger & Company, LLC
2464 Taylor Rd., Ste. 106
Wildwood, MO 63040
(314)249-7076
E-mail: brook@mabirsinger.com
Website: http://www.mabirsinger.com

Nebraska

McDermott & Miller, P.C.
2722 S Locust St.
Grand Island, NE 68802
(308)382-7850
Fax: (308)382-7240
E-mail: nsaale@mmcpas.com
Website: http://www.mmcpas.com

McDermott & Miller, P.C.
747 N Burlington Ave., Ste. 401
Hastings, NE 68902
(402)462-4154
Fax: (402)462-5057
E-mail: nsaale@mmcpas.com
Website: http://www.mmcpas.com

McDermott & Miller, P.C.
404 E 25th St.
Kearney, NE 68848
(308)234-5565
Fax: (308)234-2990

E-mail: nsaale@mmcpas.com
Website: http://www.mmcpas.com

Lincoln Partnership for Economic Development (LPED)
3 Landmark Centre
1128 Lincoln Mall, Ste. 100
Lincoln, NE 68508
(402)436-2350
E-mail: info@selectlincoln.org
Website: http://www.selectlincoln.org

Farm Credit Services of America
5015 S 118th St.
Omaha, NE 68137
Free: 800-884-FARM
Website: https://www.fcsamerica.com

McDermott & Miller, P.C.
11602 W Center Rd., Ste. 125
Omaha, NE 68144
(402)391-1207
Fax: (402)391-3424
E-mail: nsaale@mmcpas.com
Website: http://www.mmcpas.com

Nebraska Credit Union League (NCUL)
4885 S 118th St., Ste. 150
Omaha, NE 68137
(402)333-9331
Fax: (402)333-9431
Free: 800-950-4455
E-mail: ssullivan@nebrcul.org
Website: http://www.nebrcul.org

Steier & Prchal, Ltd.
1015 N 98th St., Ste. 100
Omaha, NE 68114
(402)390-9090
Fax: (402)505-5044
E-mail: info@steiertax.com
Website: http://www.steiertax.com/
bizplan.php

Nevada

Anderson Business Advisors, PLLC
3225 McLeod Dr., Ste. 100
Las Vegas, NV 89121
Free: 800-706-4741
Fax: (702)664-0545
E-mail: info@andersonadvisors.com
Website: https://andersonadvisors.com

Stone Law Offices, Ltd.
3295 N Fort Apache Rd., Ste. 150
Las Vegas, NV 89129
Free: 877-800-3424
Fax: (702)998-0443
Website: http://nvestateplan.com

Wise Business Plans
7251 W Lake Mead Blvd., Ste. 300

Las Vegas, NV 89128
Free: 800-496-1056 (United States)
Free: 702-562-4247 (International)
E-mail: info@wisebusinessplans.com
Website: https://wisebusinessplans.com

Drew Aguilar, CPA
1663 Hwy. 395, Ste. 201
Minden, NV 89423
(775)782-7874
Fax: (775)782-8374
E-mail: drew@carsonvalleyaccounting
.com
Website: http://www.carsonvalley
accounting.com

Thunder Vick & Co.
1325 Airmotive Way, Ste. 125
Reno, NV 89502
(775)323-4440
Fax: (775)323-8977
E-mail: admin@thunderrandcpa.com
Website: http://www.thundervickcpa
.com

New Hampshire

HJ Marshall Associates
136 Sewalls Falls Rd.
Concord, NH 03301
(603)224-7073
E-mail: franmarshall@comcast.net
Website: http://www.hjmarshallassociates
.com

Rodger O. Howells, LLC
6 Loudon Rd., Ste. 205
Concord, New Hampshire 03301
(603)224-3224
Free: 877-224-3224
E-mail: info@rhowellsconsulting.com
Website: http://www.rhowellsconsulting
.com

Nathan Wechsler & Co.
70 Commercial St., 4th Fl.
Concord, NH 03301
(603)224-5357
Fax: (603)224-3792
Website: http://www.nathanwechsler
.com

Kieschnick Consulting Services
9 Woodland Rd.
Dover, NH 03820
(603)749-2922
E-mail: peggy@kieschnickconsulting.com
Website: http://www.kieschnickconsulting
.com

Trojan Consulting Group LLC
PO Box 27

Dover, NH 03821
(603)343-1707
E-mail: MNT@TrojanConsultingGroup
.com
Website: http://trojanconsultinggroup.com

Executive Service Corps (ESC)
80 Locke Rd.
Hampton, NH 03842
(603)926-0752
Website: http://www.nonprofit-
consultants.org

Hannah Grimes Center for Entrepreneurship
25 Roxbury St.
Keene, NH 03431
(603)352-5063
Fax: (603)352-5538
E-mail: info@hannahgrimes.com
Website: https://www.hannahgrimes
.com/

Nathan Wechsler & Co.
59 Emerald St.
Keene, NH 03431
(603)357-7665
Fax: (603)358-6800
Website: http://www.nathanwechsler
.com

Nathan Wechsler & Co.
44 School St.
Lebanon, NH 03766
(603)448-2650
Fax: (603)448-2476
Website: http://www.nathanwechsler
.com

Blue Ribbon Consulting, LDO, LLC
PO Box 435
New Ipswich, NH 03071
(603)878-1694
E-mail: lisa@blueribbonconsulting.com
Website: www.blueribbonconsulting.com

Dare Mighty Things, LLC
1 New Hampshire Ave., Ste. 125
Portsmouth, NH 03801
(603)431-4331
Fax: (603)431-4332
E-mail: info@daremightythings.com
Website: http://www.daremightythings
.com

New Jersey

Huffman & Huffman LLC
Changebridge Plaza
2 Changebridge Rd., Ste. 204
Montville, NJ 07045
(973)334-2600

Fax: (973)334-2627
E-mail: jhuffman@huffmancompany.com
Website: http://www.huffmancompany
.com

New Venture Design
Sperro Corporate Ctr.
2 Skyline Dr.
Montville, NJ 07045
(973)331-0022
Fax: (973)335-2656
Free: 866-639-3527
E-mail: info@newventuredesign.com
Website: http://www.newventuredesign
.com

Patterson & Associates LLC
Glendale Executive Campus
1000 White Horse Rd., Ste. 304
Voorhees, NJ 08043-4409
(856)435-2700
Fax: (856)435-1190
E-mail: info@pattersonassociatesllc.com
Website: http://www.pattersonassociatesllc
.com

New Mexico

Hinkle + Landers, P.C.
2500 9th St. NW
Albuquerque, NM 87102
(505)883-8788
Fax: (505)883-8797
E-mail: info@HL-cpas.com
Website: http://www.hl-cpas.com

Vaughn CPA
6605 Uptown Blvd., Ste. 370
Albuquerque, NM 87110
(505)828-0900
E-mail: vaughn@vaughncpa.com
Website: http://vaughncpa.com

WESST
WESST Enterprise Center
609 Broadway Blvd. NE
Albuquerque, NM 87102
(505)246-6900
Fax: (505)243-3035
Free: 800-GO-WESST
Website: https://www.wesst.org

WESST Farmington
San Juan College Quality Center for
Business
5101 College Blvd., Ste. 5060
Farmington, NM 87402
(505)566-3715
Fax: (505)566-3698
Website: https://www.wesst.org/farmington

WESST Las Cruces
221 N Main St., #104a
Las Cruces, NM 88001
(575)541-1583
Website: https://www.wesst.org/las-cruces

WESST Rio Rancho
New Mexico Bank & Trust Bldg.
4001 Southern Blvd. SE, Ste. B
Rio Rancho, NM 87124-2069
(505)892-1238
Fax: (505)892-6157
Website: https://www.wesst.org/rio-rancho

WESST Roswell
Bank of America Bldg.
500 N Main St., Ste. 700
Roswell, NM 88201
Fax: (575)624-9850
Free: 575-624-9845
Website: https://www.wesst.org/roswell

Hinkle + Landers, P.C.
404 Brunn School Rd., Bldg. B
Santa Fe, NM 87505
(505)883-8788
Fax: (505)883-8797
E-mail: info@HL-cpas.com
Website: http://www.hl-cpas.com

WESST Santa Fe
Santa Fe Business Incubator
3900 Paseo del Sol, Ste. 351
Santa Fe, NM 87507
(505)474-6556
Fax: (505)474-6687
Website: https://www.wesst.org/santa-fe

New York

Key Accounting of New York
2488 Grand Concourse, Ste. 320B
Bronx, NY 10458
(718)584-8097
Fax: (866)496-5624
E-mail: info@keyaccnewyork.com
Website: http://keyaccnewyork.com

Soundview Business Consulting
53 Prospect Park W, Ste. 4A
Brooklyn, NY 11215
(718)499-0809
Fax: (718)499-0829
E-mail: brendan@soundviewfirm.com
Website: http://www.soundviewfirm.com

Addenda Solutions
5297 Parkside Dr., Ste. 412
Canandaigua, NY 14424
(585)394-4950
Free: 888-851-0414
Website: http://addendasolutions.com

Aspire Consulting, Ltd.
1 Horseshoe Dr.
Hyde Park, NY 12538
(845)803-0438
Fax: (845)229-8262
E-mail: info@AspireAdvantage.com
Website: http://www.aspireadvantage
.com/index.html

Capacity Business Consulting
3 Wallkill Ave.
Montgomery, NY 12549
(845)764-9484
E-mail: info@capacityconsultinginc
.com
Website: http://www.capacitybusiness
consulting.com

Growthink Inc.
27 Radio Circle Dr., Ste. 202
Mount Kisco, NY 10549
Free: 800-647-6983
E-mail: services@growthink.com
Website: http://www.growthink.com

Gershon Consulting
833 Broadway, 2nd Fl.
New York, NY 10003
Free: 800-701-0176
E-mail: info@gershonconsulting.com
Website: http://www.gershonconsulting
.com

New York Business Consultants LLC
Chrysler Bldg.
405 Lexington Ave.
New York, NY 10174
(315)572-1938
Fax: (888)201-9524
Free: 800-481-2707
E-mail: info@newyorkbusiness
consultants.com
Website: http://www.newyorkbusiness
consultants.com/index.html

The Wright Consultants
394 Broadway
New York, NY 10013
(415)928-2071
Website: http://www.thewrightconsultants
.com

Addenda Solutions
1100 University Ave., Ste. 122
Rochester, NY 14607
(585)461-2654
Free: 888-851-0414
Website: http://addendasolutions.com

Addenda Solutions
126 Kiwassa Rd.
Saranac Lake, NY 12983

(518)891-1681
Free: 888-851-0414
Website: http://addendasolutions.com

North Carolina

Birds Eye Business Planning & Adventures
153 S Lexington Ave.
Asheville, NC 28801
(828)367-7248
E-mail: info@birdseye.info
Website: http://www.birdseye.info

Mountain BizWorks
153 S Lexington Ave.
Asheville, NC 28801
(828)253-2834
Free: 855-296-0048
E-mail: info@mountainbizworks.org
Website: https://www.mountainbizworks
.org

Allied Tax & Accounting Consultants, LLC
5550 77 Center Dr., Ste. 245
Charlotte, NC 28217
(704)676-1882
Fax: (704)676-1884
Free: 888-849-5119
E-mail: help@alliedtaxaccounting.com
Website: http://www.alliedtaxaccounting
.com/services/business-consulting

Brewery Business Plan
9205 Cub Run Dr.
Concord, NC 28027
(704)960-4032
Website: https://brewerybusinessplan.com

EMD Consulting
140 Foothills Dr.
Hendersonville, NC 28792
E-mail: info@emdconsulting.com
Website: http://www.emdconsulting.com

Anagard Business Consulting, LLC
9360 Falls of Neuse Rd., Ste. 205
Raleigh, NC 27615
(919)876-1314
E-mail: info@ANAGARD.com
Website: http://www.anagard.com/
index.html

Davis Group, PA, CPAs
640 Statesville Blvd., Ste. 1
Salisbury, NC 28145-1307
(704)636-1040
Fax: (704)637-3084
E-mail: gary@dgcpa.com
Website: https://www.dgcpa.com/
business-advisory

North Dakota

Center for Innovation
Ina Mae Rude Entrepreneur Ctr.
4200 James Ray Dr.
Grand Forks, ND 58203
(701)777-3132
Fax: (701)777-2339
E-mail: info@innovators.net
Website: http://www.innovators.net

Ohio

Brown Consulting Group LLC
7965 North High St., Ste. 130
Columbus, OH 43235
(614)205-5323
E-mail: keith@browngroupcpa.com
Website: http://browngroupcpa.com

Oklahoma

Wymer Brownlee
3650 SE Camelot Dr.
Bartlesville, OK 74006
(918)333-7291
Fax: (918)333-7295
E-mail: info@wymerbrownlee.com
Website: http://www.wymerbrownlee.com

Wymer Brownlee
201 N Grand, Ste. 100
Enid, OK 73701
(580)237-0060
Fax: (580)237-0092
E-mail: info@wymerbrownlee.com
Website: http://www.wymerbrownlee.com

Wymer Brownlee
126 S Main
Fairview, OK 73737
(580)227-4709
Fax: (580)227-2166
E-mail: info@wymerbrownlee.com
Website: http://www.wymerbrownlee.com

Entrepot
5711 E 72nd Ct.
Tulsa, Oklahoma 74136
(918)497-1748
Website: http://www.entrepotusa.com

Wymer Brownlee
7645 E 63rd St., Ste. 120
Tulsa, OK 74133
(918)392-8600
Fax: (918)392-8601
E-mail: info@wymerbrownlee.com
Website: http://www.wymerbrownlee.com

Wymer Brownlee
10936 NW Expressway
Yukon, OK 73099

(405)283-0100
Fax: (405)283-0200
E-mail: info@wymerbrownlee.com
Website: http://www.wymerbrownlee.com

Oregon

Timothy J. Berry
44 W Broadway Ste. 500
Eugene, OR, 97401
(541)683-6162
Website: http://timberry.com/business-
plan-expert

Advanced Trainers & Consultants, LLC (ATAC)
116 SE Hood
Gresham, OR 97080
(503)661-4013
Fax: (503)665-0775
E-mail: info@advancedtrainers.com
Website: http://www.advancedtrainers.com

Alten Sakai & Company LLP
10260 SW Greenburg Rd., Ste. 300
Portland, OR 97223
(503)297-1072
Fax: (503)297-6634
E-mail: info@altensakai.com
Website: http://www.altensakai.com

Pointman Consulting, LLC
1130 SW Morrison
Portland, OR 97205
(503)804-2074
E-mail: noah@pointmanconsulting.com
Website: http://www.pointmanconsulting
.com/index.htm

GVNW Oregon
8050 SW Warm Springs St.
Tualatin, OR 97062
(503)612-4400
E-mail: jrennard@gvnw.com
Website: http://www.gvnw.com

Pennsylvania

Main Line Rail Management, Inc.
116 N Bellevue Ave., Ste. 206
Langhorne, PA 19047
(215)741-6007
Fax: (215)741-6009
E-mail: dsg@voicenet.com
Website: http://www.mlrail.com

Fairmount Ventures, Inc.
2 Penn Ctr.
1500 JFK Blvd., Ste. 1150
Philadelphia, PA 19102
(215)717-2299
E-mail: info@fairmountinc.com
Website: http://fairmountinc.com

RINK Consulting
1420 Locust St., Ste. 31N
Philadelphia, PA 19102
(215)546-5863
Website: http://www.lindarink.com

FlagShip Business Plans and Consulting
2 Gateway Ctr.
?603 Stanwix St., Ste. 1626
Pittsburgh, PA 15222
(412)219-8157
E-mail: info@flagshipbusinessplans.com
Website: http://www.flagshipbusiness
plans.com/page.html

Puerto Rico

Manuel L. Porrata & Associates
898 Muñoz Rivera Ave., Ste. 300
San Juan, PR 00927
(787)765-2140
Fax: (787)754-3285
E-mail: mporrata@manuelporrata.com
Website: http://www.manuelporrata
.com/home.html

Rhode Island

Ledoux, Petruska & Co., Inc.
1006 Charles St.
North Providence, RI 02904
(401)727-8100
Fax: (401)727-8181
E-mail: beancounter@lpcpari.com
Website: http://www.lpcpari.com/
services/business-consulting-and-
solutions

South Carolina

Fluent Decisions, LLC
701 Gervais St., Ste. 150-157
Columbia, SC 29201
(803)748-2933
Website: https://www.fluentdecisions.com

South Dakota

South Dakota Enterprise Institute
Research Park at South Dakota State
University
2301 Research Park Way, Ste. 114
Brookings, SD 57006
(605)697-5015
E-mail: info@sdei.org
Website: http://www.sdei.org

Tennessee

Jackson Thorton Nashville Office
333 Commerce St., Ste. 1050
Nashville, TN 37201

(615)869-2050
Website: http://www.jacksonthornton.com

Texas

Zaetric Business Solutions LLC
27350 Blueberry Hill, Ste. 14
Conroe, TX 77385
(281)298-1878
Fax: (713)621-4885
E-mail: inquiries@zaetric.com
Website: http://www.zaetric.com

Optimus Business Plans
13355 Noel Rd., Ste. 1100
Dallas, TX 75240
(844)760-0903
Website: http://optimusbusinessplans.com

GVNW Texas
1001 Water St., Ste. A-100
Kerrville, TX 78028
(830)896-5200
E-mail: sgatto@gvnw.com
Website: http://www.gvnw.com

Butler Consultants
555 Republic Dr., Ste. 200
Plano, TX 75074
(214)491-4001
E-mail: Info@Financial-Projections.com
Website: http://contact.financial-
projections.com

Central Texas Business Consultants (CTBC)
PO Box 2213
Wimberley, TX 78676
(512)626-2938
Fax: (512)847-5541
E-mail: info@centraltexasbusiness
consulting.com
Website: http://www.centraltexasbusiness
consulting.com

Utah

Vector Resources
7651 S Main St., Ste. 106
Midvale, UT 84047-7158
(801)352-8500
Fax: (801)352-8506
E-mail: info@vectorresources.com
Website: http://www.vectorresources.com

Ron Woodbury Consulting, Inc.
2899 E 3240 South St.
Saint George, UT 84790
(435)275-2978
E-mail: ron@ronwoodburyconsulting.com
Website: http://ronwoodburyconsulting
.com

Vermont

CDS Consulting Co-op
659 Old Codding Rd.
Putney, VT 05346
(802)387-6013
Website: http://www.cdsconsulting.coop

Virginia

The Profit Partner, LLC
3900 Jermantown Rd., Ste. 300
Fairfax, VA 22030
(703)934-4630
Website: http://www.theprofitpartner.com

Dare Mighty Things, LLC
805 Park Ave.
Herndon, VA 20170
(703)424-3119
Fax: (603)431-4332
E-mail: info@daremightythings.com
Website: http://www.daremightythings.com

Washington

ECG Management Consultants Inc.
1111 3rd Ave., Ste. 2700
Seattle, WA 98101-3201
(206)689-2200
Fax: (206)689-2209
E-mail: ecg@ecgmc.com
Website: http://www.ecgmc.com

West Virginia

Cava & Banko, PLLC
117 E Main St.
Bridgeport, WV 26330
(304)842-4499
Fax: (304)842-4585
Website: http://cavabankocpa.com

Wisconsin

Virtual Management Solutions
959 Primrose Center Rd.
Belleville, WI 53508-9376
(608)832-8003
E-mail: davelind@chorus.net
Website: http://www.virtualmanagement
solutions.com

Wyoming

CPA Consulting Group, LLP
300 Country Club Rd., Ste. 302
Casper, WY 82609
(307)577-4040
E-mail: taxes@cpawyo.com
Website: http://www.cpacasper.com

CA Boner Business Plans
3218 Rock Springs St.
Cheyenne, WY 82001
(307)214-2043
Website: http://caboner.biz

CPA Group of Laramie, LLC
1273 N 15th St., Ste. 121
Laramie, WY 82072
(307)745-7241
Fax: (307)745-7292
Website: http://www.cpalaramie.com/
index.php

Small business administration regional offices

This section contains a listing of Small Business Administration offices arranged numerically by region. Service areas are provided. Contact the appropriate office for a referral to the nearest field office, or visit the Small Business Administration online at www.sba.gov.

Region I

U.S. Small Business Administration New England Office
10 Causeway St., Ste. 265A
Boston, MA 02222
Phone: (617)565-8416
Fax: (617)565-8420
Website: http://www.sba.gov/offices/
regional/i
Serves Connecticut, Maine, Massachusetts, New Hampshire, Rhode Island, and Vermont.

Region II

U.S. Small Business Administration Atlantic Office
26 Federal Plaza, Ste. 3108
New York, NY 10278
Phone: (212)264-1450
Website: http://www.sba.gov/offices/
regional/ii
Serves New Jersey, New York, Puerto Rico, and the U.S. Virgin Islands.

Region III

U.S. Small Business Administration Mid-Atlantic Office
1150 1st Ave., Ste. 1001
King of Prussia, PA 19406
(610)382-3092
Website: http://www.sba.gov/offices/
regional/iii

Serves Delaware, Maryland, Pennsylvania, Virginia, Washington, DC, and West Virginia.

Region IV

U.S. Small Business Administration Southeast Office
233 Peachtree St. NE, Ste. 1800
Atlanta, GA 30303
Phone: (404)331-4999
Fax: (404)331-2354
Website: http://www.sba.gov/offices/
regional/iv
Serves Alabama, Florida, Georgia, Kentucky, Mississippi, North Carolina, South Carolina, and Tennessee.

Region V

U.S. Small Business Administration Great Lakes Office
500 W Madison St., Ste. 1150
Chicago, IL 60661
Phone: (312)353-0357
Fax: (312)353-3426
Website: http://www.sba.gov/offices/
regional/v
Serves Illinois, Indiana, Michigan, Minnesota, Ohio, and Wisconsin.

Region VI

U.S. Small Business Administration South Central Office
4300 Amon Carter Blvd., Ste. 108
Fort Worth, TX 76155
Phone: (817)684-5581
Fax: (817)684-5588
TTY/TDD: (817)684-5552
Website: http://www.sba.gov/offices/
regional/vi
Serves Arkansas, Louisiana, New Mexico, Oklahoma, and Texas.

Region VII

U.S. Small Business Administration Great Plains Office
1000 Walnut, Ste. 530
Kansas City, MO 64106
Phone: (816)426-4840
Fax: (816)426-4848
Website: http://www.sba.gov/offices/
regional/vii
Serves Iowa, Kansas, Missouri, and Nebraska.

Region VIII

U.S. Small Business Administration Rocky Mountains Office
721 19th St., Ste. 400
Denver, CO 80202
Fax: (303)844-0506
Website: http://www.sba.gov/offices/
regional/viii
Serves Colorado, Montana, North Dakota, South Dakota, Utah, and Wyoming.

Region IX

U.S. Small Business Administration Pacific Office
330 N Brand Blvd., Ste. 1200
Glendale, CA 91203
Phone: (818)552-3437
Fax: (202)481-0344
Website: http://www.sba.gov/offices/
regional/ix
Serves Arizona, California, Guam, Hawaii, and Nevada.

Region X

U.S. Small Business Administration Pacific Northwest Office
2401 4th Ave., Ste. 400
Seattle, WA 98121
Phone: (206)553-5676
Fax: (206)553-4155
Website: http://www.sba.gov/offices/
regional/x
Serves Alaska, Idaho, Oregon, and Washington.

Small business development centers

This section contains a listing of all Small Business Development Centers, organized alphabetically by state/U.S. territory, then by city, then by agency name.

Alabama

Alabama SBDC

UNIVERSITY OF ALABAMA
2800 Milan Court Suite 124
Birmingham, AL 35211-6908
Phone: 205-943-6750
Fax: 205-943-6752
E-Mail: wcampbell@provost.uab.edu
Website: http://www.asbdc.org
Mr. William Campbell Jr, State Director

Alaska

Alaska SBDC

UNIVERSITY OF ALASKA - ANCHORAGE
430 West Seventh Avenue, Suite 110
Anchorage, AK 99501
Phone: 907-274 -7232
Fax: 907-272-0565
E-Mail: Isaac.Vanderburg@aksbdc.org
Website: http://www.aksbdc.org
Isaac Vanderburg, State Director

American Samoa

American Samoa SBDC

AMERICAN SAMOA COMMUNITY COLLEGE
P.O. Box 2609
Pago Pago, American Samoa 96799
Phone: 011-684-699-4830
Fax: 011-684-699-6132
E-Mail: hthweatt.sbdc@hotmail.com
Website: www.as-sbdc.org
Mr. Herbert Thweatt, Director

Arizona

Arizona SBDC

MARICOPA COUNTY COMMUNITY COLLEGE
2411 West 14th Street, Suite 114
Tempe, AZ 85281
Phone: (480)731-8720
Fax: (480)731-8729
E-Mail: janice.washington@domail
.maricopa.edu
Website: http://www.azsbdc.net
Janice Washington, State Director

Arkansas

Arkansas SBDC

UNIVERSITY OF ARKANSAS
2801 South University Avenue
Little Rock, AR 72204
Phone: 501-683-7700
Fax: 501-683-7720
E-Mail: jmroderick@ualr.edu
Website: http://asbtdc.org
Ms. Janet M. Roderick, State Director

California

California - Northern California Regional SBDC

Northern California SBDC

HUMBOLDT STATE UNIVERSITY
1 Harpst Street 2006A, 209 Siemens Hall

Arcata, CA, 95521
Phone: 707-826-3920
Fax: 707-826-3912
E-Mail: Kristin.Johnson@humboldt.edu
Website: https://www.norcalsbdc.org
Kristin Johnson, Regional Director

California - Northern California SBDC

CALIFORNIA STATE UNIVERSITY - CHICO
35 Main St., Rm 203rr
Chico, CA 95929-0765
Phone: 530-898-5443
Fax: 530-898-4734
E-Mail: dripke@csuchico.edu
Website: https://www.necsbdc.org
Mr. Dan Ripke, Interim Regional
Director

California - San Diego and Imperial SBDC

SOUTHWESTERN COMMUNITY COLLEGE
880 National City Boulevard, Suite 103
National City, CA 91950
Phone: 619-216-6721
Fax: 619-216-6692
E-Mail: awilson@swccd.edu
Website: http://www.SBDCRegional
Network.org
Aleta Wilson, Regional Director

California - UC Merced SBDC

UC Merced Lead Center

UNIVERSITY OF CALIFORNIA - MERCED
550 East Shaw, Suite 105A
Fresno, CA 93710
Phone: 559-241-6590
Fax: 559-241-7422
E-Mail: dhowerton@ucmerced.edu
Website: http://sbdc.ucmerced.edu
Diane Howerton, State Director

California - Orange County/Inland Empire SBDC

Tri-County Lead SBDC

CALIFORNIA STATE UNIVERSITY - FULLERTON
800 North State College Boulevard,
SGMH 5313
Fullerton, CA 92834
Phone: 714-278-5168
Fax: 714-278-7101
E-Mail: kmpayne@fullerton.edu
Website: http://www.leadsbdc.org
Katrina Payne Smith, Lead Center Director

California - Los Angeles Region SBDC

LONG BEACH CITY COLLEGE
4900 E Conant Street, Building 2
Long Beach, CA 90808
Phone: 562-938-5006
Fax: 562-938-5030
E-Mail: jtorres@lbcc.edu
Website: http://www.smallbizla.org
Jesse Torres, Lead Center Director

Colorado

Colorado SBDC

COLORADO SBDC
1625 Broadway, Suite 2700
Denver, CO 80202
Phone: 303-892-3864
Fax: 303-892-3848
E-Mail: Kelly.Manning@state.co.us
Website: http://www.www.coloradosbdc
.org
Ms. Kelly Manning, State Director

Connecticut

Connecticut SBDC

UNIVERSITY OF CONNECTICUT
2100 Hillside Road, Unit 1044
Storrs, CT 06269
Phone: 855-428-7232
E-Mail: ecarter@uconn.edu
Website: www.ctsbdc.com
Emily Carter, State Director

Delaware

Delaware SBDC

DELAWARE TECHNOLOGY PARK
1 Innovation Way, Suite 301
Newark, DE 19711
Phone: 302-831-4283
Fax: 302-831-1423
E-Mail: jmbowman@udel.edu
Website: http://www.delawaresbdc.org
Mike Bowman, State Director

District of Columbia

District of Columbia SBDC

HOWARD UNIVERSITY
2600 6th Street, NW Room 128
Washington, DC 20059
Phone: 202-806-1550
Fax: 202-806-1777
E-Mail: darrell.brown@howard.edu
Website: http://www.dcsbdc.com
Darrell Brown, Executive Director

Florida

Florida SBDC

UNIVERSITY OF WEST FLORIDA
11000 University Parkway, Building 38
Pensacola, FL 32514
Phone: 850-473-7800
Fax: 850-473-7813
E-Mail: mmyhre@uwf.edu
Website: http://www.floridasbdc.com
Michael Myhre, State Director

Georgia

Georgia SBDC

UNIVERSITY OF GEORGIA
1180 East Broad Street
Athens, GA 30602
Phone: 706-542-6762
Fax: 706-542-7935
E-mail: aadams@georgiasbdc.org
Website: http://www.georgiasbdc.org
Mr. Allan Adams, State Director

Guam

Guam Small Business Development Center

UNIVERSITY OF GUAM
Pacific Islands SBDC
P.O. Box 5014 - U.O.G. Station
Mangilao, GU 96923
Phone: 671-735-2590
Fax: 671-734-2002
E-mail: casey@pacificsbdc.com
Website: http://www.uog.edu/sbdc
Mr. Casey Jeszenka, Director

Hawaii

Hawaii SBDC

UNIVERSITY OF HAWAII - HILO
200 W Kawili Street, Suite 107
Hilo, HI 96720
Phone: 808-974-7515
Fax: 808-974-7683
E-Mail: cathy.wiltse@hisbdc.org
Website: http://www.hisbdc.org
Cathy Wiltse, State Director

Idaho

Idaho SBDC

BOISE STATE UNIVERSITY
1910 University Drive
Boise, ID 83725
Phone: 208-426-3838
Fax: 208-426-3877
E-mail: ksewell@boisestate.edu

Website: http://www.idahosbdc.org
Katie Sewell, State Director

Illinois

Illinois SBDC

DEPARTMENT OF COMMERCE AND ECONOMIC OPPORTUNITY
500 E Monroe
Springfield, IL 62701
Phone: 217-524-5700
Fax: 217-524-0171
E-mail: mark.petrilli@illinois.gov
Website: http://www.ilsbdc.biz
Mr. Mark Petrilli, State Director

Indiana

Indiana SBDC

INDIANA ECONOMIC DEVELOPMENT CORPORATION
One North Capitol, Suite 700
Indianapolis, IN 46204
Phone: 317-232-8805
Fax: 317-232-8872
E-mail: JSchpok@iedc.in.gov
Website: http://www.isbdc.org
Jacob Schpok, State Director

Iowa

Iowa SBDC

IOWA STATE UNIVERSITY
2321 North Loop Drive, Suite 202
Ames, IA 50010
Phone: 515-294-2030
Fax: 515-294-6522
E-mail: lshimkat@iastate.edu
Website: http://www.iowasbdc.org
Lisa Shimkat, State Director

Kansas

Kansas SBDC

FORT HAYS STATE UNIVERSITY
214 SW Sixth Street, Suite 301
Topeka, KS 66603
Phone: 785-296-6514
Fax: 785-291-3261
E-mail: panichello@ksbdc.net
Website: http://www.fhsu.edu/ksbdc
Greg Panichello, State Director

Kentucky

Kentucky SBDC

UNIVERSITY OF KENTUCKY
One Quality Street
Lexington, KY 40507

Phone: 859-257-7668
Fax: 859-323-1907
E-mail: lrnaug0@uky.edu
Website: http://www.ksbdc.org
Becky Naugle, State Director

Louisiana

Louisiana SBDC

UNIVERSITY OF LOUISIANA - MONROE

College of Business Administration
700 University Avenue
Monroe, LA 71209
Phone: 318-342-5507
Fax: 318-342-5510
E-mail: rkessler@lsbdc.org
Website: http://www.lsbdc.org
Rande Kessler, State Director

Maine

Maine SBDC

UNIVERSITY OF SOUTHERN MAINE
96 Falmouth Street P.O. Box 9300
Portland, ME 04104
Phone: 207-780-4420
Fax: 207-780-4810
E-mail: mark.delisle@maine.edu
Website: http://www.mainesbdc.org
Mark Delisle, State Director

Maryland

Maryland SBDC

UNIVERSITY OF MARYLAND
7100 Baltimore Avenue, Suite 401
College Park, MD 20742
Phone: 301-403-8300
Fax: 301-403-8303
E-mail: rsprow@mdsbdc.umd.edu
Website: http://www.mdsbdc.umd.edu
Renee Sprow, State Director

Massachusetts

Massachusetts SBDC

UNIVERSITY OF MASSACHUSETTS
23 Tillson Farm Road
Amherst, MA 01003
Phone: 413-545-6301
Fax: 413-545-1273
E-mail: gparkin@msbdc.umass.edu
Website: http://www.www.msbdc.org
Georgianna Parkin, State Director

Michigan

Michigan SBTDC

GRAND VALLEY STATE UNIVERSITY
510 West Fulton Avenue
Grand Rapids, MI 49504
Phone: 616-331-7480
Fax: 616-331-7485
E-mail: boesen@gvsu.edu
Website: http://www.misbtdc.org
Nancy Boese, State Director

Minnesota

Minnesota SBDC

MINNESOTA SMALL BUSINESS DEVELOPMENT CENTER
1st National Bank Building
332 Minnesota Street, Suite E200
Saint Paul, MN 55101-1349
Phone: 651-259-7420
Fax: 651-296-5287
E-mail: Bruce.Strong@state.mn.us
Website: http://www.mnsbdc.com
Bruce H. Strong, State Director

Mississippi

Mississippi SBDC

UNIVERSITY OF MISSISSIPPI
122 Jeanette Phillips Drive
P.O. Box 1848
University, MS 38677
Phone: 662-915-5001
Fax: 662-915-5650
E-mail: wgurley@olemiss.edu
Website: http://www.mssbdc.org
Doug Gurley, Jr., State Director

Missouri

Missouri SBDC

UNIVERSITY OF MISSOURI
410 South 6th Street, ?200 Engineering North
Columbia, MO 65211
Phone: 573-882-9206
Fax: 573-884-4297
E-mail: bouchardc@missouri.edu
Website: http://www.missouribusiness.net
Chris Bouchard, State Director

Montana

Montana SBDC

DEPARTMENT OF COMMERCE
301 S Park Avenue, Room 114
Helena, MT 59601

Phone: 406-841-2746
Fax: 406-841-2728
E-mail: adesch@mt.gov
Website: http://www.sbdc.mt.gov
Ms. Ann Desch, State Director

Nebraska

Nebraska SBDC

UNIVERSITY OF NEBRASKA - OMAHA
200 Mammel Hall, 67th & Pine Streets
Omaha, NE 68182
Phone: 402-554-2521
Fax: 402-554-3473
E-mail: rbernier@unomaha.edu
Website: http://nbdc.unomaha.edu
Robert Bernier, State Director

Nevada

Nevada SBDC

UNIVERSITY OF NEVADA - RENO
Reno College of Business, Room 411
Reno, NV 89557-0100
Phone: 775-784-1717
Fax: 775-784-4337
E-mail: males@unr.edu
Website: http://www.nsbdc.org
Sam Males, State Director

New Hampshire

New Hampshire SBDC

UNIVERSITY OF NEW HAMPSHIRE
10 Garrison Avenue
Durham, NH 03824-3593
Phone: 603-862-2200
Fax: 603-862-4876
E-mail: Mary.Collins@unh.edu
Website: http://www.nhsbdc.org
Mary Collins, State Director

New Jersey

New Jersey SBDC

RUTGERS UNIVERSITY
1 Washington Park, 3rd Floor
Newark, NJ 07102
Phone: 973-353-1927
Fax: 973-353-1110
E-mail: bhopper@njsbdc.com
Website: http://www.njsbdc.com
Brenda Hopper, State Director

New Mexico

New Mexico SBDC

SANTA FE COMMUNITY COLLEGE
6401 Richards Avenue
Santa Fe, NM 87508

Phone: 505-428-1362
Fax: 505-428-1469
E-mail: russell.wyrick@sfcc.edu
Website: http://www.nmsbdc.org
Russell Wyrick, State Director

New York

New York SBDC

STATE UNIVERSITY OF NEW YORK
22 Corporate Woods, 3rd Floor
Albany, NY 12246
Phone: 518-443-5398
Fax: 518-443-5275
E-mail: j.king@nyssbdc.org
Website: http://www.nyssbdc.org
Jim King, State Director

North Carolina

North Carolina SBDTC

UNIVERSITY OF NORTH CAROLINA
5 West Hargett Street, Suite 600
Raleigh, NC 27601
Phone: 919-715-7272
Fax: 919-715-7777
E-mail: sdaugherty@sbtdc.org
Website: http://www.sbtdc.org
Scott Daugherty, State Director

North Dakota

North Dakota SBDC

UNIVERSITY OF NORTH DAKOTA
1200 Memorial Highway, PO Box 5509
Bismarck, ND 58506
Phone: 701-328-5375
Fax: 701-250-4304
E-mail: dkmartin@ndsbdc.org
Website: http://www.ndsbdc.org
David Martin, State Director

Ohio

Ohio SBDC

OHIO DEPARTMENT OF DEVELOPMENT
77 South High Street, 28th Floor
Columbus, OH 43216
Phone: 614-466-2711
Fax: 614-466-1789
E-mail: ezra.escudero@development.ohio.gov
Website: http://www.ohiosbdc.org
Ezra Escudero, State Director

Oklahoma

Oklahoma SBDC

SOUTHEAST OKLAHOMA STATE UNIVERSITY
1405 N. 4th Avenue, PMB 2584
Durant, OK 74701
Phone: 580-745-2955
Fax: 580-745-7471
E-mail: wcarter@se.edu
Website: http://www.osbdc.org
Grady Pennington, State Director

Oregon

Oregon SBDC

LANE COMMUNITY COLLEGE
1445 Willamette Street, Suite 5
Eugene, OR 97401
Phone: 541-463-5250
Fax: 541-345-6006
E-mail: gregorym@lanecc.edu
Website: http://www.bizcenter.org
Mark Gregory, State Director

Pennsylvania

Pennsylvania SBDC

UNIVERSITY OF PENNSYLVANIA

The Wharton School
3819-33 Chestnut Street, Suite 325
Philadelphia, PA 19104
Phone: 215-898-1219
Fax: 215-573-2135
E-mail: cconroy@wharton.upenn.edu
Website: http://pasbdc.org
Christian Conroy, State Director

Puerto Rico

Puerto Rico SBDC

INTER-AMERICAN UNIVERSITY OF PUERTO RICO
416 Ponce de Leon Avenue, Union Plaza,
Tenth Floor
Hato Rey, PR 00918
Phone: 787-763-6811
Fax: 787-763-6875
E-mail: cmarti@prsbdc.org
Website: http://www.prsbdc.org
Carmen Marti, Executive Director

Rhode Island

Rhode Island SBDC

UNIVERSITY OF RHODE ISLAND
75 Lower College Road, 2nd Floor
Kingston, RI 02881

Phone: 401-874-4576
E-mail: gsonnenfeld@uri.edu
Website: http://www.risbdc.org
Gerald Sonnenfeld, State Director

South Carolina

South Carolina SBDC

UNIVERSITY OF SOUTH CAROLINA

Moore School of Business
1014 Greene Street
Columbia, SC 29208
Phone: 803-777-0749
Fax: 803-777-6876
E-mail: michele.abraham@moore.sc.edu
Website: http://www.scsbdc.com
Michele Abraham, State Director

South Dakota

South Dakota SBDC

UNIVERSITY OF SOUTH DAKOTA
414 East Clark Street, Patterson Hall
Vermillion, SD 57069
Phone: 605-677-5103
Fax: 605-677-5427
E-mail: jeff.eckhoff@usd.edu
Website: http://www.usd.edu/sbdc
Jeff Eckhoff, State Director

Tennessee

Tennessee SBDC

MIDDLE TENNESSEE STATE UNIVERSITY
3050 Medical Center Parkway, Ste. 200
Nashville, TN 37129
Phone: 615-849-9999
Fax: 615-893-7089
E-mail: pgeho@tsbdc.org
Website: http://www.tsbdc.org
Patrick Geho, State Director

Texas

Texas-North SBDC

DALLAS COUNTY COMMUNITY COLLEGE
1402 Corinth Street
Dallas, TX 75215
Phone: 214-860-5832
Fax: 214-860-5813
E-mail: m.langford@dcccd.edu
Website: http://www.ntsbdc.org
Mark Langford, Region Director

Texas Gulf Coast SBDC

UNIVERSITY OF HOUSTON
2302 Fannin, Suite 200
Houston, TX 77002
Phone: 713-752-8444
Fax: 713-756-1500
E-mail: fyoung@uh.edu
Website: http://sbdcnetwork.uh.edu
Mike Young, Executive Director

Texas-NW SBDC

TEXAS TECH UNIVERSITY
2579 South Loop 289, Suite 114
Lubbock, TX 79423
Phone: 806-745-3973
Fax: 806-745-6207
E-mail: c.bean@nwtsbdc.org
Website: http://www.nwtsbdc.org
Craig Bean, Executive Director

Texas-South-West Texas Border Region SBDC

UNIVERSITY OF TEXAS - SAN ANTONIO
501 West Durango Boulevard
San Antonio, TX 78207-4415
Phone: 210-458-2480
Fax: 210-458-2425
E-mail: albert.salgado@utsa.edu
Website: https://www.txsbdc.org
Alberto Salgado, Region Director

Utah

Utah SBDC

SALT LAKE COMMUNITY COLLEGE
9750 South 300 West
Salt Lake City, UT 84070
Phone: 801-957-5384
Fax: 801-985-5300
E-mail: Sherm.Wilkinson@slcc.edu
Website: http://www.utahsbdc.org
Sherm Wilkinson, State Director

Vermont

Vermont SBDC

VERMONT TECHNICAL COLLEGE
PO Box 188, 1 Main Street
Randolph Center, VT 05061-0188
Phone: 802-728-9101
Fax: 802-728-3026
E-mail: lrossi@vtsbdc.org
Website: http://www.vtsbdc.org
Linda Rossi, State Director

Virgin Islands

Virgin Islands SBDC

UNIVERSITY OF THE VIRGIN ISLANDS
8000 Nisky Center, Suite 720
Saint Thomas, VI 00802
Phone: 340-776-3206
Fax: 340-775-3756
E-mail: ldottin@uvi.edu
Website: http://www.sbdcvi.org
Leonor Dottin, State Director

Virginia

Virginia SBDC

GEORGE MASON UNIVERSITY
4031 University Drive, Suite100
Fairfax, VA 22030
Phone: 703-277-7727
Fax: 703-352-8518
E-mail: jkeenan@gmu.edu
Website: http://www.virginiasbdc.org
Jody Keenan, Director

Washington

Washington SBDC

WASHINGTON STATE UNIVERSITY
1235 N. Post Street, Suite 201
Spokane, WA 99201
Phone: 509-358-7765
Fax: 509-358-7764
E-mail: duane.fladland@wsbdc.org
Website: http://www.wsbdc.org
Duane Fladland, State Director

West Virginia

West Virginia SBDC

WEST VIRGINIA DEVELOPMENT OFFICE
Capital Complex, Building 6, Room 652
1900 Kanawha Boulevard
Charleston, WV 25305
Phone: 304-957-2087
Fax: 304-558-0127
E-mail: Kristina.J.Oliver@wv.gov
Website: http://www.wvsbdc.org
Mr. Conley Salyor, State Director

Wisconsin

Wisconsin SBDC

UNIVERSITY OF WISCONSIN
432 North Lake Street, Room 423
Madison, WI 53706
Phone: 608-263-7794
Fax: 608-263-7830

E-mail: bon.wikenheiser@uwex.edu
Website: http://www.uwex.edu/sbdc
Bon Wikenheiser, State Director

Wyoming

Wyoming SBDC

UNIVERSITY OF WYOMING
1000 E University Ave., Dept. 3922
Laramie, WY 82071-3922
Phone: (307)766-3405
Fax: (307)766-3406
E-mail: jkline@uwyo.edu
Website: http://www.wyomingentre
preneur.biz
Jill Kline, Acting State Director

Service corps of retired executives (score) offices

This section contains a listing of all SCORE offices organized alphabetically by state/U.S. territory, then by city, then by agency name.

Alabama

SCORE Office (Northeast Alabama)
1400 Commerce Blvd., Northeast
Anniston, AL 36207
(256)241-6111

SCORE Office (North Alabama)
1731 1st Ave. North, Ste. 200
Birmingham, AL 35203
(205)264-8425
Fax: (205)934-0538

SCORE Office (Baldwin County)
327 Fairhope Avenue
Fairhope, AL 36532
(251)928-6387

SCORE Office (Mobile)
451 Government Street
Mobile, AL 36652
(251)431-8614
Fax: (251)431-8646

SCORE Office (Alabama Capitol City)
600 S Court St.
Montgomery, AL 36104
(334)240-6868
Fax: (334)240-6869

SCORE Office (Tuscaloosa)
2200 University Blvd.
Tuscaloosa, AL 35402
(205)758-7588

Alaska

SCORE Office (Anchorage)
420 L St., Ste. 300
Anchorage, AK 99501
(907)271-4022
Fax: (907)271-4545

Arizona

SCORE Office (Greater Phoenix)
2828 N. Central Ave., Ste. 800
Phoenix, AZ 85004
(602)745-7250
Fax: (602)745-7210
E-mail: e-mail@SCORE-phoenix.org
Website: http://www.greaterphoenix
.score.org

SCORE Office (Northern Arizona)
1228 Willow Creek Rd., Ste. 2
Prescott, AZ 86301
(928)778-7438
Fax: (928)778-0812
Website: http://www.northernarizona
.score.org

SCORE Office (Southern Arizona)
1400 W Speedway Blvd.
Tucson, AZ 85745
(520)505-3636
Fax: (520)670-5011
Website: http://www.southernarizona
.score.org

Arkansas

SCORE Office (South Central)
201 N. Jackson Ave.
El Dorado, AR 71730-5803
(870)863-6113
Fax: (870)863-6115

SCORE Office (Northwest Arkansas)
614 E Emma St., Room M412
Springdale, AR 72764
(479)725-1809
Website: http://www.northwestarkansas
.score.org

SCORE Office (Little Rock)
2120 Riverfront Dr., Ste. 250
Little Rock, AR 72202-1747
(501)324-7379
Fax: (501)324-5199
Website: http://www.littlerock.score.org

SCORE Office (Southeast Arkansas)
P.O. Box 5069
Pine Bluff, AR 71611-5069
(870)535-0110
Fax: (870)535-1643

California

SCORE Office (Bakersfield)
P.O. Box 2426
Bakersfield, CA 93303
(661)861-9249
Fax: (661)395-4134
Website: http://www.bakersfield.score.org

SCORE Office (Santa Cruz County)
716 G Capitola Ave.
Capitola, CA 95010
(831)621-3735
Fax: (831)475-6530
Website: http://santacruzcounty.score.org

SCORE Office (Greater Chico Area)
1324 Mangrove St., Ste. 114
Chico, CA 95926
(530)342-8932
Fax: (530)342-8932
Website: http://www.greaterchicoarea.score
.org

SCORE Office (El Centro)
1850 W Main St, Ste. C
El Centro, CA 92243
(760)337-2692
Website: http://www.sandiego.score.org

SCORE Office (Central Valley)
801 R St., Ste. 201
Fresno, CA 93721
(559)487-5605
Fax: (559)487-5636
Website: http://www.centralvalley.score.org

SCORE Office (Los Angeles)
330 N. Brand Blvd., Ste. 190
Glendale, CA 91203-2304
(818)552-3206
Fax: (818)552-3323
Website: http://www.greaterlosangeles
.score.org

SCORE Office (Modesto Merced)
1880 W Wardrobe Ave.
Merced, CA 95340
(209)725-2033
Fax: (209)577-2673
Website: http://www.modestomerced
.score.org

SCORE Office (Monterey Bay)
Monterey Chamber of Commerce
30 Ragsdale Dr.
Monterey, CA 93940
(831)648-5360
Website: http://www.montereybay
.score.org

SCORE Office (East Bay)
492 9th St., Ste. 350

Oakland, CA 94607
(510)273-6611
Fax: (510)273-6015
E-mail: webmaster@eastbayscore.org
Website: http://www.eastbay.score.org

SCORE Office (Ventura County)
400 E Esplanade Dr., Ste. 301
Oxnard, CA 93036
(805)204-6022
Fax: (805)650-1414
Website: http://www.ventura.score.org

SCORE Office (Coachella)
43100 Cook St., Ste. 104
Palm Desert, CA 92211
(760)773-6507
Fax: (760)773-6514
Website: http://www.coachellavalley
.score.org

SCORE Office (Antelope Valley)
1212 E Avenue, S Ste. A3
Palmdale, CA 93550
(661)947-7679
Website: http://www.antelopevalley
.score.org

SCORE Office (Inland Empire)
11801 Pierce St., 2nd Fl.
Riverside, CA 92505
(951)-652-4390
Fax: (951)929-8543
Website: http://www.inlandempire
.score.org

SCORE Office (Sacramento)
4990 Stockton Blvd.
Sacramento, CA 95820
(916)635-9085
Fax: (916)635-9089
Website: http://www.sacramento
.score.org

SCORE Office (San Diego)
550 West C. St., Ste. 550
San Diego, CA 92101-3540
(619)557-7272
Website: http://www.sandiego.score.org

SCORE Office (San Francisco)
455 Market St., 6th Fl.
San Francisco, CA 94105
(415)744-6827
Fax: (415)744-6750
E-mail: sfscore@sfscore.
Website: http://www.sanfrancisco
.score.org

SCORE Office (Silicon Valley)
234 E Gish Rd., Ste. 100
San Jose, CA 95112

(408)453-6237
Fax: (408)494-0214
E-mail: info@svscore.org
Website: http://www.siliconvalley
.score.org

SCORE Office (San Luis Obispo)
711 Tank Farm Rd., Ste. 210
San Luis Obispo, CA 93401
(805)547-0779
Website: http://www.sanluisobispo
.score.org

SCORE Office (Orange County)
200 W Santa Anna Blvd., Ste. 700
Santa Ana, CA 92701
(714)550-7369
Fax: (714)550-0191
Website: http://www.orangecounty
.score.org

SCORE Office (Santa Barbara)
924 Anacapa St.
Santa Barbara, CA 93101
(805)563-0084
Website: http://www.santabarbara
.score.org

SCORE Office (North Coast)
777 Sonoma Ave., Rm. 115E
Santa Rosa, CA 95404
(707)571-8342
Fax: (707)541-0331
Website: http://www.northcoast
.score.org

SCORE Office (Tuolumne County)
222 S Shepherd St.
Sonora, CA 95370
(209)532-4316
Fax: (209)588-0673
Website: http://www.tuolumnecounty
.score.org

Colorado

SCORE Office (Colorado Springs)
3595 E Fountain Blvd., Ste. E-1
Colorado Springs, CO 80910
(719)636-3074
Fax: (719)635-1571
Website: http://www.coloradosprings
.score.org

SCORE Office (Denver)
US Custom's House, 4th Fl.
721 19th St.
Denver, CO 80202
(303)844-3985
Fax: (303)844-6490
Website: http://www.denver.score.org

SCORE Office (Tri-River)
1102 Grand Ave.
Glenwood Springs, CO 81601
(970)945-6589

SCORE Office (Grand Junction)
2591 B & 3/4 Rd.
Grand Junction, CO 81503
(970)243-5242

SCORE Office (Gunnison)
608 N. 11th
Gunnison, CO 81230
(303)641-4422

SCORE Office (Montrose)
1214 Peppertree Dr.
Montrose, CO 81401
(970)249-6080

SCORE Office (Pagosa Springs)
PO Box 4381
Pagosa Springs, CO 81157
(970)731-4890

SCORE Office (Rifle)
0854 W Battlement Pky., Apt. C106
Parachute, CO 81635
(970)285-9390

SCORE Office (Pueblo)
302 N. Santa Fe
Pueblo, CO 81003
(719)542-1704
Fax: (719)542-1624
Website: http://www.pueblo.score.org

SCORE Office (Ridgway)
143 Poplar Pl.
Ridgway, CO 81432

SCORE Office (Silverton)
PO Box 480
Silverton, CO 81433
(303)387-5430

SCORE Office (Minturn)
PO Box 2066
Vail, CO 81658
(970)476-1224

Connecticut

SCORE Office (Greater Bridgeport)
230 Park Ave.
Bridgeport, CT 06604
(203)450-9484
Fax: (203)576-4388

SCORE Office (Western Connecticut)
155 Deer Hill Ave.
Danbury, CT 06010
(203)794-1404

Website: http://www.westernconnecticut
.score.org

SCORE Office (Greater Hartford County)
330 Main St., 2nd Fl.
Hartford, CT 06106
(860)240-4700
Fax: (860)240-4659
Website: http://www.greaterhartford
.score.org

SCORE Office (Manchester)
20 Hartford Rd.
Manchester, CT 06040
(203)646-2223
Fax: (203)646-5871

SCORE Office (New Britain)
185 Main St., Ste. 431
New Britain, CT 06051
(203)827-4492
Fax: (203)827-4480

SCORE Office (New Haven)
60 Sargent Dr.
New Haven, CT 06511
(203)865-7645
Website: http://www.newhaven.score.org

SCORE Office (Fairfield County)
111 East Ave.
Norwalk, CT 06851
(203)847-7348
Fax: (203)849-9308
Website: http://www.fairfieldcounty
score.org

SCORE Office (Southeastern Connecticut)
665 Boston Post Rd.
Old Saybrook, CT 06475
(860)388-9508
Website: http://www.southeastern
connecticut.score.org

SCORE Office (Northwest Connecticut)
333 Kennedy Dr.
Torrington, CT 06790
(560)482-6586
Website: http://www.northwest
connecticut.score.org

Delaware

SCORE Office (Dover)
Treadway Towers
PO Box 576
Dover, DE 19903
(302)678-0892
Fax: (302)678-0189

SCORE Office (Lewes)
PO Box 1
Lewes, DE 19958
(302)645-8073
Fax: (302)645-8412

SCORE Office (Milford)
204 NE Front St.
Milford, DE 19963
(302)422-3301

SCORE Office (Wilmington)
824 Market St., Ste. 610
Wilmington, DE 19801
(302)573-6652
Fax: (302)573-6092
Website: http://www.scoredelaware.com

District of Columbia

SCORE Office (George Mason University)
409 3rd St. SW, 4th Fl.
Washington, DC 20024
800-634-0245

SCORE Office (Washington DC)
1110 Vermont Ave. NW, 9th Fl.
Washington, DC 20043
(202)606-4000
Fax: (202)606-4225
E-mail: dcscore@hotmail.com
Website: http://www.scoredc.org

Florida

SCORE Office (Desota County Chamber of Commerce)
16 South Velucia Ave.
Arcadia, FL 34266
(941)494-4033

SCORE Office (Suncoast/Pinellas)
Airport Business Ctr.
4707 - 140th Ave. N, No. 311
Clearwater, FL 33755
(813)532-6800
Fax: (813)532-6800

SCORE Office (DeLand)
336 N. Woodland Blvd.
DeLand, FL 32720
(904)734-4331
Fax: (904)734-4333

SCORE Office (South Palm Beach)
1050 S Federal Hwy., Ste. 132
Delray Beach, FL 33483
(561)278-7752
Fax: (561)278-0288

SCORE Office (Fort Lauderdale)
Federal Bldg., Ste. 123
299 E Broward Blvd.

Fort Lauderdale, FL 33301
(954)356-7263
Fax: (954)356-7145

SCORE Office (Southwest Florida)
The Renaissance
8695 College Pky., Ste. 345 & 346
Fort Myers, FL 33919
(941)489-2935
Fax: (941)489-1170

SCORE Office (Treasure Coast)
Professional Center, Ste. 2
3220 S US, No. 1
Fort Pierce, FL 34982
(561)489-0548

SCORE Office (Gainesville)
101 SE 2nd Pl., Ste. 104
Gainesville, FL 32601
(904)375-8278

SCORE Office (Hialeah Dade Chamber)
59 W 5th St.
Hialeah, FL 33010
(305)887-1515
Fax: (305)887-2453

SCORE Office (Daytona Beach)
921 Nova Rd., Ste. A
Holly Hills, FL 32117
(904)255-6889
Fax: (904)255-0229
E-mail: score87@dbeach.com

SCORE Office (South Broward)
3475 Sheridian St., Ste. 203
Hollywood, FL 33021
(305)966-8415

SCORE Office (Citrus County)
5 Poplar Ct.
Homosassa, FL 34446
(352)382-1037

SCORE Office (Jacksonville)
7825 Baymeadows Way, Ste. 100-B
Jacksonville, FL 32256
(904)443-1911
Fax: (904)443-1980
E-mail: scorejax@juno.com
Website: http://www.scorejax.org

SCORE Office (Jacksonville Satellite)
3 Independent Dr.
Jacksonville, FL 32256
(904)366-6600
Fax: (904)632-0617

SCORE Office (Central Florida)
5410 S Florida Ave., No. 3
Lakeland, FL 33801
(941)687-5783
Fax: (941)687-6225

SCORE Office (Lakeland)
100 Lake Morton Dr.
Lakeland, FL 33801
(941)686-2168

SCORE Office (Saint Petersburg)
800 W Bay Dr., Ste. 505
Largo, FL 33712
(813)585-4571

SCORE Office (Leesburg)
9501 US Hwy. 441
Leesburg, FL 34788-8751
(352)365-3556
Fax: (352)365-3501

SCORE Office (Cocoa)
1600 Farno Rd., Unit 205
Melbourne, FL 32935
(407)254-2288

SCORE Office (Melbourne)
Melbourne Professional Complex
1600 Sarno, Ste. 205
Melbourne, FL 32935
(407)254-2288
Fax: (407)245-2288

SCORE Office (Merritt Island)
1600 Sarno Rd., Ste. 205
Melbourne, FL 32935
(407)254-2288
Fax: (407)254-2288

SCORE Office (Space Coast)
Melbourn Professional Complex
1600 Sarno, Ste. 205
Melbourne, FL 32935
(407)254-2288
Fax: (407)254-2288

SCORE Office (Dade)
49 NW 5th St.
Miami, FL 33128
(305)371-6889
Fax: (305)374-1882
E-mail: score@netrox.net
Website: http://www.netrox.net/~score

SCORE Office (Naples of Collier)
International College
2654 Tamiami Trl. E
Naples, FL 34112
(941)417-1280
Fax: (941)417-1281
E-mail: score@naples.net
Website: http://www.naples.net/clubs/
score/index.htm

SCORE Office (Pasco County)
6014 US Hwy. 19, Ste. 302
New Port Richey, FL 34652
(813)842-4638

SCORE Office (Southeast Volusia)
115 Canal St.
New Smyrna Beach, FL 32168
(904)428-2449
Fax: (904)423-3512

SCORE Office (Ocala)
110 E Silver Springs Blvd.
Ocala, FL 34470
(352)629-5959

Clay County SCORE Office
Clay County Chamber of Commerce
1734 Kingsdey Ave.
PO Box 1441
Orange Park, FL 32073
(904)264-2651
Fax: (904)269-0363

SCORE Office (Orlando)
80 N. Hughey Ave.
Rm. 445 Federal Bldg.
Orlando, FL 32801
(407)648-6476
Fax: (407)648-6425

SCORE Office (Emerald Coast)
19 W Garden St., No. 325
Pensacola, FL 32501
(904)444-2060
Fax: (904)444-2070

SCORE Office (Charlotte County)
201 W Marion Ave., Ste. 211
Punta Gorda, FL 33950
(941)575-1818
E-mail: score@gls3c.com
Website: http://www.charlotte-
florida.com/business/scorepg01.htm

SCORE Office (Saint Augustine)
1 Riberia St.
Saint Augustine, FL 32084
(904)829-5681
Fax: (904)829-6477

SCORE Office (Bradenton)
2801 Fruitville, Ste. 280
Sarasota, FL 34237
(813)955-1029

SCORE Office (Manasota)
2801 Fruitville Rd., Ste. 280
Sarasota, FL 34237
(941)955-1029
Fax: (941)955-5581
E-mail: score116@gte.net
Website: http://www.score-suncoast.org

SCORE Office (Tallahassee)
200 W Park Ave.
Tallahassee, FL 32302
(850)487-2665

SCORE Office (Hillsborough)
4732 Dale Mabry Hwy. N, Ste. 400
Tampa, FL 33614-6509
(813)870-0125

SCORE Office (Lake Sumter)
122 E Main St.
Tavares, FL 32778-3810
(352)365-3556

SCORE Office (Titusville)
2000 S Washington Ave.
Titusville, FL 32780
(407)267-3036
Fax: (407)264-0127

SCORE Office (Venice)
257 N. Tamiami Trl.
Venice, FL 34285
(941)488-2236
Fax: (941)484-5903

SCORE Office (Palm Beach)
500 Australian Ave. S, Ste. 100
West Palm Beach, FL 33401
(561)833-1672
Fax: (561)833-1712

SCORE Office (Wildwood)
103 N. Webster St.
Wildwood, FL 34785

Georgia

SCORE Office (Atlanta)
Harris Tower, Suite 1900
233 Peachtree Rd., NE
Atlanta, GA 30309
(404)347-2442
Fax: (404)347-1227

SCORE Office (Augusta)
3126 Oxford Rd.
Augusta, GA 30909
(706)869-9100

SCORE Office (Columbus)
School Bldg.
PO Box 40
Columbus, GA 31901
(706)327-3654

SCORE Office (Dalton-Whitfield)
305 S Thorton Ave.
Dalton, GA 30720
(706)279-3383

SCORE Office (Gainesville)
PO Box 374
Gainesville, GA 30503
(770)532-6206
Fax: (770)535-8419

SCORE Office (Macon)
711 Grand Bldg.
Macon, GA 31201
(912)751-6160

SCORE Office (Brunswick)
4 Glen Ave.
Saint Simons Island, GA 31520
(912)265-0620
Fax: (912)265-0629

SCORE Office (Savannah)
111 E Liberty St., Ste. 103
Savannah, GA 31401
(912)652-4335
Fax: (912)652-4184
E-mail: info@scoresav.org
Website: http://www.coastalempire.com/
score/index.htm

Guam

SCORE Office (Guam)
Pacific News Bldg., Rm. 103
238 Archbishop Flores St.
Agana, GU 96910-5100
(671)472-7308

Hawaii

SCORE Office (Hawaii, Inc.)
1111 Bishop St., Ste. 204
PO Box 50207
Honolulu, HI 96813
(808)522-8132
Fax: (808)522-8135
E-mail: hnlscore@juno.com

SCORE Office (Kahului)
250 Alamaha, Unit N16A
Kahului, HI 96732
(808)871-7711

SCORE Office (Maui, Inc.)
590 E Lipoa Pkwy., Ste. 227
Kihei, HI 96753
(808)875-2380

Idaho

SCORE Office (Treasure Valley)
1020 Main St., No. 290
Boise, ID 83702
(208)334-1696
Fax: (208)334-9353

SCORE Office (Eastern Idaho)
2300 N. Yellowstone, Ste. 119
Idaho Falls, ID 83401
(208)523-1022
Fax: (208)528-7127

Illinois

SCORE Office (Fox Valley)
40 W Downer Pl.
PO Box 277
Aurora, IL 60506
(630)897-9214
Fax: (630)897-7002

SCORE Office (Greater Belvidere)
419 S State St.
Belvidere, IL 61008
(815)544-4357
Fax: (815)547-7654

SCORE Office (Bensenville)
1050 Busse Hwy. Suite 100
Bensenville, IL 60106
(708)350-2944
Fax: (708)350-2979

SCORE Office (Central Illinois)
402 N. Hershey Rd.
Bloomington, IL 61704
(309)644-0549
Fax: (309)663-8270
E-mail: webmaster@central-illinois-
score.org
Website: http://www.central-illinois-
score.org

SCORE Office (Southern Illinois)
150 E Pleasant Hill Rd.
Box 1
Carbondale, IL 62901
(618)453-6654
Fax: (618)453-5040

SCORE Chicago
500 W Madison St., Ste. 1150
Chicago, IL 60661
(312)353-7724
Fax: (312)886-4879
E-mail: info@scorechicago.org
Website: http://scorechicago.org

SCORE Office (Danville)
28 W N. Street
Danville, IL 61832
(217)442-7232
Fax: (217)442-6228

SCORE Office (Decatur)
Milliken University
1184 W Main St.
Decatur, IL 62522
(217)424-6297
Fax: (217)424-3993
E-mail: charding@mail.millikin.edu
Website: http://www.millikin.edu/
academics/Tabor/score.html

SCORE Office (Downers Grove)
925 Curtis
Downers Grove, IL 60515
(708)968-4050
Fax: (708)968-8368

SCORE Office (Elgin)
24 E Chicago, 3rd Fl.
PO Box 648
Elgin, IL 60120
(847)741-5660
Fax: (847)741-5677

SCORE Office (Freeport Area)
26 S Galena Ave.
Freeport, IL 61032
(815)233-1350
Fax: (815)235-4038

SCORE Office (Galesburg)
292 E Simmons St.
PO Box 749
Galesburg, IL 61401
(309)343-1194
Fax: (309)343-1195

SCORE Office (Glen Ellyn)
500 Pennsylvania
Glen Ellyn, IL 60137
(708)469-0907
Fax: (708)469-0426

SCORE Office (Greater Alton)
Alden Hall
5800 Godfrey Rd.
Godfrey, IL 62035-2466
(618)467-2280
Fax: (618)466-8289
Website: http://www.altonweb.com/score

SCORE Office (Grayslake)
19351 W Washington St.
Grayslake, IL 60030
(708)223-3633
Fax: (708)223-9371

SCORE Office (Harrisburg)
303 S Commercial
Harrisburg, IL 62946-1528
(618)252-8528
Fax: (618)252-0210

SCORE Office (Joliet)
100 N. Chicago
Joliet, IL 60432
(815)727-5371
Fax: (815)727-5374

SCORE Office (Kankakee)
101 S Schuyler Ave.
Kankakee, IL 60901
(815)933-0376
Fax: (815)933-0380

SCORE Office (Macomb)
216 Seal Hall, Rm. 214
Macomb, IL 61455
(309)298-1128
Fax: (309)298-2520

SCORE Office (Matteson)
210 Lincoln Mall
Matteson, IL 60443
(708)709-3750
Fax: (708)503-9322

SCORE Office (Mattoon)
1701 Wabash Ave.
Mattoon, IL 61938
(217)235-5661
Fax: (217)234-6544

SCORE Office (Quad Cities)
622 19th St.
Moline, IL 61265
(309)797-0082
Fax: (309)757-5435
E-mail: score@qconline.com
Website: http://www.qconline.com/
business/score

SCORE Office (Naperville)
131 W Jefferson Ave.
Naperville, IL 60540
(708)355-4141
Fax: (708)355-8355

SCORE Office (Northbrook)
2002 Walters Ave.
Northbrook, IL 60062
(847)498-5555
Fax: (847)498-5510

SCORE Office (Palos Hills)
10900 S 88th Ave.
Palos Hills, IL 60465
(847)974-5468
Fax: (847)974-0078

SCORE Office (Peoria)
124 SW Adams, Ste. 300
Peoria, IL 61602
(309)676-0755
Fax: (309)676-7534

SCORE Office (Prospect Heights)
1375 Wolf Rd.
Prospect Heights, IL 60070
(847)537-8660
Fax: (847)537-7138

SCORE Office (Quincy Tri-State)
300 Civic Center Plz., Ste. 245
Quincy, IL 62301
(217)222-8093
Fax: (217)222-3033

SCORE Office (River Grove)
2000 5th Ave.
River Grove, IL 60171
(708)456-0300
Fax: (708)583-3121

SCORE Office (Northern Illinois)
515 N. Court St.
Rockford, IL 61103
(815)962-0122
Fax: (815)962-0122

SCORE Office (Saint Charles)
103 N. 1st Ave.
Saint Charles, IL 60174-1982
(847)584-8384
Fax: (847)584-6065

SCORE Office (Springfield)
511 W Capitol Ave., Ste. 302
Springfield, IL 62704
(217)492-4416
Fax: (217)492-4867

SCORE Office (Sycamore)
112 Somunak St.
Sycamore, IL 60178
(815)895-3456
Fax: (815)895-0125

SCORE Office (University)
Hwy. 50 & Stuenkel Rd. Ste. C3305
University Park, IL 60466
(708)534-5000
Fax: (708)534-8457

Indiana

SCORE Office (Anderson)
205 W 11th St.
Anderson, IN 46015
(317)642-0264

SCORE Office (Bloomington)
Star Center
216 W Allen
Bloomington, IN 47403
(812)335-7334
E-mail: wtfische@indiana.edu
Website: http://www.brainfreezemedia
.com/score527

SCORE Office (South East Indiana)
500 Franklin St.
Box 29
Columbus, IN 47201
(812)379-4457

SCORE Office (Corydon)
310 N. Elm St.
Corydon, IN 47112
(812)738-2137
Fax: (812)738-6438

SCORE Office (Crown Point)
Old Courthouse Sq. Ste. 206
PO Box 43
Crown Point, IN 46307
(219)663-1800

SCORE Office (Elkhart)
418 S Main St.
Elkhart, IN 46515
(219)293-1531
Fax: (219)294-1859

SCORE Office (Evansville)
1100 W Lloyd Expy., Ste. 105
Evansville, IN 47708
(812)426-6144

SCORE Office (Fort Wayne)
1300 S Harrison St.
Fort Wayne, IN 46802
(219)422-2601
Fax: (219)422-2601

SCORE Office (Gary)
973 W 6th Ave., Rm. 326
Gary, IN 46402
(219)882-3918

SCORE Office (Hammond)
7034 Indianapolis Blvd.
Hammond, IN 46324
(219)931-1000
Fax: (219)845-9548

SCORE Office (Indianapolis)
429 N. Pennsylvania St., Ste. 100
Indianapolis, IN 46204-1873
(317)226-7264
Fax: (317)226-7259
E-mail: inscore@indy.net
Website: http://www.score-indianapolis
.org

SCORE Office (Jasper)
PO Box 307
Jasper, IN 47547-0307
(812)482-6866

SCORE Office (Kokomo/Howard Counties)
106 N. Washington St.
Kokomo, IN 46901
(765)457-5301
Fax: (765)452-4564

SCORE Office (Logansport)
300 E Broadway, Ste. 103
Logansport, IN 46947
(219)753-6388

SCORE Office (Madison)
301 E Main St.
Madison, IN 47250

(812)265-3135
Fax: (812)265-2923

SCORE Office (Marengo)
Rt. 1 Box 224D
Marengo, IN 47140
Fax: (812)365-2793

SCORE Office (Marion/Grant Counties)
215 S Adams
Marion, IN 46952
(765)664-5107

SCORE Office (Merrillville)
255 W 80th Pl.
Merrillville, IN 46410
(219)769-8180
Fax: (219)736-6223

SCORE Office (Michigan City)
200 E Michigan Blvd.
Michigan City, IN 46360
(219)874-6221
Fax: (219)873-1204

SCORE Office (South Central Indiana)
4100 Charleston Rd.
New Albany, IN 47150-9538
(812)945-0066

SCORE Office (Rensselaer)
104 W Washington
Rensselaer, IN 47978

SCORE Office (Salem)
210 N. Main St.
Salem, IN 47167
(812)883-4303
Fax: (812)883-1467

SCORE Office (South Bend)
300 N. Michigan St.
South Bend, IN 46601
(219)282-4350
E-mail: chair@southbend-score.org
Website: http://www.southbend-
score.org

SCORE Office (Valparaiso)
150 Lincolnway
Valparaiso, IN 46383
(219)462-1105
Fax: (219)469-5710

SCORE Office (Vincennes)
27 N. 3rd
PO Box 553
Vincennes, IN 47591
(812)882-6440
Fax: (812)882-6441

SCORE Office (Wabash)
PO Box 371
Wabash, IN 46992

(219)563-1168
Fax: (219)563-6920

Iowa

SCORE Office (Burlington)
Federal Bldg.
300 N. Main St.
Burlington, IA 52601
(319)752-2967

SCORE Office (Cedar Rapids)
2750 1st Ave. NE, Ste 350
Cedar Rapids, IA 52401-1806
(319)362-6405
Fax: (319)362-7861
E:mail: score@scorecr.org
Website: http://www.scorecr.org

SCORE Office (Illowa)
333 4th Ave. S
Clinton, IA 52732
(319)242-5702

SCORE Office (Council Bluffs)
7 N. 6th St.
Council Bluffs, IA 51502
(712)325-1000

SCORE Office (Northeast Iowa)
3404 285th St.
Cresco, IA 52136
(319)547-3377

SCORE Office (Des Moines)
Federal Bldg., Rm. 749
210 Walnut St.
Des Moines, IA 50309-2186
(515)284-4760

SCORE Office (Fort Dodge)
Federal Bldg., Rm. 436
205 S 8th St.
Fort Dodge, IA 50501
(515)955-2622

SCORE Office (Independence)
110 1st. St. E
Independence, IA 50644
(319)334-7178
Fax: (319)334-7179

SCORE Office (Iowa City)
210 Federal Bldg.
PO Box 1853
Iowa City, IA 52240-1853
(319)338-1662

SCORE Office (Keokuk)
401 Main St.
Pierce Bldg., No. 1
Keokuk, IA 52632
(319)524-5055

SCORE Office (Central Iowa)
Fisher Community College
709 S Center
Marshalltown, IA 50158
(515)753-6645

SCORE Office (River City)
15 West State St.
Mason City, IA 50401
(515)423-5724

SCORE Office (South Central)
SBDC, Indian Hills Community
College
525 Grandview Ave.
Ottumwa, IA 52501
(515)683-5127
Fax: (515)683-5263

SCORE Office (Dubuque)
10250 Sundown Rd.
Peosta, IA 52068
(319)556-5110

SCORE Office (Southwest Iowa)
614 W Sheridan
Shenandoah, IA 51601
(712)246-3260

SCORE Office (Sioux City)
Federal Bldg.
320 6th St.
Sioux City, IA 51101
(712)277-2324
Fax: (712)277-2325

SCORE Office (Iowa Lakes)
122 W 5th St.
Spencer, IA 51301
(712)262-3059

SCORE Office (Vista)
119 W 6th St.
Storm Lake, IA 50588
(712)732-3780

SCORE Office (Waterloo)
215 E 4th
Waterloo, IA 50703
(319)233-8431

Kansas

SCORE Office (Southwest Kansas)
501 W Spruce
Dodge City, KS 67801
(316)227-3119

SCORE Office (Emporia)
811 Homewood
Emporia, KS 66801
(316)342-1600

SCORE Office (Golden Belt)
1307 Williams
Great Bend, KS 67530
(316)792-2401

SCORE Office (Hays)
PO Box 400
Hays, KS 67601
(913)625-6595

SCORE Office (Hutchinson)
1 E 9th St.
Hutchinson, KS 67501
(316)665-8468
Fax: (316)665-7619

SCORE Office (Southeast Kansas)
404 Westminster Pl.
PO Box 886
Independence, KS 67301
(316)331-4741

SCORE Office (McPherson)
306 N. Main
PO Box 616
McPherson, KS 67460
(316)241-3303

SCORE Office (Salina)
120 Ash St.
Salina, KS 67401
(785)243-4290
Fax: (785)243-1833

SCORE Office (Topeka)
1700 College
Topeka, KS 66621
(785)231-1010

SCORE Office (Wichita)
100 E English, Ste. 510
Wichita, KS 67202
(316)269-6273
Fax: (316)269-6499

SCORE Office (Ark Valley)
205 E 9th St.
Winfield, KS 67156
(316)221-1617

Kentucky

SCORE Office (Ashland)
PO Box 830
Ashland, KY 41105
(606)329-8011
Fax: (606)325-4607

SCORE Office (Bowling Green)
812 State St.
PO Box 51
Bowling Green, KY 42101
(502)781-3200
Fax: (502)843-0458

SCORE Office (Tri-Lakes)
508 Barbee Way
Danville, KY 40422-1548
(606)231-9902

SCORE Office (Glasgow)
301 W Main St.
Glasgow, KY 42141
(502)651-3161
Fax: (502)651-3122

SCORE Office (Hazard)
B & I Technical Center
100 Airport Gardens Rd.
Hazard, KY 41701
(606)439-5856
Fax: (606)439-1808

SCORE Office (Lexington)
410 W Vine St., Ste. 290, Civic C
Lexington, KY 40507
(606)231-9902
Fax: (606)253-3190
E-mail: scorelex@uky.campus.mci.net

SCORE Office (Louisville)
188 Federal Office Bldg.
600 Dr. Martin L. King Jr. Pl.
Louisville, KY 40202
(502)582-5976

SCORE Office (Madisonville)
257 N. Main
Madisonville, KY 42431
(502)825-1399
Fax: (502)825-1396

SCORE Office (Paducah)
Federal Office Bldg.
501 Broadway, Rm. B-36
Paducah, KY 42001
(502)442-5685

Louisiana

SCORE Office (Central Louisiana)
802 3rd St.
Alexandria, LA 71309
(318)442-6671

SCORE Office (Baton Rouge)
564 Laurel St.
PO Box 3217
Baton Rouge, LA 70801
(504)381-7130
Fax: (504)336-4306

SCORE Office (North Shore)
2 W Thomas
Hammond, LA 70401
(504)345-4457
Fax: (504)345-4749

SCORE Office (Lafayette)
804 St. Mary Blvd.
Lafayette, LA 70505-1307
(318)233-2705
Fax: (318)234-8671
E-mail: score302@aol.com

SCORE Office (Lake Charles)
120 W Pujo St.
Lake Charles, LA 70601
(318)433-3632

SCORE Office (New Orleans)
365 Canal St., Ste. 3100
New Orleans, LA 70130
(504)589-2356
Fax: (504)589-2339

SCORE Office (Shreveport)
400 Edwards St.
Shreveport, LA 71101
(318)677-2536
Fax: (318)677-2541

Maine

SCORE Office (Augusta)
40 Western Ave.
Augusta, ME 04330
(207)622-8509

SCORE Office (Bangor)
Peabody Hall, Rm. 229
One College Cir.
Bangor, ME 04401
(207)941-9707

SCORE Office (Central & Northern Arroostock)
111 High St.
Caribou, ME 04736
(207)492-8010
Fax: (207)492-8010

SCORE Office (Penquis)
South St.
Dover Foxcroft, ME 04426
(207)564-7021

SCORE Office (Maine Coastal)
Mill Mall
Box 1105
Ellsworth, ME 04605-1105
(207)667-5800
E-mail: score@arcadia.net

SCORE Office (Lewiston-Auburn)
BIC of Maine-Bates Mill Complex
35 Canal St.
Lewiston, ME 04240-7764
(207)782-3708
Fax: (207)783-7745

SCORE Office (Portland)
66 Pearl St., Rm. 210
Portland, ME 04101
(207)772-1147
Fax: (207)772-5581
E-mail: Score53@score.maine.org
Website: http://www.score.maine.org/chapter53

SCORE Office (Western Mountains)
255 River St.
PO Box 252
Rumford, ME 04257-0252
(207)369-9976

SCORE Office (Oxford Hills)
166 Main St.
South Paris, ME 04281
(207)743-0499

Maryland

SCORE Office (Southern Maryland)
2525 Riva Rd., Ste. 110
Annapolis, MD 21401
(410)266-9553
Fax: (410)573-0981
E-mail: score390@aol.com
Website: http://members.aol.com/score390/index.htm

SCORE Office (Baltimore)
The City Crescent Bldg., 6th Fl.
10 S Howard St.
Baltimore, MD 21201
(410)962-2233
Fax: (410)962-1805

SCORE Office (Bel Air)
108 S Bond St.
Bel Air, MD 21014
(410)838-2020
Fax: (410)893-4715

SCORE Office (Bethesda)
7910 Woodmont Ave., Ste. 1204
Bethesda, MD 20814
(301)652-4900
Fax: (301)657-1973

SCORE Office (Bowie)
6670 Race Track Rd.
Bowie, MD 20715
(301)262-0920
Fax: (301)262-0921

SCORE Office (Dorchester County)
203 Sunburst Hwy.
Cambridge, MD 21613
(410)228-3575

SCORE Office (Upper Shore)
210 Marlboro Ave.
Easton, MD 21601

(410)822-4606
Fax: (410)822-7922

SCORE Office (Frederick County)
43A S Market St.
Frederick, MD 21701
(301)662-8723
Fax: (301)846-4427

SCORE Office (Gaithersburg)
9 Park Ave.
Gaithersburg, MD 20877
(301)840-1400
Fax: (301)963-3918

SCORE Office (Glen Burnie)
103 Crain Hwy. SE
Glen Burnie, MD 21061
(410)766-8282
Fax: (410)766-9722

SCORE Office (Hagerstown)
111 W Washington St.
Hagerstown, MD 21740
(301)739-2015
Fax: (301)739-1278

SCORE Office (Laurel)
7901 Sandy Spring Rd. Ste. 501
Laurel, MD 20707
(301)725-4000
Fax: (301)725-0776

SCORE Office (Salisbury)
300 E Main St.
Salisbury, MD 21801
(410)749-0185
Fax: (410)860-9925

Massachusetts

SCORE Office (NE Massachusetts)
100 Cummings Ctr., Ste. 101 K
Beverly, MA 01923
(978)922-9441
Website: http://www1.shore.net/~score

SCORE Office (Boston)
10 Causeway St., Rm. 265
Boston, MA 02222-1093
(617)565-5591
Fax: (617)565-5598
E-mail: boston-score-20@worldnet.att.net
Website: http://www.scoreboston.org

SCORE office (Bristol/Plymouth County)
53 N. 6th St., Federal Bldg.
Bristol, MA 02740
(508)994-5093

SCORE Office (SE Massachusetts)
60 School St.
Brockton, MA 02401
(508)587-2673
Fax: (508)587-1340
Website: http://
www.metrosouthchamber.com/
score.html

SCORE Office (North Adams)
820 N. State Rd.
Cheshire, MA 01225
(413)743-5100

SCORE Office (Clinton Satellite)
1 Green St.
Clinton, MA 01510
Fax: (508)368-7689

SCORE Office (Greenfield)
PO Box 898
Greenfield, MA 01302
(413)773-5463
Fax: (413)773-7008

SCORE Office (Haverhill)
87 Winter St.
Haverhill, MA 01830
(508)373-5663
Fax: (508)373-8060

SCORE Office (Hudson Satellite)
PO Box 578
Hudson, MA 01749
(508)568-0360
Fax: (508)568-0360

SCORE Office (Cape Cod)
Independence Pk., Ste. 5B
270 Communications Way
Hyannis, MA 02601
(508)775-4884
Fax: (508)790-2540

SCORE Office (Lawrence)
264 Essex St.
Lawrence, MA 01840
(508)686-0900
Fax: (508)794-9953

SCORE Office (Leominster Satellite)
110 Erdman Way
Leominster, MA 01453
(508)840-4300
Fax: (508)840-4896

SCORE Office (Bristol/Plymouth Counties)
53 N. 6th St., Federal Bldg.
New Bedford, MA 02740
(508)994-5093

SCORE Office (Newburyport)
29 State St.
Newburyport, MA 01950
(617)462-6680

SCORE Office (Pittsfield)
66 West St.
Pittsfield, MA 01201
(413)499-2485

SCORE Office (Haverhill-Salem)
32 Derby Sq.
Salem, MA 01970
(508)745-0330
Fax: (508)745-3855

SCORE Office (Springfield)
1350 Main St.
Federal Bldg.
Springfield, MA 01103
(413)785-0314

SCORE Office (Carver)
12 Taunton Green, Ste. 201
Taunton, MA 02780
(508)824-4068
Fax: (508)824-4069

SCORE Office (Worcester)
33 Waldo St.
Worcester, MA 01608
(508)753-2929
Fax: (508)754-8560

Michigan

SCORE Office (Allegan)
PO Box 338
Allegan, MI 49010
(616)673-2479

SCORE Office (Ann Arbor)
425 S Main St., Ste. 103
Ann Arbor, MI 48104
(313)665-4433

SCORE Office (Battle Creek)
34 W Jackson Ste. 4A
Battle Creek, MI 49017-3505
(616)962-4076
Fax: (616)962-6309

SCORE Office (Cadillac)
222 Lake St.
Cadillac, MI 49601
(616)775-9776
Fax: (616)768-4255

SCORE Office (Detroit)
477 Michigan Ave., Rm. 515
Detroit, MI 48226
(313)226-7947
Fax: (313)226-3448

SCORE Office (Flint)
708 Root Rd., Rm. 308
Flint, MI 48503
(810)233-6846

SCORE Office (Grand Rapids)
111 Pearl St. NW
Grand Rapids, MI 49503-2831
(616)771-0305
Fax: (616)771-0328
E-mail: scoreone@iserv.net
Website: http://www.iserv.net/~scoreone

SCORE Office (Holland)
480 State St.
Holland, MI 49423
(616)396-9472

SCORE Office (Jackson)
209 East Washington
PO Box 80
Jackson, MI 49204
(517)782-8221
Fax: (517)782-0061

SCORE Office (Kalamazoo)
345 W Michigan Ave.
Kalamazoo, MI 49007
(616)381-5382
Fax: (616)384-0096
E-mail: score@nucleus.net

SCORE Office (Lansing)
117 E Allegan
PO Box 14030
Lansing, MI 48901
(517)487-6340
Fax: (517)484-6910

SCORE Office (Livonia)
15401 Farmington Rd.
Livonia, MI 48154
(313)427-2122
Fax: (313)427-6055

SCORE Office (Madison Heights)
26345 John R
Madison Heights, MI 48071
(810)542-5010
Fax: (810)542-6821

SCORE Office (Monroe)
111 E 1st
Monroe, MI 48161
(313)242-3366
Fax: (313)242-7253

SCORE Office (Mount Clemens)
58 S/B Gratiot
Mount Clemens, MI 48043
(810)463-1528
Fax: (810)463-6541

SCORE Office (Muskegon)
PO Box 1087
230 Terrace Plz.
Muskegon, MI 49443
(616)722-3751
Fax: (616)728-7251

SCORE Office (Petoskey)
401 E Mitchell St.
Petoskey, MI 49770
(616)347-4150

SCORE Office (Pontiac)
Executive Office Bldg.
1200 N. Telegraph Rd.
Pontiac, MI 48341
(810)975-9555

SCORE Office (Pontiac)
PO Box 430025
Pontiac, MI 48343
(810)335-9600

SCORE Office (Port Huron)
920 Pinegrove Ave.
Port Huron, MI 48060
(810)985-7101

SCORE Office (Rochester)
71 Walnut Ste. 110
Rochester, MI 48307
(810)651-6700
Fax: (810)651-5270

SCORE Office (Saginaw)
901 S Washington Ave.
Saginaw, MI 48601
(517)752-7161
Fax: (517)752-9055

SCORE Office (Upper Peninsula)
2581 I-75 Business Spur
Sault Ste. Marie, MI 49783
(906)632-3301

SCORE Office (Southfield)
21000 W 10 Mile Rd.
Southfield, MI 48075
(810)204-3050
Fax: (810)204-3099

SCORE Office (Traverse City)
202 E Grandview Pkwy.
PO Box 387
Traverse City, MI 49685
(616)947-5075
Fax: (616)946-2565

SCORE Office (Warren)
30500 Van Dyke, Ste. 118
Warren, MI 48093
(810)751-3939

Minnesota

SCORE Office (Aitkin)
Aitkin, MN 56431
(218)741-3906

SCORE Office (Albert Lea)
202 N. Broadway Ave.
Albert Lea, MN 56007
(507)373-7487

SCORE Office (Austin)
PO Box 864
Austin, MN 55912
(507)437-4561
Fax: (507)437-4869

SCORE Office (South Metro)
Ames Business Ctr.
2500 W County Rd., No. 42
Burnsville, MN 55337
(612)898-5645
Fax: (612)435-6972
E-mail: southmetro@scoreminn.org
Website: http://www.scoreminn.org/
southmetro

SCORE Office (Duluth)
1717 Minnesota Ave.
Duluth, MN 55802
(218)727-8286
Fax: (218)727-3113
E-mail: duluth@scoreminn.org
Website: http://www.scoreminn.org

SCORE Office (Fairmont)
PO Box 826
Fairmont, MN 56031
(507)235-5547
Fax: (507)235-8411

SCORE Office (Southwest Minnesota)
112 Riverfront St.
Box 999
Mankato, MN 56001
(507)345-4519
Fax: (507)345-4451
Website: http://www.scoreminn.org

SCORE Office (Minneapolis)
North Plaza Bldg., Ste. 51
5217 Wayzata Blvd.
Minneapolis, MN 55416
(612)591-0539
Fax: (612)544-0436
Website: http://www.scoreminn.org

SCORE Office (Owatonna)
PO Box 331
Owatonna, MN 55060
(507)451-7970
Fax: (507)451-7972

SCORE Office (Red Wing)
2000 W Main St., Ste. 324
Red Wing, MN 55066
(612)388-4079

SCORE Office (Southeastern Minnesota)
220 S Broadway, Ste. 100
Rochester, MN 55901
(507)288-1122
Fax: (507)282-8960
Website: http://www.scoreminn.org

SCORE Office (Brainerd)
Saint Cloud, MN 56301

SCORE Office (Central Area)
1527 Northway Dr.
Saint Cloud, MN 56301
(320)240-1332
Fax: (320)255-9050
Website: http://www.scoreminn.org

SCORE Office (Saint Paul)
350 St. Peter St., No. 295
Lowry Professional Bldg.
Saint Paul, MN 55102
(651)223-5010
Fax: (651)223-5048
Website: http://www.scoreminn.org

SCORE Office (Winona)
Box 870
Winona, MN 55987
(507)452-2272
Fax: (507)454-8814

SCORE Office (Worthington)
1121 3rd Ave.
Worthington, MN 56187
(507)372-2919
Fax: (507)372-2827

Mississippi

SCORE Office (Delta)
915 Washington Ave.
PO Box 933
Greenville, MS 38701
(601)378-3141

SCORE Office (Gulfcoast)
1 Government Plaza
2909 13th St., Ste. 203
Gulfport, MS 39501
(228)863-0054

SCORE Office (Jackson)
1st Jackson Center, Ste. 400
101 W Capitol St.
Jackson, MS 39201
(601)965-5533

SCORE Office (Meridian)
5220 16th Ave.
Meridian, MS 39305
(601)482-4412

Missouri

SCORE Office (Lake of the Ozark)
University Extension
113 Kansas St.
PO Box 1405
Camdenton, MO 65020
(573)346-2644
Fax: (573)346-2694
E-mail: score@cdoc.net
Website: http://sites.cdoc.net/score

Chamber of Commerce (Cape Girardeau)
PO Box 98
Cape Girardeau, MO 63702-0098
(314)335-3312

SCORE Office (Mid-Missouri)
1705 Halstead Ct.
Columbia, MO 65203
(573)874-1132

SCORE Office (Ozark-Gateway)
1486 Glassy Rd.
Cuba, MO 65453-1640
(573)885-4954

SCORE Office (Kansas City)
323 W 8th St., Ste. 104
Kansas City, MO 64105
(816)374-6675
Fax: (816)374-6692
E-mail: SCOREBIC@AOL.COM
Website: http://www.crn.org/score

SCORE Office (Sedalia)
Lucas Place
323 W 8th St., Ste.104
Kansas City, MO 64105
(816)374-6675

SCORE office (Tri-Lakes)
PO Box 1148
Kimberling, MO 65686
(417)739-3041

SCORE Office (Tri-Lakes)
HCRI Box 85
Lampe, MO 65681
(417)858-6798

SCORE Office (Mexico)
111 N. Washington St.
Mexico, MO 65265
(314)581-2765

SCORE Office (Southeast Missouri)
Rte. 1, Box 280
Neelyville, MO 63954
(573)989-3577

SCORE office (Poplar Bluff Area)
806 Emma St.
Poplar Bluff, MO 63901
(573)686-8892

SCORE Office (Saint Joseph)
3003 Frederick Ave.
Saint Joseph, MO 64506
(816)232-4461

SCORE Office (Saint Louis)
815 Olive St., Rm. 242
Saint Louis, MO 63101-1569
(314)539-6970
Fax: (314)539-3785
E-mail: info@stlscore.org
Website: http://www.stlscore.org

SCORE Office (Lewis & Clark)
425 Spencer Rd.
Saint Peters, MO 63376
(314)928-2900
Fax: (314)928-2900
E-mail: score01@mail.win.org

SCORE Office (Springfield)
620 S Glenstone, Ste. 110
Springfield, MO 65802-3200
(417)864-7670
Fax: (417)864-4108

SCORE office (Southeast Kansas)
1206 W First St.
Webb City, MO 64870
(417)673-3984

Montana

SCORE Office (Billings)
815 S 27th St.
Billings, MT 59101
(406)245-4111

SCORE Office (Bozeman)
1205 E Main St.
Bozeman, MT 59715
(406)586-5421

SCORE Office (Butte)
1000 George St.
Butte, MT 59701
(406)723-3177

SCORE Office (Great Falls)
710 First Ave. N
Great Falls, MT 59401
(406)761-4434
E-mail: scoregtf@in.tch.com

SCORE Office (Havre, Montana)
518 First St.
Havre, MT 59501
(406)265-4383

SCORE Office (Helena)
Federal Bldg.
301 S Park
Helena, MT 59626-0054
(406)441-1081

SCORE Office (Kalispell)
2 Main St.
Kalispell, MT 59901
(406)756-5271
Fax: (406)752-6665

SCORE Office (Missoula)
723 Ronan
Missoula, MT 59806
(406)327-8806
E-mail: score@safeshop.com
Website: http://missoula.bigsky.net/score

Nebraska

SCORE Office (Columbus)
Columbus, NE 68601
(402)564-2769

SCORE Office (Fremont)
92 W 5th St.
Fremont, NE 68025
(402)721-2641

SCORE Office (Hastings)
Hastings, NE 68901
(402)463-3447

SCORE Office (Lincoln)
8800 O St.
Lincoln, NE 68520
(402)437-2409

SCORE Office (Panhandle)
150549 CR 30
Minatare, NE 69356
(308)632-2133
Website: http://www.tandt.com/SCORE

SCORE Office (Norfolk)
3209 S 48th Ave.
Norfolk, NE 68106
(402)564-2769

SCORE Office (North Platte)
3301 W 2nd St.
North Platte, NE 69101
(308)532-4466

SCORE Office (Omaha)
11145 Mill Valley Rd.
Omaha, NE 68154
(402)221-3606

Fax: (402)221-3680
E-mail: infoctr@ne.uswest.net
Website: http://www.tandt.com/score

Nevada

SCORE Office (Incline Village)
969 Tahoe Blvd.
Incline Village, NV 89451
(702)831-7327
Fax: (702)832-1605

SCORE Office (Carson City)
301 E Stewart
PO Box 7527
Las Vegas, NV 89125
(702)388-6104

SCORE Office (Las Vegas)
300 Las Vegas Blvd. S, Ste. 1100
Las Vegas, NV 89101
(702)388-6104

SCORE Office (Northern Nevada)
SBDC, College of Business
Administration
Univ. of Nevada
Reno, NV 89557-0100
(702)784-4436
Fax: (702)784-4337

New Hampshire

SCORE Office (North Country)
PO Box 34
Berlin, NH 03570
(603)752-1090

SCORE Office (Concord)
143 N. Main St., Rm. 202A
PO Box 1258
Concord, NH 03301
(603)225-1400
Fax: (603)225-1409

SCORE Office (Dover)
299 Central Ave.
Dover, NH 03820
(603)742-2218
Fax: (603)749-6317

SCORE Office (Monadnock)
34 Mechanic St.
Keene, NH 03431-3421
(603)352-0320

SCORE Office (Lakes Region)
67 Water St., Ste. 105
Laconia, NH 03246
(603)524-9168

SCORE Office (Upper Valley)
Citizens Bank Bldg., Rm. 310
20 W Park St.

Lebanon, NH 03766
(603)448-3491
Fax: (603)448-1908
E-mail: billt@valley.net
Website: http://www.valley.net/~score

SCORE Office (Merrimack Valley)
275 Chestnut St., Rm. 618
Manchester, NH 03103
(603)666-7561
Fax: (603)666-7925

SCORE Office (Mount Washington Valley)
PO Box 1066
North Conway, NH 03818
(603)383-0800

SCORE Office (Seacoast)
195 Commerce Way, Unit-A
Portsmouth, NH 03801-3251
(603)433-0575

New Jersey

SCORE Office (Somerset)
Paritan Valley Community College, Rte. 28
Branchburg, NJ 08807
(908)218-8874
E-mail: nj-score@grizbiz.com.
Website: http://www.nj-score.org

SCORE Office (Chester)
5 Old Mill Rd.
Chester, NJ 07930
(908)879-7080

SCORE Office (Greater Princeton)
4 A George Washington Dr.
Cranbury, NJ 08512
(609)520-1776

SCORE Office (Freehold)
36 W Main St.
Freehold, NJ 07728
(908)462-3030
Fax: (908)462-2123

SCORE Office (North West)
Picantinny Innovation Ctr.
3159 Schrader Rd.
Hamburg, NJ 07419
(973)209-8525
Fax: (973)209-7252
E-mail: nj-score@grizbiz.com
Website: http://www.nj-score.org

SCORE Office (Monmouth)
765 Newman Springs Rd.
Lincroft, NJ 07738
(908)224-2573
E-mail: nj-score@grizbiz.com
Website: http://www.nj-score.org

SCORE Office (Manalapan)
125 Symmes Dr.
Manalapan, NJ 07726
(908)431-7220

SCORE Office (Jersey City)
2 Gateway Ctr., 4th Fl.
Newark, NJ 07102
(973)645-3982
Fax: (973)645-2375

SCORE Office (Newark)
2 Gateway Center, 15th Fl.
Newark, NJ 07102-5553
(973)645-3982
Fax: (973)645-2375
E-mail: nj-score@grizbiz.com
Website: http://www.nj-score.org

SCORE Office (Bergen County)
327 E Ridgewood Ave.
Paramus, NJ 07652
(201)599-6090
E-mail: nj-score@grizbiz.com
Website: http://www.nj-score.org

SCORE Office (Pennsauken)
4900 Rte. 70
Pennsauken, NJ 08109
(609)486-3421

SCORE Office (Southern New Jersey)
4900 Rte. 70
Pennsauken, NJ 08109
(609)486-3421
E-mail: nj-score@grizbiz.com
Website: http://www.nj-score.org

SCORE Office (Greater Princeton)
216 Rockingham Row
Princeton Forrestal Village
Princeton, NJ 08540
(609)520-1776
Fax: (609)520-9107
E-mail: nj-score@grizbiz.com
Website: http://www.nj-score.org

SCORE Office (Shrewsbury)
Hwy. 35
Shrewsbury, NJ 07702
(908)842-5995
Fax: (908)219-6140

SCORE Office (Ocean County)
33 Washington St.
Toms River, NJ 08754
(732)505-6033
E-mail: nj-score@grizbiz.com
Website: http://www.nj-score.org

SCORE Office (Wall)
2700 Allaire Rd.
Wall, NJ 07719
(908)449-8877

SCORE Office (Wayne)
2055 Hamburg Tpke.
Wayne, NJ 07470
(201)831-7788
Fax: (201)831-9112

New Mexico

SCORE Office (Albuquerque)
525 Buena Vista, SE
Albuquerque, NM 87106
(505)272-7999
Fax: (505)272-7963

SCORE Office (Las Cruces)
Loretto Towne Center
505 S Main St., Ste. 125
Las Cruces, NM 88001
(505)523-5627
Fax: (505)524-2101
E-mail: score.397@zianet.com

SCORE Office (Roswell)
Federal Bldg., Rm. 237
Roswell, NM 88201
(505)625-2112
Fax: (505)623-2545

SCORE Office (Santa Fe)
Montoya Federal Bldg.
120 Federal Place, Rm. 307
Santa Fe, NM 87501
(505)988-6302
Fax: (505)988-6300

New York

SCORE Office (Northeast)
1 Computer Dr. S
Albany, NY 12205
(518)446-1118
Fax: (518)446-1228

SCORE Office (Auburn)
30 South St.
PO Box 675
Auburn, NY 13021
(315)252-7291

SCORE Office (South Tier Binghamton)
Metro Center, 2nd Fl.
49 Court St.
PO Box 995
Binghamton, NY 13902
(607)772-8860

SCORE Office (Queens County City)
12055 Queens Blvd., Rm. 333
Borough Hall, NY 11424
(718)263-8961

SCORE Office (Buffalo)
Federal Bldg., Rm. 1311
111 W Huron St.
Buffalo, NY 14202
(716)551-4301
Website: http://www2.pcom.net/score/
buf45.html

SCORE Office (Canandaigua)
Chamber of Commerce Bldg.
113 S Main St.
Canandaigua, NY 14424
(716)394-4400
Fax: (716)394-4546

SCORE Office (Chemung)
333 E Water St., 4th Fl.
Elmira, NY 14901
(607)734-3358

SCORE Office (Geneva)
Chamber of Commerce Bldg.
PO Box 587
Geneva, NY 14456
(315)789-1776
Fax: (315)789-3993

SCORE Office (Glens Falls)
84 Broad St.
Glens Falls, NY 12801
(518)798-8463
Fax: (518)745-1433

SCORE Office (Orange County)
40 Matthews St.
Goshen, NY 10924
(914)294-8080
Fax: (914)294-6121

SCORE Office (Huntington Area)
151 W Carver St.
Huntington, NY 11743
(516)423-6100

SCORE Office (Tompkins County)
904 E Shore Dr.
Ithaca, NY 14850
(607)273-7080

SCORE Office (Long Island City)
120-55 Queens Blvd.
Jamaica, NY 11424
(718)263-8961
Fax: (718)263-9032

SCORE Office (Chatauqua)
101 W 5th St.
Jamestown, NY 14701
(716)484-1103

SCORE Office (Westchester)
2 Caradon Ln.
Katonah, NY 10536
(914)948-3907

Fax: (914)948-4645
E-mail: score@w-w-w.com
Website: http://w-w-w.com/score

SCORE Office (Queens County)
Queens Borough Hall
120-55 Queens Blvd. Rm. 333
Kew Gardens, NY 11424
(718)263-8961
Fax: (718)263-9032

SCORE Office (Brookhaven)
3233 Rte. 112
Medford, NY 11763
(516)451-6563
Fax: (516)451-6925

SCORE Office (Melville)
35 Pinelawn Rd., Rm. 207-W
Melville, NY 11747
(516)454-0771

SCORE Office (Nassau County)
400 County Seat Dr., No. 140
Mineola, NY 11501
(516)571-3303
E-mail: Counse1998@aol.com
Website: http://members.aol.com/
Counse1998/Default.htm

SCORE Office (Mount Vernon)
4 N. 7th Ave.
Mount Vernon, NY 10550
(914)667-7500

SCORE Office (New York)
26 Federal Plz., Rm. 3100
New York, NY 10278
(212)264-4507
Fax: (212)264-4963
E-mail: score1000@erols.com
Website: http://users.erols.com/score-nyc

SCORE Office (Newburgh)
47 Grand St.
Newburgh, NY 12550
(914)562-5100

SCORE Office (Owego)
188 Front St.
Owego, NY 13827
(607)687-2020

SCORE Office (Peekskill)
1 S Division St.
Peekskill, NY 10566
(914)737-3600
Fax: (914)737-0541

SCORE Office (Penn Yan)
2375 Rte. 14A
Penn Yan, NY 14527
(315)536-3111

SCORE Office (Dutchess)
110 Main St.
Poughkeepsie, NY 12601
(914)454-1700

SCORE Office (Rochester)
601 Keating Federal Bldg., Rm. 410
100 State St.
Rochester, NY 14614
(716)263-6473
Fax: (716)263-3146
Website: http://www.ggw.org/score

SCORE Office (Saranac Lake)
30 Main St.
Saranac Lake, NY 12983
(315)448-0415

SCORE Office (Suffolk)
286 Main St.
Setauket, NY 11733
(516)751-3886

SCORE Office (Staten Island)
130 Bay St.
Staten Island, NY 10301
(718)727-1221

SCORE Office (Ulster)
Clinton Bldg., Rm. 107
Stone Ridge, NY 12484
(914)687-5035
Fax: (914)687-5015
Website: http://www.scoreulster.org

SCORE Office (Syracuse)
401 S Salina, 5th Fl.
Syracuse, NY 13202
(315)471-9393

SCORE Office (Utica)
SUNY Institute of Technology, Route 12
Utica, NY 13504-3050
(315)792-7553

SCORE Office (Watertown)
518 Davidson St.
Watertown, NY 13601
(315)788-1200
Fax: (315)788-8251

North Carolina

SCORE office (Asheboro)
317 E Dixie Dr.
Asheboro, NC 27203
(336)626-2626
Fax: (336)626-7077

SCORE Office (Asheville)
Federal Bldg., Rm. 259
151 Patton
Asheville, NC 28801-5770

(828)271-4786
Fax: (828)271-4009

SCORE Office (Chapel Hill)
104 S Estes Dr.
PO Box 2897
Chapel Hill, NC 27514
(919)967-7075

SCORE Office (Coastal Plains)
PO Box 2897
Chapel Hill, NC 27515
(919)967-7075
Fax: (919)968-6874

SCORE Office (Charlotte)
200 N. College St., Ste. A-2015
Charlotte, NC 28202
(704)344-6576
Fax: (704)344-6769
E-mail: CharlotteSCORE47@AOL.com
Website: http://www.charweb.org/
business/score

SCORE Office (Durham)
411 W Chapel Hill St.
Durham, NC 27707
(919)541-2171

SCORE Office (Gastonia)
PO Box 2168
Gastonia, NC 28053
(704)864-2621
Fax: (704)854-8723

SCORE Office (Greensboro)
400 W Market St., Ste. 103
Greensboro, NC 27401-2241
(910)333-5399

SCORE Office (Henderson)
PO Box 917
Henderson, NC 27536
(919)492-2061
Fax: (919)430-0460

SCORE Office (Hendersonville)
Federal Bldg., Rm. 108
W 4th Ave. & Church St.
Hendersonville, NC 28792
(828)693-8702
E-mail: score@circle.net
Website: http://www.wncguide.com/
score/Welcome.html

SCORE Office (Unifour)
PO Box 1828
Hickory, NC 28603
(704)328-6111

SCORE Office (High Point)
1101 N. Main St.
High Point, NC 27262

(336)882-8625
Fax: (336)889-9499

SCORE Office (Outer Banks)
Collington Rd. and Mustain
Kill Devil Hills, NC 27948
(252)441-8144

SCORE Office (Down East)
312 S Front St., Ste. 6
New Bern, NC 28560
(252)633-6688
Fax: (252)633-9608

SCORE Office (Kinston)
PO Box 95
New Bern, NC 28561
(919)633-6688

SCORE Office (Raleigh)
Century Post Office Bldg., Ste. 306
300 Federal St. Mall
Raleigh, NC 27601
(919)856-4739
E-mail: jendres@ibm.net
Website: http://www.intrex.net/score96/
score96.htm

SCORE Office (Sanford)
1801 Nash St.
Sanford, NC 27330
(919)774-6442
Fax: (919)776-8739

SCORE Office (Sandhills Area)
1480 Hwy. 15-501
PO Box 458
Southern Pines, NC 28387
(910)692-3926

SCORE Office (Wilmington)
Corps of Engineers Bldg.
96 Darlington Ave., Ste. 207
Wilmington, NC 28403
(910)815-4576
Fax: (910)815-4658

North Dakota

SCORE Office (Bismarck-Mandan)
700 E Main Ave., 2nd Fl.
PO Box 5509
Bismarck, ND 58506-5509
(701)250-4303

SCORE Office (Fargo)
657 2nd Ave., Rm. 225
Fargo, ND 58108-3083
(701)239-5677

SCORE Office (Upper Red River)
4275 Technology Dr., Rm. 156
Grand Forks, ND 58202-8372
(701)777-3051

SCORE Office (Minot)
100 1st St. SW
Minot, ND 58701-3846
(701)852-6883
Fax: (701)852-6905

Ohio

SCORE Office (Akron)
1 Cascade Plz., 7th Fl.
Akron, OH 44308
(330)379-3163
Fax: (330)379-3164

SCORE Office (Ashland)
Gill Center
47 W Main St.
Ashland, OH 44805
(419)281-4584

SCORE Office (Canton)
116 Cleveland Ave. NW, Ste. 601
Canton, OH 44702-1720
(330)453-6047

SCORE Office (Chillicothe)
165 S Paint St.
Chillicothe, OH 45601
(614)772-4530

SCORE Office (Cincinnati)
Ameritrust Bldg., Rm. 850
525 Vine St.
Cincinnati, OH 45202
(513)684-2812
Fax: (513)684-3251
Website: http://www.score.chapter34.org

SCORE Office (Cleveland)
Eaton Center, Ste. 620
1100 Superior Ave.
Cleveland, OH 44114-2507
(216)522-4194
Fax: (216)522-4844

SCORE Office (Columbus)
2 Nationwide Plz., Ste. 1400
Columbus, OH 43215-2542
(614)469-2357
Fax: (614)469-2391
E-mail: info@scorecolumbus.org
Website: http://www.scorecolumbus.org

SCORE Office (Dayton)
Dayton Federal Bldg., Rm. 505
200 W Second St.
Dayton, OH 45402-1430
(513)225-2887
Fax: (513)225-7667

SCORE Office (Defiance)
615 W 3rd St.
PO Box 130

Defiance, OH 43512
(419)782-7946

SCORE Office (Findlay)
123 E Main Cross St.
PO Box 923
Findlay, OH 45840
(419)422-3314

SCORE Office (Lima)
147 N. Main St.
Lima, OH 45801
(419)222-6045
Fax: (419)229-0266

SCORE Office (Mansfield)
55 N. Mulberry St.
Mansfield, OH 44902
(419)522-3211

SCORE Office (Marietta)
Thomas Hall
Marietta, OH 45750
(614)373-0268

SCORE Office (Medina)
County Administrative Bldg.
144 N. Broadway
Medina, OH 44256
(216)764-8650

SCORE Office (Licking County)
50 W Locust St.
Newark, OH 43055
(614)345-7458

SCORE Office (Salem)
2491 State Rte. 45 S
Salem, OH 44460
(216)332-0361

SCORE Office (Tiffin)
62 S Washington St.
Tiffin, OH 44883
(419)447-4141
Fax: (419)447-5141

SCORE Office (Toledo)
608 Madison Ave, Ste. 910
Toledo, OH 43624
(419)259-7598
Fax: (419)259-6460

SCORE Office (Heart of Ohio)
377 W Liberty St.
Wooster, OH 44691
(330)262-5735
Fax: (330)262-5745

SCORE Office (Youngstown)
306 Williamson Hall
Youngstown, OH 44555
(330)746-2687

Oklahoma

SCORE Office (Anadarko)
PO Box 366
Anadarko, OK 73005
(405)247-6651

SCORE Office (Ardmore)
410 W Main
Ardmore, OK 73401
(580)226-2620

SCORE Office (Northeast Oklahoma)
210 S Main
Grove, OK 74344
(918)787-2796
Fax: (918)787-2796
E-mail: Score595@greencis.net

SCORE Office (Lawton)
4500 W Lee Blvd., Bldg. 100, Ste. 107
Lawton, OK 73505
(580)353-8727
Fax: (580)250-5677

SCORE Office (Oklahoma City)
210 Park Ave., No. 1300
Oklahoma City, OK 73102
(405)231-5163
Fax: (405)231-4876
E-mail: score212@usa.net

SCORE Office (Stillwater)
439 S Main
Stillwater, OK 74074
(405)372-5573
Fax: (405)372-4316

SCORE Office (Tulsa)
616 S Boston, Ste. 406
Tulsa, OK 74119
(918)581-7462
Fax: (918)581-6908
Website: http://www.ionet.net/~tulscore

Oregon

SCORE Office (Bend)
63085 N. Hwy. 97
Bend, OR 97701
(541)923-2849
Fax: (541)330-6900

SCORE Office (Willamette)
1401 Willamette St.
PO Box 1107
Eugene, OR 97401-4003
(541)465-6600
Fax: (541)484-4942

SCORE Office (Florence)
3149 Oak St.
Florence, OR 97439

(503)997-8444
Fax: (503)997-8448

SCORE Office (Southern Oregon)
33 N. Central Ave., Ste. 216
Medford, OR 97501
(541)776-4220
E-mail: pgr134f@prodigy.com

SCORE Office (Portland)
1515 SW 5th Ave., Ste. 1050
Portland, OR 97201
(503)326-3441
Fax: (503)326-2808
E-mail: gr134@prodigy.com

SCORE Office (Salem)
416 State St. (corner of Liberty)
Salem, OR 97301
(503)370-2896

Pennsylvania

SCORE Office (Altoona-Blair)
1212 12th Ave.
Altoona, PA 16601-3493
(814)943-8151

SCORE Office (Lehigh Valley)
Rauch Bldg. 37
Lehigh University
621 Taylor St.
Bethlehem, PA 18015
(610)758-4496
Fax: (610)758-5205

SCORE Office (Butler County)
100 N. Main St.
PO Box 1082
Butler, PA 16003
(412)283-2222
Fax: (412)283-0224

SCORE Office (Harrisburg)
4211 Trindle Rd.
Camp Hill, PA 17011
(717)761-4304
Fax: (717)761-4315

SCORE Office (Cumberland Valley)
75 S 2nd St.
Chambersburg, PA 17201
(717)264-2935

SCORE Office (Monroe County-Stroudsburg)
556 Main St.
East Stroudsburg, PA 18301
(717)421-4433

SCORE Office (Erie)
120 W 9th St.
Erie, PA 16501

(814)871-5650
Fax: (814)871-7530

SCORE Office (Bucks County)
409 Hood Blvd.
Fairless Hills, PA 19030
(215)943-8850
Fax: (215)943-7404

SCORE Office (Hanover)
146 Broadway
Hanover, PA 17331
(717)637-6130
Fax: (717)637-9127

SCORE Office (Harrisburg)
100 Chestnut, Ste. 309
Harrisburg, PA 17101
(717)782-3874

SCORE Office (East Montgomery County)
Baederwood Shopping Center
1653 The Fairways, Ste. 204
Jenkintown, PA 19046
(215)885-3027

SCORE Office (Kittanning)
2 Butler Rd.
Kittanning, PA 16201
(412)543-1305
Fax: (412)543-6206

SCORE Office (Lancaster)
118 W Chestnut St.
Lancaster, PA 17603
(717)397-3092

SCORE Office (Westmoreland County)
300 Fraser Purchase Rd.
Latrobe, PA 15650-2690
(412)539-7505
Fax: (412)539-1850

SCORE Office (Lebanon)
252 N. 8th St.
PO Box 899
Lebanon, PA 17042-0899
(717)273-3727
Fax: (717)273-7940

SCORE Office (Lewistown)
3 W Monument Sq., Ste. 204
Lewistown, PA 17044
(717)248-6713
Fax: (717)248-6714

SCORE Office (Delaware County)
602 E Baltimore Pike
Media, PA 19063
(610)565-3677
Fax: (610)565-1606

SCORE Office (Milton Area)
112 S Front St.
Milton, PA 17847
(717)742-7341
Fax: (717)792-2008

SCORE Office (Mon-Valley)
435 Donner Ave.
Monessen, PA 15062
(412)684-4277
Fax: (412)684-7688

SCORE Office (Monroeville)
William Penn Plaza
2790 Mosside Blvd., Ste. 295
Monroeville, PA 15146
(412)856-0622
Fax: (412)856-1030

SCORE Office (Airport Area)
986 Brodhead Rd.
Moon Township, PA 15108-2398
(412)264-6270
Fax: (412)264-1575

SCORE Office (Northeast)
8601 E Roosevelt Blvd.
Philadelphia, PA 19152
(215)332-3400
Fax: (215)332-6050

SCORE Office (Philadelphia)
1315 Walnut St., Ste. 500
Philadelphia, PA 19107
(215)790-5050
Fax: (215)790-5057
E-mail: score46@bellatlantic.net
Website: http://www.pgweb.net/score46

SCORE Office (Pittsburgh)
1000 Liberty Ave., Rm. 1122
Pittsburgh, PA 15222
(412)395-6560
Fax: (412)395-6562

SCORE Office (Tri-County)
801 N. Charlotte St.
Pottstown, PA 19464
(610)327-2673

SCORE Office (Reading)
601 Penn St.
Reading, PA 19601
(610)376-3497

SCORE Office (Scranton)
Oppenheim Bldg.
116 N. Washington Ave., Ste. 650
Scranton, PA 18503
(717)347-4611
Fax: (717)347-4611

SCORE Office (Central Pennsylvania)
200 Innovation Blvd., Ste. 242-B
State College, PA 16803
(814)234-9415
Fax: (814)238-9686
Website: http://countrystore.org/
business/score.htm

SCORE Office (Monroe-Stroudsburg)
556 Main St.
Stroudsburg, PA 18360
(717)421-4433

SCORE Office (Uniontown)
Federal Bldg.
Pittsburg St.
PO Box 2065 DTS
Uniontown, PA 15401
(412)437-4222
E-mail: uniontownscore@lcsys.net

SCORE Office (Warren County)
315 2nd Ave.
Warren, PA 16365
(814)723-9017

SCORE Office (Waynesboro)
323 E Main St.
Waynesboro, PA 17268
(717)762-7123
Fax: (717)962-7124

SCORE Office (Chester County)
Government Service Center, Ste. 281
601 Westtown Rd.
West Chester, PA 19382-4538
(610)344-6910
Fax: (610)344-6919
E-mail: score@locke.ccil.org

SCORE Office (Wilkes-Barre)
7 N. Wilkes-Barre Blvd.
Wilkes Barre, PA 18702-5241
(717)826-6502
Fax: (717)826-6287

SCORE Office (North Central Pennsylvania)
240 W 3rd St., Rm. 227
PO Box 725
Williamsport, PA 17703
(717)322-3720
Fax: (717)322-1607
E-mail: score234@mail.csrlink.net
Website: http://www.lycoming.org/score

SCORE Office (York)
Cyber Center
2101 Pennsylvania Ave.
York, PA 17404
(717)845-8830
Fax: (717)854-9333

Puerto Rico

SCORE Office (Puerto Rico & Virgin Islands)
PO Box 12383-96
San Juan, PR 00914-0383
(787)726-8040
Fax: (787)726-8135

Rhode Island

SCORE Office (Barrington)
281 County Rd.
Barrington, RI 02806
(401)247-1920
Fax: (401)247-3763

SCORE Office (Woonsocket)
640 Washington Hwy.
Lincoln, RI 02865
(401)334-1000
Fax: (401)334-1009

SCORE Office (Wickford)
8045 Post Rd.
North Kingstown, RI 02852
(401)295-5566
Fax: (401)295-8987

SCORE Office (J.G.E. Knight)
380 Westminster St.
Providence, RI 02903
(401)528-4571
Fax: (401)528-4539
Website: http://www.riscore.org

SCORE Office (Warwick)
3288 Post Rd.
Warwick, RI 02886
(401)732-1100
Fax: (401)732-1101

SCORE Office (Westerly)
74 Post Rd.
Westerly, RI 02891
(401)596-7761
800-732-7636
Fax: (401)596-2190

South Carolina

SCORE Office (Aiken)
PO Box 892
Aiken, SC 29802
(803)641-1111
800-542-4536
Fax: (803)641-4174

SCORE Office (Anderson)
Anderson Mall
3130 N. Main St.
Anderson, SC 29621
(864)224-0453

SCORE Office (Coastal)
284 King St.
Charleston, SC 29401
(803)727-4778
Fax: (803)853-2529

SCORE Office (Midlands)
Strom Thurmond Bldg., Rm. 358
1835 Assembly St., Rm 358
Columbia, SC 29201
(803)765-5131
Fax: (803)765-5962
Website: http://www.scoremidlands
.org

SCORE Office (Piedmont)
Federal Bldg., Rm. B-02
300 E Washington St.
Greenville, SC 29601
(864)271-3638

SCORE Office (Greenwood)
PO Drawer 1467
Greenwood, SC 29648
(864)223-8357

SCORE Office (Hilton Head Island)
52 Savannah Trail
Hilton Head, SC 29926
(803)785-7107
Fax: (803)785-7110

SCORE Office (Grand Strand)
937 Broadway
Myrtle Beach, SC 29577
(803)918-1079
Fax: (803)918-1083
E-mail: score381@aol.com

SCORE Office (Spartanburg)
PO Box 1636
Spartanburg, SC 29304
(864)594-5000
Fax: (864)594-5055

South Dakota

SCORE Office (West River)
Rushmore Plz. Civic Ctr.
444 Mount Rushmore Rd., No. 209
Rapid City, SD 57701
(605)394-5311
E-mail: score@gwtc.net

SCORE Office (Sioux Falls)
First Financial Center
110 S Phillips Ave., Ste. 200
Sioux Falls, SD 57104-6727
(605)330-4231
Fax: (605)330-4231

Tennessee

SCORE Office (Chattanooga)
Federal Bldg., Rm. 26
900 Georgia Ave.
Chattanooga, TN 37402
(423)752-5190
Fax: (423)752-5335

SCORE Office (Cleveland)
PO Box 2275
Cleveland, TN 37320
(423)472-6587
Fax: (423)472-2019

SCORE Office (Upper Cumberland Center)
1225 S Willow Ave.
Cookeville, TN 38501
(615)432-4111
Fax: (615)432-6010

SCORE Office (Unicoi County)
PO Box 713
Erwin, TN 37650
(423)743-3000
Fax: (423)743-0942

SCORE Office (Greeneville)
115 Academy St.
Greeneville, TN 37743
(423)638-4111
Fax: (423)638-5345

SCORE Office (Jackson)
194 Auditorium St.
Jackson, TN 38301
(901)423-2200

SCORE Office (Northeast Tennessee)
1st Tennessee Bank Bldg.
2710 S Roan St., Ste. 584
Johnson City, TN 37601
(423)929-7686
Fax: (423)461-8052

SCORE Office (Kingsport)
151 E Main St.
Kingsport, TN 37662
(423)392-8805

SCORE Office (Greater Knoxville)
Farragot Bldg., Ste. 224
530 S Gay St.
Knoxville, TN 37902
(423)545-4203
E-mail: scoreknox@ntown.com
Website: http://www.scoreknox.org

SCORE Office (Maryville)
201 S Washington St.
Maryville, TN 37804-5728
(423)983-2241

800-525-6834
Fax: (423)984-1386

SCORE Office (Memphis)
Federal Bldg., Ste. 390
167 N. Main St.
Memphis, TN 38103
(901)544-3588

SCORE Office (Nashville)
50 Vantage Way, Ste. 201
Nashville, TN 37228-1500
(615)736-7621

Texas

SCORE Office (Abilene)
2106 Federal Post Office and Court Bldg.
Abilene, TX 79601
(915)677-1857

SCORE Office (Austin)
2501 S Congress
Austin, TX 78701
(512)442-7235
Fax: (512)442-7528

SCORE Office (Golden Triangle)
450 Boyd St.
Beaumont, TX 77704
(409)838-6581
Fax: (409)833-6718

SCORE Office (Brownsville)
3505 Boca Chica Blvd., Ste. 305
Brownsville, TX 78521
(210)541-4508

SCORE Office (Brazos Valley)
3000 Briarcrest, Ste. 302
Bryan, TX 77802
(409)776-8876
E-mail: 102633.2612@compuserve.com

SCORE Office (Cleburne)
Watergarden Pl., 9th Fl., Ste. 400
Cleburne, TX 76031
(817)871-6002

SCORE Office (Corpus Christi)
651 Upper North Broadway, Ste. 654
Corpus Christi, TX 78477
(512)888-4322
Fax: (512)888-3418

SCORE Office (Dallas)
6260 E Mockingbird
Dallas, TX 75214-2619
(214)828-2471
Fax: (214)821-8033

SCORE Office (El Paso)
10 Civic Center Plaza
El Paso, TX 79901

(915)534-0541
Fax: (915)534-0513

SCORE Office (Bedford)
100 E 15th St., Ste. 400
Fort Worth, TX 76102
(817)871-6002

SCORE Office (Fort Worth)
100 E 15th St., No. 24
Fort Worth, TX 76102
(817)871-6002
Fax: (817)871-6031
E-mail: fwbac@onramp.net

SCORE Office (Garland)
2734 W Kingsley Rd.
Garland, TX 75041
(214)271-9224

SCORE Office (Granbury Chamber of Commerce)
416 S Morgan
Granbury, TX 76048
(817)573-1622
Fax: (817)573-0805

SCORE Office (Lower Rio Grande Valley)
222 E Van Buren, Ste. 500
Harlingen, TX 78550
(956)427-8533
Fax: (956)427-8537

SCORE Office (Houston)
9301 Southwest Fwy., Ste. 550
Houston, TX 77074
(713)773-6565
Fax: (713)773-6550

SCORE Office (Irving)
3333 N. MacArthur Blvd., Ste. 100
Irving, TX 75062
(214)252-8484
Fax: (214)252-6710

SCORE Office (Lubbock)
1205 Texas Ave., Rm. 411D
Lubbock, TX 79401
(806)472-7462
Fax: (806)472-7487

SCORE Office (Midland)
Post Office Annex
200 E Wall St., Rm. P121
Midland, TX 79701
(915)687-2649

SCORE Office (Orange)
1012 Green Ave.
Orange, TX 77630-5620
(409)883-3536
800-528-4906
Fax: (409)886-3247

SCORE Office (Plano)
1200 E 15th St.
PO Drawer 940287
Plano, TX 75094-0287
(214)424-7547
Fax: (214)422-5182

SCORE Office (Port Arthur)
4749 Twin City Hwy., Ste. 300
Port Arthur, TX 77642
(409)963-1107
Fax: (409)963-3322

SCORE Office (Richardson)
411 Belle Grove
Richardson, TX 75080
(214)234-4141
800-777-8001
Fax: (214)680-9103

SCORE Office (San Antonio)
Federal Bldg., Rm. A527
727 E Durango
San Antonio, TX 78206
(210)472-5931
Fax: (210)472-5935

SCORE Office (Texarkana State College)
819 State Line Ave.
Texarkana, TX 75501
(903)792-7191
Fax: (903)793-4304

SCORE Office (East Texas)
RTDC
1530 SSW Loop 323, Ste. 100
Tyler, TX 75701
(903)510-2975
Fax: (903)510-2978

SCORE Office (Waco)
401 Franklin Ave.
Waco, TX 76701
(817)754-8898
Fax: (817)756-0776
Website: http://www.brc-waco.com

SCORE Office (Wichita Falls)
Hamilton Bldg.
900 8th St.
Wichita Falls, TX 76307
(940)723-2741
Fax: (940)723-8773

Utah

SCORE Office (Northern Utah)
160 N. Main
Logan, UT 84321
(435)746-2269

SCORE Office (Ogden)
1701 E Windsor Dr.
Ogden, UT 84604
(801)629-8613
E-mail: score158@netscape.net

SCORE Office (Central Utah)
1071 E Windsor Dr.
Provo, UT 84604
(801)373-8660

SCORE Office (Southern Utah)
225 South 700 East
Saint George, UT 84770
(435)652-7751

SCORE Office (Salt Lake)
310 S Main St.
Salt Lake City, UT 84101
(801)746-2269
Fax: (801)746-2273

Vermont

SCORE Office (Champlain Valley)
Winston Prouty Federal Bldg.
11 Lincoln St., Rm. 106
Essex Junction, VT 05452
(802)951-6762

SCORE Office (Montpelier)
87 State St., Rm. 205
PO Box 605
Montpelier, VT 05601
(802)828-4422
Fax: (802)828-4485

SCORE Office (Marble Valley)
256 N. Main St.
Rutland, VT 05701-2413
(802)773-9147

SCORE Office (Northeast Kingdom)
20 Main St.
PO Box 904
Saint Johnsbury, VT 05819
(802)748-5101

Virgin Islands

SCORE Office (Saint Croix)
United Plaza Shopping Center
PO Box 4010, Christiansted
Saint Croix, VI 00822
(809)778-5380

SCORE Office (Saint Thomas-Saint John)
Federal Bldg., Rm. 21
Veterans Dr.
Saint Thomas, VI 00801
(809)774-8530

Virginia

SCORE Office (Arlington)
2009 N. 14th St., Ste. 111
Arlington, VA 22201
(703)525-2400

SCORE Office (Blacksburg)
141 Jackson St.
Blacksburg, VA 24060
(540)552-4061

SCORE Office (Bristol)
20 Volunteer Pkwy.
Bristol, VA 24203
(540)989-4850

SCORE Office (Central Virginia)
1001 E Market St., Ste. 101
Charlottesville, VA 22902
(804)295-6712
Fax: (804)295-7066

SCORE Office (Alleghany Satellite)
241 W Main St.
Covington, VA 24426
(540)962-2178
Fax: (540)962-2179

SCORE Office (Central Fairfax)
3975 University Dr., Ste. 350
Fairfax, VA 22030
(703)591-2450

SCORE Office (Falls Church)
PO Box 491
Falls Church, VA 22040
(703)532-1050
Fax: (703)237-7904

SCORE Office (Glenns)
Glenns Campus
Box 287
Glenns, VA 23149
(804)693-9650

SCORE Office (Peninsula)
6 Manhattan Sq.
PO Box 7269
Hampton, VA 23666
(757)766-2000
Fax: (757)865-0339
E-mail: score100@seva.net

SCORE Office (Tri-Cities)
108 N. Main St.
Hopewell, VA 23860
(804)458-5536

SCORE Office (Lynchburg)
Federal Bldg.
1100 Main St.
Lynchburg, VA 24504-1714
(804)846-3235

SCORE Office (Greater Prince William)
8963 Center St
Manassas, VA 20110
(703)368-4813
Fax: (703)368-4733

SCORE Office (Martinsvile)
115 Broad St.
Martinsville, VA 24112-0709
(540)632-6401
Fax: (540)632-5059

SCORE Office (Hampton Roads)
Federal Bldg., Rm. 737
200 Grandby St.
Norfolk, VA 23510
(757)441-3733
Fax: (757)441-3733
E-mail: scorehr60@juno.com

SCORE Office (Norfolk)
Federal Bldg., Rm. 737
200 Granby St.
Norfolk, VA 23510
(757)441-3733
Fax: (757)441-3733

SCORE Office (Virginia Beach)
Chamber of Commerce
200 Grandby St., Rm 737
Norfolk, VA 23510
(804)441-3733

SCORE Office (Radford)
1126 Norwood St.
Radford, VA 24141
(540)639-2202

SCORE Office (Richmond)
Federal Bldg.
400 N. 8th St., Ste. 1150
PO Box 10126
Richmond, VA 23240-0126
(804)771-2400
Fax: (804)771-8018
E-mail: scorechapter12@yahoo.com
Website: http://www.cvco.org/score

SCORE Office (Roanoke)
Federal Bldg., Rm. 716
250 Franklin Rd.
Roanoke, VA 24011
(540)857-2834
Fax: (540)857-2043
E-mail: scorerva@juno.com
Website: http://hometown.aol.com/
scorerv/Index.html

SCORE Office (Fairfax)
8391 Old Courthouse Rd., Ste. 300
Vienna, VA 22182
(703)749-0400

SCORE Office (Greater Vienna)
513 Maple Ave. West
Vienna, VA 22180
(703)281-1333
Fax: (703)242-1482

SCORE Office (Shenandoah Valley)
301 W Main St.
Waynesboro, VA 22980
(540)949-8203
Fax: (540)949-7740
E-mail: score427@intelos.net

SCORE Office (Williamsburg)
201 Penniman Rd.
Williamsburg, VA 23185
(757)229-6511
E-mail: wacc@williamsburgcc.com

SCORE Office (Northern Virginia)
1360 S Pleasant Valley Rd.
Winchester, VA 22601
(540)662-4118

Washington

SCORE Office (Gray's Harbor)
506 Duffy St.
Aberdeen, WA 98520
(360)532-1924
Fax: (360)533-7945

SCORE Office (Bellingham)
101 E Holly St.
Bellingham, WA 98225
(360)676-3307

SCORE Office (Everett)
2702 Hoyt Ave.
Everett, WA 98201-3556
(206)259-8000

SCORE Office (Gig Harbor)
3125 Judson St.
Gig Harbor, WA 98335
(206)851-6865

SCORE Office (Kennewick)
PO Box 6986
Kennewick, WA 99336
(509)736-0510

SCORE Office (Puyallup)
322 2nd St. SW
PO Box 1298
Puyallup, WA 98371
(206)845-6755
Fax: (206)848-6164

SCORE Office (Seattle)
1200 6th Ave., Ste. 1700
Seattle, WA 98101
(206)553-7320

Fax: (206)553-7044
E-mail: score55@aol.com
Website: http://www.scn.org/civic/score-
online/index55.html

SCORE Office (Spokane)
801 W Riverside Ave., No. 240
Spokane, WA 99201
(509)353-2820
Fax: (509)353-2600
E-mail: score@dmi.net
Website: http://www.dmi.net/score

SCORE Office (Clover Park)
PO Box 1933
Tacoma, WA 98401-1933
(206)627-2175

SCORE Office (Tacoma)
1101 Pacific Ave.
Tacoma, WA 98402
(253)274-1288
Fax: (253)274-1289

SCORE Office (Fort Vancouver)
1701 Broadway, S-1
Vancouver, WA 98663
(360)699-1079

SCORE Office (Walla Walla)
500 Tausick Way
Walla Walla, WA 99362
(509)527-4681

SCORE Office (Mid-Columbia)
1113 S 14th Ave.
Yakima, WA 98907
(509)574-4944
Fax: (509)574-2943
Website: http://www.ellensburg.com/
~score

West Virginia

SCORE Office (Charleston)
1116 Smith St.
Charleston, WV 25301
(304)347-5463
E-mail: score256@juno.com

SCORE Office (Virginia Street)
1116 Smith St., Ste. 302
Charleston, WV 25301
(304)347-5463

SCORE Office (Marion County)
PO Box 208
Fairmont, WV 26555-0208
(304)363-0486

SCORE Office (Upper Monongahela Valley)
1000 Technology Dr., Ste. 1111
Fairmont, WV 26555

(304)363-0486

E-mail: score537@hotmail.com

SCORE Office (Huntington)

1101 6th Ave., Ste. 220

Huntington, WV 25701-2309

(304)523-4092

SCORE Office (Wheeling)

1310 Market St.

Wheeling, WV 26003

(304)233-2575

Fax: (304)233-1320

Wisconsin

SCORE Office (Fox Cities)

227 S Walnut St.

Appleton, WI 54913

(920)734-7101

Fax: (920)734-7161

SCORE Office (Beloit)

136 W Grand Ave., Ste. 100

PO Box 717

Beloit, WI 53511

(608)365-8835

Fax: (608)365-9170

SCORE Office (Eau Claire)

Federal Bldg., Rm. B11

510 S Barstow St.

Eau Claire, WI 54701

(715)834-1573

E-mail: score@ecol.net

Website: http://www.ecol.net/
~score

SCORE Office (Fond du Lac)

207 N. Main St.

Fond du Lac, WI 54935

(414)921-9500

Fax: (414)921-9559

SCORE Office (Green Bay)

835 Potts Ave.

Green Bay, WI 54304

(414)496-8930

Fax: (414)496-6009

SCORE Office (Janesville)

20 S Main St., Ste. 11

PO Box 8008

Janesville, WI 53547

(608)757-3160

Fax: (608)757-3170

SCORE Office (La Crosse)

712 Main St.

La Crosse, WI 54602-0219

(608)784-4880

SCORE Office (Madison)

505 S Rosa Rd.

Madison, WI 53719

(608)441-2820

SCORE Office (Manitowoc)

1515 Memorial Dr.

PO Box 903

Manitowoc, WI 54221-0903

(414)684-5575

Fax: (414)684-1915

SCORE Office (Milwaukee)

310 W Wisconsin Ave., Ste. 425

Milwaukee, WI 53203

(414)297-3942

Fax: (414)297-1377

SCORE Office (Central Wisconsin)

1224 Lindbergh Ave.

Stevens Point, WI 54481

(715)344-7729

SCORE Office (Superior)

Superior Business Center Inc.

1423 N. 8th St.

Superior, WI 54880

(715)394-7388

Fax: (715)393-7414

SCORE Office (Waukesha)

223 Wisconsin Ave.

Waukesha, WI 53186-4926

(414)542-4249

SCORE Office (Wausau)

300 3rd St., Ste. 200

Wausau, WI 54402-6190

(715)845-6231

SCORE Office (Wisconsin Rapids)

2240 Kingston Rd.

Wisconsin Rapids, WI 54494

(715)423-1830

Wyoming

SCORE Office (Casper)

Federal Bldg., No. 2215

100 East B St.

Casper, WY 82602

(307)261-6529

Fax: (307)261-6530

Venture capital & financing companies

This section contains a listing of financing and loan companies in the United States and Canada. These listing are arranged
alphabetically by country, then by state or province, then by city, then by organization name.

Canada

Alberta

Launchworks Inc.

1902J 11th St., SE

Calgary, AB, Canada T2G 3G2

(403)269-1119

Fax: (403)269-1141

Website: http://www.launchworks.com

Native Venture Capital Company, Inc.

21 Artist View Point, Box 7

Site 25, RR 12

Calgary, AB, Canada T3E 6W3

(903)208-5380

Miralta Capital Inc.

4445 Calgary Trail South

888 Terrace Plaza Alberta

Edmonton, AB, Canada T6H 5R7

(780)438-3535

Fax: (780)438-3129

Vencap Equities Alberta Ltd.

10180-101st St., Ste. 1980

Edmonton, AB, Canada T5J 3S4

(403)420-1171

Fax: (403)429-2541

British Columbia

Discovery Capital

5th Fl., 1199 West Hastings

Vancouver, BC, Canada V6E 3T5

(604)683-3000

Fax: (604)662-3457

E-mail: info@discoverycapital.com

Website: http://
www.discoverycapital.com

Greenstone Venture Partners

1177 West Hastings St.

Ste. 400

Vancouver, BC, Canada V6E 2K3

(604)717-1977

Fax: (604)717-1976

Website: http://www.greenstonevc.com

Growthworks Capital

2600-1055 West Georgia St.

Box 11170 Royal Centre

Vancouver, BC, Canada V6E 3R5

(604)895-7259

Fax: (604)669-7605

Website: http://www.wofund.com

MDS Discovery Venture Management, Inc.
555 W Eighth Ave., Ste. 305
Vancouver, BC, Canada V5Z 1C6
(604)872-8464
Fax: (604)872-2977
E-mail: info@mds-ventures.com

Ventures West Management Inc.
1285 W Pender St., Ste. 280
Vancouver, BC, Canada V6E 4B1
(604)688-9495
Fax: (604)687-2145
Website: http://www.ventureswest.com

Nova Scotia

ACF Equity Atlantic Inc.
Purdy's Wharf Tower II
Ste. 2106
Halifax, NS, Canada B3J 3R7
(902)421-1965
Fax: (902)421-1808

Montgomerie, Huck & Co.
146 Bluenose Dr.
PO Box 538
Lunenburg, NS, Canada B0J 2C0
(902)634-7125
Fax: (902)634-7130

Ontario

IPS Industrial Promotion Services Ltd.
60 Columbia Way, Ste. 720
Markham, ON, Canada L3R 0C9
(905)475-9400
Fax: (905)475-5003

Betwin Investments Inc.
Box 23110
Sault Ste. Marie, ON, Canada P6A 6W6
(705)253-0744
Fax: (705)253-0744

Bailey & Company, Inc.
594 Spadina Ave.
Toronto, ON, Canada M5S 2H4
(416)921-6930
Fax: (416)925-4670

BCE Capital
200 Bay St.
South Tower, Ste. 3120
Toronto, ON, Canada M5J 2J2
(416)815-0078
Fax: (416)941-1073
Website: http://www.bcecapital.com

Castlehill Ventures
55 University Ave., Ste. 500
Toronto, ON, Canada M5J 2H7

(416)862-8574
Fax: (416)862-8875

CCFL Mezzanine Partners of Canada
70 University Ave.
Ste. 1450
Toronto, ON, Canada M5J 2M4
(416)977-1450
Fax: (416)977-6764
E-mail: info@ccfl.com
Website: http://www.ccfl.com

Celtic House International
100 Simcoe St., Ste. 100
Toronto, ON, Canada M5H 3G2
(416)542-2436
Fax: (416)542-2435
Website: http://www.celtic-house.com

Clairvest Group Inc.
22 St. Clair Ave. East
Ste. 1700
Toronto, ON, Canada M4T 2S3
(416)925-9270
Fax: (416)925-5753

Crosbie & Co., Inc.
One First Canadian Place
9th Fl.
PO Box 116
Toronto, ON, Canada M5X 1A4
(416)362-7726
Fax: (416)362-3447
E-mail: info@crosbieco.com
Website: http://www.crosbieco.com

Drug Royalty Corp.
Eight King St. East
Ste. 202
Toronto, ON, Canada M5C 1B5
(416)863-1865
Fax: (416)863-5161

Grieve, Horner, Brown & Asculai
8 King St. E, Ste. 1704
Toronto, ON, Canada M5C 1B5
(416)362-7668
Fax: (416)362-7660

Jefferson Partners
77 King St. West
Ste. 4010
PO Box 136
Toronto, ON, Canada M5K 1H1
(416)367-1533
Fax: (416)367-5827
Website: http://www.jefferson.com

J.L. Albright Venture Partners
Canada Trust Tower, 161 Bay St.
Ste. 4440
PO Box 215

Toronto, ON, Canada M5J 2S1
(416)367-2440
Fax: (416)367-4604
Website: http://www.jlaventures.com

McLean Watson Capital Inc.
One First Canadian Place
Ste. 1410
PO Box 129
Toronto, ON, Canada M5X 1A4
(416)363-2000
Fax: (416)363-2010
Website: http://www.mcleanwatson.com

Middlefield Capital Fund
One First Canadian Place
85th Fl.
PO Box 192
Toronto, ON, Canada M5X 1A6
(416)362-0714
Fax: (416)362-7925
Website: http://www.middlefield.com

Mosaic Venture Partners
24 Duncan St.
Ste. 300
Toronto, ON, Canada M5V 3M6
(416)597-8889
Fax: (416)597-2345

Onex Corp.
161 Bay St.
PO Box 700
Toronto, ON, Canada M5J 2S1
(416)362-7711
Fax: (416)362-5765

Penfund Partners Inc.
145 King St. West
Ste. 1920
Toronto, ON, Canada M5H 1J8
(416)865-0300
Fax: (416)364-6912
Website: http://www.penfund.com

Primaxis Technology Ventures Inc.
1 Richmond St. West, 8th Fl.
Toronto, ON, Canada M5H 3W4
(416)313-5210
Fax: (416)313-5218
Website: http://www.primaxis.com

Priveq Capital Funds
240 Duncan Mill Rd., Ste. 602
Toronto, ON, Canada M3B 3P1
(416)447-3330
Fax: (416)447-3331
E-mail: priveq@sympatico.ca

Roynat Ventures
40 King St. West, 26th Fl.
Toronto, ON, Canada M5H 1H1

(416)933-2667
Fax: (416)933-2783
Website: http://www.roynatcapital.com

Tera Capital Corp.
366 Adelaide St. East, Ste. 337
Toronto, ON, Canada M5A 3X9
(416)368-1024
Fax: (416)368-1427

Working Ventures Canadian Fund Inc.
250 Bloor St. East, Ste. 1600
Toronto, ON, Canada M4W 1E6
(416)934-7718
Fax: (416)929-0901
Website: http://www.workingventures.ca

Quebec

Altamira Capital Corp.
202 University
Niveau de Maisoneuve, Bur. 201
Montreal, QC, Canada H3A 2A5
(514)499-1656
Fax: (514)499-9570

Federal Business Development Bank
Venture Capital Division
Five Place Ville Marie, Ste. 600
Montreal, QC, Canada H3B 5E7
(514)283-1896
Fax: (514)283-5455

Hydro-Quebec Capitech Inc.
75 Boul, Rene Levesque Quest
Montreal, QC, Canada H2Z 1A4
(514)289-4783
Fax: (514)289-5420
Website: http://www.hqcapitech.com

Investissement Desjardins
2 complexe Desjardins
C.P. 760
Montreal, QC, Canada H5B 1B8
(514)281-7131
Fax: (514)281-7808
Website: http://www.desjardins.com/id

Marleau Lemire Inc.
One Place Ville-Marie, Ste. 3601
Montreal, QC, Canada H3B 3P2
(514)877-3800
Fax: (514)875-6415

Speirs Consultants Inc.
365 Stanstead
Montreal, QC, Canada H3R 1X5
(514)342-3858
Fax: (514)342-1977

Tecnocap Inc.
4028 Marlowe
Montreal, QC, Canada H4A 3M2

(514)483-6009
Fax: (514)483-6045
Website: http://www.technocap.com

Telsoft Ventures
1000, Rue de la Gauchetiere
Quest, 25eme Etage
Montreal, QC, Canada H3B 4W5
(514)397-8450
Fax: (514)397-8451

Saskatchewan

**Saskatchewan Government
Growth Fund**
1801 Hamilton St., Ste. 1210
Canada Trust Tower
Regina, SK, Canada S4P 4B4
(306)787-2994
Fax: (306)787-2086

United states

Alabama

FHL Capital Corp.
600 20th Street North
Suite 350
Birmingham, AL 35203
(205)328-3098
Fax: (205)323-0001

Harbert Management Corp.
One Riverchase Pkwy. South
Birmingham, AL 35244
(205)987-5500
Fax: (205)987-5707
Website: http://www.harbert.net

Jefferson Capital Fund
PO Box 13129
Birmingham, AL 35213
(205)324-7709

Private Capital Corp.
100 Brookwood Pl., 4th Fl.
Birmingham, AL 35209
(205)879-2722
Fax: (205)879-5121

21st Century Health Ventures
One Health South Pkwy.
Birmingham, AL 35243
(256)268-6250
Fax: (256)970-8928

FJC Growth Capital Corp.
200 Westside Sq., Ste. 340
Huntsville, AL 35801
(256)922-2918
Fax: (256)922-2909

Hickory Venture Capital Corp.
301 Washington St. NW
Suite 301
Huntsville, AL 35801
(256)539-1931
Fax: (256)539-5130
E-mail: hvcc@hvcc.com
Website: http://www.hvcc.com

Southeastern Technology Fund
7910 South Memorial Pkwy., Ste. F
Huntsville, AL 35802
(256)883-8711
Fax: (256)883-8558

Cordova Ventures
4121 Carmichael Rd., Ste. 301
Montgomery, AL 36106
(334)271-6011
Fax: (334)260-0120
Website: http://www.cordovaventures
.com

**Small Business Clinic of Alabama/AG
Bartholomew & Associates**
PO Box 231074
Montgomery, AL 36123-1074
(334)284-3640

Arizona

Miller Capital Corp.
4909 E McDowell Rd.
Phoenix, AZ 85008
(602)225-0504
Fax: (602)225-9024
Website: http://www.themillergroup.com

The Columbine Venture Funds
9449 North 90th St., Ste. 200
Scottsdale, AZ 85258
(602)661-9222
Fax: (602)661-6262

Koch Ventures
17767 N. Perimeter Dr., Ste. 101
Scottsdale, AZ 85255
(480)419-3600
Fax: (480)419-3606
Website: http://www.kochventures.com

McKee & Co.
7702 E Doubletree Ranch Rd.
Suite 230
Scottsdale, AZ 85258
(480)368-0333
Fax: (480)607-7446

Merita Capital Ltd.
7350 E Stetson Dr., Ste. 108-A
Scottsdale, AZ 85251
(480)947-8700
Fax: (480)947-8766

Valley Ventures / Arizona Growth Partners L.P.
6720 N. Scottsdale Rd., Ste. 208
Scottsdale, AZ 85253
(480)661-6600
Fax: (480)661-6262

Estreetcapital.com
660 South Mill Ave., Ste. 315
Tempe, AZ 85281
(480)968-8400
Fax: (480)968-8480
Website: http://www.estreetcapital.com

Coronado Venture Fund
PO Box 65420
Tucson, AZ 85728-5420
(520)577-3764
Fax: (520)299-8491

Arkansas

Arkansas Capital Corp.
225 South Pulaski St.
Little Rock, AR 72201
(501)374-9247
Fax: (501)374-9425
Website: http://www.arcapital.com

California

Sundance Venture Partners, L.P.
100 Clocktower Place, Ste. 130
Carmel, CA 93923
(831)625-6500
Fax: (831)625-6590

Westar Capital (Costa Mesa)
949 South Coast Dr., Ste. 650
Costa Mesa, CA 92626
(714)481-5160
Fax: (714)481-5166
E-mail: mailbox@westarcapital.com
Website: http://www.westarcapital.com

Alpine Technology Ventures
20300 Stevens Creek Boulevard, Ste. 495
Cupertino, CA 95014
(408)725-1810
Fax: (408)725-1207
Website: http://www.alpineventures.com

Bay Partners
10600 N. De Anza Blvd.
Cupertino, CA 95014-2031
(408)725-2444
Fax: (408)446-4502
Website: http://www.baypartners.com

Novus Ventures
20111 Stevens Creek Blvd., Ste. 130
Cupertino, CA 95014
(408)252-3900

Fax: (408)252-1713
Website: http://www.novusventures.com

Triune Capital
19925 Stevens Creek Blvd., Ste. 200
Cupertino, CA 95014
(310)284-6800
Fax: (310)284-3290

Acorn Ventures
268 Bush St., Ste. 2829
Daly City, CA 94014
(650)994-7801
Fax: (650)994-3305
Website: http://www.acornventures.com

Digital Media Campus
2221 Park Place
El Segundo, CA 90245
(310)426-8000
Fax: (310)426-8010
E-mail: info@thecampus.com
Website: http://www.digitalmediacampus
.com

BankAmerica Ventures / BA Venture Partners
950 Tower Ln., Ste. 700
Foster City, CA 94404
(650)378-6000
Fax: (650)378-6040
Website: http://www.baventurepartners
.com

Starting Point Partners
666 Portofino Lane
Foster City, CA 94404
(650)722-1035
Website: http://www.startingpointpartners
.com

Opportunity Capital Partners
2201 Walnut Ave., Ste. 210
Fremont, CA 94538
(510)795-7000
Fax: (510)494-5439
Website: http://www.ocpcapital.com

Imperial Ventures Inc.
9920 S La Cienega Boulevar, 14th Fl.
Inglewood, CA 90301
(310)417-5409
Fax: (310)338-6115

Ventana Global (Irvine)
18881 Von Karman Ave., Ste. 1150
Irvine, CA 92612
(949)476-2204
Fax: (949)752-0223
Website: http://www.ventanaglobal.com

Integrated Consortium Inc.
50 Ridgecrest Rd.
Kentfield, CA 94904

(415)925-0386
Fax: (415)461-2726

Enterprise Partners
979 Ivanhoe Ave., Ste. 550
La Jolla, CA 92037
(858)454-8833
Fax: (858)454-2489
Website: http://www.epvc.com

Domain Associates
28202 Cabot Rd., Ste. 200
Laguna Niguel, CA 92677
(949)347-2446
Fax: (949)347-9720
Website: http://www.domainvc.com

Cascade Communications Ventures
60 E Sir Francis Drake Blvd., Ste. 300
Larkspur, CA 94939
(415)925-6500
Fax: (415)925-6501

Allegis Capital
One First St., Ste. Two
Los Altos, CA 94022
(650)917-5900
Fax: (650)917-5901
Website: http://www.allegiscapital.com

Aspen Ventures
1000 Fremont Ave., Ste. 200
Los Altos, CA 94024
(650)917-5670
Fax: (650)917-5677
Website: http://www.aspenventures.com

AVI Capital L.P.
1 First St., Ste. 2
Los Altos, CA 94022
(650)949-9862
Fax: (650)949-8510
Website: http://www.avicapital.com

Bastion Capital Corp.
1999 Avenue of the Stars, Ste. 2960
Los Angeles, CA 90067
(310)788-5700
Fax: (310)277-7582
E-mail: ga@bastioncapital.com
Website: http://www.bastioncapital.com

Davis Group
PO Box 69953
Los Angeles, CA 90069-0953
(310)659-6327
Fax: (310)659-6337

Developers Equity Corp.
1880 Century Park East, Ste. 211
Los Angeles, CA 90067
(213)277-0300

Far East Capital Corp.
350 S Grand Ave., Ste. 4100
Los Angeles, CA 90071
(213)687-1361
Fax: (213)617-7939
E-mail: free@fareastnationalbank.com

Kline Hawkes & Co.
11726 San Vicente Blvd., Ste. 300
Los Angeles, CA 90049
(310)442-4700
Fax: (310)442-4707
Website: http://www.klinehawkes.com

Lawrence Financial Group
701 Teakwood
PO Box 491773
Los Angeles, CA 90049
(310)471-4060
Fax: (310)472-3155

Riordan Lewis & Haden
300 S Grand Ave., 29th Fl.
Los Angeles, CA 90071
(213)229-8500
Fax: (213)229-8597

Union Venture Corp.
445 S Figueroa St., 9th Fl.
Los Angeles, CA 90071
(213)236-4092
Fax: (213)236-6329

Wedbush Capital Partners
1000 Wilshire Blvd.
Los Angeles, CA 90017
(213)688-4545
Fax: (213)688-6642
Website: http://www.wedbush.com

Advent International Corp.
2180 Sand Hill Rd., Ste. 420
Menlo Park, CA 94025
(650)233-7500
Fax: (650)233-7515
Website: http://
www.adventinternational.com

Altos Ventures
2882 Sand Hill Rd., Ste. 100
Menlo Park, CA 94025
(650)234-9771
Fax: (650)233-9821
Website: http://www.altosvc.com

Applied Technology
1010 El Camino Real, Ste. 300
Menlo Park, CA 94025
(415)326-8622
Fax: (415)326-8163

APV Technology Partners
535 Middlefield, Ste. 150
Menlo Park, CA 94025

(650)327-7871
Fax: (650)327-7631
Website: http://www.apvtp.com

August Capital Management
2480 Sand Hill Rd., Ste. 101
Menlo Park, CA 94025
(650)234-9900
Fax: (650)234-9910
Website: http://www.augustcap.com

Baccharis Capital Inc.
2420 Sand Hill Rd., Ste. 100
Menlo Park, CA 94025
(650)324-6844
Fax: (650)854-3025

Benchmark Capital
2480 Sand Hill Rd., Ste. 200
Menlo Park, CA 94025
(650)854-8180
Fax: (650)854-8183
E-mail: info@benchmark.com
Website: http://www.benchmark.com

Bessemer Venture Partners (Menlo Park)
535 Middlefield Rd., Ste. 245
Menlo Park, CA 94025
(650)853-7000
Fax: (650)853-7001
Website: http://www.bvp.com

The Cambria Group
1600 El Camino Real Rd., Ste. 155
Menlo Park, CA 94025
(650)329-8600
Fax: (650)329-8601
Website: http://www.cambriagroup.com

Canaan Partners
2884 Sand Hill Rd., Ste. 115
Menlo Park, CA 94025
(650)854-8092
Fax: (650)854-8127
Website: http://www.canaan.com

Capstone Ventures
3000 Sand Hill Rd., Bldg. One, Ste. 290
Menlo Park, CA 94025
(650)854-2523
Fax: (650)854-9010
Website: http://www.capstonevc.com

Comdisco Venture Group (Silicon Valley)
3000 Sand Hill Rd., Bldg. 1, Ste. 155
Menlo Park, CA 94025
(650)854-9484
Fax: (650)854-4026

Commtech International
535 Middlefield Rd., Ste. 200
Menlo Park, CA 94025

(650)328-0190
Fax: (650)328-6442

Compass Technology Partners
1550 El Camino Real, Ste. 275
Menlo Park, CA 94025-4111
(650)322-7595
Fax: (650)322-0588
Website: http://www.compasstechpartners.com

Convergence Partners
3000 Sand Hill Rd., Ste. 235
Menlo Park, CA 94025
(650)854-3010
Fax: (650)854-3015
Website: http://www.convergencepartners.com

The Dakota Group
PO Box 1025
Menlo Park, CA 94025
(650)853-0600
Fax: (650)851-4899
E-mail: info@dakota.com

Delphi Ventures
3000 Sand Hill Rd.
Bldg. One, Ste. 135
Menlo Park, CA 94025
(650)854-9650
Fax: (650)854-2961
Website: http://www.delphiventures.com

El Dorado Ventures
2884 Sand Hill Rd., Ste. 121
Menlo Park, CA 94025
(650)854-1200
Fax: (650)854-1202
Website: http://www.eldoradoventures.com

Glynn Ventures
3000 Sand Hill Rd., Bldg. 4, Ste. 235
Menlo Park, CA 94025
(650)854-2215

Indosuez Ventures
2180 Sand Hill Rd., Ste. 450
Menlo Park, CA 94025
(650)854-0587
Fax: (650)323-5561
Website: http://www.indosuezventures.com

Institutional Venture Partners
3000 Sand Hill Rd., Bldg. 2, Ste. 290
Menlo Park, CA 94025
(650)854-0132
Fax: (650)854-5762
Website: http://www.ivp.com

Interwest Partners (Menlo Park)
3000 Sand Hill Rd., Bldg. 3, Ste. 255

Menlo Park, CA 94025-7112
(650)854-8585
Fax: (650)854-4706
Website: http://www.interwest.com

**Kleiner Perkins Caufield & Byers
(Menlo Park)**
2750 Sand Hill Rd.
Menlo Park, CA 94025
(650)233-2750
Fax: (650)233-0300
Website: http://www.kpcb.com

Magic Venture Capital LLC
1010 El Camino Real, Ste. 300
Menlo Park, CA 94025
(650)325-4149

Matrix Partners
2500 Sand Hill Rd., Ste. 113
Menlo Park, CA 94025
(650)854-3131
Fax: (650)854-3296
Website: http://www.matrixpartners.com

Mayfield Fund
2800 Sand Hill Rd.
Menlo Park, CA 94025
(650)854-5560
Fax: (650)854-5712
Website: http://www.mayfield.com

**McCown De Leeuw and Co. (Menlo
Park)**
3000 Sand Hill Rd., Bldg. 3, Ste. 290
Menlo Park, CA 94025-7111
(650)854-6000
Fax: (650)854-0853
Website: http://www.mdcpartners.com

Menlo Ventures
3000 Sand Hill Rd., Bldg. 4, Ste. 100
Menlo Park, CA 94025
(650)854-8540
Fax: (650)854-7059
Website: http://www.menloventures.com

Merrill Pickard Anderson & Eyre
2480 Sand Hill Rd., Ste. 200
Menlo Park, CA 94025
(650)854-8600
Fax: (650)854-0345

New Enterprise Associates (Menlo Park)
2490 Sand Hill Rd.
Menlo Park, CA 94025
(650)854-9499
Fax: (650)854-9397
Website: http://www.nea.com

Onset Ventures
2400 Sand Hill Rd., Ste. 150
Menlo Park, CA 94025

(650)529-0700
Fax: (650)529-0777
Website: http://www.onset.com

Paragon Venture Partners
3000 Sand Hill Rd., Bldg. 1, Ste. 275
Menlo Park, CA 94025
(650)854-8000
Fax: (650)854-7260

**Pathfinder Venture Capital Funds
(Menlo Park)**
3000 Sand Hill Rd., Bldg. 3, Ste. 255
Menlo Park, CA 94025
(650)854-0650
Fax: (650)854-4706

Rocket Ventures
3000 Sandhill Rd., Bldg. 1, Ste. 170
Menlo Park, CA 94025
(650)561-9100
Fax: (650)561-9183
Website: http://www.rocketventures.com

Sequoia Capital
3000 Sand Hill Rd., Bldg. 4, Ste. 280
Menlo Park, CA 94025
(650)854-3927
Fax: (650)854-2977
E-mail: sequoia@sequioacap.com
Website: http://www.sequoiacap.com

Sierra Ventures
3000 Sand Hill Rd., Bldg. 4, Ste. 210
Menlo Park, CA 94025
(650)854-1000
Fax: (650)854-5593
Website: http://www.sierraventures.com

Sigma Partners
2884 Sand Hill Rd., Ste. 121
Menlo Park, CA 94025-7022
(650)853-1700
Fax: (650)853-1717
E-mail: info@sigmapartners.com
Website: http://www.sigmapartners.com

Sprout Group (Menlo Park)
3000 Sand Hill Rd.
Bldg. 3, Ste. 170
Menlo Park, CA 94025
(650)234-2700
Fax: (650)234-2779
Website: http://www.sproutgroup.com

TA Associates (Menlo Park)
70 Willow Rd., Ste. 100
Menlo Park, CA 94025
(650)328-1210
Fax: (650)326-4933
Website: http://www.ta.com

Thompson Clive & Partners Ltd.
3000 Sand Hill Rd., Bldg. 1, Ste. 185
Menlo Park, CA 94025-7102
(650)854-0314
Fax: (650)854-0670
E-mail: mail@tcvc.com
Website: http://www.tcvc.com

Trinity Ventures Ltd.
3000 Sand Hill Rd., Bldg. 1, Ste. 240
Menlo Park, CA 94025
(650)854-9500
Fax: (650)854-9501
Website: http://www.trinityventures.com

U.S. Venture Partners
2180 Sand Hill Rd., Ste. 300
Menlo Park, CA 94025
(650)854-9080
Fax: (650)854-3018
Website: http://www.usvp.com

USVP-Schlein Marketing Fund
2180 Sand Hill Rd., Ste. 300
Menlo Park, CA 94025
(415)854-9080
Fax: (415)854-3018
Website: http://www.usvp.com

Venrock Associates
2494 Sand Hill Rd., Ste. 200
Menlo Park, CA 94025
(650)561-9580
Fax: (650)561-9180
Website: http://www.venrock.com

Brad Peery Capital Inc.
145 Chapel Pkwy.
Mill Valley, CA 94941
(415)389-0625
Fax: (415)389-1336

Dot Edu Ventures
650 Castro St., Ste. 270
Mountain View, CA 94041
(650)575-5638
Fax: (650)325-5247
Website: http://
www.doteduventures.com

Forrest, Binkley & Brown
840 Newport Ctr. Dr., Ste. 480
Newport Beach, CA 92660
(949)729-3222
Fax: (949)729-3226
Website: http://www.fbbvc.com

Marwit Capital LLC
180 Newport Center Dr., Ste. 200
Newport Beach, CA 92660
(949)640-6234
Fax: (949)720-8077
Website: http://www.marwit.com

Kaiser Permanente / National Venture Development
1800 Harrison St., 22nd Fl.
Oakland, CA 94612
(510)267-4010
Fax: (510)267-4036
Website: http://www.kpventures.com

Nu Capital Access Group, Ltd.
7677 Oakport St., Ste. 105
Oakland, CA 94621
(510)635-7345
Fax: (510)635-7068

Inman and Bowman
4 Orinda Way, Bldg. D, Ste. 150
Orinda, CA 94563
(510)253-1611
Fax: (510)253-9037

Accel Partners (San Francisco)
428 University Ave.
Palo Alto, CA 94301
(650)614-4800
Fax: (650)614-4880
Website: http://www.accel.com

Advanced Technology Ventures
485 Ramona St., Ste. 200
Palo Alto, CA 94301
(650)321-8601
Fax: (650)321-0934
Website: http://www.atvcapital.com

Anila Fund
400 Channing Ave.
Palo Alto, CA 94301
(650)833-5790
Fax: (650)833-0590
Website: http://www.anila.com

Asset Management Company Venture Capital
2275 E Bayshore, Ste. 150
Palo Alto, CA 94303
(650)494-7400
Fax: (650)856-1826
E-mail: postmaster@assetman.com
Website: http://www.assetman.com

BancBoston Capital / BancBoston Ventures
435 Tasso St., Ste. 250
Palo Alto, CA 94305
(650)470-4100
Fax: (650)853-1425
Website: http://www.bancbostoncapital
.com

Charter Ventures
525 University Ave., Ste. 1400
Palo Alto, CA 94301

(650)325-6953
Fax: (650)325-4762
Website: http://
www.charterventures.com

Communications Ventures
505 Hamilton Avenue, Ste. 305
Palo Alto, CA 94301
(650)325-9600
Fax: (650)325-9608
Website: http://www.comven.com

HMS Group
2468 Embarcadero Way
Palo Alto, CA 94303-3313
(650)856-9862
Fax: (650)856-9864

Jafco America Ventures, Inc.
505 Hamilton Ste. 310
Palto Alto, CA 94301
(650)463-8800
Fax: (650)463-8801
Website: http://www.jafco.com

New Vista Capital
540 Cowper St., Ste. 200
Palo Alto, CA 94301
(650)329-9333
Fax: (650)328-9434
E-mail: fgreene@nvcap.com
Website: http://www.nvcap.com

Norwest Equity Partners (Palo Alto)
245 Lytton Ave., Ste. 250
Palo Alto, CA 94301-1426
(650)321-8000
Fax: (650)321-8010
Website: http://www.norwestvp.com

Oak Investment Partners
525 University Ave., Ste. 1300
Palo Alto, CA 94301
(650)614-3700
Fax: (650)328-6345
Website: http://www.oakinv.com

Patricof & Co. Ventures, Inc. (Palo Alto)
2100 Geng Rd., Ste. 150
Palo Alto, CA 94303
(650)494-9944
Fax: (650)494-6751
Website: http://www.patricof.com

RWI Group
835 Page Mill Rd.
Palo Alto, CA 94304
(650)251-1800
Fax: (650)213-8660
Website: http://www.rwigroup.com

Summit Partners (Palo Alto)
499 Hamilton Ave., Ste. 200
Palo Alto, CA 94301
(650)321-1166
Fax: (650)321-1188
Website: http://
www.summitpartners.com

Sutter Hill Ventures
755 Page Mill Rd., Ste. A-200
Palo Alto, CA 94304
(650)493-5600
Fax: (650)858-1854
E-mail: shv@shv.com

Vanguard Venture Partners
525 University Ave., Ste. 600
Palo Alto, CA 94301
(650)321-2900
Fax: (650)321-2902
Website: http://www.vanguardventures
.com

Venture Growth Associates
2479 East Bayshore St., Ste. 710
Palo Alto, CA 94303
(650)855-9100
Fax: (650)855-9104

Worldview Technology Partners
435 Tasso St., Ste. 120
Palo Alto, CA 94301
(650)322-3800
Fax: (650)322-3880
Website: http://www.worldview.com

Draper, Fisher, Jurvetson / Draper Associates
400 Seaport Ct., Ste.250
Redwood City, CA 94063
(415)599-9000
Fax: (415)599-9726
Website: http://www.dfj.com

Gabriel Venture Partners
350 Marine Pkwy., Ste. 200
Redwood Shores, CA 94065
(650)551-5000
Fax: (650)551-5001
Website: http://www.gabrielvp.com

Hallador Venture Partners, L.L.C.
740 University Ave., Ste. 110
Sacramento, CA 95825-6710
(916)920-0191
Fax: (916)920-5188
E-mail: chris@hallador.com

Emerald Venture Group
12396 World Trade Dr., Ste. 116
San Diego, CA 92128
(858)451-1001

Fax: (858)451-1003
Website: http://www.emeraldventure.com

Forward Ventures
9255 Towne Centre Dr.
San Diego, CA 92121
(858)677-6077
Fax: (858)452-8799
E-mail: info@forwardventure.com
Website: http://www.forwardventure.com

Idanta Partners Ltd.
4660 La Jolla Village Dr., Ste. 850
San Diego, CA 92122
(619)452-9690
Fax: (619)452-2013
Website: http://www.idanta.com

Kingsbury Associates
3655 Nobel Dr., Ste. 490
San Diego, CA 92122
(858)677-0600
Fax: (858)677-0800

Kyocera International Inc.
Corporate Development
8611 Balboa Ave.
San Diego, CA 92123
(858)576-2600
Fax: (858)492-1456

Sorrento Associates, Inc.
4370 LaJolla Village Dr., Ste. 1040
San Diego, CA 92122
(619)452-3100
Fax: (619)452-7607
Website: http://www.sorrentoventures.com

Western States Investment Group
9191 Towne Ctr. Dr., Ste. 310
San Diego, CA 92122
(619)678-0800
Fax: (619)678-0900

Aberdare Ventures
One Embarcadero Center, Ste. 4000
San Francisco, CA 94111
(415)392-7442
Fax: (415)392-4264
Website: http://www.aberdare.com

Acacia Venture Partners
101 California St., Ste. 3160
San Francisco, CA 94111
(415)433-4200
Fax: (415)433-4250
Website: http://www.acaciavp.com

Access Venture Partners
319 Laidley St.
San Francisco, CA 94131
(415)586-0132
Fax: (415)392-6310

Website: http://www.accessventure
partners.com

Alta Partners
One Embarcadero Center, Ste. 4050
San Francisco, CA 94111
(415)362-4022
Fax: (415)362-6178
E-mail: alta@altapartners.com
Website: http://www.altapartners.com

Bangert Dawes Reade Davis & Thom
220 Montgomery St., Ste. 424
San Francisco, CA 94104
(415)954-9900
Fax: (415)954-9901
E-mail: bdrdt@pacbell.net

Berkeley International Capital Corp.
650 California St., Ste. 2800
San Francisco, CA 94108-2609
(415)249-0450
Fax: (415)392-3929
Website: http://www.berkeleyvc.com

Blueprint Ventures LLC
456 Montgomery St., 22nd Fl.
San Francisco, CA 94104
(415)901-4000
Fax: (415)901-4035
Website: http://www.blueprintventures
.com

Blumberg Capital Ventures
580 Howard St., Ste. 401
San Francisco, CA 94105
(415)905-5007
Fax: (415)357-5027
Website: http://www.blumberg-
capital.com

Burr, Egan, Deleage, and Co. (San Francisco)
1 Embarcadero Center, Ste. 4050
San Francisco, CA 94111
(415)362-4022
Fax: (415)362-6178

Burrill & Company
120 Montgomery St., Ste. 1370
San Francisco, CA 94104
(415)743-3160
Fax: (415)743-3161
Website: http://www.burrillandco.com

CMEA Ventures
235 Montgomery St., Ste. 920
San Francisco, CA 94401
(415)352-1520
Fax: (415)352-1524
Website: http://www.cmeaventures.com

Crocker Capital
1 Post St., Ste. 2500
San Francisco, CA 94101
(415)956-5250
Fax: (415)959-5710

Dominion Ventures, Inc.
44 Montgomery St., Ste. 4200
San Francisco, CA 94104
(415)362-4890
Fax: (415)394-9245

Dorset Capital
Pier 1
Bay 2
San Francisco, CA 94111
(415)398-7101
Fax: (415)398-7141
Website: http://www.dorsetcapital.com

Gatx Capital
Four Embarcadero Center, Ste. 2200
San Francisco, CA 94904
(415)955-3200
Fax: (415)955-3449

IMinds
135 Main St., Ste. 1350
San Francisco, CA 94105
(415)547-0000
Fax: (415)227-0300
Website: http://www.iminds.com

LF International Inc.
360 Post St., Ste. 705
San Francisco, CA 94108
(415)399-0110
Fax: (415)399-9222
Website: http://www.lfvc.com

Newbury Ventures
535 Pacific Ave., 2nd Fl.
San Francisco, CA 94133
(415)296-7408
Fax: (415)296-7416
Website: http://www.newburyven.com

Quest Ventures (San Francisco)
333 Bush St., Ste. 1750
San Francisco, CA 94104
(415)782-1414
Fax: (415)782-1415

Robertson-Stephens Co.
555 California St., Ste. 2600
San Francisco, CA 94104
(415)781-9700
Fax: (415)781-2556
Website: http://www.omegaadventures.com

Rosewood Capital, L.P.
One Maritime Plaza, Ste. 1330
San Francisco, CA 94111-3503

(415)362-5526
Fax: (415)362-1192
Website: http://www.rosewoodvc.com

Ticonderoga Capital Inc.
555 California St., No. 4950
San Francisco, CA 94104
(415)296-7900
Fax: (415)296-8956

21st Century Internet Venture Partners
Two South Park
2nd Floor
San Francisco, CA 94107
(415)512-1221
Fax: (415)512-2650
Website: http://www.21vc.com

VK Ventures
600 California St., Ste.1700
San Francisco, CA 94111
(415)391-5600
Fax: (415)397-2744

Walden Group of Venture Capital Funds
750 Battery St., Seventh Floor
San Francisco, CA 94111
(415)391-7225
Fax: (415)391-7262

Acer Technology Ventures
2641 Orchard Pkwy.
San Jose, CA 95134
(408)433-4945
Fax: (408)433-5230

Authosis
226 Airport Pkwy., Ste. 405
San Jose, CA 95110
(650)814-3603
Website: http://www.authosis.com

Western Technology Investment
2010 N. First St., Ste. 310
San Jose, CA 95131
(408)436-8577
Fax: (408)436-8625
E-mail: mktg@westerntech.com

Drysdale Enterprises
177 Bovet Rd., Ste. 600
San Mateo, CA 94402
(650)341-6336
Fax: (650)341-1329
E-mail: drysdale@aol.com

Greylock
2929 Campus Dr., Ste. 400
San Mateo, CA 94401
(650)493-5525
Fax: (650)493-5575
Website: http://www.greylock.com

Technology Funding
2000 Alameda de las Pulgas, Ste. 250
San Mateo, CA 94403
(415)345-2200
Fax: (415)345-1797

2M Invest Inc.
1875 S Grant St.
Suite 750
San Mateo, CA 94402
(650)655-3765
Fax: (650)372-9107
E-mail: 2minfo@2minvest.com
Website: http://www.2minvest.com

Phoenix Growth Capital Corp.
2401 Kerner Blvd.
San Rafael, CA 94901
(415)485-4569
Fax: (415)485-4663

NextGen Partners LLC
1705 East Valley Rd.
Santa Barbara, CA 93108
(805)969-8540
Fax: (805)969-8542
Website: http://www.nextgenpartners.com

Denali Venture Capital
1925 Woodland Ave.
Santa Clara, CA 95050
(408)690-4838
Fax: (408)247-6979
E-mail: wael@denaliventurecapital.com
Website: http://www.denaliventurecapital
.com

Dotcom Ventures LP
3945 Freedom Circle, Ste. 740
Santa Clara, CA 95045
(408)919-9855
Fax: (408)919-9857
Website: http://www.dotcomventuresatl.com

Silicon Valley Bank
3003 Tasman
Santa Clara, CA 95054
(408)654-7400
Fax: (408)727-8728

Al Shugart International
920 41st Ave.
Santa Cruz, CA 95062
(831)479-7852
Fax: (831)479-7852
Website: http://www.alshugart.com

Leonard Mautner Associates
1434 Sixth St.
Santa Monica, CA 90401
(213)393-9788
Fax: (310)459-9918

Palomar Ventures
100 Wilshire Blvd., Ste. 450
Santa Monica, CA 90401
(310)260-6050
Fax: (310)656-4150
Website: http://www.palomarventures.com

Medicus Venture Partners
12930 Saratoga Ave., Ste. D8
Saratoga, CA 95070
(408)447-8600
Fax: (408)447-8599
Website: http://www.medicusvc.com

Redleaf Venture Management
14395 Saratoga Ave., Ste. 130
Saratoga, CA 95070
(408)868-0800
Fax: (408)868-0810
E-mail: nancy@redleaf.com
Website: http://www.redleaf.com

Artemis Ventures
207 Second St., Ste. E
3rd Fl.
Sausalito, CA 94965
(415)289-2500
Fax: (415)289-1789
Website: http://www.artemisventures.com

Deucalion Venture Partners
19501 Brooklime
Sonoma, CA 95476
(707)938-4974
Fax: (707)938-8921

Windward Ventures
PO Box 7688
Thousand Oaks, CA 91359-7688
(805)497-3332
Fax: (805)497-9331

National Investment Management, Inc.
2601 Airport Dr., Ste.210
Torrance, CA 90505
(310)784-7600
Fax: (310)784-7605

Southern California Ventures
406 Amapola Ave. Ste. 125
Torrance, CA 90501
(310)787-4381
Fax: (310)787-4382

Sandton Financial Group
21550 Oxnard St., Ste. 300
Woodland Hills, CA 91367
(818)702-9283

Woodside Fund
850 Woodside Dr.
Woodside, CA 94062
(650)368-5545

Fax: (650)368-2416
Website: http://www.woodsidefund.com

Colorado

Colorado Venture Management
Ste. 300
Boulder, CO 80301
(303)440-4055
Fax: (303)440-4636

Dean & Associates
4362 Apple Way
Boulder, CO 80301
Fax: (303)473-9900

Roser Ventures LLC
1105 Spruce St.
Boulder, CO 80302
(303)443-6436
Fax: (303)443-1885
Website: http://www.roserventures.com

Sequel Venture Partners
4430 Arapahoe Ave., Ste. 220
Boulder, CO 80303
(303)546-0400
Fax: (303)546-9728
E-mail: tom@sequelvc.com
Website: http://www.sequelvc.com

New Venture Resources
445C E Cheyenne Mtn. Blvd.
Colorado Springs, CO 80906-4570
(719)598-9272
Fax: (719)598-9272

The Centennial Funds
1428 15th St.
Denver, CO 80202-1318
(303)405-7500
Fax: (303)405-7575
Website: http://www.centennial.com

Rocky Mountain Capital Partners
1125 17th St., Ste. 2260
Denver, CO 80202
(303)291-5200
Fax: (303)291-5327

Sandlot Capital LLC
600 South Cherry St., Ste. 525
Denver, CO 80246
(303)893-3400
Fax: (303)893-3403
Website: http://www.sandlotcapital.com

Wolf Ventures
50 South Steele St., Ste. 777
Denver, CO 80209
(303)321-4800
Fax: (303)321-4848
E-mail: businessplan@wolfventures.com
Website: http://www.wolfventures.com

The Columbine Venture Funds
5460 S Quebec St., Ste. 270
Englewood, CO 80111
(303)694-3222
Fax: (303)694-9007

Investment Securities of Colorado, Inc.
4605 Denice Dr.
Englewood, CO 80111
(303)796-9192

Kinship Partners
6300 S Syracuse Way, Ste. 484
Englewood, CO 80111
(303)694-0268
Fax: (303)694-1707
E-mail: block@vailsys.com

Boranco Management, L.L.C.
1528 Hillside Dr.
Fort Collins, CO 80524-1969
(970)221-2297
Fax: (970)221-4787

Aweida Ventures
890 West Cherry St., Ste. 220
Louisville, CO 80027
(303)664-9520
Fax: (303)664-9530
Website: http://www.aweida.com

Access Venture Partners
8787 Turnpike Dr., Ste. 260
Westminster, CO 80030
(303)426-8899
Fax: (303)426-8828

Connecticut

Medmax Ventures, LP
1 Northwestern Dr., Ste. 203
Bloomfield, CT 06002
(860)286-2960
Fax: (860)286-9960

James B. Kobak & Co.
Four Mansfield Place
Darien, CT 06820
(203)656-3471
Fax: (203)655-2905

Orien Ventures
1 Post Rd.
Fairfield, CT 06430
(203)259-9933
Fax: (203)259-5288

ABP Acquisition Corporation
115 Maple Ave.
Greenwich, CT 06830
(203)625-8287
Fax: (203)447-6187

Catterton Partners
9 Greenwich Office Park
Greenwich, CT 06830
(203)629-4901
Fax: (203)629-4903
Website: http://www.cpequity.com

Consumer Venture Partners
3 Pickwick Plz.
Greenwich, CT 06830
(203)629-8800
Fax: (203)629-2019

Insurance Venture Partners
31 Brookside Dr., Ste. 211
Greenwich, CT 06830
(203)861-0030
Fax: (203)861-2745

The NTC Group
Three Pickwick Plaza
Ste. 200
Greenwich, CT 06830
(203)862-2800
Fax: (203)622-6538

Regulus International Capital Co., Inc.
140 Greenwich Ave.
Greenwich, CT 06830
(203)625-9700
Fax: (203)625-9706

Axiom Venture Partners
City Place II
185 Asylum St., 17th Fl.
Hartford, CT 06103
(860)548-7799
Fax: (860)548-7797
Website: http://www.axiomventures.com

Conning Capital Partners
City Place II
185 Asylum St.
Hartford, CT 06103-4105
(860)520-1289
Fax: (860)520-1299
E-mail: pe@conning.com
Website: http://www.conning.com

First New England Capital L.P.
100 Pearl St.
Hartford, CT 06103
(860)293-3333
Fax: (860)293-3338
E-mail: info@firstnewenglandcapital.com
Website: http://www.firstnewenglandcapital
.com

Northeast Ventures
One State St., Ste. 1720
Hartford, CT 06103
(860)547-1414
Fax: (860)246-8755

Windward Holdings
38 Sylvan Rd.
Madison, CT 06443
(203)245-6870
Fax: (203)245-6865

Advanced Materials Partners, Inc.
45 Pine St.
PO Box 1022
New Canaan, CT 06840
(203)966-6415
Fax: (203)966-8448
E-mail: wkb@amplink.com

RFE Investment Partners
36 Grove St.
New Canaan, CT 06840
(203)966-2800
Fax: (203)966-3109
Website: http://www.rfeip.com

Connecticut Innovations, Inc.
999 West St.
Rocky Hill, CT 06067
(860)563-5851
Fax: (860)563-4877
E-mail: pamela.hartley@ctinnovations
.com
Website: http://www.ctinnovations.com

Canaan Partners
105 Rowayton Ave.
Rowayton, CT 06853
(203)855-0400
Fax: (203)854-9117
Website: http://www.canaan.com

Landmark Partners, Inc.
10 Mill Pond Ln.
Simsbury, CT 06070
(860)651-9760
Fax: (860)651-8890
Website: http://www.landmarkpartners.com

Sweeney & Company
PO Box 567
Southport, CT 06490
(203)255-0220
Fax: (203)255-0220
E-mail: sweeney@connix.com

Baxter Associates, Inc.
PO Box 1333
Stamford, CT 06904
(203)323-3143
Fax: (203)348-0622

Beacon Partners Inc.
6 Landmark Sq., 4th Fl.
Stamford, CT 06901-2792
(203)359-5776
Fax: (203)359-5876

Collinson, Howe, and Lennox, LLC
1055 Washington Blvd., 5th Fl.
Stamford, CT 06901
(203)324-7700
Fax: (203)324-3636
E-mail: info@chlmedical.com
Website: http://www.chlmedical.com

Prime Capital Management Co.
550 West Ave.
Stamford, CT 06902
(203)964-0642
Fax: (203)964-0862

Saugatuck Capital Co.
1 Canterbury Green
Stamford, CT 06901
(203)348-6669
Fax: (203)324-6995
Website: http://
www.saugatuckcapital.com

Soundview Financial Group Inc.
22 Gatehouse Rd.
Stamford, CT 06902
(203)462-7200
Fax: (203)462-7350
Website: http://www.sndv.com

TSG Ventures, L.L.C.
177 Broad St., 12th Fl.
Stamford, CT 06901
(203)406-1500
Fax: (203)406-1590

Whitney & Company
177 Broad St.
Stamford, CT 06901
(203)973-1400
Fax: (203)973-1422
Website: http://www.jhwhitney.com

Cullinane & Donnelly Venture Partners L.P.
970 Farmington Ave.
West Hartford, CT 06107
(860)521-7811

The Crestview Investment and Financial Group
431 Post Rd. E, Ste. 1
Westport, CT 06880-4403
(203)222-0333
Fax: (203)222-0000

Marketcorp Venture Associates, L.P. (MCV)
274 Riverside Ave.
Westport, CT 06880
(203)222-3030
Fax: (203)222-3033

Oak Investment Partners (Westport)
1 Gorham Island
Westport, CT 06880
(203)226-8346
Fax: (203)227-0372
Website: http://www.oakinv.com

Oxford Bioscience Partners
315 Post Rd. W
Westport, CT 06880-5200
(203)341-3300
Fax: (203)341-3309
Website: http://www.oxbio.com

Prince Ventures (Westport)
25 Ford Rd.
Westport, CT 06880
(203)227-8332
Fax: (203)226-5302

LTI Venture Leasing Corp.
221 Danbury Rd.
Wilton, CT 06897
(203)563-1100
Fax: (203)563-1111
Website: http://www.ltileasing.com

Delaware

Blue Rock Capital
5803 Kennett Pike, Ste. A
Wilmington, DE 19807
(302)426-0981
Fax: (302)426-0982
Website: http://
www.bluerockcapital.com

District of Columbia

Allied Capital Corp.
1919 Pennsylvania Ave. NW
Washington, DC 20006-3434
(202)331-2444
Fax: (202)659-2053
Website: http://www.alliedcapital.com

Atlantic Coastal Ventures, L.P.
3101 South St. NW
Washington, DC 20007
(202)293-1166
Fax: (202)293-1181
Website: http://www.atlanticcv.com

Columbia Capital Group, Inc.
1660 L St. NW, Ste. 308
Washington, DC 20036
(202)775-8815
Fax: (202)223-0544

Core Capital Partners
901 15th St., NW
9th Fl.
Washington, DC 20005

(202)589-0090
Fax: (202)589-0091
Website: http://www.core-capital.com

Next Point Partners
701 Pennsylvania Ave. NW, Ste. 900
Washington, DC 20004
(202)661-8703
Fax: (202)434-7400
E-mail: mf@nextpoint.vc
Website: http://www.nextpointvc.com

Telecommunications Development Fund
2020 K. St. NW
Ste. 375
Washington, DC 20006
(202)293-8840
Fax: (202)293-8850
Website: http://www.tdfund.com

Wachtel & Co., Inc.
1101 4th St. NW
Washington, DC 20005-5680
(202)898-1144

Winslow Partners LLC
1300 Connecticut Ave. NW
Washington, DC 20036-1703
(202)530-5000
Fax: (202)530-5010
E-mail: winslow@winslowpartners.com

Women's Growth Capital Fund
1054 31st St., NW
Ste. 110
Washington, DC 20007
(202)342-1431
Fax: (202)341-1203
Website: http://www.wgcf.com

Florida

Sigma Capital Corp.
22668 Caravelle Circle
Boca Raton, FL 33433
(561)368-9783

North American Business Development Co., L.L.C.
111 East Las Olas Blvd.
Fort Lauderdale, FL 33301
(305)463-0681
Fax: (305)527-0904
Website: http://
www.northamericanfund.com

Chartwell Capital Management Co. Inc.
1 Independent Dr., Ste. 3120
Jacksonville, FL 32202
(904)355-3519
Fax: (904)353-5833
E-mail: info@chartwellcap.com

CEO Advisors
1061 Maitland Center Commons
Ste. 209
Maitland, FL 32751
(407)660-9327
Fax: (407)660-2109

Henry & Co.
8201 Peters Rd., Ste. 1000
Plantation, FL 33324
(954)797-7400

Avery Business Development Services
2506 St. Michel Ct.
Ponte Vedra, FL 32082
(904)285-6033

New South Ventures
5053 Ocean Blvd.
Sarasota, FL 34242
(941)358-6000
Fax: (941)358-6078
Website: http://www.newsouthventures
.com

Venture Capital Management Corp.
PO Box 2626
Satellite Beach, FL 32937
(407)777-1969

Florida Capital Venture Ltd.
325 Florida Bank Plaza
100 W Kennedy Blvd.
Tampa, FL 33602
(813)229-2294
Fax: (813)229-2028

Quantum Capital Partners
339 South Plant Ave.
Tampa, FL 33606
(813)250-1999
Fax: (813)250-1998
Website: http://www.quantumcapital
partners.com

South Atlantic Venture Fund
614 W Bay St.
Tampa, FL 33606-2704
(813)253-2500
Fax: (813)253-2360
E-mail: venture@southatlantic.com
Website: http://www.southatlantic.com

LM Capital Corp.
120 S Olive, Ste. 400
West Palm Beach, FL 33401
(561)833-9700
Fax: (561)655-6587
Website: http://www.lmcapitalsecurities
.com

Georgia

Venture First Associates
4811 Thornwood Dr.
Acworth, GA 30102
(770)928-3733
Fax: (770)928-6455

Alliance Technology Ventures
8995 Westside Pkwy., Ste. 200
Alpharetta, GA 30004
(678)336-2000
Fax: (678)336-2001
E-mail: info@atv.com
Website: http://www.atv.com

Cordova Ventures
2500 North Winds Pkwy., Ste. 475
Alpharetta, GA 30004
(678)942-0300
Fax: (678)942-0301
Website: http://www.cordovaventures
.com

Advanced Technology Development Fund
1000 Abernathy, Ste. 1420
Atlanta, GA 30328-5614
(404)668-2333
Fax: (404)668-2333

CGW Southeast Partners
12 Piedmont Center, Ste. 210
Atlanta, GA 30305
(404)816-3255
Fax: (404)816-3258
Website: http://www.cgwlp.com

Cyberstarts
1900 Emery St., NW
3rd Fl.
Atlanta, GA 30318
(404)267-5000
Fax: (404)267-5200
Website: http://www.cyberstarts.com

EGL Holdings, Inc.
10 Piedmont Center, Ste. 412
Atlanta, GA 30305
(404)949-8300
Fax: (404)949-8311

Equity South
1790 The Lenox Bldg.
3399 Peachtree Rd. NE
Atlanta, GA 30326
(404)237-6222
Fax: (404)261-1578

Five Paces
3400 Peachtree Rd., Ste. 200
Atlanta, GA 30326
(404)439-8300

Fax: (404)439-8301
Website: http://www.fivepaces.com

Frontline Capital, Inc.
3475 Lenox Rd., Ste. 400
Atlanta, GA 30326
(404)240-7280
Fax: (404)240-7281

Fuqua Ventures LLC
1201 W Peachtree St. NW, Ste. 5000
Atlanta, GA 30309
(404)815-4500
Fax: (404)815-4528
Website: http://www.fuquaventures.com

Noro-Moseley Partners
4200 Northside Pkwy., Bldg. 9
Atlanta, GA 30327
(404)233-1966
Fax: (404)239-9280
Website: http://www.noro-moseley.com

Renaissance Capital Corp.
34 Peachtree St. NW, Ste. 2230
Atlanta, GA 30303
(404)658-9061
Fax: (404)658-9064

River Capital, Inc.
Two Midtown Plaza
1360 Peachtree St. NE, Ste. 1430
Atlanta, GA 30309
(404)873-2166
Fax: (404)873-2158

State Street Bank & Trust Co.
3414 Peachtree Rd. NE, Ste. 1010
Atlanta, GA 30326
(404)364-9500
Fax: (404)261-4469

UPS Strategic Enterprise Fund
55 Glenlake Pkwy. NE
Atlanta, GA 30328
(404)828-8814
Fax: (404)828-8088
E-mail: jcacyce@ups.com
Website: http://www.ups.com/sef/sef_home

Wachovia
191 Peachtree St. NE, 26th Fl.
Atlanta, GA 30303
(404)332-1000
Fax: (404)332-1392
Website: http://www.wachovia.com/wca

Brainworks Ventures
4243 Dunwoody Club Dr.
Chamblee, GA 30341
(770)239-7447

First Growth Capital Inc.
Best Western Plaza, Ste. 105
PO Box 815
Forsyth, GA 31029
(912)781-7131

Financial Capital Resources, Inc.
21 Eastbrook Bend, Ste. 116
Peachtree City, GA 30269
(404)487-6650

Hawaii

HMS Hawaii Management Partners
Davies Pacific Center
841 Bishop St., Ste. 860
Honolulu, HI 96813
(808)545-3755
Fax: (808)531-2611

Idaho

Sun Valley Ventures
160 Second St.
Ketchum, ID 83340
(208)726-5005
Fax: (208)726-5094

Illinois

Open Prairie Ventures
115 N. Neil St., Ste. 209
Champaign, IL 61820
(217)351-7000
Fax: (217)351-7051
E-mail: inquire@openprairie.com
Website: http://www.openprairie.com

ABN AMRO Private Equity
208 S La Salle St., 10th Fl.
Chicago, IL 60604
(312)855-7079
Fax: (312)553-6648
Website: http://www.abnequity.com

Alpha Capital Partners, Ltd.
122 S Michigan Ave., Ste. 1700
Chicago, IL 60603
(312)322-9800
Fax: (312)322-9808
E-mail: acp@alphacapital.com

Ameritech Development Corp.
30 S Wacker Dr., 37th Fl.
Chicago, IL 60606
(312)750-5083
Fax: (312)609-0244

Apex Investment Partners
225 W Washington, Ste. 1450
Chicago, IL 60606
(312)857-2800
Fax: (312)857-1800

E-mail: apex@apexvc.com
Website: http://www.apexvc.com

Arch Venture Partners
8725 W Higgins Rd., Ste. 290
Chicago, IL 60631
(773)380-6600
Fax: (773)380-6606
Website: http://www.archventure.com

The Bank Funds
208 South LaSalle St., Ste. 1680
Chicago, IL 60604
(312)855-6020
Fax: (312)855-8910

Batterson Venture Partners
303 W Madison St., Ste. 1110
Chicago, IL 60606-3309
(312)269-0300
Fax: (312)269-0021
Website: http://www.battersonvp.com

William Blair Capital Partners, L.L.C.
222 W Adams St., Ste. 1300
Chicago, IL 60606
(312)364-8250
Fax: (312)236-1042
E-mail: privateequity@wmblair.com
Website: http://www.wmblair.com

Bluestar Ventures
208 South LaSalle St., Ste. 1020
Chicago, IL 60604
(312)384-5000
Fax: (312)384-5005
Website: http://www.bluestarventures.com

The Capital Strategy Management Co.
233 S Wacker Dr.
Box 06334
Chicago, IL 60606
(312)444-1170

DN Partners
77 West Wacker Dr., Ste. 4550
Chicago, IL 60601
(312)332-7960
Fax: (312)332-7979

Dresner Capital Inc.
29 South LaSalle St., Ste. 310
Chicago, IL 60603
(312)726-3600
Fax: (312)726-7448

Eblast Ventures LLC
11 South LaSalle St., 5th Fl.
Chicago, IL 60603
(312)372-2600
Fax: (312)372-5621
Website: http://www.eblastventures.com

Essex Woodlands Health Ventures, L.P.
190 S LaSalle St., Ste. 2800
Chicago, IL 60603
(312)444-6040
Fax: (312)444-6034
Website: http://www.essexwoodlands
.com

First Analysis Venture Capital
233 S Wacker Dr., Ste. 9500
Chicago, IL 60606
(312)258-1400
Fax: (312)258-0334
Website: http://www.firstanalysis.com

Frontenac Co.
135 S LaSalle St., Ste.3800
Chicago, IL 60603
(312)368-0044
Fax: (312)368-9520
Website: http://www.frontenac.com

GTCR Golder Rauner, LLC
6100 Sears Tower
Chicago, IL 60606
(312)382-2200
Fax: (312)382-2201
Website: http://www.gtcr.com

High Street Capital LLC
311 South Wacker Dr., Ste. 4550
Chicago, IL 60606
(312)697-4990
Fax: (312)697-4994
Website: http://www.highstr.com

IEG Venture Management, Inc.
70 West Madison
Chicago, IL 60602
(312)644-0890
Fax: (312)454-0369
Website: http://www.iegventure.com

JK&B Capital
180 North Stetson, Ste. 4500
Chicago, IL 60601
(312)946-1200
Fax: (312)946-1103
E-mail: gspencer@jkbcapital.com
Website: http://www.jkbcapital.com

Kettle Partners L.P.
350 W Hubbard, Ste. 350
Chicago, IL 60610
(312)329-9300
Fax: (312)527-4519
Website: http://www.kettlevc.com

Lake Shore Capital Partners
20 N. Wacker Dr., Ste. 2807
Chicago, IL 60606
(312)803-3536
Fax: (312)803-3534

LaSalle Capital Group Inc.
70 W Madison St., Ste. 5710
Chicago, IL 60602
(312)236-7041
Fax: (312)236-0720

Linc Capital, Inc.
303 E Wacker Pkwy., Ste. 1000
Chicago, IL 60601
(312)946-2670
Fax: (312)938-4290
E-mail: bdemars@linccap.com

Madison Dearborn Partners, Inc.
3 First National Plz., Ste. 3800
Chicago, IL 60602
(312)895-1000
Fax: (312)895-1001
E-mail: invest@mdcp.com
Website: http://www.mdcp.com

Mesirow Private Equity Investments Inc.
350 N. Clark St.
Chicago, IL 60610
(312)595-6950
Fax: (312)595-6211
Website: http://www.meisrowfinancial.com

Mosaix Ventures LLC
1822 North Mohawk
Chicago, IL 60614
(312)274-0988
Fax: (312)274-0989
Website: http://www.mosaixventures.com

Nesbitt Burns
111 West Monroe St.
Chicago, IL 60603
(312)416-3855
Fax: (312)765-8000
Website: http://www.harrisbank.com

Polestar Capital, Inc.
180 N. Michigan Ave., Ste. 1905
Chicago, IL 60601
(312)984-9090
Fax: (312)984-9877
E-mail: wl@polestarvc.com
Website: http://www.polestarvc.com

Prince Ventures (Chicago)
10 S Wacker Dr., Ste. 2575
Chicago, IL 60606-7407
(312)454-1408
Fax: (312)454-9125

Prism Capital
444 N. Michigan Ave.
Chicago, IL 60611
(312)464-7900
Fax: (312)464-7915
Website: http://www.prismfund.com

Third Coast Capital
900 N. Franklin St., Ste. 700
Chicago, IL 60610
(312)337-3303
Fax: (312)337-2567
E-mail: manic@earthlink.com
Website: http://www.thirdcoastcapital
.com

Thoma Cressey Equity Partners
4460 Sears Tower, 92nd Fl.
233 S Wacker Dr.
Chicago, IL 60606
(312)777-4444
Fax: (312)777-4445
Website: http://www.thomacressey.com

Tribune Ventures
435 N. Michigan Ave., Ste. 600
Chicago, IL 60611
(312)527-8797
Fax: (312)222-5993
Website: http://www.tribuneventures.com

Wind Point Partners (Chicago)
676 N. Michigan Ave., Ste. 330
Chicago, IL 60611
(312)649-4000
Website: http://www.wppartners.com

Marquette Venture Partners
520 Lake Cook Rd., Ste. 450
Deerfield, IL 60015
(847)940-1700
Fax: (847)940-1724
Website: http://www.marquetteventures
.com

Duchossois Investments Limited, LLC
845 Larch Ave.
Elmhurst, IL 60126
(630)530-6105
Fax: (630)993-8644
Website: http://www.duchtec.com

Evanston Business Investment Corp.
1840 Oak Ave.
Evanston, IL 60201
(847)866-1840
Fax: (847)866-1808
E-mail: t-parkinson@nwu.com
Website: http://www.ebic.com

Inroads Capital Partners L.P.
1603 Orrington Ave., Ste. 2050
Evanston, IL 60201-3841
(847)864-2000
Fax: (847)864-9692

The Cerulean Fund/WGC Enterprises
1701 E Lake Ave., Ste. 170
Glenview, IL 60025

(847)657-8002
Fax: (847)657-8168

Ventana Financial Resources, Inc.
249 Market Sq.
Lake Forest, IL 60045
(847)234-3434

Beecken, Petty & Co.
901 Warrenville Rd., Ste. 205
Lisle, IL 60532
(630)435-0300
Fax: (630)435-0370
E-mail: hep@bpcompany.com
Website: http://www.bpcompany.com

Allstate Private Equity
3075 Sanders Rd., Ste. G5D
Northbrook, IL 60062-7127
(847)402-8247
Fax: (847)402-0880

KB Partners
1101 Skokie Blvd., Ste. 260
Northbrook, IL 60062-2856
(847)714-0444
Fax: (847)714-0445
E-mail: keith@kbpartners.com
Website: http://www.kbpartners.com

Transcap Associates Inc.
900 Skokie Blvd., Ste. 210
Northbrook, IL 60062
(847)753-9600
Fax: (847)753-9090

**Graystone Venture Partners, L.L.C. /
Portage Venture Partners**
One Northfield Plaza, Ste. 530
Northfield, IL 60093
(847)446-9460
Fax: (847)446-9470
Website: http://www.portageventures.com

Motorola Inc.
1303 E Algonquin Rd.
Schaumburg, IL 60196-1065
(847)576-4929
Fax: (847)538-2250
Website: http://www.mot.com/mne

Indiana

Irwin Ventures LLC
500 Washington St.
Columbus, IN 47202
(812)373-1434
Fax: (812)376-1709
Website: http://www.irwinventures.com

Cambridge Venture Partners
4181 East 96th St., Ste. 200
Indianapolis, IN 46240

(317)814-6192
Fax: (317)944-9815

CID Equity Partners
One American Square, Ste. 2850
Box 82074
Indianapolis, IN 46282
(317)269-2350
Fax: (317)269-2355
Website: http://www.cidequity.com

Gazelle Techventures
6325 Digital Way, Ste. 460
Indianapolis, IN 46278
(317)275-6800
Fax: (317)275-1101
Website: http://www.gazellevc.com

Monument Advisors Inc.
Bank One Center/Circle
111 Monument Circle, Ste. 600
Indianapolis, IN 46204-5172
(317)656-5065
Fax: (317)656-5060
Website: http://www.monumentadv.com

MWV Capital Partners
201 N. Illinois St., Ste. 300
Indianapolis, IN 46204
(317)237-2323
Fax: (317)237-2325
Website: http://www.mwvcapital.com

First Source Capital Corp.
100 North Michigan St.
PO Box 1602
South Bend, IN 46601
(219)235-2180
Fax: (219)235-2227

Iowa

Allsop Venture Partners
118 Third Ave. SE, Ste. 837
Cedar Rapids, IA 52401
(319)368-6675
Fax: (319)363-9515

InvestAmerica Investment Advisors, Inc.
101 2nd St. SE, Ste. 800
Cedar Rapids, IA 52401
(319)363-8249
Fax: (319)363-9683

Pappajohn Capital Resources
2116 Financial Center
Des Moines, IA 50309
(515)244-5746
Fax: (515)244-2346
Website: http://www.pappajohn.com

Berthel Fisher & Company Planning Inc.
701 Tama St.
PO Box 609

Marion, IA 52302
(319)497-5700
Fax: (319)497-4244

Kansas

Enterprise Merchant Bank
7400 West 110th St., Ste. 560
Overland Park, KS 66210
(913)327-8500
Fax: (913)327-8505

**Kansas Venture Capital, Inc.
(Overland Park)**
6700 Antioch Plz., Ste. 460
Overland Park, KS 66204
(913)262-7117
Fax: (913)262-3509
E-mail: jdalton@kvci.com

Child Health Investment Corp.
6803 W 64th St., Ste. 208
Shawnee Mission, KS 66202
(913)262-1436
Fax: (913)262-1575
Website: http://www.chca.com

Kansas Technology Enterprise Corp.
214 SW 6th, 1st Fl.
Topeka, KS 66603-3719
(785)296-5272
Fax: (785)296-1160
E-mail: ktec@ktec.com
Website: http://www.ktec.com

Kentucky

**Kentucky Highlands Investment
Corp.**
362 Old Whitley Rd.
London, KY 40741
(606)864-5175
Fax: (606)864-5194
Website: http://www.khic.org

Chrysalis Ventures, L.L.C.
1850 National City Tower
Louisville, KY 40202
(502)583-7644
Fax: (502)583-7648
E-mail: bobsany@chrysalisventures.com
Website: http://www.chrysalisventures
.com

Humana Venture Capital
500 West Main St.
Louisville, KY 40202
(502)580-3922
Fax: (502)580-2051
E-mail: gemont@humana.com
George Emont, Director

Summit Capital Group, Inc.
6510 Glenridge Park Pl., Ste. 8

Louisville, KY 40222
(502)332-2700

Louisiana

Bank One Equity Investors, Inc.
451 Florida St.
Baton Rouge, LA 70801
(504)332-4421
Fax: (504)332-7377

Advantage Capital Partners
LLE Tower
909 Poydras St., Ste. 2230
New Orleans, LA 70112
(504)522-4850
Fax: (504)522-4950
Website: http://www.advantagecap.com

Maine

CEI Ventures / Coastal Ventures LP
2 Portland Fish Pier, Ste. 201
Portland, ME 04101
(207)772-5356
Fax: (207)772-5503
Website: http://www.ceiventures.com

Commwealth Bioventures, Inc.
4 Milk St.
Portland, ME 04101
(207)780-0904
Fax: (207)780-0913

Maryland

Annapolis Ventures LLC
151 West St., Ste. 302
Annapolis, MD 21401
(443)482-9555
Fax: (443)482-9565
Website: http://www.annapolisventures.com

Delmag Ventures
220 Wardour Dr.
Annapolis, MD 21401
(410)267-8196
Fax: (410)267-8017
Website: http://www.delmagventures.com

Abell Venture Fund
111 S Calvert St., Ste. 2300
Baltimore, MD 21202
(410)547-1300
Fax: (410)539-6579
Website: http://www.abell.org

ABS Ventures (Baltimore)
1 South St., Ste. 2150
Baltimore, MD 21202
(410)895-3895
Fax: (410)895-3899
Website: http://www.absventures.com

Anthem Capital, L.P.
16 S Calvert St., Ste. 800
Baltimore, MD 21202-1305
(410)625-1510
Fax: (410)625-1735
Website: http://www.anthemcapital.com

Catalyst Ventures
1119 St. Paul St.
Baltimore, MD 21202
(410)244-0123
Fax: (410)752-7721

Maryland Venture Capital Trust
217 E Redwood St., Ste. 2200
Baltimore, MD 21202
(410)767-6361
Fax: (410)333-6931

New Enterprise Associates (Baltimore)
1119 St. Paul St.
Baltimore, MD 21202
(410)244-0115
Fax: (410)752-7721
Website: http://www.nea.com

T. Rowe Price Threshold Partnerships
100 E Pratt St., 8th Fl.
Baltimore, MD 21202
(410)345-2000
Fax: (410)345-2800

Spring Capital Partners
16 W Madison St.
Baltimore, MD 21201
(410)685-8000
Fax: (410)727-1436
E-mail: mailbox@springcap.com

Arete Corporation
3 Bethesda Metro Ctr., Ste. 770
Bethesda, MD 20814
(301)657-6268
Fax: (301)657-6254
Website: http://www.arete-microgen.com

Embryon Capital
7903 Sleaford Place
Bethesda, MD 20814
(301)656-6837
Fax: (301)656-8056

Potomac Ventures
7920 Norfolk Ave., Ste. 1100
Bethesda, MD 20814
(301)215-9240
Website: http://www.potomacventures.com

Toucan Capital Corp.
3 Bethesda Metro Center, Ste. 700
Bethesda, MD 20814

(301)961-1970
Fax: (301)961-1969
Website: http://www.toucancapital.com

Kinetic Ventures LLC
2 Wisconsin Cir., Ste. 620
Chevy Chase, MD 20815
(301)652-8066
Fax: (301)652-8310
Website: http://www.kineticventures.com

Boulder Ventures Ltd.
4750 Owings Mills Blvd.
Owings Mills, MD 21117
(410)998-3114
Fax: (410)356-5492
Website: http://www.boulderventures.com

Grotech Capital Group
9690 Deereco Rd., Ste. 800
Timonium, MD 21093
(410)560-2000
Fax: (410)560-1910
Website: http://www.grotech.com

Massachusetts

Adams, Harkness & Hill, Inc.
60 State St.
Boston, MA 02109
(617)371-3900

Advent International
75 State St., 29th Fl.
Boston, MA 02109
(617)951-9400
Fax: (617)951-0566
Website: http://www.adventinernational.com

American Research and Development
30 Federal St.
Boston, MA 02110-2508
(617)423-7500
Fax: (617)423-9655

Ascent Venture Partners
255 State St., 5th Fl.
Boston, MA 02109
(617)270-9400
Fax: (617)270-9401
E-mail: info@ascentvp.com
Website: http://www.ascentvp.com

Atlas Venture
222 Berkeley St.
Boston, MA 02116
(617)488-2200
Fax: (617)859-9292
Website: http://www.atlasventure.com

Axxon Capital
28 State St., 37th Fl.
Boston, MA 02109
(617)722-0980
Fax: (617)557-6014
Website: http://www.axxoncapital.com

BancBoston Capital/BancBoston Ventures
175 Federal St., 10th Fl.
Boston, MA 02110
(617)434-2509
Fax: (617)434-6175
Website: http://
www.bancbostoncapital.com

Boston Capital Ventures
Old City Hall
45 School St.
Boston, MA 02108
(617)227-6550
Fax: (617)227-3847
E-mail: info@bcv.com
Website: http://www.bcv.com

Boston Financial & Equity Corp.
20 Overland St.
PO Box 15071
Boston, MA 02215
(617)267-2900
Fax: (617)437-7601
E-mail: debbie@bfec.com

Boston Millennia Partners
30 Rowes Wharf
Boston, MA 02110
(617)428-5150
Fax: (617)428-5160
Website: http://www.millenniapartners
.com

Bristol Investment Trust
842A Beacon St.
Boston, MA 02215-3199
(617)566-5212
Fax: (617)267-0932

Brook Venture Management LLC
50 Federal St., 5th Fl.
Boston, MA 02110
(617)451-8989
Fax: (617)451-2369
Website: http://www.brookventure.com

Burr, Egan, Deleage, and Co. (Boston)
200 Clarendon St., Ste. 3800
Boston, MA 02116
(617)262-7770
Fax: (617)262-9779

Cambridge/Samsung Partners
One Exeter Plaza
Ninth Fl.

Boston, MA 02116
(617)262-4440
Fax: (617)262-5562

Chestnut Street Partners, Inc.
75 State St., Ste. 2500
Boston, MA 02109
(617)345-7220
Fax: (617)345-7201
E-mail: chestnut@chestnutp.com

Claflin Capital Management, Inc.
10 Liberty Sq., Ste. 300
Boston, MA 02109
(617)426-6505
Fax: (617)482-0016
Website: http://www.claflincapital.com

Copley Venture Partners
99 Summer St., Ste. 1720
Boston, MA 02110
(617)737-1253
Fax: (617)439-0699

Corning Capital / Corning Technology Ventures
121 High Street, Ste. 400
Boston, MA 02110
(617)338-2656
Fax: (617)261-3864
Website: http://www.corningventures.com

Downer & Co.
211 Congress St.
Boston, MA 02110
(617)482-6200
Fax: (617)482-6201
E-mail: cdowner@downer.com
Website: http://www.downer.com

Fidelity Ventures
82 Devonshire St.
Boston, MA 02109
(617)563-6370
Fax: (617)476-9023
Website: http://www.fidelityventures.com

Greylock Management Corp. (Boston)
1 Federal St.
Boston, MA 02110-2065
(617)423-5525
Fax: (617)482-0059

Gryphon Ventures
222 Berkeley St., Ste.1600
Boston, MA 02116
(617)267-9191
Fax: (617)267-4293
E-mail: all@gryphoninc.com

Halpern, Denny & Co.
500 Boylston St.
Boston, MA 02116

(617)536-6602
Fax: (617)536-8535

Harbourvest Partners, LLC
1 Financial Center, 44th Fl.
Boston, MA 02111
(617)348-3707
Fax: (617)350-0305
Website: http://www.hvpllc.com

Highland Capital Partners
2 International Pl.
Boston, MA 02110
(617)981-1500
Fax: (617)531-1550
E-mail: info@hcp.com
Website: http://www.hcp.com

Lee Munder Venture Partners
John Hancock Tower T-53
200 Clarendon St.
Boston, MA 02103
(617)380-5600
Fax: (617)380-5601
Website: http://www.leemunder.com

M/C Venture Partners
75 State St., Ste. 2500
Boston, MA 02109
(617)345-7200
Fax: (617)345-7201
Website: http://www.mcventurepartners
.com

Massachusetts Capital Resources Co.
420 Boylston St.
Boston, MA 02116
(617)536-3900
Fax: (617)536-7930

Massachusetts Technology Development Corp. (MTDC)
148 State St.
Boston, MA 02109
(617)723-4920
Fax: (617)723-5983
E-mail: jhodgman@mtdc.com
Website: http://www.mtdc.com

New England Partners
One Boston Place, Ste. 2100
Boston, MA 02108
(617)624-8400
Fax: (617)624-8999
Website: http://www.nepartners.com

North Hill Ventures
Ten Post Office Square
11th Fl.
Boston, MA 02109
(617)788-2112
Fax: (617)788-2152

Website: http://www.northhillventures
.com

OneLiberty Ventures
150 Cambridge Park Dr.
Boston, MA 02140
(617)492-7280
Fax: (617)492-7290
Website: http://www.oneliberty.com

Schroder Ventures
Life Sciences
60 State St., Ste. 3650
Boston, MA 02109
(617)367-8100
Fax: (617)367-1590
Website: http://www.shroderventures
.com

Shawmut Capital Partners
75 Federal St., 18th Fl.
Boston, MA 02110
(617)368-4900
Fax: (617)368-4910
Website: http://www.shawmutcapital.com

Solstice Capital LLC
15 Broad St., 3rd Fl.
Boston, MA 02109
(617)523-7733
Fax: (617)523-5827
E-mail: solticecapital@solcap.com

Spectrum Equity Investors
One International Pl., 29th Fl.
Boston, MA 02110
(617)464-4600
Fax: (617)464-4601
Website: http://www.spectrumequity
.com

Spray Venture Partners
One Walnut St.
Boston, MA 02108
(617)305-4140
Fax: (617)305-4144
Website: http://www.sprayventure.com

The Still River Fund
100 Federal St., 29th Fl.
Boston, MA 02110
(617)348-2327
Fax: (617)348-2371
Website: http://www.stillriverfund.com

Summit Partners
600 Atlantic Ave., Ste. 2800
Boston, MA 02210-2227
(617)824-1000
Fax: (617)824-1159
Website: http://www.summitpartners.com

TA Associates, Inc. (Boston)
High Street Tower
125 High St., Ste. 2500
Boston, MA 02110
(617)574-6700
Fax: (617)574-6728
Website: http://www.ta.com

TVM Techno Venture Management
101 Arch St., Ste. 1950
Boston, MA 02110
(617)345-9320
Fax: (617)345-9377
E-mail: info@tvmvc.com
Website: http://www.tvmvc.com

UNC Ventures
64 Burough St.
Boston, MA 02130-4017
(617)482-7070
Fax: (617)522-2176

**Venture Investment Management
Company (VIMAC)**
177 Milk St.
Boston, MA 02190-3410
(617)292-3300
Fax: (617)292-7979
E-mail: bzeisig@vimac.com
Website: http://www.vimac.com

MDT Advisers, Inc.
125 Cambridge Park Dr.
Cambridge, MA 02140-2314
(617)234-2200
Fax: (617)234-2210
Website: http://www.mdtai.com

TTC Ventures
One Main St., 6th Fl.
Cambridge, MA 02142
(617)528-3137
Fax: (617)577-1715
E-mail: info@ttcventures.com

Zero Stage Capital Co. Inc.
101 Main St., 17th Fl.
Cambridge, MA 02142
(617)876-5355
Fax: (617)876-1248
Website: http://www.zerostage.com

Atlantic Capital
164 Cushing Hwy.
Cohasset, MA 02025
(617)383-9449
Fax: (617)383-6040
E-mail: info@atlanticcap.com
Website: http://www.atlanticcap.com

Seacoast Capital Partners
55 Ferncroft Rd.
Danvers, MA 01923

(978)750-1300
Fax: (978)750-1301
E-mail: gdeli@seacoastcapital.com
Website: http://www.seacoastcapital.com

Sage Management Group
44 South Street
PO Box 2026
East Dennis, MA 02641
(508)385-7172
Fax: (508)385-7272
E-mail: sagemgt@capecod.net

Applied Technology
1 Cranberry Hill
Lexington, MA 02421-7397
(617)862-8622
Fax: (617)862-8367

Royalty Capital Management
5 Downing Rd.
Lexington, MA 02421-6918
(781)861-8490

Argo Global Capital
210 Broadway, Ste. 101
Lynnfield, MA 01940
(781)592-5250
Fax: (781)592-5230
Website: http://www.gsmcapital.com

Industry Ventures
6 Bayne Lane
Newburyport, MA 01950
(978)499-7606
Fax: (978)499-0686
Website: http://www.industryventures
.com

Softbank Capital Partners
10 Langley Rd., Ste. 202
Newton Center, MA 02459
(617)928-9300
Fax: (617)928-9305
E-mail: clax@bvc.com

**Advanced Technology Ventures
(Boston)**
281 Winter St., Ste. 350
Waltham, MA 02451
(781)290-0707
Fax: (781)684-0045
E-mail: info@atvcapital.com
Website: http://www.atvcapital.com

Castile Ventures
890 Winter St., Ste. 140
Waltham, MA 02451
(781)890-0060
Fax: (781)890-0065
Website: http://www.castileventures.com

Charles River Ventures
1000 Winter St., Ste. 3300
Waltham, MA 02451
(781)487-7060
Fax: (781)487-7065
Website: http://www.crv.com

Comdisco Venture Group (Waltham)
Totton Pond Office Center
400-1 Totten Pond Rd.
Waltham, MA 02451
(617)672-0250
Fax: (617)398-8099

Marconi Ventures
890 Winter St., Ste. 310
Waltham, MA 02451
(781)839-7177
Fax: (781)522-7477
Website: http://www.marconi.com

Matrix Partners
Bay Colony Corporate Center
1000 Winter St., Ste.4500
Waltham, MA 02451
(781)890-2244
Fax: (781)890-2288
Website: http://www.matrixpartners.com

North Bridge Venture Partners
950 Winter St. Ste. 4600
Waltham, MA 02451
(781)290-0004
Fax: (781)290-0999
E-mail: eta@nbvp.com

Polaris Venture Partners
Bay Colony Corporate Ctr.
1000 Winter St., Ste. 3500
Waltham, MA 02451
(781)290-0770
Fax: (781)290-0880
E-mail: partners@polarisventures.com
Website: http://www.polarisventures.com

Seaflower Ventures
Bay Colony Corporate Ctr.
1000 Winter St. Ste. 1000
Waltham, MA 02451
(781)466-9552
Fax: (781)466-9553
E-mail: moot@seaflower.com
Website: http://www.seaflower.com

Ampersand Ventures
55 William St., Ste. 240
Wellesley, MA 02481
(617)239-0700
Fax: (617)239-0824
E-mail: info@ampersandventures.com
Website: http://www.ampersandventures
.com

Battery Ventures (Boston)
20 William St., Ste. 200
Wellesley, MA 02481
(781)577-1000
Fax: (781)577-1001
Website: http://www.battery.com

Commonwealth Capital Ventures, L.P.
20 William St., Ste.225
Wellesley, MA 02481
(781)237-7373
Fax: (781)235-8627
Website: http://www.ccvlp.com

Fowler, Anthony & Company
20 Walnut St.
Wellesley, MA 02481
(781)237-4201
Fax: (781)237-7718

Gemini Investors
20 William St.
Wellesley, MA 02481
(781)237-7001
Fax: (781)237-7233

Grove Street Advisors Inc.
20 William St., Ste. 230
Wellesley, MA 02481
(781)263-6100
Fax: (781)263-6101
Website: http://www.grovestreetadvisors
.com

Mees Pierson Investeringsmaat B.V.
20 William St., Ste. 210
Wellesley, MA 02482
(781)239-7600
Fax: (781)239-0377

Norwest Equity Partners
40 William St., Ste. 305
Wellesley, MA 02481-3902
(781)237-5870
Fax: (781)237-6270
Website: http://www.norwestvp.com

Bessemer Venture Partners (Wellesley Hills)
83 Walnut St.
Wellesley Hills, MA 02481
(781)237-6050
Fax: (781)235-7576
E-mail: travis@bvpny.com
Website: http://www.bvp.com

Venture Capital Fund of New England
20 Walnut St., Ste. 120
Wellesley Hills, MA 02481-2175
(781)239-8262
Fax: (781)239-8263

Prism Venture Partners
100 Lowder Brook Dr., Ste. 2500
Westwood, MA 02090
(781)302-4000
Fax: (781)302-4040
E-mail: dwbaum@prismventure.com

Palmer Partners LP
200 Unicorn Park Dr.
Woburn, MA 01801
(781)933-5445
Fax: (781)933-0698

Michigan

Arbor Partners, L.L.C.
130 South First St.
Ann Arbor, MI 48104
(734)668-9000
Fax: (734)669-4195
Website: http://www.arborpartners.com

EDF Ventures
425 N. Main St.
Ann Arbor, MI 48104
(734)663-3213
Fax: (734)663-7358
E-mail: edf@edfvc.com
Website: http://www.edfvc.com

White Pines Management, L.L.C.
2401 Plymouth Rd., Ste. B
Ann Arbor, MI 48105
(734)747-9401
Fax: (734)747-9704
E-mail: ibund@whitepines.com
Website: http://www.whitepines.com

Wellmax, Inc.
3541 Bendway Blvd., Ste. 100
Bloomfield Hills, MI 48301
(248)646-3554
Fax: (248)646-6220

Venture Funding, Ltd.
Fisher Bldg.
3011 West Grand Blvd., Ste. 321
Detroit, MI 48202
(313)871-3606
Fax: (313)873-4935

Investcare Partners L.P. / GMA Capital LLC
32330 W Twelve Mile Rd.
Farmington Hills, MI 48334
(248)489-9000
Fax: (248)489-8819
E-mail: gma@gmacapital.com
Website: http://www.gmacapital.com

Liberty Bidco Investment Corp.
30833 Northwestern Highway, Ste. 211
Farmington Hills, MI 48334

(248)626-6070
Fax: (248)626-6072

Seaflower Ventures
5170 Nicholson Rd.
PO Box 474
Fowlerville, MI 48836
(517)223-3335
Fax: (517)223-3337
E-mail: gibbons@seaflower.com
Website: http://www.seaflower.com

Ralph Wilson Equity Fund LLC
15400 E Jefferson Ave.
Gross Pointe Park, MI 48230
(313)821-9122
Fax: (313)821-9101
Website: http://www.RalphWilsonEquity
Fund.com
J. Skip Simms, President

Minnesota

Development Corp. of Austin
1900 Eighth Ave., NW
Austin, MN 55912
(507)433-0346
Fax: (507)433-0361
E-mail: dca@smig.net
Website: http://www.spamtownusa.com

Northeast Ventures Corp.
802 Alworth Bldg.
Duluth, MN 55802
(218)722-9915
Fax: (218)722-9871

Medical Innovation Partners, Inc.
6450 City West Pkwy.
Eden Prairie, MN 55344-3245
(612)828-9616
Fax: (612)828-9596

St. Paul Venture Capital, Inc.
10400 Vicking Dr., Ste. 550
Eden Prairie, MN 55344
(612)995-7474
Fax: (612)995-7475
Website: http://www.stpaulvc.com

Cherry Tree Investments, Inc.
7601 France Ave. S, Ste. 150
Edina, MN 55435
(612)893-9012
Fax: (612)893-9036
Website: http://www.cherrytree.com

Shared Ventures, Inc.
6550 York Ave. S
Edina, MN 55435
(612)925-3411

Sherpa Partners LLC
5050 Lincoln Dr., Ste. 490
Edina, MN 55436
(952)942-1070
Fax: (952)942-1071
Website: http://www.sherpapartners.com

Affinity Capital Management
901 Marquette Ave., Ste. 1810
Minneapolis, MN 55402
(612)252-9900
Fax: (612)252-9911
Website: http://www.affinitycapital.com

Artesian Capital
1700 Foshay Tower
821 Marquette Ave.
Minneapolis, MN 55402
(612)334-5600
Fax: (612)334-5601
E-mail: artesian@artesian.com

Coral Ventures
60 S 6th St., Ste. 3510
Minneapolis, MN 55402
(612)335-8666
Fax: (612)335-8668
Website: http://www.coralventures.com

Crescendo Venture Management, L.L.C.
800 LaSalle Ave., Ste. 2250
Minneapolis, MN 55402
(612)607-2800
Fax: (612)607-2801
Website: http://www.crescendoventures
.com

Gideon Hixon Venture
1900 Foshay Tower
821 Marquette Ave.
Minneapolis, MN 55402
(612)904-2314
Fax: (612)204-0913

Norwest Equity Partners
3600 IDS Center
80 S 8th St.
Minneapolis, MN 55402
(612)215-1600
Fax: (612)215-1601
Website: http://www.norwestvp.com

Oak Investment Partners
(Minneapolis)
4550 Norwest Center
90 S 7th St.
Minneapolis, MN 55402
(612)339-9322
Fax: (612)337-8017
Website: http://www.oakinv.com

Pathfinder Venture Capital Funds
(Minneapolis)
7300 Metro Blvd., Ste. 585
Minneapolis, MN 55439
(612)835-1121
Fax: (612)835-8389
E-mail: jahrens620@aol.com

U.S. Bancorp Piper Jaffray
Ventures, Inc.
800 Nicollet Mall, Ste. 800
Minneapolis, MN 55402
(612)303-5686
Fax: (612)303-1350
Website: http://
www.paperjaffreyventures.com

The Food Fund, Ltd. Partnership
5720 Smatana Dr., Ste. 300
Minnetonka, MN 55343
(612)939-3950
Fax: (612)939-8106

Mayo Medical Ventures
200 First St. SW
Rochester, MN 55905
(507)266-4586
Fax: (507)284-5410
Website: http://www.mayo.edu

Missouri

Bankers Capital Corp.
3100 Gillham Rd.
Kansas City, MO 64109
(816)531-1600
Fax: (816)531-1334

Capital for Business, Inc. (Kansas City)
1000 Walnut St., 18th Fl.
Kansas City, MO 64106
(816)234-2357
Fax: (816)234-2952
Website: http://www.capitalforbusiness
.com

De Vries & Co. Inc.
800 West 47th St.
Kansas City, MO 64112
(816)756-0055
Fax: (816)756-0061

InvestAmerica Venture Group Inc.
(Kansas City)
Commerce Tower
911 Main St., Ste. 2424
Kansas City, MO 64105
(816)842-0114
Fax: (816)471-7339

Kansas City Equity Partners
233 W 47th St.
Kansas City, MO 64112

(816)960-1771
Fax: (816)960-1777
Website: http://www.kcep.com

Bome Investors, Inc.
8000 Maryland Ave., Ste. 1190
Saint Louis, MO 63105
(314)721-5707
Fax: (314)721-5135
Website: http://www.gatewayventures.com

Capital for Business, Inc. (Saint Louis)
11 S Meramac St., Ste. 1430
Saint Louis, MO 63105
(314)746-7427
Fax: (314)746-8739
Website: http://www.capitalforbusiness
.com

Crown Capital Corp.
540 Maryville Centre Dr., Ste. 120
Saint Louis, MO 63141
(314)576-1201
Fax: (314)576-1525
Website: http://www.crown-cap.com

Gateway Associates L.P.
8000 Maryland Ave., Ste. 1190
Saint Louis, MO 63105
(314)721-5707
Fax: (314)721-5135

Harbison Corp.
8112 Maryland Ave., Ste. 250
Saint Louis, MO 63105
(314)727-8200
Fax: (314)727-0249

Nebraska

Heartland Capital Fund, Ltd.
PO Box 642117
Omaha, NE 68154
(402)778-5124
Fax: (402)445-2370
Website: http://www.heartlandcapital
fund.com

Odin Capital Group
1625 Farnam St., Ste. 700
Omaha, NE 68102
(402)346-6200
Fax: (402)342-9311
Website: http://www.odincapital.com

Nevada

Edge Capital Investment Co. LLC
1350 E Flamingo Rd., Ste. 3000
Las Vegas, NV 89119
(702)438-3343
E-mail: info@edgecapital.net
Website: http://www.edgecapital.net

The Benefit Capital Companies Inc.
PO Box 542
Logandale, NV 89021
(702)398-3222
Fax: (702)398-3700

Millennium Three Venture Group LLC
6880 South McCarran Blvd., Ste. A-11
Reno, NV 89509
(775)954-2020
Fax: (775)954-2023
Website: http://www.m3vg.com

New Jersey

Alan I. Goldman & Associates
497 Ridgewood Ave.
Glen Ridge, NJ 07028
(973)857-5680
Fax: (973)509-8856

CS Capital Partners LLC
328 Second St., Ste. 200
Lakewood, NJ 08701
(732)901-1111
Fax: (212)202-5071
Website: http://www.cs-capital.com

Edison Venture Fund
1009 Lenox Dr., Ste. 4
Lawrenceville, NJ 08648
(609)896-1900
Fax: (609)896-0066
E-mail: info@edisonventure.com
Website: http://www.edisonventure.com

Tappan Zee Capital Corp. (New Jersey)
201 Lower Notch Rd.
PO Box 416
Little Falls, NJ 07424
(973)256-8280
Fax: (973)256-2841

The CIT Group/Venture Capital, Inc.
650 CIT Dr.
Livingston, NJ 07039
(973)740-5429
Fax: (973)740-5555
Website: http://www.cit.com

Capital Express, L.L.C.
1100 Valleybrook Ave.
Lyndhurst, NJ 07071
(201)438-8228
Fax: (201)438-5131
E-mail: niles@capitalexpress.com
Website: http://www.capitalexpress.com

Westford Technology Ventures, L.P.
17 Academy St.
Newark, NJ 07102
(973)624-2131
Fax: (973)624-2008

Accel Partners
1 Palmer Sq.
Princeton, NJ 08542
(609)683-4500
Fax: (609)683-4880
Website: http://www.accel.com

Cardinal Partners
221 Nassau St.
Princeton, NJ 08542
(609)924-6452
Fax: (609)683-0174
Website: http://
www.cardinalhealthpartners.com

Domain Associates L.L.C.
One Palmer Sq., Ste. 515
Princeton, NJ 08542
(609)683-5656
Fax: (609)683-9789
Website: http://www.domainvc.com

Johnston Associates, Inc.
181 Cherry Valley Rd.
Princeton, NJ 08540
(609)924-3131
Fax: (609)683-7524
E-mail: jaincorp@aol.com

Kemper Ventures
Princeton Forrestal Village
155 Village Blvd.
Princeton, NJ 08540
(609)936-3035
Fax: (609)936-3051

Penny Lane Parnters
One Palmer Sq., Ste. 309
Princeton, NJ 08542
(609)497-4646
Fax: (609)497-0611

Early Stage Enterprises L.P.
995 Route 518
Skillman, NJ 08558
(609)921-8896
Fax: (609)921-8703
Website: http://www.esevc.com

MBW Management Inc.
1 Springfield Ave.
Summit, NJ 07901
(908)273-4060
Fax: (908)273-4430

BCI Advisors, Inc.
Glenpointe Center W.
Teaneck, NJ 07666
(201)836-3900
Fax: (201)836-6368
E-mail: info@bciadvisors.com
Website: http://www.bcipartners.com

Demuth, Folger & Wetherill / DFW Capital Partners
Glenpointe Center E., 5th Fl.
300 Frank W. Burr Blvd.
Teaneck, NJ 07666
(201)836-2233
Fax: (201)836-5666
Website: http://www.dfwcapital.com

First Princeton Capital Corp.
189 Berdan Ave., No. 131
Wayne, NJ 07470-3233
(973)278-3233
Fax: (973)278-4290
Website: http://www.lytellcatt.net

Edelson Technology Partners
300 Tice Blvd.
Woodcliff Lake, NJ 07675
(201)930-9898
Fax: (201)930-8899
Website: http://www.edelsontech.com

New Mexico

Bruce F. Glaspell & Associates
10400 Academy Rd. NE, Ste. 313
Albuquerque, NM 87111
(505)292-4505
Fax: (505)292-4258

High Desert Ventures, Inc.
6101 Imparata St. NE, Ste. 1721
Albuquerque, NM 87111
(505)797-3330
Fax: (505)338-5147

New Business Capital Fund, Ltd.
5805 Torreon NE
Albuquerque, NM 87109
(505)822-8445

SBC Ventures
10400 Academy Rd. NE, Ste. 313
Albuquerque, NM 87111
(505)292-4505
Fax: (505)292-4528

Technology Ventures Corp.
1155 University Blvd. SE
Albuquerque, NM 87106
(505)246-2882
Fax: (505)246-2891

New York

Small Business Technology Investment Fund
99 Washington Ave., Ste. 1731
Albany, NY 12210
(518)473-9741
Fax: (518)473-6876

Rand Capital Corp.
2200 Rand Bldg.
Buffalo, NY 14203
(716)853-0802
Fax: (716)854-8480
Website: http://www.randcapital.com

Seed Capital Partners
620 Main St.
Buffalo, NY 14202
(716)845-7520
Fax: (716)845-7539
Website: http://www.seedcp.com

Coleman Venture Group
5909 Northern Blvd.
PO Box 224
East Norwich, NY 11732
(516)626-3642
Fax: (516)626-9722

Vega Capital Corp.
45 Knollwood Rd.
Elmsford, NY 10523
(914)345-9500
Fax: (914)345-9505

Herbert Young Securities, Inc.
98 Cuttermill Rd.
Great Neck, NY 11021
(516)487-8300
Fax: (516)487-8319

Sterling/Carl Marks Capital, Inc.
175 Great Neck Rd., Ste. 408
Great Neck, NY 11021
(516)482-7374
Fax: (516)487-0781
E-mail: stercrlmar@aol.com
Website: http://
www.serlingcarlmarks.com

Impex Venture Management Co.
PO Box 1570
Green Island, NY 12183
(518)271-8008
Fax: (518)271-9101

Corporate Venture Partners L.P.
200 Sunset Park
Ithaca, NY 14850
(607)257-6323
Fax: (607)257-6128

Arthur P. Gould & Co.
One Wilshire Dr.
Lake Success, NY 11020
(516)773-3000
Fax: (516)773-3289

Dauphin Capital Partners
108 Forest Ave.
Locust Valley, NY 11560

(516)759-3339
Fax: (516)759-3322
Website: http://www.dauphincapital.com

550 Digital Media Ventures
555 Madison Ave., 10th Fl.
New York, NY 10022
Website: http://www.550dmv.com

Aberlyn Capital Management Co., Inc.
500 Fifth Ave.
New York, NY 10110
(212)391-7750
Fax: (212)391-7762

Adler & Company
342 Madison Ave., Ste. 807
New York, NY 10173
(212)599-2535
Fax: (212)599-2526

Alimansky Capital Group, Inc.
605 Madison Ave., Ste. 300
New York, NY 10022-1901
(212)832-7300
Fax: (212)832-7338

Allegra Partners
515 Madison Ave., 29th Fl.
New York, NY 10022
(212)826-9080
Fax: (212)759-2561

The Argentum Group
The Chyrsler Bldg.
405 Lexington Ave.
New York, NY 10174
(212)949-6262
Fax: (212)949-8294
Website: http://www.argentumgroup.com

Axavision Inc.
14 Wall St., 26th Fl.
New York, NY 10005
(212)619-4000
Fax: (212)619-7202

Bedford Capital Corp.
18 East 48th St., Ste. 1800
New York, NY 10017
(212)688-5700
Fax: (212)754-4699
E-mail: info@bedfordnyc.com
Website: http://www.bedfordnyc.com

Bloom & Co.
950 Third Ave.
New York, NY 10022
(212)838-1858
Fax: (212)838-1843

Bristol Capital Management
300 Park Ave., 17th Fl.
New York, NY 10022

(212)572-6306
Fax: (212)705-4292

Citicorp Venture Capital Ltd. (New York City)
399 Park Ave., 14th Fl.
Zone 4
New York, NY 10043
(212)559-1127
Fax: (212)888-2940

CM Equity Partners
135 E 57th St.
New York, NY 10022
(212)909-8428
Fax: (212)980-2630

Cohen & Co., L.L.C.
800 Third Ave.
New York, NY 10022
(212)317-2250
Fax: (212)317-2255
E-mail: nlcohen@aol.com

Cornerstone Equity Investors, L.L.C.
717 5th Ave., Ste. 1100
New York, NY 10022
(212)753-0901
Fax: (212)826-6798
Website: http://www.cornerstone-equity.com

CW Group, Inc.
1041 3rd Ave., 2nd fl.
New York, NY 10021
(212)308-5266
Fax: (212)644-0354
Website: http://www.cwventures.com

DH Blair Investment Banking Corp.
44 Wall St., 2nd Fl.
New York, NY 10005
(212)495-5000
Fax: (212)269-1438

Dresdner Kleinwort Capital
75 Wall St.
New York, NY 10005
(212)429-3131
Fax: (212)429-3139
Website: http://www.dresdnerkb.com

East River Ventures, L.P.
645 Madison Ave., 22nd Fl.
New York, NY 10022
(212)644-2322
Fax: (212)644-5498

Easton Hunt Capital Partners
641 Lexington Ave., 21st Fl.
New York, NY 10017
(212)702-0950
Fax: (212)702-0952
Website: http://www.eastoncapital.com

Elk Associates Funding Corp.
747 3rd Ave., Ste. 4C
New York, NY 10017
(212)355-2449
Fax: (212)759-3338

EOS Partners, L.P.
320 Park Ave., 22nd Fl.
New York, NY 10022
(212)832-5800
Fax: (212)832-5815
E-mail: mfirst@eospartners.com
Website: http://www.eospartners.com

Euclid Partners
45 Rockefeller Plaza, Ste. 3240
New York, NY 10111
(212)218-6880
Fax: (212)218-6877
E-mail: graham@euclidpartners.com
Website: http://www.euclidpartners.com

Evergreen Capital Partners, Inc.
150 East 58th St.
New York, NY 10155
(212)813-0758
Fax: (212)813-0754

Exeter Capital L.P.
10 E 53rd St.
New York, NY 10022
(212)872-1172
Fax: (212)872-1198
E-mail: exeter@usa.net

Financial Technology Research Corp.
518 Broadway
Penthouse
New York, NY 10012
(212)625-9100
Fax: (212)431-0300
E-mail: fintek@financier.com

4C Ventures
237 Park Ave., Ste. 801
New York, NY 10017
(212)692-3680
Fax: (212)692-3685
Website: http://www.4cventures.com

Fusient Ventures
99 Park Ave., 20th Fl.
New York, NY 10016
(212)972-8999
Fax: (212)972-9876
E-mail: info@fusient.com
Website: http://www.fusient.com

Generation Capital Partners
551 Fifth Ave., Ste. 3100
New York, NY 10176
(212)450-8507

Fax: (212)450-8550
Website: http://www.genpartners.com

Golub Associates, Inc.
555 Madison Ave.
New York, NY 10022
(212)750-6060
Fax: (212)750-5505

Hambro America Biosciences Inc.
650 Madison Ave., 21st Floor
New York, NY 10022
(212)223-7400
Fax: (212)223-0305

Hanover Capital Corp.
505 Park Ave., 15th Fl.
New York, NY 10022
(212)755-1222
Fax: (212)935-1787

Harvest Partners, Inc.
280 Park Ave, 33rd Fl.
New York, NY 10017
(212)559-6300
Fax: (212)812-0100
Website: http://www.harvpart.com

Holding Capital Group, Inc.
10 E 53rd St., 30th Fl.
New York, NY 10022
(212)486-6670
Fax: (212)486-0843

Hudson Venture Partners
660 Madison Ave., 14th Fl.
New York, NY 10021-8405
(212)644-9797
Fax: (212)644-7430
Website: http://www.hudsonptr.com

IBJS Capital Corp.
1 State St., 9th Fl.
New York, NY 10004
(212)858-2018
Fax: (212)858-2768

InterEquity Capital Partners, L.P.
220 5th Ave.
New York, NY 10001
(212)779-2022
Fax: (212)779-2103
Website: http://www.interequity-capital.com

The Jordan Edmiston Group Inc.
150 East 52nd St., 18th Fl.
New York, NY 10022
(212)754-0710
Fax: (212)754-0337

Josephberg, Grosz and Co., Inc.
633 3rd Ave., 13th Fl.
New York, NY 10017

(212)974-9926
Fax: (212)397-5832

J.P. Morgan Capital Corp.
60 Wall St.
New York, NY 10260-0060
(212)648-9000
Fax: (212)648-5002
Website: http://www.jpmorgan.com

The Lambda Funds
380 Lexington Ave., 54th Fl.
New York, NY 10168
(212)682-3454
Fax: (212)682-9231

Lepercq Capital Management Inc.
1675 Broadway
New York, NY 10019
(212)698-0795
Fax: (212)262-0155

Loeb Partners Corp.
61 Broadway, Ste. 2400
New York, NY 10006
(212)483-7000
Fax: (212)574-2001

Madison Investment Partners
660 Madison Ave.
New York, NY 10021
(212)223-2600
Fax: (212)223-8208

MC Capital Inc.
520 Madison Ave., 16th Fl.
New York, NY 10022
(212)644-0841
Fax: (212)644-2926

**McCown, De Leeuw and Co.
(New York)**
65 E 55th St., 36th Fl.
New York, NY 10022
(212)355-5500
Fax: (212)355-6283
Website: http://www.mdcpartners.com

Morgan Stanley Venture Partners
1221 Avenue of the Americas, 33rd Fl.
New York, NY 10020
(212)762-7900
Fax: (212)762-8424
E-mail: msventures@ms.com
Website: http://www.msvp.com

Nazem and Co.
645 Madison Ave., 12th Fl.
New York, NY 10022
(212)371-7900
Fax: (212)371-2150

Needham Capital Management, L.L.C.
445 Park Ave.
New York, NY 10022
(212)371-8300
Fax: (212)705-0299
Website: http://www.needhamco.com

Norwood Venture Corp.
1430 Broadway, Ste. 1607
New York, NY 10018
(212)869-5075
Fax: (212)869-5331
E-mail: nvc@mail.idt.net
Website: http://www.norven.com

Noveltek Venture Corp.
521 Fifth Ave., Ste. 1700
New York, NY 10175
(212)286-1963

Paribas Principal, Inc.
787 7th Ave.
New York, NY 10019
(212)841-2005
Fax: (212)841-3558

**Patricof & Co. Ventures, Inc.
(New York)**
445 Park Ave.
New York, NY 10022
(212)753-6300
Fax: (212)319-6155
Website: http://www.patricof.com

The Platinum Group, Inc.
350 Fifth Ave, Ste. 7113
New York, NY 10118
(212)736-4300
Fax: (212)736-6086
Website: http://www.platinumgroup
.com

Pomona Capital
780 Third Ave., 28th Fl.
New York, NY 10017
(212)593-3639
Fax: (212)593-3987
Website: http://www.pomonacapital.com

Prospect Street Ventures
10 East 40th St., 44th Fl.
New York, NY 10016
(212)448-0702
Fax: (212)448-9652
E-mail: wkohler@prospectstreet.com
Website: http://www.prospectstreet.com

Regent Capital Management
505 Park Ave., Ste. 1700
New York, NY 10022
(212)735-9900
Fax: (212)735-9908

Rothschild Ventures, Inc.
1251 Avenue of the Americas, 51st Fl.
New York, NY 10020
(212)403-3500
Fax: (212)403-3652
Website: http://www.nmrothschild
.com

Sandler Capital Management
767 Fifth Ave., 45th Fl.
New York, NY 10153
(212)754-8100
Fax: (212)826-0280

Siguler Guff & Company
630 Fifth Ave., 16th Fl.
New York, NY 10111
(212)332-5100
Fax: (212)332-5120

Spencer Trask Ventures Inc.
535 Madison Ave.
New York, NY 10022
(212)355-5565
Fax: (212)751-3362
Website: http://www.spencertrask.com

Sprout Group (New York City)
277 Park Ave.
New York, NY 10172
(212)892-3600
Fax: (212)892-3444
E-mail: info@sproutgroup.com
Website: http://www.sproutgroup.com

US Trust Private Equity
114 W.47th St.
New York, NY 10036
(212)852-3949
Fax: (212)852-3759
Website: http://www.ustrust.com/
privateequity

Vencon Management Inc.
301 West 53rd St., Ste. 10F
New York, NY 10019
(212)581-8787
Fax: (212)397-4126
Website: http://www.venconinc.com

Venrock Associates
30 Rockefeller Plaza, Ste. 5508
New York, NY 10112
(212)649-5600
Fax: (212)649-5788
Website: http://www.venrock.com

Venture Capital Fund of America, Inc.
509 Madison Ave., Ste. 812
New York, NY 10022
(212)838-5577
Fax: (212)838-7614

E-mail: mail@vcfa.com
Website: http://www.vcfa.com

Venture Opportunities Corp.
150 E 58th St.
New York, NY 10155
(212)832-3737
Fax: (212)980-6603

Warburg Pincus Ventures, Inc.
466 Lexington Ave., 11th Fl.
New York, NY 10017
(212)878-9309
Fax: (212)878-9200
Website: http://www.warburgpincus.com

Wasserstein, Perella & Co. Inc.
31 W 52nd St., 27th Fl.
New York, NY 10019
(212)702-5691
Fax: (212)969-7879

Welsh, Carson, Anderson, & Stowe
320 Park Ave., Ste. 2500
New York, NY 10022-6815
(212)893-9500
Fax: (212)893-9575

Whitney and Co. (New York)
630 Fifth Ave. Ste. 3225
New York, NY 10111
(212)332-2400
Fax: (212)332-2422
Website: http://www.jhwitney.com

Winthrop Ventures
74 Trinity Place, Ste. 600
New York, NY 10006
(212)422-0100

The Pittsford Group
8 Lodge Pole Rd.
Pittsford, NY 14534
(716)223-3523

Genesee Funding
70 Linden Oaks, 3rd Fl.
Rochester, NY 14625
(716)383-5550
Fax: (716)383-5305

Gabelli Multimedia Partners
One Corporate Center
Rye, NY 10580
(914)921-5395
Fax: (914)921-5031

Stamford Financial
108 Main St.
Stamford, NY 12167
(607)652-3311
Fax: (607)652-6301

Website: http://www.stamfordfinancial
.com

Northwood Ventures LLC
485 Underhill Blvd., Ste. 205
Syosset, NY 11791
(516)364-5544
Fax: (516)364-0879
E-mail: northwood@northwood.com
Website: http://www.northwoodventures
.com

Exponential Business Development Co.
216 Walton St.
Syracuse, NY 13202-1227
(315)474-4500
Fax: (315)474-4682
E-mail: dirksonn@aol.com
Website: http://www.exponential-ny.com

Onondaga Venture Capital Fund Inc.
714 State Tower Bldg.
Syracuse, NY 13202
(315)478-0157
Fax: (315)478-0158

Bessemer Venture Partners (Westbury)
1400 Old Country Rd., Ste. 109
Westbury, NY 11590
(516)997-2300
Fax: (516)997-2371
E-mail: bob@bvpny.com
Website: http://www.bvp.com

Ovation Capital Partners
120 Bloomingdale Rd., 4th Fl.
White Plains, NY 10605
(914)258-0011
Fax: (914)684-0848
Website: http://www.ovationcapital.com

North Carolina

Carolinas Capital Investment Corp.
1408 Biltmore Dr.
Charlotte, NC 28207
(704)375-3888
Fax: (704)375-6226

First Union Capital Partners
1st Union Center, 12th Fl.
301 S College St.
Charlotte, NC 28288-0732
(704)383-0000
Fax: (704)374-6711
Website: http://www.fucp.com

Frontier Capital LLC
525 North Tryon St., Ste. 1700
Charlotte, NC 28202
(704)414-2880
Fax: (704)414-2881
Website: http://www.frontierfunds.com

Kitty Hawk Capital
2700 Coltsgate Rd., Ste. 202
Charlotte, NC 28211
(704)362-3909
Fax: (704)362-2774
Website: http://www.kittyhawkcapital.com

Piedmont Venture Partners
One Morrocroft Centre
6805 Morisson Blvd., Ste. 380
Charlotte, NC 28211
(704)731-5200
Fax: (704)365-9733
Website: http://www.piedmontvp.com

Ruddick Investment Co.
1800 Two First Union Center
Charlotte, NC 28282
(704)372-5404
Fax: (704)372-6409

The Shelton Companies Inc.
3600 One First Union Center
301 S College St.
Charlotte, NC 28202
(704)348-2200
Fax: (704)348-2260

Wakefield Group
1110 E Morehead St.
PO Box 36329
Charlotte, NC 28236
(704)372-0355
Fax: (704)372-8216
Website: http://www.wakefieldgroup.com

Aurora Funds, Inc.
2525 Meridian Pkwy., Ste. 220
Durham, NC 27713
(919)484-0400
Fax: (919)484-0444
Website: http://www.aurorafunds.com

Intersouth Partners
3211 Shannon Rd., Ste. 610
Durham, NC 27707
(919)493-6640
Fax: (919)493-6649
E-mail: info@intersouth.com
Website: http://www.intersouth.com

Geneva Merchant Banking Partners
PO Box 21962
Greensboro, NC 27420
(336)275-7002
Fax: (336)275-9155
Website: http://
www.genevamerchantbank.com

The North Carolina Enterprise Fund, L.P.
3600 Glenwood Ave., Ste. 107
Raleigh, NC 27612

(919)781-2691
Fax: (919)783-9195
Website: http://www.ncef.com

Ohio

Senmend Medical Ventures
4445 Lake Forest Dr., Ste. 600
Cincinnati, OH 45242
(513)563-3264
Fax: (513)563-3261

The Walnut Group
312 Walnut St., Ste. 1151
Cincinnati, OH 45202
(513)651-3300
Fax: (513)929-4441
Website: http://www.thewalnutgroup
.com

Brantley Venture Partners
20600 Chagrin Blvd., Ste. 1150
Cleveland, OH 44122
(216)283-4800
Fax: (216)283-5324

Clarion Capital Corp.
1801 E 9th St., Ste. 1120
Cleveland, OH 44114
(216)687-1096
Fax: (216)694-3545

Crystal Internet Venture Fund, L.P.
1120 Chester Ave., Ste. 418
Cleveland, OH 44114
(216)263-5515
Fax: (216)263-5518
E-mail: jf@crystalventure.com
Website: http://www.crystalventure.com

Key Equity Capital Corp.
127 Public Sq., 28th Fl.
Cleveland, OH 44114
(216)689-3000
Fax: (216)689-3204
Website: http://www.keybank.com

Morgenthaler Ventures
Terminal Tower
50 Public Square, Ste. 2700
Cleveland, OH 44113
(216)416-7500
Fax: (216)416-7501
Website: http://www.morgenthaler.com

National City Equity Partners Inc.
1965 E 6th St.
Cleveland, OH 44114
(216)575-2491
Fax: (216)575-9965
E-mail: nccap@aol.com
Website: http://www.nccapital.com

Primus Venture Partners, Inc.
5900 LanderBrook Dr., Ste. 2000
Cleveland, OH 44124-4020
(440)684-7300
Fax: (440)684-7342
E-mail: info@primusventure.com
Website: http://www.primusventure.com

Banc One Capital Partners (Columbus)
150 East Gay St., 24th Fl.
Columbus, OH 43215
(614)217-1100
Fax: (614)217-1217

Battelle Venture Partners
505 King Ave.
Columbus, OH 43201
(614)424-7005
Fax: (614)424-4874

Ohio Partners
62 E Board St., 3rd Fl.
Columbus, OH 43215
(614)621-1210
Fax: (614)621-1240

Capital Technology Group, L.L.C.
400 Metro Place North, Ste. 300
Dublin, OH 43017
(614)792-6066
Fax: (614)792-6036
E-mail: info@capitaltech.com
Website: http://www.capitaltech.com

Northwest Ohio Venture Fund
4159 Holland-Sylvania R., Ste. 202
Toledo, OH 43623
(419)824-8144
Fax: (419)882-2035
E-mail: bwalsh@novf.com

Oklahoma

Moore & Associates
1000 W Wilshire Blvd., Ste. 370
Oklahoma City, OK 73116
(405)842-3660
Fax: (405)842-3763

Chisholm Private Capital Partners
100 West 5th St., Ste. 805
Tulsa, OK 74103
(918)584-0440
Fax: (918)584-0441
Website: http://www.chisholmvc.com

Davis, Tuttle Venture Partners (Tulsa)
320 S Boston, Ste. 1000
Tulsa, OK 74103-3703
(918)584-7272
Fax: (918)582-3404
Website: http://www.davistuttle.com

RBC Ventures
2627 E 21st St.
Tulsa, OK 74114
(918)744-5607
Fax: (918)743-8630

Oregon

Utah Ventures II LP
10700 SW Beaverton-Hillsdale Hwy., Ste.
548
Beaverton, OR 97005
(503)574-4125
E-mail: adishlip@uven.com
Website: http://www.uven.com

Orien Ventures
14523 SW Westlake Dr.
Lake Oswego, OR 97035
(503)699-1680
Fax: (503)699-1681

OVP Venture Partners (Lake Oswego)
340 Oswego Pointe Dr., Ste. 200
Lake Oswego, OR 97034
(503)697-8766
Fax: (503)697-8863
E-mail: info@ovp.com
Website: http://www.ovp.com

Oregon Resource and Technology Development Fund
4370 NE Halsey St., Ste. 233
Portland, OR 97213-1566
(503)282-4462
Fax: (503)282-2976

Shaw Venture Partners
400 SW 6th Ave., Ste. 1100
Portland, OR 97204-1636
(503)228-4884
Fax: (503)227-2471
Website: http://www.shawventures.com

Pennsylvania

Mid-Atlantic Venture Funds
125 Goodman Dr.
Bethlehem, PA 18015
(610)865-6550
Fax: (610)865-6427
Website: http://www.mavf.com

Newspring Ventures
100 W Elm St., Ste. 101
Conshohocken, PA 19428
(610)567-2380
Fax: (610)567-2388
Website: http://www.newsprintventures.com

Patricof & Co. Ventures, Inc.
455 S Gulph Rd., Ste. 410
King of Prussia, PA 19406

(610)265-0286
Fax: (610)265-4959
Website: http://www.patricof.com

Loyalhanna Venture Fund
527 Cedar Way, Ste. 104
Oakmont, PA 15139
(412)820-7035
Fax: (412)820-7036

Innovest Group Inc.
2000 Market St., Ste. 1400
Philadelphia, PA 19103
(215)564-3960
Fax: (215)569-3272

Keystone Venture Capital Management Co.
1601 Market St., Ste. 2500
Philadelphia, PA 19103
(215)241-1200
Fax: (215)241-1211
Website: http://www.keystonevc.com

Liberty Venture Partners
2005 Market St., Ste. 200
Philadelphia, PA 19103
(215)282-4484
Fax: (215)282-4485
E-mail: info@libertyvp.com
Website: http://www.libertyvp.com

Penn Janney Fund, Inc.
1801 Market St., 11th Fl.
Philadelphia, PA 19103
(215)665-4447
Fax: (215)557-0820

Philadelphia Ventures, Inc.
The Bellevue
200 S Broad St.
Philadelphia, PA 19102
(215)732-4445
Fax: (215)732-4644

Birchmere Ventures Inc.
2000 Technology Dr.
Pittsburgh, PA 15219-3109
(412)803-8000
Fax: (412)687-8139
Website: http://www.birchmerevc.com

CEO Venture Fund
2000 Technology Dr., Ste. 160
Pittsburgh, PA 15219-3109
(412)687-3451
Fax: (412)687-8139
E-mail: ceofund@aol.com
Website: http://www.ceoventurefund.com

Innovation Works Inc.
2000 Technology Dr., Ste. 250
Pittsburgh, PA 15219

(412)681-1520
Fax: (412)681-2625
Website: http://www.innovationworks.org

Keystone Minority Capital Fund L.P.
1801 Centre Ave., Ste. 201
Williams Sq.
Pittsburgh, PA 15219
(412)338-2230
Fax: (412)338-2224

Mellon Ventures, Inc.
One Mellon Bank Ctr., Rm. 3500
Pittsburgh, PA 15258
(412)236-3594
Fax: (412)236-3593
Website: http://www.mellonventures.com

Pennsylvania Growth Fund
5850 Ellsworth Ave., Ste. 303
Pittsburgh, PA 15232
(412)661-1000
Fax: (412)361-0676

Point Venture Partners
The Century Bldg.
130 Seventh St., 7th Fl.
Pittsburgh, PA 15222
(412)261-1966
Fax: (412)261-1718

Cross Atlantic Capital Partners
5 Radnor Corporate Center, Ste. 555
Radnor, PA 19087
(610)995-2650
Fax: (610)971-2062
Website: http://www.xacp.com

Meridian Venture Partners (Radnor)
The Radnor Court Bldg., Ste. 140
259 Radnor-Chester Rd.
Radnor, PA 19087
(610)254-2999
Fax: (610)254-2996
E-mail: mvpart@ix.netcom.com

TDH
919 Conestoga Rd., Bldg. 1, Ste. 301
Rosemont, PA 19010
(610)526-9970
Fax: (610)526-9971

Adams Capital Management
500 Blackburn Ave.
Sewickley, PA 15143
(412)749-9454
Fax: (412)749-9459
Website: http://www.acm.com

S.R. One, Ltd.
Four Tower Bridge
200 Barr Harbor Dr., Ste. 250
W Conshohocken, PA 19428

(610)567-1000
Fax: (610)567-1039

Greater Philadelphia Venture Capital Corp.
351 East Conestoga Rd.
Wayne, PA 19087
(610)688-6829
Fax: (610)254-8958

PA Early Stage
435 Devon Park Dr., Bldg. 500, Ste. 510
Wayne, PA 19087
(610)293-4075
Fax: (610)254-4240
Website: http://www.paearlystage.com

The Sandhurst Venture Fund, L.P.
351 E Constoga Rd.
Wayne, PA 19087
(610)254-8900
Fax: (610)254-8958

TL Ventures
700 Bldg.
435 Devon Park Dr.
Wayne, PA 19087-1990
(610)975-3765
Fax: (610)254-4210
Website: http://www.tlventures.com

Rockhill Ventures, Inc.
100 Front St., Ste. 1350
West Conshohocken, PA 19428
(610)940-0300
Fax: (610)940-0301

Puerto Rico

Advent-Morro Equity Partners
Banco Popular Bldg.
206 Tetuan St., Ste. 903
San Juan, PR 00902
(787)725-5285
Fax: (787)721-1735

North America Investment Corp.
Mercantil Plaza, Ste. 813
PO Box 191831
San Juan, PR 00919
(787)754-6178
Fax: (787)754-6181

Rhode Island

Manchester Humphreys, Inc.
40 Westminster St., Ste. 900
Providence, RI 02903
(401)454-0400
Fax: (401)454-0403

Navis Partners
50 Kennedy Plaza, 12th Fl.
Providence, RI 02903

(401)278-6770
Fax: (401)278-6387
Website: http://www.navispartners.com

South Carolina

Capital Insights, L.L.C.
PO Box 27162
Greenville, SC 29616-2162
(864)242-6832
Fax: (864)242-6755
E-mail: jwarner@capitalinsights.com
Website: http://www.capitalinsights.com

Transamerica Mezzanine Financing
7 N. Laurens St., Ste. 603
Greenville, SC 29601
(864)232-6198
Fax: (864)241-4444

Tennessee

Valley Capital Corp.
Krystal Bldg.
100 W Martin Luther King Blvd., Ste. 212
Chattanooga, TN 37402
(423)265-1557
Fax: (423)265-1588

Coleman Swenson Booth Inc.
237 2nd Ave. S
Franklin, TN 37064-2649
(615)791-9462
Fax: (615)791-9636
Website: http://www.colemanswenson.com

Capital Services & Resources, Inc.
5159 Wheelis Dr., Ste. 106
Memphis, TN 38117
(901)761-2156
Fax: (907)767-0060

Paradigm Capital Partners LLC
6410 Poplar Ave., Ste. 395
Memphis, TN 38119
(901)682-6060
Fax: (901)328-3061

SSM Ventures
845 Crossover Ln., Ste. 140
Memphis, TN 38117
(901)767-1131
Fax: (901)767-1135
Website: http://www.ssmventures.com

Capital Across America L.P.
501 Union St., Ste. 201
Nashville, TN 37219
(615)254-1414
Fax: (615)254-1856
Website: http://www.capitalacross
america.com

Equitas L.P.
2000 Glen Echo Rd., Ste. 101
PO Box 158838
Nashville, TN 37215-8838
(615)383-8673
Fax: (615)383-8693

Massey Burch Capital Corp.
One Burton Hills Blvd., Ste. 350
Nashville, TN 37215
(615)665-3221
Fax: (615)665-3240
E-mail: tcalton@masseyburch.com
Website: http://www.masseyburch.com

Nelson Capital Corp.
3401 West End Ave., Ste. 300
Nashville, TN 37203
(615)292-8787
Fax: (615)385-3150

Texas

Phillips-Smith Specialty Retail Group
5080 Spectrum Dr., Ste. 805 W
Addison, TX 75001
(972)387-0725
Fax: (972)458-2560
E-mail: pssrg@aol.com
Website: http://www.phillips-smith.com

Austin Ventures, L.P.
701 Brazos St., Ste. 1400
Austin, TX 78701
(512)485-1900
Fax: (512)476-3952
E-mail: info@ausven.com
Website: http://www.austinventures.com

The Capital Network
3925 West Braker Lane, Ste. 406
Austin, TX 78759-5321
(512)305-0826
Fax: (512)305-0836

Techxas Ventures LLC
5000 Plaza on the Lake
Austin, TX 78746
(512)343-0118
Fax: (512)343-1879
E-mail: bruce@techxas.com
Website: http://www.techxas.com

Alliance Financial of Houston
218 Heather Ln.
Conroe, TX 77385-9013
(936)447-3300
Fax: (936)447-4222

Amerimark Capital Corp.
1111 W Mockingbird, Ste. 1111
Dallas, TX 75247
(214)638-7878

Fax: (214)638-7612
E-mail: amerimark@amcapital.com
Website: http://www.amcapital.com

AMT Venture Partners / AMT Capital Ltd.
5220 Spring Valley Rd., Ste. 600
Dallas, TX 75240
(214)905-9757
Fax: (214)905-9761
Website: http://www.amtcapital.com

Arkoma Venture Partners
5950 Berkshire Lane, Ste. 1400
Dallas, TX 75225
(214)739-3515
Fax: (214)739-3572
E-mail: joelf@arkomavp.com

Capital Southwest Corp.
12900 Preston Rd., Ste. 700
Dallas, TX 75230
(972)233-8242
Fax: (972)233-7362
Website: http://www.capitalsouthwest.com

Dali, Hook Partners
One Lincoln Center, Ste. 1550
5400 LBJ Freeway
Dallas, TX 75240
(972)991-5457
Fax: (972)991-5458
E-mail: dhook@hookpartners.com
Website: http://www.hookpartners.com

HO2 Partners
Two Galleria Tower
13455 Noel Rd., Ste. 1670
Dallas, TX 75240
(972)702-1144
Fax: (972)702-8234
Website: http://www.ho2.com

Interwest Partners (Dallas)
2 Galleria Tower
13455 Noel Rd., Ste. 1670
Dallas, TX 75240
(972)392-7279
Fax: (972)490-6348
Website: http://www.interwest.com

Kahala Investments, Inc.
8214 Westchester Dr., Ste. 715
Dallas, TX 75225
(214)987-0077
Fax: (214)987-2332

MESBIC Ventures Holding Co.
2435 North Central Expressway, Ste. 200
Dallas, TX 75080
(972)991-1597
Fax: (972)991-4770
Website: http://www.mvhc.com

North Texas MESBIC, Inc.
9500 Forest Lane, Ste. 430
Dallas, TX 75243
(214)221-3565
Fax: (214)221-3566

Richard Jaffe & Company, Inc,
7318 Royal Cir.
Dallas, TX 75230
(214)265-9397
Fax: (214)739-1845

Sevin Rosen Management Co.
13455 Noel Rd., Ste. 1670
Dallas, TX 75240
(972)702-1100
Fax: (972)702-1103
E-mail: info@srfunds.com
Website: http://www.srfunds.com

Stratford Capital Partners, L.P.
300 Crescent Ct., Ste. 500
Dallas, TX 75201
(214)740-7377
Fax: (214)720-7393
E-mail: stratcap@hmtf.com

Sunwestern Investment Group
12221 Merit Dr., Ste. 935
Dallas, TX 75251
(972)239-5650
Fax: (972)701-0024

Wingate Partners
750 N St. Paul St., Ste. 1200
Dallas, TX 75201
(214)720-1313
Fax: (214)871-8799

Buena Venture Associates
201 Main St., 32nd Fl.
Fort Worth, TX 76102
(817)339-7400
Fax: (817)390-8408
Website: http://www.buenaventure.com

The Catalyst Group
3 Riverway, Ste. 770
Houston, TX 77056
(713)623-8133
Fax: (713)623-0473
E-mail: herman@thecatalystgroup.net
Website: http://www.thecatalystgroup.net

Cureton & Co., Inc.
1100 Louisiana, Ste. 3250
Houston, TX 77002
(713)658-9806
Fax: (713)658-0476

Davis, Tuttle Venture Partners (Dallas)
8 Greenway Plaza, Ste. 1020
Houston, TX 77046

(713)993-0440
Fax: (713)621-2297
Website: http://www.davistuttle.com

Houston Partners
401 Louisiana, 8th Fl.
Houston, TX 77002
(713)222-8600
Fax: (713)222-8932

Southwest Venture Group
10878 Westheimer, Ste. 178
Houston, TX 77042
(713)827-8947
(713)461-1470

AM Fund
4600 Post Oak Place, Ste. 100
Houston, TX 77027
(713)627-9111
Fax: (713)627-9119

Ventex Management, Inc.
3417 Milam St.
Houston, TX 77002-9531
(713)659-7870
Fax: (713)659-7855

MBA Venture Group
1004 Olde Town Rd., Ste. 102
Irving, TX 75061
(972)986-6703

First Capital Group Management Co.
750 East Mulberry St., Ste. 305
PO Box 15616
San Antonio, TX 78212
(210)736-4233
Fax: (210)736-5449

The Southwest Venture Partnerships
16414 San Pedro, Ste. 345
San Antonio, TX 78232
(210)402-1200
Fax: (210)402-1221
E-mail: swvp@aol.com

Medtech International Inc.
1742 Carriageway
Sugarland, TX 77478
(713)980-8474
Fax: (713)980-6343

Utah

First Security Business Investment Corp.
15 East 100 South, Ste. 100
Salt Lake City, UT 84111
(801)246-5737
Fax: (801)246-5740

Utah Ventures II, L.P.
423 Wakara Way, Ste. 206
Salt Lake City, UT 84108
(801)583-5922
Fax: (801)583-4105
Website: http://www.uven.com

Wasatch Venture Corp.
1 S Main St., Ste. 1400
Salt Lake City, UT 84133
(801)524-8939
Fax: (801)524-8941
E-mail: mail@wasatchvc.com

Vermont

North Atlantic Capital Corp.
76 Saint Paul St., Ste. 600
Burlington, VT 05401
(802)658-7820
Fax: (802)658-5757
Website: http://www.northatlantic
capital.com

Green Mountain Advisors Inc.
PO Box 1230
Quechee, VT 05059
(802)296-7800
Fax: (802)296-6012
Website: http://www.gmtcap.com

Virginia

Oxford Financial Services Corp.
Alexandria, VA 22314
(703)519-4900
Fax: (703)519-4910
E-mail: oxford133@aol.com

Continental SBIC
4141 N. Henderson Rd.
Arlington, VA 22203
(703)527-5200
Fax: (703)527-3700

Novak Biddle Venture Partners
1750 Tysons Blvd., Ste. 1190
McLean, VA 22102
(703)847-3770
Fax: (703)847-3771
E-mail: roger@novakbiddle.com
Website: http://www.novakbiddle.com

Spacevest
11911 Freedom Dr., Ste. 500
Reston, VA 20190
(703)904-9800
Fax: (703)904-0571
E-mail: spacevest@spacevest.com
Website: http://www.spacevest.com

Virginia Capital
1801 Libbie Ave., Ste. 201
Richmond, VA 23226

(804)648-4802
Fax: (804)648-4809
E-mail: webmaster@vacapital.com
Website: http://www.vacapital.com

Calvert Social Venture Partners
402 Maple Ave. W
Vienna, VA 22180
(703)255-4930
Fax: (703)255-4931
E-mail: calven2000@aol.com

Fairfax Partners
8000 Towers Crescent Dr., Ste. 940
Vienna, VA 22182
(703)847-9486
Fax: (703)847-0911

Global Internet Ventures
8150 Leesburg Pike, Ste. 1210
Vienna, VA 22182
(703)442-3300
Fax: (703)442-3388
Website: http://www.givinc.com

Walnut Capital Corp. (Vienna)
8000 Towers Crescent Dr., Ste. 1070
Vienna, VA 22182
(703)448-3771
Fax: (703)448-7751

Washington

Encompass Ventures
777 108th Ave. NE, Ste. 2300
Bellevue, WA 98004
(425)486-3900
Fax: (425)486-3901
E-mail: info@evpartners.com
Website: http://www.encompassventures
.com

Fluke Venture Partners
11400 SE Sixth St., Ste. 230
Bellevue, WA 98004
(425)453-4590
Fax: (425)453-4675
E-mail: gabelein@flukeventures.com
Website: http://www.flukeventures.com

Pacific Northwest Partners SBIC, L.P.
15352 SE 53rd St.

Bellevue, WA 98006
(425)455-9967
Fax: (425)455-9404

Materia Venture Associates, L.P.
3435 Carillon Pointe
Kirkland, WA 98033-7354
(425)822-4100
Fax: (425)827-4086

OVP Venture Partners (Kirkland)
2420 Carillon Pt.
Kirkland, WA 98033
(425)889-9192
Fax: (425)889-0152
E-mail: info@ovp.com
Website: http://www.ovp.com

Digital Partners
999 3rd Ave., Ste. 1610
Seattle, WA 98104
(206)405-3607
Fax: (206)405-3617
Website: http://www.digitalpartners.com

Frazier & Company
601 Union St., Ste. 3300
Seattle, WA 98101
(206)621-7200
Fax: (206)621-1848
E-mail: jon@frazierco.com

Kirlan Venture Capital, Inc.
221 First Ave. W, Ste. 108
Seattle, WA 98119-4223
(206)281-8610
Fax: (206)285-3451
Website: http://www.kirlanventure
.com

Phoenix Partners
1000 2nd Ave., Ste. 3600
Seattle, WA 98104
(206)624-8968
Fax: (206)624-1907

Voyager Capital
800 5th St., Ste. 4100
Seattle, WA 98103
(206)470-1180
Fax: (206)470-1185

E-mail: info@voyagercap.com
Website: http://www.voyagercap.com

Northwest Venture Associates
221 N. Wall St., Ste. 628
Spokane, WA 99201
(509)747-0728
Fax: (509)747-0758
Website: http://www.nwva.com

Wisconsin

Venture Investors Management, L.L.C.
University Research Park
505 S Rosa Rd.
Madison, WI 53719
(608)441-2700
Fax: (608)441-2727
E-mail: roger@ventureinvestors.com
Website: http://www.ventureinvesters
.com

Capital Investments, Inc.
1009 West Glen Oaks Lane, Ste. 103
Mequon, WI 53092
(414)241-0303
Fax: (414)241-8451
Website: http://www.capitalinvest
mentsinc.com

Future Value Venture, Inc.
2745 N. Martin Luther King Dr., Ste. 204
Milwaukee, WI 53212-2300
(414)264-2252
Fax: (414)264-2253
E-mail: fvvventures@aol.com
William Beckett, President

Lubar and Co., Inc.
700 N. Water St., Ste. 1200
Milwaukee, WI 53202
(414)291-9000
Fax: (414)291-9061

GCI
20875 Crossroads Cir., Ste. 100
Waukesha, WI 53186
(262)798-5080
Fax: (262)798-5087

Glossary of Small Business Terms

Absolute liability
Liability that is incurred due to product defects or negligent actions. Manufacturers or retail establishments are held responsible, even though the defect or action may not have been intentional or negligent.

ACE
See Active Corps of Executives

Accident and health benefits
Benefits offered to employees and their families in order to offset the costs associated with accidental death, accidental injury, or sickness.

Account statement
A record of transactions, including payments, new debt, and deposits, incurred during a defined period of time.

Accounting system
System capturing the costs of all employees and/or machinery included in business expenses.

Accounts payable
See Trade credit

Accounts receivable
Unpaid accounts which arise from unsettled claims and transactions from the sale of a company's products or services to its customers.

Active Corps of Executives (ACE)
A group of volunteers for a management assistance program of the U.S. Small Business Administration; volunteers provide one-on-one counseling and teach workshops and seminars for small firms.

ADA
See Americans with Disabilities Act

Adaptation
The process whereby an invention is modified to meet the needs of users.

Adaptive engineering
The process whereby an invention is modified to meet the manufacturing and commercial requirements of a targeted market.

Adverse selection
The tendency for higher-risk individuals to purchase health care and more comprehensive plans, resulting in increased costs.

Advertising
A marketing tool used to capture public attention and influence purchasing decisions for a product or service. Utilizes various forms of media to generate consumer response, such as flyers, magazines, newspapers, radio, and television.

Age discrimination
The denial of the rights and privileges of employment based solely on the age of an individual.

Agency costs
Costs incurred to insure that the lender or investor maintains control over assets while allowing the borrower or entrepreneur to use them. Monitoring and information costs are the two major types of agency costs.

Agribusiness
The production and sale of commodities and products from the commercial farming industry.

Americans with Disabilities Act (ADA)
Law designed to ensure equal access and opportunity to handicapped persons.

Annual report
Yearly financial report prepared by a business that adheres to the requirements set forth by the Securities and Exchange Commission (SEC).

295

Antitrust immunity
Exemption from prosecution under antitrust laws. In the transportation industry, firms with antitrust immunity are permitted under certain conditions to set schedules and sometimes prices for the public benefit.

Applied research
Scientific study targeted for use in a product or process.

Assets
Anything of value owned by a company.

Audit
The verification of accounting records and business procedures conducted by an outside accounting service.

Average cost
Total production costs divided by the quantity produced.

Balance Sheet
A financial statement listing the total assets and liabilities of a company at a given time.

Bankruptcy
The condition in which a business cannot meet its debt obligations and petitions a federal district court either for reorganization of its debts (Chapter 11) or for liquidation of its assets (Chapter 7).

Basket clause
A provision specifying the amount of public pension funds that may be placed in investments not included on a state's legal list (see separate citation).

BDC
See Business development corporation

Benefit
Various services, such as health care, flextime, day care, insurance, and vacation, offered to employees as part of a hiring package. Typically subsidized in whole or in part by the business.

BIDCO
See Business and industrial development company

Billing cycle
A system designed to evenly distribute customer billing throughout the month, preventing clerical backlogs.

Blue chip security
A low-risk, low-yield security representing an interest in a very stable company.

Blue sky laws
A general term that denotes various states' laws regulating securities.

Bond
A written instrument executed by a bidder or contractor (the principal) and a second party (the surety or sureties) to assure fulfillment of the principal's obligations to a third party (the obligee or government) identified in the bond. If the principal's obligations are not met, the bond assures payment to the extent stipulated of any loss sustained by the obligee.

Bonding requirements
Terms contained in a bond (see separate citation).

Bonus
An amount of money paid to an employee as a reward for achieving certain business goals or objectives.

Brainstorming
A group session where employees contribute their ideas for solving a problem or meeting a company objective without fear of retribution or ridicule.

Brand name
The part of a brand, trademark, or service mark that can be spoken. It can be a word, letter, or group of words or letters.

Bridge financing
A short-term loan made in expectation of intermediateterm or long-term financing. Can be used when a company plans to go public in the near future.

Broker
One who matches resources available for innovation with those who need them.

Budget
An estimate of the spending necessary to complete a project or offer a service in comparison to cash-on-hand and expected earnings for the coming year, with an emphasis on cost control.

Business and industrial development company (BIDCO)
A private, for-profit financing corporation chartered by the state to provide both equity and long-term debt capital to small business owners (see separate citations for equity and debt capital).

Business birth

The formation of a new establishment or enterprise. The appearance of a new establishment or enterprise in the Small Business Data Base (see separate citation).

Business conditions

Outside factors that can affect the financial performance of a business.

Business contractions

The number of establishments that have decreased in employment during a specified time.

Business cycle

A period of economic recession and recovery. These cycles vary in duration.

Business death

The voluntary or involuntary closure of a firm or establishment. The disappearance of an establishment or enterprise from the Small Business Data Base (see separate citation).

Business development corporation (BDC)

A business financing agency, usually composed of the financial institutions in an area or state, organized to assist in financing businesses unable to obtain assistance through normal channels; the risk is spread among various members of the business development corporation, and interest rates may vary somewhat from those charged by member institutions. A venture capital firm in which shares of ownership are publicly held and to which the Investment Act of 1940 applies.

Business dissolution

For enumeration purposes, the absence of a business that was present in the prior time period from any current record.

Business entry

See Business birth

Business ethics

Moral values and principles espoused by members of the business community as a guide to fair and honest business practices.

Business exit

See Business death

Business expansions

The number of establishments that added employees during a specified time.

Business failure

Closure of a business causing a loss to at least one creditor.

Business format franchising

The purchase of the name, trademark, and an ongoing business plan of the parent corporation or franchisor by the franchisee.

Business license

A legal authorization issued by municipal and state governments and required for business operations.

Business name

Enterprises must register their business names with local governments usually on a "doing business as" (DBA) form. (This name is sometimes referred to as a "fictional name.") The procedure is part of the business licensing process and prevents any other business from using that same name for a similar business in the same locality.

Business norms

See Financial ratios

Business permit

See Business license

Business plan

A document that spells out a company's expected course of action for a specified period, usually including a detailed listing and analysis of risks and uncertainties. For the small business, it should examine the proposed products, the market, the industry, the management policies, the marketing policies, production needs, and financial needs. Frequently, it is used as a prospectus for potential investors and lenders.

Business proposal

See Business plan

Business service firm

An establishment primarily engaged in rendering services to other business organizations on a fee or contract basis.

Business start

For enumeration purposes, a business with a name or similar designation that did not exist in a prior time period.

Cafeteria plan
See Flexible benefit plan

Capacity
Level of a firm's, industry's, or nation's output corresponding to full practical utilization of available resources.

Capital
Assets less liabilities, representing the ownership interest in a business. A stock of accumulated goods, especially at a specified time and in contrast to income received during a specified time period. Accumulated goods devoted to production. Accumulated possessions calculated to bring income.

Capital expenditure
Expenses incurred by a business for improvements that will depreciate over time.

Capital gain
The monetary difference between the purchase price and the selling price of capital. Capital gains are taxed at a rate of 28% by the federal government.

Capital intensity
The relative importance of capital in the production process, usually expressed as the ratio of capital to labor but also sometimes as the ratio of capital to output.

Capital resource
The equipment, facilities and labor used to create products and services.

Catastrophic care
Medical and other services for acute and long-term illnesses that cost more than insurance coverage limits or that cost the amount most families may be expected to pay with their own resources.

CDC
See Certified development corporation

Certified development corporation (CDC)
A local area or statewide corporation or authority (for profit or nonprofit) that packages U.S. Small Business Administration (SBA), bank, state, and/or private money into financial assistance for existing business capital improvements. The SBA holds the second lien on its maximum share of 40 percent

involvement. Each state has at least one certified development corporation. This program is called the SBA 504 Program.

Certified lenders
Banks that participate in the SBA guaranteed loan program (see separate citation). Such banks must have a good track record with the U.S. Small Business Administration (SBA) and must agree to certain conditions set forth by the agency. In return, the SBA agrees to process any guaranteed loan application within three business days.

Channel of distribution
The means used to transport merchandise from the manufacturer to the consumer.

Chapter 7 of the 1978 Bankruptcy Act
Provides for a court-appointed trustee who is responsible for liquidating a company's assets in order to settle outstanding debts.

Chapter 11 of the 1978 Bankruptcy Act
Allows the business owners to retain control of the company while working with their creditors to reorganize their finances and establish better business practices to prevent liquidation of assets.

Closely held corporation
A corporation in which the shares are held by a few persons, usually officers, employees, or others close to the management; these shares are rarely offered to the public.

Code of Federal Regulations
Codification of general and permanent rules of the federal government published in the Federal Register.

Code sharing
See Computer code sharing

Coinsurance
Upon meeting the deductible payment, health insurance participants may be required to make additional health care cost-sharing payments. Coinsurance is a payment of a fixed percentage of the cost of each service; copayment is usually a fixed amount to be paid with each service.

Collateral
Securities, evidence of deposit, or other property pledged by a borrower to secure repayment of a loan.

Collective ratemaking
The establishment of uniform charges for services by a group of businesses in the same industry.

Commercial insurance plan
See Underwriting

Commercial loans
Short-term renewable loans used to finance specific capital needs of a business.

Commercialization
The final stage of the innovation process, including production and distribution.

Common stock
The most frequently used instrument for purchasing ownership in private or public companies. Common stock generally carries the right to vote on certain corporate actions and may pay dividends, although it rarely does in venture investments. In liquidation, common stockholders are the last to share in the proceeds from the sale of a corporation's assets; bondholders and preferred shareholders have priority. Common stock is often used in firstround start-up financing.

Community development corporation
A corporation established to develop economic programs for a community and, in most cases, to provide financial support for such development.

Competitor
A business whose product or service is marketed for the same purpose/use and to the same consumer group as the product or service of another.

Consignment
A merchandising agreement, usually referring to secondhand shops, where the dealer pays the owner of an item a percentage of the profit when the item is sold.

Consortium
A coalition of organizations such as banks and corporations for ventures requiring large capital resources.

Consultant
An individual that is paid by a business to provide advice and expertise in a particular area.

Consumer price index
A measure of the fluctuation in prices between two points in time.

Consumer research
Research conducted by a business to obtain information about existing or potential consumer markets.

Continuation coverage
Health coverage offered for a specified period of time to employees who leave their jobs and to their widows, divorced spouses, or dependents.

Contractions
See Business contractions

Convertible preferred stock
A class of stock that pays a reasonable dividend and is convertible into common stock (see separate citation). Generally the convertible feature may only be exercised after being held for a stated period of time. This arrangement is usually considered second-round financing when a company needs equity to maintain its cash flow.

Convertible securities
A feature of certain bonds, debentures, or preferred stocks that allows them to be exchanged by the owner for another class of securities at a future date and in accordance with any other terms of the issue.

Copayment
See Coinsurance

Copyright
A legal form of protection available to creators and authors to safeguard their works from unlawful use or claim of ownership by others. Copyrights may be acquired for works of art, sculpture, music, and published or unpublished manuscripts. All copyrights should be registered at the Copyright Office of the Library of Congress.

Corporate financial ratios
The relationship between key figures found in a company's financial statement expressed as a

numeric value. Used to evaluate risk and company performance. Also known as Financial averages, Operating ratios, and Business ratios.

Corporation

A legal entity, chartered by a state or the federal government, recognized as a separate entity having its own rights, privileges, and liabilities distinct from those of its members.

Cost containment

Actions taken by employers and insurers to curtail rising health care costs; for example, increasing employee cost sharing (see separate citation), requiring second opinions, or preadmission screening.

Cost sharing

The requirement that health care consumers contribute to their own medical care costs through deductibles and coinsurance (see separate citations). Cost sharing does not include the amounts paid in premiums. It is used to control utilization of services; for example, requiring a fixed amount to be paid with each health care service.

Cottage industry

Businesses based in the home in which the family members are the labor force and family-owned equipment is used to process the goods.

Credit Rating

A letter or number calculated by an organization (such as Dun & Bradstreet) to represent the ability and disposition of a business to meet its financial obligations.

Customer service

Various techniques used to ensure the satisfaction of a customer.

Cyclical peak

The upper turning point in a business cycle.

Cyclical trough

The lower turning point in a business cycle.

DBA (Doing business as)

See Business name

Death

See Business death

Debenture

A certificate given as acknowledgment of a debt (see separate citation) secured by the general credit of the issuing corporation. A bond, usually without security, issued by a corporation and sometimes convertible to common stock.

Debt

Something owed by one person to another. Financing in which a company receives capital that must be repaid; no ownership is transferred.

Debt capital

Business financing that normally requires periodic interest payments and repayment of the principal within a specified time.

Debt financing

See Debt capital

Debt securities

Loans such as bonds and notes that provide a specified rate of return for a specified period of time.

Deductible

A set amount that an individual must pay before any benefits are received.

Demand shock absorbers

A term used to describe the role that some small firms play by expanding their output levels to accommodate a transient surge in demand.

Demographics

Statistics on various markets, including age, income, and education, used to target specific products or services to appropriate consumer groups.

Demonstration

Showing that a product or process has been modified sufficiently to meet the needs of users.

Deregulation

The lifting of government restrictions; for example, the lifting of government restrictions on the entry of new businesses, the expansion of services, and the setting of prices in particular industries.

Disaster loans

Various types of physical and economic assistance available to individuals and businesses through the U.S. Small Business Administration (SBA). This is the only SBA loan program available for residential purposes.

Discrimination
The denial of the rights and privileges of employment based on factors such as age, race, religion, or gender.

Diseconomies of scale
The condition in which the costs of production increase faster than the volume of production.

Dissolution
See Business dissolution

Distribution
Delivering a product or process to the user.

Distributor
One who delivers merchandise to the user.

Diversified company
A company whose products and services are used by several different markets.

Doing business as (DBA)
See Business name

Dow Jones
An information services company that publishes the Wall Street Journal and other sources of financial information.

Dow Jones Industrial Average
An indicator of stock market performance.

Earned income
A tax term that refers to wages and salaries earned by the recipient, as opposed to monies earned through interest and dividends.

Economic efficiency
The use of productive resources to the fullest practical extent in the provision of the set of goods and services that is most preferred by purchasers in the economy.

Economic indicators
Statistics used to express the state of the economy. These include the length of the average work week, the rate of unemployment, and stock prices.

Economically disadvantaged
See Socially and economically disadvantaged

Economies of scale
See Scale economies

EEOC
See Equal Employment Opportunity Commission

8(a) Program
A program authorized by the Small Business Act that directs federal contracts to small businesses owned and operated by socially and economically disadvantaged individuals.

Electronic mail (e-mail)
The electronic transmission of mail via phone lines.

E-mail
See Electronic mail

Employee leasing
A contract by which employers arrange to have their workers hired by a leasing company and then leased back to them for a management fee. The leasing company typically assumes the administrative burden of payroll and provides a benefit package to the workers.

Employee tenure
The length of time an employee works for a particular employer.

Employer identification number
The business equivalent of a social security number. Assigned by the U.S. Internal Revenue Service.

Enterprise
An aggregation of all establishments owned by a parent company. An enterprise may consist of a single, independent establishment or include subsidiaries and other branches under the same ownership and control.

Enterprise zone
A designated area, usually found in inner cities and other areas with significant unemployment, where businesses receive tax credits and other incentives to entice them to establish operations there.

Entrepreneur
A person who takes the risk of organizing and operating a new business venture.

Entry
See Business entry

Equal Employment Opportunity Commission (EEOC)
A federal agency that ensures nondiscrimination in the hiring and firing practices of a business.

Equal opportunity employer
An employer who adheres to the standards set by the Equal Employment Opportunity Commission (see separate citation).

Equity
The ownership interest. Financing in which partial or total ownership of a company is surrendered in exchange for capital. An investor's financial return comes from dividend payments and from growth in the net worth of the business.

Equity capital
See Equity; Equity midrisk venture capital

Equity financing
See Equity; Equity midrisk venture capital

Equity midrisk venture capital
An unsecured investment in a company. Usually a purchase of ownership interest in a company that occurs in the later stages of a company's development.

Equity partnership
A limited partnership arrangement for providing start-up and seed capital to businesses.

Equity securities
See Equity

Equity-type
Debt financing subordinated to conventional debt.

Establishment
A single-location business unit that may be independent (a single-establishment enterprise) or owned by a parent enterprise.

Establishment and Enterprise Microdata File
See U.S. Establishment and Enterprise Microdata File

Establishment birth
See Business birth

Establishment Longitudinal Microdata File
See U.S. Establishment Longitudinal Microdata File

Ethics
See Business ethics

Evaluation
Determining the potential success of translating an invention into a product or process.

Exit
See Business exit

Experience rating
See Underwriting

Export
A product sold outside of the country.

Export license
A general or specific license granted by the U.S. Department of Commerce required of anyone wishing to export goods. Some restricted articles need approval from the U.S. Departments of State, Defense, or Energy.

Failure
See Business failure

Fair share agreement
An agreement reached between a franchisor and a minority business organization to extend business ownership to minorities by either reducing the amount of capital required or by setting aside certain marketing areas for minority business owners.

Feasibility study
A study to determine the likelihood that a proposed product or development will fulfill the objectives of a particular investor.

Federal Trade Commission (FTC)
Federal agency that promotes free enterprise and competition within the U.S.

Federal Trade Mark Act of 1946
See Lanham Act

Fictional name
See Business name

Fiduciary
An individual or group that hold assets in trust for a beneficiary.

Financial analysis
The techniques used to determine money needs in a business. Techniques include ratio analysis, calculation of return on investment, guides for measuring

profitability, and break-even analysis to determine ultimate success.

Financial intermediary
A financial institution that acts as the intermediary between borrowers and lenders. Banks, savings and loan associations, finance companies, and venture capital companies are major financial intermediaries in the United States.

Financial ratios
See Corporate financial ratios; Industry financial ratios

Financial statement
A written record of business finances, including balance sheets and profit and loss statements.

Financing
See First-stage financing; Second-stage financing; Thirdstage financing

First-stage financing
Financing provided to companies that have expended their initial capital, and require funds to start full-scale manufacturing and sales. Also known as First-round financing.

Fiscal year
Any twelve-month period used by businesses for accounting purposes.

504 Program
See Certified development corporation

Flexible benefit plan
A plan that offers a choice among cash and/or qualified benefits such as group term life insurance, accident and health insurance, group legal services, dependent care assistance, and vacations.

FOB
See Free on board

Format franchising
See Business format franchising; Franchising

401(k) plan
A financial plan where employees contribute a percentage of their earnings to a fund that is invested in stocks, bonds, or money markets for the purpose of saving money for retirement.

Four Ps
Marketing terms referring to Product, Price, Place, and Promotion.

Franchising
A form of licensing by which the owner-the franchisor- distributes or markets a product, method, or service through affiliated dealers called franchisees. The product, method, or service being marketed is identified by a brand name, and the franchisor maintains control over the marketing methods employed. The franchisee is often given exclusive access to a defined geographic area.

Free on board (FOB)
A pricing term indicating that the quoted price includes the cost of loading goods into transport vessels at a specified place.

Frictional unemployment
See Unemployment

FTC
See Federal Trade Commission

Fulfillment
The systems necessary for accurate delivery of an ordered item, including subscriptions and direct marketing.

Full-time workers
Generally, those who work a regular schedule of more than 35 hours per week.

Garment registration number
A number that must appear on every garment sold in the U.S. to indicate the manufacturer of the garment, which may or may not be the same as the label under which the garment is sold. The U.S. Federal Trade Commission assigns and regulates garment registration numbers.

Gatekeeper
A key contact point for entry into a network.

GDP
See Gross domestic product

General obligation bond
A municipal bond secured by the taxing power of the municipality. The Tax Reform Act of 1986 limits the

purposes for which such bonds may be issued and establishes volume limits on the extent of their issuance.

GNP
See Gross national product

Good Housekeeping Seal
Seal appearing on products that signifies the fulfillment of the standards set by the Good Housekeeping Institute to protect consumer interests.

Goods sector
All businesses producing tangible goods, including agriculture, mining, construction, and manufacturing businesses.

GPO
See Gross product originating

Gross domestic product (GDP)
The part of the nation's gross national product (see separate citation) generated by private business using resources from within the country.

Gross national product (GNP)
The most comprehensive single measure of aggregate economic output. Represents the market value of the total output of goods and services produced by a nation's economy.

Gross product originating (GPO)
A measure of business output estimated from the income or production side using employee compensation, profit income, net interest, capital consumption, and indirect business taxes.

HAL
See Handicapped assistance loan program

Handicapped assistance loan program (HAL)
Low-interest direct loan program through the U.S. Small Business Administration (SBA) for handicapped persons. The SBA requires that these persons demonstrate that their disability is such that it is impossible for them to secure employment, thus making it necessary to go into their own business to make a living.

Health maintenance organization (HMO)
Organization of physicians and other health care professionals that provides health services to subscribers and their dependents on a prepaid basis.

Health provider
An individual or institution that gives medical care. Under Medicare, an institutional provider is a hospital, skilled nursing facility, home health agency, or provider of certain physical therapy services.

Hispanic
A person of Cuban, Mexican, Puerto Rican, Latin American (Central or South American), European Spanish, or other Spanish-speaking origin or ancestry.

HMO
See Health maintenance organization

Home-based business
A business with an operating address that is also a residential address (usually the residential address of the proprietor).

Hub-and-spoke system
A system in which flights of an airline from many different cities (the spokes) converge at a single airport (the hub). After allowing passengers sufficient time to make connections, planes then depart for different cities.

Human Resources Management
A business program designed to oversee recruiting, pay, benefits, and other issues related to the company's work force, including planning to determine the optimal use of labor to increase production, thereby increasing profit.

Idea
An original concept for a new product or process.

Import
Products produced outside the country in which they are consumed.

Income
Money or its equivalent, earned or accrued, resulting from the sale of goods and services.

Income statement
A financial statement that lists the profits and losses of a company at a given time.

Incorporation
The filing of a certificate of incorporation with a state's secretary of state, thereby limiting the business owner's liability.

Incubator
A facility designed to encourage entrepreneurship and minimize obstacles to new business formation and growth, particularly for high-technology firms, by housing a number of fledgling enterprises that share an array of services, such as meeting areas, secretarial services, accounting, research library, on-site financial and management counseling, and word processing facilities.

Independent contractor
An individual considered self-employed (see separate citation) and responsible for paying Social Security taxes and income taxes on earnings.

Indirect health coverage
Health insurance obtained through another individual's health care plan; for example, a spouse's employersponsored plan.

Industrial development authority
The financial arm of a state or other political subdivision established for the purpose of financing economic development in an area, usually through loans to nonprofit organizations, which in turn provide facilities for manufacturing and other industrial operations.

Industry financial ratios
Corporate financial ratios averaged for a specified industry. These are used for comparison purposes and reveal industry trends and identify differences between the performance of a specific company and the performance of its industry. Also known as Industrial averages, Industry ratios, Financial averages, and Business or Industrial norms.

Inflation
Increases in volume of currency and credit, generally resulting in a sharp and continuing rise in price levels.

Informal capital
Financing from informal, unorganized sources; includes informal debt capital such as trade credit or loans from friends and relatives and equity capital from informal investors.

Initial public offering (IPO)
A corporation's first offering of stock to the public.

Innovation
The introduction of a new idea into the marketplace in the form of a new product or service or an improvement in organization or process.

Intellectual property
Any idea or work that can be considered proprietary in nature and is thus protected from infringement by others.

Internal capital
Debt or equity financing obtained from the owner or through retained business earnings.

Internet
A government-designed computer network that contains large amounts of information and is accessible through various vendors for a fee.

Intrapreneurship
The state of employing entrepreneurial principles to nonentrepreneurial situations.

Invention
The tangible form of a technological idea, which could include a laboratory prototype, drawings, formulas, etc.

IPO
See Initial public offering

Job description
The duties and responsibilities required in a particular position.

Job tenure
A period of time during which an individual is continuously employed in the same job.

Joint marketing agreements
Agreements between regional and major airlines, often involving the coordination of flight schedules, fares, and baggage transfer. These agreements help regional carriers operate at lower cost.

Joint venture
Venture in which two or more people combine efforts in a particular business enterprise, usually a single transaction or a limited activity, and agree to share the profits and losses jointly or in proportion to their contributions.

Keogh plan
Designed for self-employed persons and unincorporated businesses as a tax-deferred pension account.

Labor force
Civilians considered eligible for employment who are also willing and able to work.

Labor force participation rate
The civilian labor force as a percentage of the civilian population.

Labor intensity
The relative importance of labor in the production process, usually measured as the capital-labor ratio; i.e., the ratio of units of capital (typically, dollars of tangible assets) to the number of employees. The higher the capital-labor ratio exhibited by a firm or industry, the lower the capital intensity of that firm or industry is said to be.

Labor surplus area
An area in which there exists a high unemployment rate. In procurement (see separate citation), extra points are given to firms in counties that are designated a labor surplus area; this information is requested on procurement bid sheets.

Labor union
An organization of similarly-skilled workers who collectively bargain with management over the conditions of employment.

Laboratory prototype
See Prototype

LAN
See Local Area Network

Lanham Act
Refers to the Federal Trade Mark Act of 1946. Protects registered trademarks, trade names, and other service marks used in commerce.

Large business-dominated industry
Industry in which a minimum of 60 percent of employment or sales is in firms with more than 500 workers.

LBO
See Leveraged buy-out

Leader pricing
A reduction in the price of a good or service in order to generate more sales of that good or service.

Legal list
A list of securities selected by a state in which certain institutions and fiduciaries (such as pension funds, insurance companies, and banks) may invest. Securities not on the list are not eligible for investment. Legal lists typically restrict investments to high quality securities meeting certain specifications. Generally, investment is limited to U.S. securities and investment-grade blue chip securities (see separate citation).

Leveraged buy-out (LBO)
The purchase of a business or a division of a corporation through a highly leveraged financing package.

Liability
An obligation or duty to perform a service or an act. Also defined as money owed.

License
A legal agreement granting to another the right to use a technological innovation.

Limited Liability Company
A hybrid type of legal structure that provides the limited liability features of a corporation and the tax efficiencies and operational flexibility of a partnership. Depending on the state, the members can consist of a single individual (one owner), two or more individuals, corporations or other LLCs.

Limited liability partnerships
A business organization that allows limited partners to enjoy limited personal liability while general partners have unlimited personal liability

Liquidity
The ability to convert a security into cash promptly.

Loans
See Commercial loans; Disaster loans; SBA direct loans; SBA guaranteed loans; SBA special lending institution categories Local Area Network (LAN) Computer networks contained within a single building or small area; used to facilitate the sharing of information.

Local development corporation

An organization, usually made up of local citizens of a community, designed to improve the economy of the area by inducing business and industry to locate and expand there. A local development corporation establishes a capability to finance local growth.

Long-haul rates

Rates charged by a transporter in which the distance traveled is more than 800 miles.

Long-term debt

An obligation that matures in a period that exceeds five years.

Low-grade bond

A corporate bond that is rated below investment grade by the major rating agencies (Standard and Poor's, Moody's).

Macro-efficiency

Efficiency as it pertains to the operation of markets and market systems.

Managed care

A cost-effective health care program initiated by employers whereby low-cost health care is made available to the employees in return for exclusive patronage to program doctors.

Management Assistance Programs

See SBA Management Assistance Programs

Management and technical assistance

A term used by many programs to mean business (as opposed to technological) assistance.

Mandated benefits

Specific treatments, providers, or individuals required by law to be included in commercial health plans.

Market evaluation

The use of market information to determine the sales potential of a specific product or process.

Market failure

The situation in which the workings of a competitive market do not produce the best results from the point of view of the entire society.

Market information

Data of any type that can be used for market evaluation, which could include demographic data, technology forecasting, regulatory changes, etc.

Market research

A systematic collection, analysis, and reporting of data about the market and its preferences, opinions, trends, and plans; used for corporate decision-making.

Market share

In a particular market, the percentage of sales of a specific product.

Marketing

Promotion of goods or services through various media.

Master Establishment List (MEL)

A list of firms in the United States developed by the U.S. Small Business Administration; firms can be selected by industry, region, state, standard metropolitan statistical area (see separate citation), county, and zip code.

Maturity

The date upon which the principal or stated value of a bond or other indebtedness becomes due and payable.

Medicaid (Title XIX)

A federally aided, state-operated and administered program that provides medical benefits for certain low income persons in need of health and medical care who are eligible for one of the government's welfare cash payment programs, including the aged, the blind, the disabled, and members of families with dependent children where one parent is absent, incapacitated, or unemployed.

Medicare (Title XVIII)

A nationwide health insurance program for disabled and aged persons. Health insurance is available to insured persons without regard to income. Monies from payroll taxes cover hospital insurance and monies from general revenues and beneficiary premiums pay for supplementary medical insurance.

MEL

See Master Establishment List

Merchant Status

The relationship between a company and a bank or credit card company allowing the company to accept credit card payments

MESBIC
See Minority enterprise small business investment corporation

MET
See Multiple employer trust

Metropolitan statistical area (MSA)
A means used by the government to define large population centers that may transverse different governmental jurisdictions. For example, the Washington, D.C. MSA includes the District of Columbia and contiguous parts of Maryland and Virginia because all of these geopolitical areas comprise one population and economic operating unit.

Mezzanine financing
See Third-stage financing

Micro-efficiency
Efficiency as it pertains to the operation of individual firms.

Microdata
Information on the characteristics of an individual business firm.

Microloan
An SBA loan program that helps entrepreneurs obtain loans from less than $100 to $25,000.

Mid-term debt
An obligation that matures within one to five years.

Midrisk venture capital
See Equity midrisk venture capital

Minimum premium plan
A combination approach to funding an insurance plan aimed primarily at premium tax savings. The employer self-funds a fixed percentage of estimated monthly claims and the insurance company insures the excess.

Minimum wage
The lowest hourly wage allowed by the federal government.

Minority Business Development Agency
Contracts with private firms throughout the nation to sponsor Minority Business Development Centers which provide minority firms with advice and technical assistance on a fee basis.

Minority Enterprise Small Business Investment Corporation (MESBIC)
A federally funded private venture capital firm licensed by the U.S. Small Business Administration to provide capital to minority-owned businesses (see separate citation).

Minority-owned business
Businesses owned by those who are socially or economically disadvantaged (see separate citation).

Mission statement
A short statement describing a company's function, markets and competitive advantages.

Mom and Pop business
A small store or enterprise having limited capital, principally employing family members.

Multi-employer plan
A health plan to which more than one employer is required to contribute and that may be maintained through a collective bargaining agreement and required to meet standards prescribed by the U.S. Department of Labor.

Multi-level marketing
A system of selling in which you sign up other people to assist you and they, in turn, recruit others to help them. Some entrepreneurs have built successful companies on this concept because the main focus of their activities is their product and product sales.

Multiple employer trust (MET)
A self-funded benefit plan generally geared toward small employers sharing a common interest.

NASDAQ
See National Association of Securities Dealers Automated Quotations

National Association of Securities Dealers Automated Quotations
Provides price quotes on over-the-counter securities as well as securities listed on the New York Stock Exchange.

National income
Aggregate earnings of labor and property arising from the production of goods and services in a nation's economy.

Net assets
See Net worth

Net income
The amount remaining from earnings and profits after all expenses and costs have been met or deducted. Also known as Net earnings.

Net profit
Money earned after production and overhead expenses (see separate citations) have been deducted.

Net worth
The difference between a company's total assets and its total liabilities.

Network
A chain of interconnected individuals or organizations sharing information and/or services.

New York Stock Exchange (NYSE)
The oldest stock exchange in the U.S. Allows for trading in stocks, bonds, warrants, options, and rights that meet listing requirements.

Niche
A career or business for which a person is well-suited. Also, a product which fulfills one need of a particular market segment, often with little or no competition.

Nodes
One workstation in a network, either local area or wide area (see separate citations).

Nonbank bank
A bank that either accepts deposits or makes loans, but not both. Used to create many new branch banks.

Noncompetitive awards
A method of contracting whereby the federal government negotiates with only one contractor to supply a product or service.

Nonmember bank
A state-regulated bank that does not belong to the federal bank system.

Nonprofit
An organization that has no shareholders, does not distribute profits, and is without federal and state tax liabilities.

Norms
See Financial ratios

North American Free Trade Agreement (NAFTA)
Passed in 1993, NAFTA eliminates trade barriers among businesses in the U.S., Canada, and Mexico.

NYSE
See New York Stock Exchange

Occupational Safety & Health Administration (OSHA)
Federal agency that regulates health and safety standards within the workplace.

Operating Expenses
Business expenditures not directly associated with the production of goods or services.

Optimal firm size
The business size at which the production cost per unit of output (average cost) is, in the long run, at its minimum.

Organizational chart
A hierarchical chart tracking the chain of command within an organization.

OSHA
See Occupational Safety & Health Administration

Overhead
Expenses, such as employee benefits and building utilities, incurred by a business that are unrelated to the actual product or service sold.

Owner's capital
Debt or equity funds provided by the owner(s) of a business; sources of owner's capital are personal savings, sales of assets, or loans from financial institutions.

P & L
See Profit and loss statement

Part-time workers
Normally, those who work less than 35 hours per week. The Tax Reform Act indicated that part-time workers who work less than 17.5 hours per week may be excluded from health plans for purposes of complying with federal nondiscrimination rules.

Part-year workers
Those who work less than 50 weeks per year.

Partnership
Two or more parties who enter into a legal relationship to conduct business for profit. Defined by

the U.S. Internal Revenue Code as joint ventures, syndicates, groups, pools, and other associations of two or more persons organized for profit that are not specifically classified in the IRS code as corporations or proprietorships.

Patent
A grant made by the government assuring an inventor the sole right to make, use, and sell an invention for a period of 17 years.

PC
See Professional corporation

Peak
See Cyclical peak

Pension
A series of payments made monthly, semiannually, annually, or at other specified intervals during the lifetime of the pensioner for distribution upon retirement. The term is sometimes used to denote the portion of the retirement allowance financed by the employer's contributions.

Pension fund
A fund established to provide for the payment of pension benefits; the collective contributions made by all of the parties to the pension plan.

Performance appraisal
An established set of objective criteria, based on job description and requirements, that is used to evaluate the performance of an employee in a specific job.

Permit
See Business license

Plan
See Business plan

Pooling
An arrangement for employers to achieve efficiencies and lower health costs by joining together to purchase group health insurance or self-insurance.

PPO
See Preferred provider organization

Preferred lenders program
See SBA special lending institution categories

Preferred provider organization (PPO)
A contractual arrangement with a health care services organization that agrees to discount its health care rates in return for faster payment and/or a patient base.

Premiums
The amount of money paid to an insurer for health insurance under a policy. The premium is generally paid periodically (e.g., monthly), and often is split between the employer and the employee. Unlike deductibles and coinsurance or copayments, premiums are paid for coverage whether or not benefits are actually used.

Prime-age workers
Employees 25 to 54 years of age.

Prime contract
A contract awarded directly by the U.S. Federal Government.

Private company
See Closely held corporation

Private placement
A method of raising capital by offering for sale an investment or business to a small group of investors (generally avoiding registration with the Securities and Exchange Commission or state securities registration agencies). Also known as Private financing or Private offering.

Pro forma
The use of hypothetical figures in financial statements to represent future expenditures, debts, and other potential financial expenses.

Proactive
Taking the initiative to solve problems and anticipate future events before they happen, instead of reacting to an already existing problem or waiting for a difficult situation to occur.

Procurement
A contract from an agency of the federal government for goods or services from a small business.

Product development
The stage of the innovation process where research is translated into a product or process through evaluation, adaptation, and demonstration.

Product franchising

An arrangement for a franchisee to use the name and to produce the product line of the franchisor or parent corporation.

Production

The manufacture of a product.

Production prototype

See Prototype

Productivity

A measurement of the number of goods produced during a specific amount of time.

Professional corporation (PC)

Organized by members of a profession such as medicine, dentistry, or law for the purpose of conducting their professional activities as a corporation. Liability of a member or shareholder is limited in the same manner as in a business corporation.

Profit and loss statement (P & L)

The summary of the incomes (total revenues) and costs of a company's operation during a specific period of time. Also known as Income and expense statement.

Proposal

See Business plan

Proprietorship

The most common legal form of business ownership; about 85 percent of all small businesses are proprietorships. The liability of the owner is unlimited in this form of ownership.

Prospective payment system

A cost-containment measure included in the Social Security Amendments of 1983 whereby Medicare payments to hospitals are based on established prices, rather than on cost reimbursement.

Prototype

A model that demonstrates the validity of the concept of an invention (laboratory prototype); a model that meets the needs of the manufacturing process and the user (production prototype).

Prudent investor rule or standard

A legal doctrine that requires fiduciaries to make investments using the prudence, diligence, and intelligence that would be used by a prudent person in making similar investments. Because fiduciaries make investments on behalf of third-party beneficiaries, the standard results in very conservative investments. Until recently, most state regulations required the fiduciary to apply this standard to each investment. Newer, more progressive regulations permit fiduciaries to apply this standard to the portfolio taken as a whole, thereby allowing a fiduciary to balance a portfolio with higher-yield, higher-risk investments. In states with more progressive regulations, practically every type of security is eligible for inclusion in the portfolio of investments made by a fiduciary, provided that the portfolio investments, in their totality, are those of a prudent person.

Public equity markets

Organized markets for trading in equity shares such as common stocks, preferred stocks, and warrants. Includes markets for both regularly traded and nonregularly traded securities.

Public offering

General solicitation for participation in an investment opportunity. Interstate public offerings are supervised by the U.S. Securities and Exchange Commission (see separate citation).

Quality control

The process by which a product is checked and tested to ensure consistent standards of high quality.

Rate of return

The yield obtained on a security or other investment based on its purchase price or its current market price. The total rate of return is current income plus or minus capital appreciation or depreciation.

Real property

Includes the land and all that is contained on it.

Realignment

See Resource realignment

Recession

Contraction of economic activity occurring between the peak and trough (see separate citations) of a business cycle.

Regulated market
A market in which the government controls the forces of supply and demand, such as who may enter and what price may be charged.

Regulation D
A vehicle by which small businesses make small offerings and private placements of securities with limited disclosure requirements. It was designed to ease the burdens imposed on small businesses utilizing this method of capital formation.

Regulatory Flexibility Act
An act requiring federal agencies to evaluate the impact of their regulations on small businesses before the regulations are issued and to consider less burdensome alternatives.

Research
The initial stage of the innovation process, which includes idea generation and invention.

Research and development financing
A tax-advantaged partnership set up to finance product development for start-ups as well as more mature companies.

Resource mobility
The ease with which labor and capital move from firm to firm or from industry to industry.

Resource realignment
The adjustment of productive resources to interindustry changes in demand.

Resources
The sources of support or help in the innovation process, including sources of financing, technical evaluation, market evaluation, management and business assistance, etc.

Retained business earnings
Business profits that are retained by the business rather than being distributed to the shareholders as dividends.

Return on investment
A profitability measure that evaluates the performance of a business by dividing net profit by net worth.

Revolving credit
An agreement with a lending institution for an amount of money, which cannot exceed a set maximum, over a specified period of time. Each time the borrower repays a portion of the loan, the amount of the repayment may be borrowed yet again.

Risk capital
See Venture capital

Risk management
The act of identifying potential sources of financial loss and taking action to minimize their negative impact.

Routing
The sequence of steps necessary to complete a product during production.

S corporations
See Sub chapter S corporations

SBA
See Small Business Administration

SBA direct loans
Loans made directly by the U.S. Small Business Administration (SBA); monies come from funds appropriated specifically for this purpose. In general, SBA direct loans carry interest rates slightly lower than those in the private financial markets and are available only to applicants unable to secure private financing or an SBA guaranteed loan.

SBA 504 Program
See Certified development corporation

SBA guaranteed loans
Loans made by lending institutions in which the U.S. Small Business Administration (SBA) will pay a prior agreed-upon percentage of the outstanding principal in the event the borrower of the loan defaults. The terms of the loan and the interest rate are negotiated between theborrower and the lending institution, within set parameters.

SBA loans
See Disaster loans; SBA direct loans; SBA guaranteed loans; SBA special lending institution categories

SBA Management Assistance Programs
Classes, workshops, counseling, and publications offered by the U.S. Small Business Administration.

SBA special lending institution categories
U.S. Small Business Administration (SBA) loan program in which the SBA promises certified banks a 72-hour turnaround period in giving its approval for a loan, and in which preferred lenders in a pilot program are allowed to write SBA loans without seeking prior SBA approval.

SBDB
See Small Business Data Base

SBDC
See Small business development centers

SBI
See Small business institutes program

SBIC
See Small business investment corporation

SBIR Program
See Small Business Innovation Development Act of 1982

Scale economies
The decline of the production cost per unit of output (average cost) as the volume of output increases.

Scale efficiency
The reduction in unit cost available to a firm when producing at a higher output volume.

SCORE
See Service Corps of Retired Executives

SEC
See Securities and Exchange Commission

SECA
See Self-Employment Contributions Act

Second-stage financing
Working capital for the initial expansion of a company that is producing, shipping, and has growing accounts receivable and inventories. Also known as Second-round financing.

Secondary market
A market established for the purchase and sale of outstanding securities following their initial distribution.

Secondary worker
Any worker in a family other than the person who is the primary source of income for the family.

Secondhand capital
Previously used and subsequently resold capital equipment (e.g., buildings and machinery).

Securities and Exchange Commission (SEC)
Federal agency charged with regulating the trade of securities to prevent unethical practices in the investor market.

Securitized debt
A marketing technique that converts long-term loans to marketable securities.

Seed capital
Venture financing provided in the early stages of the innovation process, usually during product development.

Self-employed person
One who works for a profit or fees in his or her own business, profession, or trade, or who operates a farm.

Self-Employment Contributions Act (SECA)
Federal law that governs the self-employment tax (see separate citation).

Self-employment income
Income covered by Social Security if a business earns a net income of at least $400.00 during the year. Taxes are paid on earnings that exceed $400.00.

Self-employment retirement plan
See Keogh plan

Self-employment tax
Required tax imposed on self-employed individuals for the provision of Social Security and Medicare. The tax must be paid quarterly with estimated income tax statements.

Self-funding
A health benefit plan in which a firm uses its own funds to pay claims, rather than transferring the financial risks of paying claims to an outside insurer in exchange for premium payments.

Service Corps of Retired Executives (SCORE)
Volunteers for the SBA Management Assistance Program who provide one-on-one counseling and teach workshops and seminars for small firms.

Service firm
See Business service firm

Service sector
Broadly defined, all U.S. industries that produce intangibles, including the five major industry divisions of transportation, communications, and utilities; wholesale trade; retail trade; finance, insurance, and real estate; and services.

Set asides
See Small business set asides

Short-haul service
A type of transportation service in which the transporter supplies service between cities where the maximum distance is no more than 200 miles.

Short-term debt
An obligation that matures in one year.

SIC codes
See Standard Industrial Classification codes

Single-establishment enterprise
See Establishment

Small business
An enterprise that is independently owned and operated, is not dominant in its field, and employs fewer than 500 people. For SBA purposes, the U.S. Small Business Administration (SBA) considers various other factors (such as gross annual sales) in determining size of a business.

Small Business Administration (SBA)
An independent federal agency that provides assistance with loans, management, and advocating interests before other federal agencies.

Small Business Data Base
A collection of microdata (see separate citation) files on individual firms developed and maintained by the U.S. Small Business Administration.

Small business development centers (SBDC)
Centers that provide support services to small businesses, such as individual counseling, SBA advice,

seminars and conferences, and other learning center activities. Most services are free of charge, or available at minimal cost.

Small business development corporation
See Certified development corporation

Small business-dominated industry
Industry in which a minimum of 60 percent of employment or sales is in firms with fewer than 500 employees.

Small Business Innovation Development Act of 1982
Federal statute requiring federal agencies with large extramural research and development budgets to allocate a certain percentage of these funds to small research and development firms. The program, called the Small Business Innovation Research (SBIR) Program, is designed to stimulate technological innovation and make greater use of small businesses in meeting national innovation needs.

Small business institutes (SBI) program
Cooperative arrangements made by U.S. Small Business Administration district offices and local colleges and universities to provide small business firms with graduate students to counsel them without charge.

Small business investment corporation (SBIC)
A privately owned company licensed and funded through the U.S. Small Business Administration and private sector sources to provide equity or debt capital to small businesses.

Small business set asides
Procurement (see separate citation) opportunities required by law to be on all contracts under $10,000 or a certain percentage of an agency's total procurement expenditure.

Smaller firms
For U.S. Department of Commerce purposes, those firms not included in the Fortune 1000.

SMSA
See Metropolitan statistical area

Socially and economically disadvantaged
Individuals who have been subjected to racial or ethnic prejudice or cultural bias without regard to

their qualities as individuals, and whose abilities to compete are impaired because of diminished opportunities to obtain capital and credit.

Sole proprietorship
An unincorporated, one-owner business, farm, or professional practice.

Special lending institution categories
See SBA special lending institution categories

Standard Industrial Classification (SIC) codes
Four-digit codes established by the U.S. Federal Government to categorize businesses by type of economic activity; the first two digits correspond to major groups such as construction and manufacturing, while the last two digits correspond to subgroups such as home construction or highway construction.

Start-up
A new business, at the earliest stages of development and financing.

Start-up costs
Costs incurred before a business can commence operations.

Start-up financing
Financing provided to companies that have either completed product development and initial marketing or have been in business for less than one year but have not yet sold their product commercially.

Stock
A certificate of equity ownership in a business.

Stop-loss coverage
Insurance for a self-insured plan that reimburses the company for any losses it might incur in its health claims beyond a specified amount.

Strategic planning
Projected growth and development of a business to establish a guiding direction for the future. Also used to determine which market segments to explore for optimal sales of products or services.

Structural unemployment
See Unemployment

Sub chapter S corporations
Corporations that are considered noncorporate for tax purposes but legally remain corporations.

Subcontract
A contract between a prime contractor and a subcontractor, or between subcontractors, to furnish supplies or services for performance of a prime contract (see separate citation) or a subcontract.

Surety bonds
Bonds providing reimbursement to an individual, company, or the government if a firm fails to complete a contract. The U.S. Small Business Administration guarantees surety bonds in a program much like the SBA guaranteed loan program (see separate citation).

Swing loan
See Bridge financing

Target market
The clients or customers sought for a business' product or service.

Targeted Jobs Tax Credit
Federal legislation enacted in 1978 that provides a tax credit to an employer who hires structurally unemployed individuals.

Tax number
A number assigned to a business by a state revenue department that enables the business to buy goods without paying sales tax.

Taxable bonds
An interest-bearing certificate of public or private indebtedness. Bonds are issued by public agencies to finance economic development.

Technical assistance
See Management and technical assistance

Technical evaluation
Assessment of technological feasibility.

Technology
The method in which a firm combines and utilizes labor and capital resources to produce goods or services; the application of science for commercial or industrial purposes.

Technology transfer
The movement of information about a technology or intellectual property from one party to another for use.

Tenure
See Employee tenure

Term
The length of time for which a loan is made.

Terms of a note
The conditions or limits of a note; includes the interest rate per annum, the due date, and transferability and convertibility features, if any.

Third-party administrator
An outside company responsible for handling claims and performing administrative tasks associated with health insurance plan maintenance.

Third-stage financing
Financing provided for the major expansion of a company whose sales volume is increasing and that is breaking even or profitable. These funds are used for further plant expansion, marketing, working capital, or development of an improved product. Also known as Third-round or Mezzanine financing.

Time management
Skills and scheduling techniques used to maximize productivity.

Trade credit
Credit extended by suppliers of raw materials or finished products. In an accounting statement, trade credit is referred to as "accounts payable."

Trade name
The name under which a company conducts business, or by which its business, goods, or services are identified. It may or may not be registered as a trademark.

Trade periodical
A publication with a specific focus on one or more aspects of business and industry.

Trade secret
Competitive advantage gained by a business through the use of a unique manufacturing process or formula.

Trade show
An exhibition of goods or services used in a particular industry. Typically held in exhibition centers where exhibitors rent space to display their merchandise.

Trademark
A graphic symbol, device, or slogan that identifies a business. A business has property rights to its trademark from the inception of its use, but it is still prudent to register all trademarks with the Trademark Office of the U.S. Department of Commerce.

Trend
A statistical measurement used to track changes that occur over time.

Trough
See Cyclical trough

UCC
See Uniform Commercial Code

UL
See Underwriters Laboratories

Underwriters Laboratories (UL)
One of several private firms that tests products and processes to determine their safety. Although various firms can provide this kind of testing service, many local and insurance codes specify UL certification.

Underwriting
A process by which an insurer determines whether or not and on what basis it will accept an application for insurance. In an experience-rated plan, premiums are based on a firm's or group's past claims; factors other than prior claims are used for community-rated or manually rated plans.

Unfair competition
Refers to business practices, usually unethical, such as using unlicensed products, pirating merchandise, or misleading the public through false advertising, which give the offending business an unequitable advantage over others.

Unfunded accrued liability
The excess of total liabilities, both present and prospective, over present and prospective assets.

Unemployment
The joblessness of individuals who are willing to work, who are legally and physically able to work, and who are seeking work. Unemployment may represent the temporary joblessness of a worker between jobs (frictional unemployment) or the joblessness of a worker whose skills are not suitable for jobs available in the labor market (structural unemployment).

Uniform Commercial Code (UCC)
A code of laws governing commercial transactions across the U.S., except Louisiana. Their purpose is to bring uniformity to financial transactions.

Uniform product code (UPC symbol)
A computer-readable label comprised of ten digits and stripes that encodes what a product is and how much it costs. The first five digits are assigned by the Uniform Product Code Council, and the last five digits by the individual manufacturer.

Unit cost
See Average cost

UPC symbol
See Uniform product code

U.S. Establishment and Enterprise Microdata (USEEM) File
A cross-sectional database containing information on employment, sales, and location for individual enterprises and establishments with employees that have a Dun & Bradstreet credit rating.

U.S. Establishment Longitudinal Microdata (USELM) File
A database containing longitudinally linked sample microdata on establishments drawn from the U.S. Establishment and Enterprise Microdata file (see separate citation).

U.S. Small Business Administration 504 Program
See Certified development corporation

USEEM
See U.S. Establishment and Enterprise Microdata File

USELM
See U.S. Establishment Longitudinal Microdata File

VCN
See Venture capital network

Venture capital
Money used to support new or unusual business ventures that exhibit above-average growth rates, significant potential for market expansion, and are in need of additional financing to sustain growth or further research and development; equity or equity-type financing traditionally provided at the commercialization stage, increasingly available prior to commercialization.

Venture capital company
A company organized to provide seed capital to a business in its formation stage, or in its first or second stage of expansion. Funding is obtained through public or private pension funds, commercial banks and bank holding companies, small business investment corporations licensed by the U.S. Small Business Administration, private venture capital firms, insurance companies, investment management companies, bank trust departments, industrial companies seeking to diversify their investment, and investment bankers acting as intermediaries for other investors or directly investing on their own behalf.

Venture capital limited partnerships
Designed for business development, these partnerships are an institutional mechanism for providing capital for young, technology-oriented businesses. The investors' money is pooled and invested in money market assets until venture investments have been selected. The general partners are experienced investment managers who select and invest the equity and debt securities of firms with high growth potential and the ability to go public in the near future.

Venture capital network (VCN)
A computer database that matches investors with entrepreneurs.

WAN
See Wide Area Network

Wide Area Network (WAN)
Computer networks linking systems throughout a state or around the world in order to facilitate the sharing of information.

Withholding

Federal, state, social security, and unemployment taxes withheld by the employer from employees' wages; employers are liable for these taxes and the corporate umbrella and bankruptcy will not exonerate an employer from paying back payroll withholding. Employers should escrow these funds in a separate account and disperse them quarterly to withholding authorities.

Workers' compensation

A state-mandated form of insurance covering workers injured in job-related accidents. In some states, the state is the insurer; in other states, insurance must be acquired from commercial insurance firms. Insurance rates are based on a number of factors, including salaries, firm history, and risk of occupation.

Working capital

Refers to a firm's short-term investment of current assets, including cash, short-term securities, accounts receivable, and inventories.

Yield

The rate of income returned on an investment, expressed as a percentage. Income yield is obtained by dividing the current dollar income by the current market price of the security. Net yield or yield to maturity is the current income yield minus any premium above par or plus any discount from par in purchase price, with the adjustment spread over the period from the date of purchase to the date of maturity.

Index

Listings in this index are arranged alphabetically by business plan type, then alphabetically by business plan name. Users are provided with the volume number in which the plan appears.

Index

Index

Index

Index

Index